FORENSIC PSYCHOLOGICAL ASSESSMENT IN PRACTICE

Case Studies

Corine de Ruiter
Nancy Kaser-Boyd

Routledge
Taylor & Francis Group

NEW YORK AND LONDON

First published 2015
by Routledge
711 Third Avenue, New York, NY 10017

and by Routledge
27 Church Road, Hove, East Sussex BN3 2FA

Routledge is an imprint of the Taylor & Francis Group, an informa business

Library of Congress Cataloging in Publication Data
Ruiter, C. de, author.
   Forensic psychological assessment in practice: case studies/Corine De
Ruiter, Nancy Kaser-Boyd.
   p. ; cm.—(International perspectives on forensic mental health)
   Includes bibliographical references and index.
   I. Kaser-Boyd, Nancy, author. II. Title.
   [DNLM: 1. Forensic Psychiatry—Case Reports. W 740]
   RA1151
   614'.15—dc23
   2014035638

ISBN: 978-0-415-89522-4 (hbk)
ISBN: 978-1-138-85275-4 (pbk)
ISBN: 978-1-315-72331-0 (ebk)

Typeset in Bembo and Stone Sans
by Florence Production Ltd, Stoodleigh, Devon, UK

CONTENTS

ABOUT THE AUTHORS

Corine de Ruiter, PhD is Professor of Forensic Psychology at Maastricht University, The Netherlands. Previously, she worked as Head of the Research Department of the Van der Hoevenkliniek, Forensic Psychiatric Centre in Utrecht, and as endowed Professor of Forensic Psychology at the University of Amsterdam. She also maintains a private forensic clinical practice through which she provides postgraduate training and consulting in forensic mental health issues, and works as an expert in criminal and civil cases.

Her research interests include the relationship between mental disorder and violence, prevention of child abuse, risk and protective factors for violence, and treatment of antisocial behavior in children, adolescents, and adults. She has authored more than 200 book chapters and peer reviewed articles. In addition, Dr. de Ruiter has served as Associate Editor of the *International Journal of Forensic Mental Health*, and she is currently Past President of the International Association of Forensic Mental Health Services. She is a Fellow of the Society for Personality Assessment.

Together with her colleagues, she started a 2-year clinical-forensic psychology Master's program at Maastricht University in 2010. She teaches graduate courses in forensic psychological assessment in criminal and family law. Website: www.corinederuiter.eu.

Nancy Kaser-Boyd, PhD is Associate Clinical Professor of Psychiatry and Biobehavioral Sciences at the David Geffen School of Medicine at UCLA, where she teaches advanced psychological assessment and violence risk management and supervises selected psychological assessments of inpatients and outpatients. She is a Fellow of the Society for Personality Assessment and a Diplomate of the American Board of Assessment Psychology. Dr. Kaser-Boyd completed her pre-doctoral clinical internship at LAC/USC County Hospital, and a Postdoctoral Fellowship in Psychology and the Law at the University of Southern California Institute of Psychiatry and Law. She was the director of clinical training at Ingleside Psychiatric Hospital. She is a member of the Psychiatric Expert Panel of Los Angeles County in Criminal Court, evaluating defendants on behalf of the Court, the prosecution, and the defense. She also serves on the Psychiatric Expert Panels in Delinquency and Dependency Courts. She has consulted on criminal cases in state and federal court in California and the western United States and Hawaii. She is a consultant to the University of Southern California Gould School of Law Post-Conviction Justice Project and has presented guest lectures to the California Department of Corrections and Rehabilitation Board of Parole, California Attorneys for Criminal Justice, and the Capital Case Defense Seminar.

Dr. Kaser-Boyd has published and lectured on women and violence, violence risk assessment, insanity, Posttraumatic Stress Disorder, and adolescent maturity.

ACKNOWLEDGEMENTS

First and foremost, we thank Dr. George Zimmar of Taylor & Francis for his encouragement and patience during the years we worked on this project. Managing to write a book like this, while maintaining a very busy academic and professional practice, required repeated postponement of manuscript deadlines. CdR is grateful to her partner Dr. Ferko Őry for unrelenting support but also critical feedback on some of the chapters, and for allowing plenty of writing time during summers, while vacationing on the beautiful Greek islands of Chios and Lesvos. Lavinia Zimmermann, MSc, is thanked for her checking of references and entering digital object identifiers (DOIs). NKB dedicates her work on this book to her mother, Dorothy Rose Kaser, whose unfailing love gave the strength to do difficult work and whose empathy for others and curiosity about human behavior provided the foundation for the practice of forensic psychology.

FOREWORD

The International Association of Forensic Mental Health Services (IAFMHS) is an interdisciplinary professional society representing forensic professionals engaged in research and practice in forensic mental health. Its membership includes psychologists, psychiatrists, social workers, nurses, and lawyers representing over 22 countries worldwide. Its goals are to promote education, training, and research in forensic mental health and to enhance the standards of forensic mental health services in the international community. IAFMHS holds an annual conference, publishes a journal (*International Journal of Forensic Mental Health*) and a book series (International Perspectives on Forensic Mental Health).

The goal of the book series is to improve the quality of health care services in forensic settings by providing a forum for discussing issues related to policy, administration, clinical practice, and research. The series covers topics such as mental health law; the organization and administration of forensic services for people with mental disorder; the development, implementation, and evaluation of treatment programs for mental disorder in civil and criminal justice settings; the assessment and management of violence risk, including risk for sexual violence and family violence; and staff selection, training, and development in forensic mental health systems.

Forensic Psychological Assessment in Practice: Case Studies, by Corine de Ruiter and Nancy Kaser-Boyd, is the latest book in the series. Their book is an exemplar of the application of the scientist-practitioner model, as it uses eight forensic criminal cases to illustrate how forensic clinicians can conduct forensic mental health assessments that are based on empirically supported best practices. The authors each present four of their own cases, providing rich clinical details about their case formulation, the assessment process and its findings, and how they responded to the psycholegal referral questions. Consistent with their scientist-practitioner approach, relevant research is also reviewed. They conclude each case with a discussion on whether the forensic assessment report made a difference in the legal outcome. These cases provide forensic practitioners with a model for approaching similar cases in their practice.

One of the unique features of this book is that the authors are experienced clinicians and scholars who work in two different legal systems, the inquisitorial legal system used in The Netherlands and the adversarial system in the United States. De Ruiter is Professor of Forensic Psychology at Maastricht University in The Netherlands and also has a part-time private practice conducting criminal forensic assessments and providing expert testimony. She served as president of the IAFMHS (2011–2013). She teaches forensic psychological assessment and has also published on this topic, including co-authoring the Structured Assessment of Protective Factors for Violence Risk (SAPROF), a widely used forensic instrument for assessing protective factors for violence risk. Kaser-Boyd is Associate Clinical Professor, Department of Psychiatry and Biobehavioral Sciences, Semel Institute for Neuroscience and Human Behavior, Geffen School of Medicine at UCLA. Her private practice focuses on the psychological assessment of adults and children. She has published on a range of forensic topics, including Post-traumatic Stress Disorder, child custody, battered women's syndrome, and children who kill. The authors point out that their two perspectives allow readers to compare the roles of forensic experts in two quite different legal systems. The first chapter of their book provides a concise overview of adversarial and inquisitorial approaches to justice. They note that while these two approaches have different legal procedures and rules, particularly the absence of juries and the more directive role of judges in the inquisitorial system, they conclude that, despite the many differences, the role of the forensic expert in each system is more similar than different.

The eight case studies in this book cover a broad range of forensic cases that may be encountered by forensic clinicians in both North America and Europe. These include neonaticide in a young immigrant woman, a firesetter in a longstay forensic facility, indecent exposure, and filicide. Other chapters add case studies on the effects of intimate partner battering, and on threat assessment.

Both authors collaborate on the final three chapters, each of which will prove valuable to forensic practitioners in preparing a forensic report and if they are called upon to testify as an expert witness in court. The first of the final two chapters reviews the essential qualities of a good forensic report, providing details of the structure and content of each of the major sections. Readers will especially find useful the separate section on communicating the results of a violence risk assessment, as the authors compare and contrast the two primary approaches to risk communications—the prediction model, which focuses on probability estimates, and the prevention model, which focuses on categorical estimates of risk and the identification of risk reduction strategies. De Ruiter and Kaser-Boyd recommend a blended approach that may report probability estimates but also focuses on dynamic risk factors and risk management strategies. The final chapter will be of value to clinicians preparing for court testimony. The authors review the literature on the characteristics of effective and ethical expert testimony, relevant ethical and professional guidelines, and present practical tips for preparing for direct testimony and cross-examination. Concrete examples of how to respond to cross-examination are provided as well as a court transcript of the testimony of one of the authors.

I am pleased to add this exceptional book to the IAFMHS book series. De Ruiter and Kaser-Boyd bring a wealth of forensic assessment experience to produce a book that will be of value to experienced clinicians as well as graduate students interested in learning about the challenges of conducting evidence-based forensic psychological assessments.

Ronald Roesch
Series Editor
International Perspectives on Forensic
Mental Health

PREFACE

What qualifies as professional and ethical forensic psychological assessment practice in criminal cases? Many textbooks have provided the frameworks, the guidelines and the standards, but not the examples, the raw reality and the pitfalls of day-to-day forensic casework. This book is our attempt to demonstrate by means of case studies what we consider professional forensic psychological practice to be, integrating present-day findings from empirical research, knowledge about current legal procedures, advanced training about mental health disorders in relation to crime and violence, and ethical principles into our casework.

Forensic psychological work in criminal cases takes place within an inherently adversarial context. The stakes for both the defendant and the prosecuting agent are high. This renders forensic mental health assessment highly vulnerable to heuristic biases and partisanship. The "hired gun" always looms large in the distance. It is our strong belief that the only way to avoid the "hired gun" fallacy is to ruthlessly choose the subject of the evaluation as our focus, that is, the person we are assessing. Even though the prosecution, the defense, or the judge may have given us the task to evaluate the individual and may be paying the bill for our work, our professional obligation to provide the best expertise we have to offer lies first and foremost with the person being assessed. Our work as forensic assessors is strongly related to their legal and civil rights and may even be a matter of life and death to them. Our forensic psychological assessment has to be performed in a thorough, balanced, objective, reliable, and accurate manner, in the interest of the assessed person. It is to him or her that we are ethically and professionally accountable. We are obliged to "find the facts" of the person's psychological make-up, with a keen eye for supportive and disconfirming facts related to mental state, and for the role of contextual factors and cultural issues. We are also obligated to perform forensic assessment in a manner that is mindful of potential risk to the public and protection of victims.

The findings from a forensic psychological assessment need to be written up accurately and transparently for the retaining party, with the ultimate goal of assisting the trier-of-fact in coming to a just legal decision. The written report, with a keen view of the interests of the individual as described above, is the outcome of a process of objective engagement between assessor and the person assessed.

Finally, we have a duty to provide clear testimony, free of confusing jargon, personal opinion, and which acknowledges possible biases or areas where the results are mixed or do not support a conclusion. In the courtroom, we also have an obligation to follow ethical principles regarding the findings of other professionals.

Forensic mental health assessment, in short, is an intensely engaging endeavor which must proceed with knowledge of the laws of a jurisdiction, awareness of relevant literature on the issues at hand, and the highest standards of professional forensic-clinical practice. It is towards these standards that this book is written. We hope it will inspire both novice and seasoned forensic-clinical psychologists to offer their best effort in the service of justice.

1

THE FORENSIC-CLINICAL PSYCHOLOGIST AS EXPERT IN CRIMINAL COURT

Corine de Ruiter

This book provides the reader with an intimate, detailed look into the casework of two forensic-clinical psychologists from different continents with different legal systems. Every clinical-forensic psychologist who offers her[1] services as an expert witness to the legal arena needs to be cognizant of the way the law and the legal system operate in her jurisdiction. Because the authors work within different systems, the adversarial system of the US and the inquisitorial system of The Netherlands, this book also provides a unique opportunity to compare the role of the expert witness, the procedures and regulations governing her work, and the practical opportunities and limitations involved. This chapter will first provide a brief overview of the most important differences between the two legal systems. Second, the role of the forensic psychologist as expert witness in both systems will be reviewed, including specific regulations which determine the legal acceptance of expert testimony. Finally, the argument will be made that despite the conceptual differences between the two systems, actual practice may be more similar than predicted from theory. The final part of this chapter is devoted to a discussion of the unique characteristics of forensic mental health assessment (FMHA) in comparison to clinical mental health assessment. Besides differences in terms of context and assessee, FMHA requires use of specialist Forensic Assessment Instruments (FAIs) and independent data from collateral sources.

Adversarial versus Inquisitorial Justice

It is important to realize first that each adversarial system differs greatly from the other, and the same applies to the different inquisitorial systems (van Koppen & Penrod, 2003). In an adversarial system, legal proceedings are essentially a contest between two opposing parties (Crombag, 2003). The contest is governed by rules of fair play and the fundamental equality of the parties involved (van Koppen & Penrod, 2003). The adversarial model often includes judgment by lay peers (the jury system) and the oral presentation of evidence (Damaška, 1973). Because lay people are the decision makers, there is a strong emphasis on rules of evidence to assure jurors are presented with reliable evidence. In an adversarial system, the judge is the arbiter who decides on the admissibility of evidence (van Koppen & Penrod, 2003).

In the inquisitorial system, legal proceedings are considered an inquiry into the truth, which is the responsibility of the court (Damaška, 1973). Thus, for instance, plea bargaining is considered irreconcilable with the inquisitorial system, because it is in conflict with the search for truth (van Cleave, 1997). And even though oral presentation of evidence is not inconsistent with an inquisitorial system, it is a fact of tradition that inquisitorial systems have a preference for written presentation of evidence (Damaška, 1973; Nijboer, 2000). Another important difference is the absence of rules of evidence in inquisitorial systems, the assumption being that the judge is trusted with the task to weigh the evidence in line with its reliability (van Koppen & Penrod, 2003).

These theoretical differences between the systems result in a large number of practical differences. One of the most remarkable of these is the fact that in The Netherlands, police officers record all witness and suspect statements into sworn statements (in Dutch: *proces-verbalen*). These statements become part of the official case file and this emphasis on written documents makes Dutch courts reluctant to hear witnesses in court (van Koppen & Penrod, 2003), unless the judge deems the written information unclear or insufficient.

Of all European criminal justice systems, the Dutch is probably one of the most inquisitorial, compared to, for instance, the German and Scandinavian systems (Geeroms, 2002; van Koppen & Penrod, 2003). Still, there have been rather profound changes in criminal procedure as a result of the European Convention on Human Rights and Fundamental Freedoms and jurisprudence of the European Court of Human Rights (ECHR) in Strasbourg (van Kampen, 2003; Swart, 1999), as a consequence of which more adversarial elements have entered the legal system. Particularly, Article 6 of the European Convention refers to notions of equality of arms and the right to a fair trial. Entirely different from countries such as the US and Germany, in The Netherlands, there is no system of constitutional review by the courts. Had there been such a system, it is likely that the European Convention and the ECHR would have played a more limited role in public debates on civil liberties and basic individual rights in The Netherlands. Swart (1999) comments as follows: "The European Convention has become to the Dutch legal system what the national Constitution is to the legal systems of the United States of America or Germany" (p. 41).

The ECHR has come to exert an important influence in transforming a number of practices in Dutch criminal procedure; basically these transformations have made the system more adversarial and more civil rights-oriented. Not all of these changes will be listed here; the reader is referred to Swart (1999) for a more detailed discussion. Here, a few examples will be highlighted. First, the practice of not hearing witnesses (including experts) in court has changed due to jurisprudence of the ECHR ruling that the statement of a witness cannot be used as evidence against the defendant, unless the defense has been given an opportunity to question the witness (*Unterpertinger v. Austria*).[2] Another area where the European Constitution and the ECHR have had a major influence on Dutch practice is access to legal counsel during police interrogations. In Art. 57, line 2 of the Code of Criminal Procedure, it is stated that: "The suspect is authorized to the assistance of counsel during the interrogation. Counsel is provided the opportunity to make the necessary remarks."[3] Still, in practice, it often happens that legal counsel is not present, especially not during the interrogations immediately after arrest, for practical reasons. In June 2009, however, the Dutch Minister of Justice wrote in a letter to parliament that in his opinion two ECHR decisions from 2008 (*Salduz v. Turkey* and *Panovits v. Cyprus*), even though not requiring the *right* to the presence of counsel during police questioning, did require adaptation of the legislation on the point of informing and providing legal assistance to suspects prior to police interrogation. The conclusion that the accused prior to the first police interrogation must have had the opportunity to discuss his trial position with counsel seemed inevitable (Letter of the Minister of Justice, June 8, 2009).[4]

Similarly, the videotaping of police interrogations has become much more common due to ECHR jurisprudence. In 2006, the Dutch Minister of Justice promised parliament the phased introduction of auditory or audiovisual registration of all police interrogations (Letter of the Minister of Justice, August 25, 2006).[5] This resulted in a major logistical operation, with 30 interrogation studios for audiovisual registration built by July 2009. Since October 1, 2006 the legal obligation to audiovisual recording of interrogations of persons under 16 and intellectually disabled individuals has been enforced.

Jury versus Professional Judges

One large difference between the legal systems of the US and The Netherlands is the fact the US has a jury system and The Netherlands has a system of professional judges. In cases of serious crime, the Dutch system employs a court comprising three judges. Lesser crimes are handled by a one-judge court, comparable to so-called "bench trials" in the US (Hans & Vidmar, 1986). The jury system brings with it one important difference between the two systems which is the two-stage justice process. First, the jury decides whether the defendant is guilty or not guilty (i.e., *actus reus*). In the second, sentencing stage, the professional judge decides on the sentence. This two-stage process has important implications for the clinical-forensic psychologist, because she may be brought into the procedure only at this second stage. In many cases, however, the forensic psychologist is asked to evaluate the defendant's mental state at the time of a crime (*mens rea*;

Packer, 2009). In such cases, the psychologist's report, or testimony, might be amended and used for sentencing. In cases where the death penalty is a possibility, or where the defense of Not Guilty By Reason of Insanity (NGRI) is raised, there are three parts to the trial (guilt, sanity, and sentencing) and the forensic psychologist could be called to testify at any stage. In death penalty cases, there is a trial focused on guilt or innocence, and if the jury finds the defendant guilty of the "special circumstances" that lead to the death penalty, there is a separate hearing, with the same jury, that focuses on mitigation (Cunningham, 2010). Then the judge holds a hearing to pronounce sentencing. In The Netherlands, the stages of guilty and sentencing are merged, and it is up to the judges to ascertain that the two evidentiary issues (guilty/not guilty and criminal responsibility/ violence risk) are considered separately. As we will see in some cases in this book (e.g., Chapter 6) judges, like all human beings, are quite prone to expectancy bias and may have difficulty with rational and objective reasoning and decision making (McAuliff & Bornstein, 2012).

How a Suspect Goes through the Systems

Van Koppen and Penrod (2003) provided a bird's eye review of the US and Dutch criminal justice systems by demonstrating how a suspect of a robbery would be dealt with by either system. We will not completely restate their review here, but point out some important highlights, as they are relevant for the present book.

Upon arrest as a suspect, American police officers have to inform the suspect of his Miranda rights (after *Miranda v. Arizona*, 1966), i.e., the right to remain silent, the right to legal counsel, free counsel if necessary, and that anything the suspect says can be used against him in court. The Dutch police have to present the suspect with the so-called *caution*, i.e., that he has the right to remain silent. Even though the American suspect has a right to have counsel present during police interrogations, this right is often not invoked, for a variety of reasons, for example, confusion about when one can have a lawyer (Leo, 1996). As pointed out above, the Dutch suspect has the right to counsel during interrogations by the police based on ECHR rulings. In The Netherlands, a suspect who does not have the financial means to pay a legal counsel herself has the right to choose one who will then be paid by the government. In the US, a defendant of limited resources will be provided with a legal counsel paid for by public funds, such as a public defender or counsel appointed from a panel of attorneys paid by the jurisdiction (county, state, or Federal).

In both jurisdictions, obtaining confession evidence is an important goal of interrogations (van Koppen & Penrod, 2003). In the US, interrogations are often taped and transcribed and the forensic psychologist has access to the live version and the transcript. In the Dutch system, the police type down the confession statement in a *proces-verbaal* (see p. 2, this chapter), and whether the defendant adds his signature on the statement is not relevant. This important difference with the US system is related to the acceptability of hearsay evidence in Dutch criminal procedure. The Dutch Supreme Court ruled in 1926 that hearsay evidence is acceptable, by reasoning that a hearsay witness personally experienced what another person said (*HR December 20, 1926, NJ 1927, 87*). Under this ruling, the sworn statement of police officers with a display of the defendant's statement is as valuable evidence as the defendant's statement itself. Thus, even statements that have subsequently been withdrawn by the defendant can be used as evidence (see Chapter 6 of this book for an example of a case in point; van Koppen & Penrod, 2003). Thus, the legal principle of immediate observation as a witness is lost in Dutch criminal procedure. As mentioned above, the recent introduction of audio-visual recording of police interrogations has reintroduced the immediacy aspect to some extent. At the least, audiovisual recording helps to prevent police from representing a biased version of the defendant's statements.

A Dutch criminal investigation is led by the public prosecutor (in Dutch: *Officier van Justitie*). All documents collected in a case, such as technical forensic evidence, information gained via wiretapping, interrogation statements, etc., are entered into a file. In more serious crimes, an investigating judge also becomes involved. This judge decides on the possible use of certain coercive measures, such as house searches, preventive detention and wiretapping. In many ways, the role of the investigating judge is similar to the role of judges in the US as they are responsible for issuing search warrants, arrest warrants, etc. (van Koppen & Penrod, 2003). In The Netherlands, the investigating judge also decides on the issue of whether or not a forensic mental health evaluation of the defendant needs to be conducted, and thus on the involvement of a forensic-clinical psychologist in a particular case.

The defense and the prosecution in The Netherlands, together with the investigating judge, play a role in building the case file. The defense can ask for additional investigations, although the prosecution always is one step ahead because they are in the lead. Just as in the US, it is the public prosecutor who decides ultimately whether to bring the case to trial. In the US, there are rules for the exchange of information gathered by each side; this is called Discovery. Typically, all materials gathered that are going to be introduced in a trial must be turned over to the other side within 30 days of the start of the trial. This includes the forensic psychologist's report and, typically, all of the "raw data," which includes interview notes, test results, emails with the attorney, notes of consultation with other experts, and so on.

In The Netherlands, there is no system of plea-bargaining. If the prosecution wants to obtain a conviction, the case has to be tried. For less serious crimes (e.g., vandalism, petty theft, driving uninsured) the prosecution can offer the defendant a so-called *transaction*, in the form of a fine or a number of hours of community service, and the case then doesn't appear before a judge. Another difference between the US and The Netherlands is the absence of bail in the latter's justice system. In The Netherlands, a suspect can be detained for 6 hours by the police.

This period can be extended by 3 days by the public prosecutor, but after this, the investigating judge has to authorize preventive detention (van Koppen & Penrod, 2003).

The trial itself reveals the most striking differences between the two legal systems. In the US, the adversarial system brings two parties in front of a jury with the judge serving the role of an arbiter responsible for ensuring that rules of evidence and procedure are followed. Both parties call witnesses and experts to present evidence and cross-examination of these by the other party is part of the procedure. In The Netherlands, a court consisting of three judges decides on more serious crimes,[6] mainly based on the prepared case file, without hearing witnesses and experts at trial. Since all participants have had access to the case file, a trial in The Netherlands takes much less time than a US trial. The court must be convinced that the defendant is guilty as charged based on the evidence as stated in the Code of Criminal Procedure. What is considered legal evidence is not very specifically defined in the Code, with one exception: at least two pieces of evidence are needed for a conviction, for instance, a confession and an eyewitness statement. Thus, in the Dutch system, the court is both determining whether it is convinced by (the quality of) the evidence and is making the ultimate legal decision (van Koppen & Penrod, 2003). In the US, the judge decides on the admissibility of the evidence on the basis of specific admissibility rules (see below), and the jury decides based on specific jury instructions which are defined by law.

Obviously, witnesses and experts are at times called to testify in a Dutch criminal court, at the request of the defense, the prosecution or the court itself. However, the court can refuse to hear witnesses or experts (see, for instance, the case of Kim V. in Chapter 6 of this book). Mostly, the judges start to ask questions of witnesses or experts, after which the prosecution and the defense are allowed to do so. In both The Netherlands and the US, the defendant also has a right to speak in court. In the US, in reality, many defense lawyers consider it too risky to put their client on the witness stand, due to the likelihood of intense, sometimes hostile, cross-examination.

In both countries, the judge decides on the sentence if the defendant is deemed guilty. In the US, this is the second, sentencing phase of the trial at which new witnesses and experts may be called. The Dutch system only has a one-phase trial. In The Netherlands, the court usually arrives at a verdict two weeks after the trial hearings have officially ended. The decision is provided in writing and must be unanimous and offer the reasoning of the Court. Still, some verdicts seem quite opaque as to their reasoning: "sometimes it remains unclear why, for instance, the court believed one witness and not another who testified to the opposite state of affairs" (van Koppen & Penrod, 2003, p. 13).

Another major difference between the two legal systems becomes apparent at the appeal stage. In The Netherlands, both the prosecution and the defense can go into appeal at the court of appeal (in Dutch: *Gerechtshof*), where the case will be tried anew.[7] In the US, most appeals are not tried *de novo*, but on the basis of appellate documents, which point to serious error at the trial, inadequate legal representation, or the discovery of new evidence. If the appellate court notes serious shortcomings, a new trial can be granted. A famous case in point is the case of Andrea Yates[8] who drowned her five children in the bathtub on June 20, 2001 under the influence of a psychotic depression. In March 2002, a Texan jury rejected the insanity defense and found her guilty. The court sentenced her to life imprisonment with eligibility for parole in 40 years. On January 6, 2005, a Texas Court of Appeals reversed the conviction, because psychiatrist and prosecution witness Dr. Park Dietz was found to have given materially false testimony at trial. Who was actually to blame for this testimony is still a bit of a mystery, but the end result was that the First Appeals Court in Houston decided that the erroneous statements may have precipitated a miscarriage of justice. Subsequently, on July 26, 2006, a new jury found Andrea Yates Not Guilty by Reason of Insanity, and she was committed to a state psychiatric hospital.

The Expert Witness

The difference between the adversarial and inquisitorial systems is also apparent in the way they approach expert evidence (van Kampen, 2003; Malsch & Freckelton, 2005). In an adversarial system such as the US system, each party presents his own expert to the trier of fact, be it a jury or a judge. In an inquisitorial system, the judge generally appoints the experts. Defendants in most cases do not actively engage experts, although they are legally allowed to do so. As we will see in many of the actual cases presented in this book (e.g., Chapter 2), the practice of criminal law as it pertains to expert evidence, may not be as different as theory suggests. For instance, recently the Dutch Code of Criminal Procedure has been extended with a special law termed the "Expert in Criminal Cases Act" (in Dutch: *Wet deskundige in strafzaken*)[9] which came into effect January 1, 2010. This Act gives the accused the right to request a second expert opinion, paid by the government. The defense should also be informed of the granting of an order for an expert investigation and is given the opportunity to influence the scope and direction of the expert's investigation. In fact, the position of the defense is strengthened by the introduction of this Act, and the courts have to deal more frequently with more than one expert report, similar to adversarial systems.

Although some proponents have argued that the adversarial system is more fair because both parties can introduce expert evidence (Freckelton, 1987) and defendants are not at the mercy of court-appointed experts (Howard, 1991), for defendants to take responsibility, both factually and financially, to secure assistance of experts is a daunting task (van Kampen, 2003). Most US states have statutes that authorize the courts to allow the defendant to secure expert assistance "upon a finding, after appropriate enquiry in an ex parte proceeding, that the services are necessary and that the person is financially unable to obtain them" [modeled after Federal Criminal Justice Act 1964 (18 USC § 3006 (e) (1)]. The US Supreme Court upheld the defendant's right to expert assistance as part of due process in the case of *Ake v. Oklahoma* (1985). For further discussion of the right to expert assistance in the US system compared to the Dutch system, the reader is referred to van Kampen (2003).

Admissibility of Expert Evidence

In both legal systems, a witness qualifies as an expert by knowledge, skill, experience, or education and may testify in the form of an opinion or otherwise (Federal Rule of Evidence 702, 1975).[10] A major difference between the two criminal justice systems is the way the quality of expert evidence is monitored by the courts. The US has a set of admissibility rules that govern whether or not certain evidence may be presented at trial. In fact, these admissibility rules work as screeners of the input to the trier of fact. In the Dutch legal system, such admissibility rules do not exist. In contrast, in the Dutch system the screening takes place afterwards, by way of decision and argumentation rules (output control). For instance, the Dutch Code of Criminal Procedure (CCP) defines what type of statements and documents may be used as evidence (Art. 339–344a CCP) and also provides basic requirements for evidence of guilt (Art. 342.2 CCP).

For expert evidence to be admissible, including evidence presented by a clinical-forensic psychologist, US courts at the state level apply different rules. All expert evidence admissibility rules serve the function to secure the reliability of the evidence that is used in court. The rules vary in terms of strictness. In California, the state where Dr. Kaser-Boyd conducts most of her expert witness evaluations, the *Frye* test is used. In *Frye v. United States* (1923), the D.C. District Court held that for expert evidence to be admissible, the method on which the expert's opinion is based has to have gained general acceptance in the particular field to which it belongs. In 1993, the US Supreme Court in the case of *Daubert v. Merrell Dow Pharmaceuticals* ruled that for scientific expert evidence to be admissible in court it must be: (1) falsifiable, i.e., a product of a testable theory or technique; (2) subjected to peer review and publication in professional journals; (3) based on a generally accepted theory; and (4) based on a technique with a known error rate (Ireland, 2010). The decision in the *Daubert* case has met with approval but also criticism (van Kampen, 2003). One of the issues raised by the decision was whether the *Daubert* criteria should also be applied to non-scientific expert evidence. In 1999, the US Supreme Court in *Kumho Tire Co. v. Carmichael* held that *Daubert* criteria should be applied to all expert evidence, whether based on science or "technical or otherwise specialized knowledge." *Daubert* has not been adopted by all US states (for example, it has not superseded *Frye* in California state courts) as of the publication of this book.

All admissibility criteria emphasize the importance of experts being explicit about the scientific foundations of their opinions and the methods they employ.

As such, they assist both the expert and the trier of fact in helping them decide on the weight that should be given to evidence. Ireland (2008, p.119) cogently argued that:

> The principles of *Daubert* are further useful in encouraging all witnesses to distinguish between what they claim is opinion based on scientific fact, and what is opinion based on specialized knowledge or conjecture. [. . .] The point being made here, however, is a simple one: if you intend to provide an opinion based on psychological tests, ensure that the tests are scientifically robust. If there are problems with the tests, you must identify these for the Court or tribunal so that they can better evaluate "expert" evidence and determine if its base is truly scientific or closer to specialized knowledge. Legal forums simply need to be assured of the basis of an opinion in case this is later relied upon.

The chapters in this book provide examples of expert evidence with varying degrees of scientific basis. For instance, the neonaticide case in Chapter 3 demonstrates how language barriers and the absence of empirical research on the use of standardized psychological tests with certain ethnic minorities may limit the validity or quality of evidence. However, the chapter also shows that the clinical-forensic psychologist, who carefully uses the empirical literature as it pertains to the case at hand, can offer an expert opinion of great relevance to the trier of fact.

In The Netherlands, as mentioned above, it is up to the trial court to decide on the selection and evaluation of the available evidence, including expert evidence. Notwithstanding this principle, there are a few Supreme Court decisions that have served to alert the lower courts to the fact that they need to justify their decisions based on expert evidence. These Supreme Court decisions resulted from criticism from defense counsel that expert evidence used was hardly scientific, that it was incomplete, or otherwise defective (van Kampen, 2003). The *Anatomically Correct Dolls* decision (*HR February 28, 1989, NJ 1989, 748*) concerned a case of a defendant accused of child sexual abuse. The expert had used so-called anatomically correct dolls when interviewing the alleged victims. At the appeal stage, defense counsel had argued that this method was unscientific and presented its own expert, as well as supportive scientific literature from peer-reviewed journals. The appellate court still convicted the defendant, using the first expert's report as one of the pieces of evidence of guilt. The defense appealed to the Supreme Court, which held that the Court of Appeal, when confronted with an argued attack upon the reliability of the method used by an expert, cannot rely upon such evidence as a basis of their decision of guilt without providing additional evidence about why the court deems the method used reliable (van Kampen, 2003).

Finally, the Dutch Supreme Court in 1998 in the now famous *Shoemaker* case (*HR January 27, 1998, NJ 1998, 404*) ruled that when courts are confronted with an attack on the expert himself (aside from his method), they need to assure whether the expert's knowledge also concerns research on, and analysis of, the substance of his testimony. In the *Shoemaker* case, a foot and shoe technician (an orthopedic shoemaker) testified at trial about shoeprint traces that had been found at the crime scene of a double homicide. The defense challenged the shoemaker's testimony to the Court of Appeal, reasoning that his method was unreliable and his level of expertise inadequate to serve as evidence in court. The Court rejected this argumentation and upheld the shoemaker's testimony. Subsequently, the Supreme Court overturned this ruling and argued that the Court of Appeal had not proven that the shoemaker, although fitting around 400 orthopedic shoes per year, had any expertise in analyzing shoe traces, that it was unclear which method the expert had used in his investigation, why the expert considered this method to be reliable, as well as to what degree the expert was capable of professionally using this method (van Kampen, 2003). Of note, the Supreme Court stated that whether or not the expert's results concur with those of other expert's findings in a case is not relevant; the trial court needs to independently determine the reliability of the expert and his method.

Obviously, many people believe admissibility standards (in the US) and Supreme Court decisions (in the US and The Netherlands) on the matter of what constitutes proper expert evidence are beneficial to fact and truth finding. Still, the question remains whether the standards and/or Supreme Court decisions actually change practice in criminal proceedings. Legal commentators in the US have argued that the real contribution of the *Daubert* decision was not in creating a stricter admissibility test, but rather in raising the overall awareness of judges to the problem of unreliable or "junk" science (Bernstein, 2001; Cheng & Yoon, 2005). Therefore, whether a jurisdiction nominally follows *Frye* or *Daubert*, the practical results are essentially the same (Cheng & Yoon, 2005).

Quality Control of Forensic Psychologists as Experts to the Court

Quality control over what is considered appropriate and scientifically sound practice is theoretically maintained by professional ethics guidelines of professional organizations. The American Psychological Association (APA) developed Specialty Guidelines for Forensic Psychologists (American Psychological Association, 1991, 2013) to provide standards for psychologists from all subdisciplines (clinical, developmental, social, experimental) when solicited as experts (Goodman-Delahunty, 1997). These Specialty Guidelines were updated after extensive peer consultation (APA, 2013). The Dutch Institute of Psychologists (*Nederlands Instituut van Psychologen*: NIP) does not have separate guidelines for forensic psychologists; they are held to the general NIP professional ethics code[11] which is tailored towards psychologists who are working with clients in a clinical/consulting setting. The recently instituted "Expert in Criminal Cases Act" (see

p. 7, this chapter) has been paired with the institutionalization of a national registry for experts to the court (in Dutch: *Nederlands Register Gerechtelijk Deskundigen*; NRGD). On its website[12] the registry claims it is "independent and transparent, and that it guarantees and promotes the consistent quality of the contribution made by court experts to the legal process." In practice, the requirements for registration as a clinical-forensic psychologist are much too lenient and basically allow entry to psychologists who have been practicing as an expert witness for a long time, but who do not meet the level of standards for certification as set by sister organizations in the US, such as the American Board of Professional Psychology.[13] In the Newsletter of the Forensic Psychology section of The Netherlands Institute of Psychologists, I have noted the NRGD "missed the opportunity" to set professional quality standards (de Ruiter, 2011).

Forensic Mental Health Assessment (FMHA)

Thus far, this chapter has focused on the differences and similarities between the two legal systems in which we practice. Some of these aspects will become apparent in the case examples we provide in this book. We close this first chapter with a discussion of the unique characteristics of forensic mental health assessments as they are exemplified in this book.

Forensic-clinical psychology is a subspecialty within clinical psychology that has grown extensively during the past few decades, both in terms of the number of clinical psychologists who started a forensic practice and in terms of specialized graduate programs in forensic psychology (Heilbrun, Kelley, Koller, Giallella, & Peterson, 2013). Currently, most psychologists practicing FMHA are originally trained as clinical psychologists, and it is extremely important to realize a number of fundamental differences between clinical and forensic psychological assessment, since these have important implications for forensic practice.

Many scholars before us have written on these essential differences (Ackerman, 1999; Greenberg & Shuman, 1997; Heilbrun, 2001; Jackson, 2008), and we refer the reader to these sources for a more extensive discussion of this issue. Here, we will highlight a number of aspects which we have found particularly helpful in our own "transformation" from clinical to forensic psychologist.

The first notable difference, which has a large impact on the FMHA process, is the purpose of the assessment. In clinical assessment this is often to diagnose an individual's symptoms and to make treatment recommendations. Forensic assessment is performed to assist the trier of fact. A forensic psychologist's role is more akin to that of an objective scientist whose function is to assist legal fact finders in making well-grounded decisions (Marczyk, DeMatteo, Kutinsky, & Heilbrun, 2008). In clinical assessment, the psychologist serves more in a therapeutic and supportive role. The fact that assessees are mostly mandated to participate in the FMHA makes the evaluator-assessee relationship potentially adversarial, which puts particular demands on the evaluator's interpersonal skills and on the test instruments employed. Because there is often a lot at stake for the assessee in an FMHA, she may have an interest in distorting (aspects of) her presentation.

A second reason why distorted response styles are more likely to occur in FMHA is related to the higher prevalence of certain types of psychopathology among assessees in a forensic context. Notably, DSM-IV-TR (American Psychiatric Association, 2000) Cluster B personality disorders (e.g., antisocial, narcissistic, borderline) and DSM-5 (American Psychiatric Association, 2013)[14] antisocial/psychopathic and borderline personality disorders (PDs), either as a primary or secondary diagnosis, are much more prevalent in forensic and correctional than in general clinical settings (Hildebrand & de Ruiter, 2004; de Ruiter & Greeven, 2000). Antisocial/psychopathic and borderline PDs are characterized by externalization of blame and diminished self-reflective abilities, which may serve as a basis for defensive and distorted responding. As a consequence of the adversarial context and the possible presence of certain personality traits, a socially desirable and defensive response style is more common in FMHA than in clinical assessment. Outright distortion in the form of faking good and faking bad may also occur, and the evaluator must take this into account when selecting a test battery.

Self-report questionnaires are highly vulnerable to distortive response styles, and FMHA requires the use of self-report instruments which allow for a judgment of response style. Questionnaires such as the Minnesota Multiphasic Personality Inventory-2 (MMPI-2; Butcher, Dahlstrom, Graham, Tellegen, & Kaemmer, 1989) and the Personality Assessment Inventory (PAI; Morey, 1991, 1998) allow for a detailed examination of response style, and should be included in FMHA for this purpose. Whenever results on instruments such as the MMPI-2 and PAI raise concern about the validity of an assessee's responses, further testing with specific symptom validity tests, such as the Structured Inventory of Malingered Symptoms (SIMS; Widows & Smith, 2005) and Structured Interview of Reported Symptoms (SIRS; Rogers, 1992; Rogers, Bagby, & Dickens, 1992) is called for. A comprehensive discussion of response style assessment is beyond the scope of this chapter, but we encourage forensic psychologists to study an excellent resource on this topic: Rogers' (2008) edited volume *Clinical assessment of malingering and deception*, now in its third edition.

Performance-based personality tests, such as the Rorschach Inkblot Method, are just as prone to response style distortion as self-report personality tests (Sewell, 2008). Scholars recommend using the response style indicators on the self-report tests to gauge possible distortion on performance-based tests. Still, performance-based personality tests can make a unique contribution to FMHA because they are comparatively less transparent to the assessee. Furthermore, using multiple methods of assessment (self-report and performance-based) allows the evaluator to examine the concordance between the findings from the two different methods. When the two concur, the evaluator has a stronger basis for the diagnostic conclusion; when they do not concur, the evaluator needs to exercise caution, either by looking for other data and/or formulating more tentative conclusions. Obviously, cross-validation of test findings is especially important in FMHA where the standard of proof is set higher than in clinical assessment. Despite the above-mentioned efforts of psychological test developers to incorporate response style indicators into their instruments, their detection rates (sensitivity and positive predictive power) are never perfect and error rates (e.g., false positives) should always be considered (Rogers, 2008).

FMHA requires the use of multiple collateral data sources, including observations of others and (medical, criminal, educational) file information, to complement the results from the psychological testing, in order for the evaluator to "weigh all the evidence." A case I examined while I was working at Van der Hoeven forensic hospital serves to illustrate the importance of collateral information in FMHA.

In 1999, Mr. A. was sentenced to 1 year's imprisonment and a mandated treatment order because of sexual assault on a student. All new patients arrive with a copy of their criminal file, including the FMHA report that was prepared during the pre-sentencing phase. The pre-sentencing report concluded that Mr. A. suffered from a mixed personality disorder with borderline and antisocial features, and alcohol abuse. He claims he doesn't remember the offense because he was too drunk. He is the youngest of four children and says he was sexually abused by his father between the ages of 6 and 12. When he was 16 years old, he got a girl pregnant and a son was born. Both the girl and Mr. A. started other relationships, and she migrated to Australia with her new partner and her son in 1984. In 1982, Mr. A. started a relationship with Helen and they had two children. Helen and the children died in a fire in 1989 and Mr. A. claimed that this was when his alcohol abuse started because he could not handle the loss. We noted that the file contained a number of inconsistencies and most of the information was from only one source: Mr. A. himself. At our forensic psychiatric hospital, all newly admitted patients were assessed by means of the Psychopathy Checklist-Revised (PCL-R; Hare, 1991, 2003), the MMPI-2 and the Rorschach Inkblot Method (Exner, 2003). The PCL-R obviously requires extensive collateral information to be able to score a number of its criteria (e.g., pathological lying, manipulativeness, exaggerated sense of self-worth). Thus, we took it upon ourselves to acquire collateral information by interviewing his siblings (his parents were both deceased) and collecting official documentation.

Our findings were quite shocking. Mr. A. had lied about most of the traumatic events in his life. His father had not sexually abused him, Helen did not exist (nor any children from this relationship), and he did not have a son in Australia. When confronted with these lies, Mr. A. claimed he made up these stories to impress people because he thought his true life story was uninteresting. Our judgment, on the basis of the FMHA we conducted, was that Mr. A. was far more cunning and manipulative than he would admit. He had successfully presented himself for many years as a victim of a difficult life, a story which he had held up during several prior admissions to addiction treatment centers and homeless shelters. He had also managed to deceive the assessor who conducted the pre-sentencing FMHA, who concluded that "Mr. A.'s lack of empathy was a result of a very tragic life history."

Last but not least, a final difference between clinical and forensic assessment is the difference in the type of referral questions and the implications these have for the choice of assessment methods. Psycholegal referral questions, such as assessment of legal competencies and risk of future violence, require use of specific forensic assessment instruments (FAIs). FAIs improve the standardization and replicability of FMHA (Grisso, 2003). FAIs are specifically developed to aid in the accurate assessment of a particular psycholegal construct. For instance, the Rogers Criminal Responsibility Assessment Scales (R-CRAS; Rogers, 1984) structures the decision making process in the assessment of legal insanity by means of a review of 28 criteria relevant to the issue of insanity (e.g., awareness of the criminality of the behavior, delusions, intellectual disability). Structured tools for risk assessment, such as the HCR-20 for violence risk (Webster, Douglas, Eaves, & Hart, 1997; Douglas, Hart, Webster, & Belfrage, 2013) and the Level of Service Inventory-Revised for general reoffending (LSI-R; Andrews & Bonta, 1995) assist in increasing the level of transparency and accountability in formulating diagnostic judgments on future risk. During the past decades, many FAIs have been developed and it is difficult for the forensic mental health practitioner to keep abreast of these developments. Good resources are the *Best Practices in Forensic Mental Health Assessment* book series (series editors: Grisso, Goldstein, & Heilbrun; Oxford University Press), Grisso (2003), for evaluating competencies, and Otto and Douglas (2010) for an overview of available risk assessment tools.

The unique characteristics of FMHA are summarized in the schema in Figure 1.1.

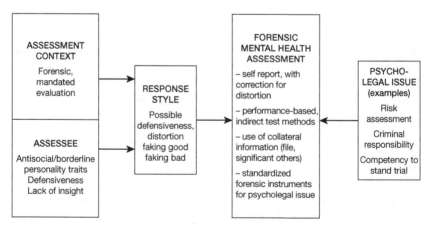

FIGURE 1.1 Guidelines for Forensic Mental Health Assessment in Relation to the Forensic Setting, the Forensic Assessee, and the Psycholegal Question.

In the case studies we provide in this book, the unique qualities of FMHA will be illustrated. Each chapter covers a specific type of offense, and the central aspects of the case are related to the existing empirical knowledge base. We aim for best-evidence practice in FMHA, yet the knowledge base in terms of normative data and psychometric qualities of many FAIs and general psychological tests for use in forensic settings is still limited. Added to this are the particular challenges and pressures of working as a mental health professional in the criminal justice legal arena. Each FMHA is a puzzle and a struggle to arrive at the psychological truth in a case. The cases presented in each chapter of this book are reflective of this striving.

Notes

1 Throughout this book, the pronouns she and he will be used interchangeably, to denote the fact that forensic psychologists can have either gender.
2 ECHR November 24, 1986, Series A 110.
3 In Dutch: De verdachte is bevoegd zich bij het verhoor door een raadsman te doen bijstaan. De raadsman wordt bij het verhoor in de gelegenheid gesteld de nodige opmerkingen te maken.
4 Accessible via https://zoek.officielebekendmakingen.nl. Vergaderjaar 2008-2009; Kamerstuk 31116 nr. G.
5 Accessible via: https://zoek.officielebekendmakingen.nl. Vergaderjaar 2006/07; Kamerstuk 30 300 VI, nr. 178.
6 Less serious crimes are decided by a one-judge court.
7 For the interested reader, Geeroms (2002) provides a thorough discussion of the differences and similarities between the criminal justice systems of Belgium, France, The Netherlands, Germany, England and the United States, and shows that getting the correct English equivalent for the different legal concepts is not an easy task. Thus, the relationship between word and concept is often not identical in the different legal languages.
8 For details, see: http://en.wikipedia.org/wiki/Andrea_Yates and www.crimelibrary. com/notorious_murders/women/andrea_yates/15.html.
9 Staatsblad van het Koninkrijk der Nederlanden. Jaargang 2009. Kamerstuk 31 116. Accessible via: www.eerstekamer.nl/behandeling/20090203/publicatie_wet_4/document3/ f=/vi2of5uelswl.pdf.
10 The Dutch Act on Experts in Criminal Cases (Art. 51i) defines the expert as someone who possesses special or particular knowledge in a certain area (in Dutch: "Op de wijze bij de wet bepaald wordt een deskundige benoemd met een opdracht tot het geven van informatie over of het doen van onderzoek op een terrein, waarvan hij specifieke of bijzondere kennis bezit.").
11 The latest update of this Ethics Code (2008) is available in English: www.psynip. nl/website-openbaar-documenten-nip-algemeen/code-of-ethics-for-psychologists.pdf.
12 www.nrgd.nl.
13 www.abfp.com.
14 DSM-5 was published in 2013 and the classification of personality disorders was not changed substantially, although several dimensional ratings are included as optional (American Psychiatric Association, 2013).

References

Ackerman, M. J. (1999). *Essentials of forensic psychological assessment.* New York: Wiley.
Ake v. Oklahoma, 470 U.S. 68 (1985). Retrieved from http://laws.findlaw.com/us/470/68.html.
American Psychiatric Association (2000). *Diagnostic and statistical manual of mental disorders* (4th ed.). Washington, DC: Author.
American Psychiatric Association (2013). *Diagnostic and statistical manual of mental disorders* (5th ed.) (DSM-5(r)). Washington, DC: Author.
American Psychological Association (1991). Specialty guidelines for forensic psychologists. *Law and Human Behavior, 15,* 655–665.
American Psychological Association (2013). Specialty guidelines for forensic psychologists. *American Psychologist, 68,* 7–19. doi: 10.1037/a0029889.
Andrews, D. A. & Bonta, J. L. (1995). *Level of service inventory-revised.* Toronto, Canada: Multi-Health Systems.
Bernstein, D. E. (2001). Frye, Frye, again: The past, present, and future of the general acceptance test. *Jurimetrics Journal, 41,* 385–404.
Butcher, J. N., Dahlstrom, W. G., Graham, J. R., Tellegen, A., & Kaemmer, B. (1989). *Minnesota multiphasic personality inventory-2 (MMPI-2): Manual for administration and scoring.* Minneapolis, MN: University of Minnesota Press.
Cheng, E. K. & Yoon, A. H. (2005). Does *Frye* or *Daubert* matter? A study of scientific admissibility standards. *Virginia Law Review, 91,* 471–513.
van Cleave, R. A. (1997). An offer you can't refuse? Punishment without trial in Italy and the United States: The search for truth and an efficient criminal justice system. *Emory International Law Review, 11,* 419–469.
Crombag, H. F. M. (2003). Adversarial or inquisitorial: Do we have a choice? In P. J. van Koppen & S. D. Penrod (Eds.), *Adversarial versus inquisitorial justice: Psychological perspectives on criminal justice systems* (pp. 21–25). New York: Kluwer Academic/Plenum.
Cunningham, M. D. (2010). *Evaluation for capital sentencing.* New York: Oxford University Press.
Damaška, M. R. (1973). Evidentiary barriers to conviction and two models of criminal procedure: A comparative study. *University of Pennsylvania Law Review,* 121, 506–589.
Daubert v. Merrell Dow Pharmaceuticals, Inc., 509 U.S. 579 (1993). Retrieved from http://laws.findlaw.com/us/509/579.html.
Douglas, K. S., Hart, S. D., Webster, C. D., & Belfrage, H. (2013). *Historical clinical risk management-20 version 3.* Vancouver, Canada: Mental Health, Law, and Policy Institute, Simon Fraser University.
Exner, J. E. (2003). *The Rorschach: A comprehensive system. Vol. 1: Basic foundations and principles of interpretation* (4th ed.). Hoboken, NJ: Wiley.
Federal Criminal Justice Act, 18 U.S.C. § 3006 (e) (1) (1964).
Freckelton, I. R. (1987). *The trial of the expert: A study of expert evidence and forensic experts.* Melbourne: Oxford University Press.
Frye v. United States, 54 App. D.C. 46, 47, 293 F. 1013 (1923).
Geeroms, S. M. F. (2002). Comparative law and legal translation: Why the terms cassation, revision and appeal should not be translated. *The American Journal of Comparative Law,* 50, 201–228. www.jstor.org/stable/840834.
Goodman-Delahunty, J. (1997). Forensic psychological expertise in the wake of Daubert. *Law and Human Behavior, 21,* 121–140. www.jstor.org/stable/1394168.

Greenberg, S. A. & Shuman, D. W. (1997). Irreconcilable conflict between therapeutic and forensic roles. *Professional Psychology: Research and Practice, 28,* 50–57.

Grisso, T. (2003). *Evaluating competencies: Forensic assessment and instruments* (2nd ed.). New York: Kluwer Academic.

Hans, V. P. & Vidmar, N. J. (1986). *Judging the jury.* New York: Plenum.

Hare, R. D. (1991). *The Hare psychopathy checklist-revised.* Toronto, ON: Multi-Health Systems.

Hare, R. D. (2003). *The Hare psychopathy checklist-revised* (2nd ed.). Toronto, ON: Multi-Health Systems.

Heilbrun, K. (2001). *Principles of forensic mental health assessment.* New York: Kluwer Academic/Plenum.

Heilbrun, K., Kelley, S. M., Koller, J. P., Giallella, C., & Peterson, L. (2013). The role of university-based forensic clinics. *International Journal of Law and Psychiatry, 36,* 195–200. doi: 10.1016/j.ijlp.2013.04.019.

Hildebrand, M. & de Ruiter, C. (2004). PCL-R psychopathy and its relation to DSM-IV Axis I and Axis II disorders in a sample of male forensic psychiatric patients in The Netherlands. *International Journal of Law and Psychiatry, 27,* 233–248. doi: 10.1016/j.ijlp.2004.03.005.

Howard, M. N. (1991). The neutral expert: A plausible threat to justice. *Criminal Law Review,* 98–105.

Ireland, J. L. (2008). Psychologists as witnesses: Background and good practice in the delivery of evidence. *Educational Psychology in Practice, 24,* 115–127.

Ireland, J. L. (2010). Legal consulting: Providing expertise in written and oral testimony. In C. A. Ireland & M. J. Fisher (Eds.), *Consulting and advising in forensic practice: Empirical and practical guidelines* (pp. 108–122). Chichester, UK: Wiley.

Jackson, R. (Ed.) (2008). *Learning forensic assessment.* New York: Routledge.

van Kampen, P. T. C. (2003). Expert evidence: The state of the law in The Netherlands and the United States. In P. J. van Koppen & S. D. Penrod (Eds.), *Adversarial versus inquisitorial justice: Psychological perspectives on criminal justice systems* (pp. 209–234). New York: Kluwer Academic/Plenum.

van Koppen, P. J. & Penrod, S. D. (2003). Adversarial or inquisitorial: Comparing systems. In P. J. van Koppen & S. D. Penrod (Eds.), *Adversarial versus inquisitorial justice: Psychological perspectives on criminal justice systems* (pp. 1–19). New York: Kluwer Academic/Plenum.

Kumho Tire Co., Ltd v. Carmichael, 97–1907, US Ct. App. 11th Cir. (1999).

Leo, R. A. (1996). Inside the interrogation room. *The Journal of Criminal Law and Criminology, 86,* 266–303.

Malsch, M. & Freckelton, I. (2005). Expert bias and partisanship: A comparison between Australia and The Netherlands. *Psychology, Public Policy and Law, 11,* 42–61. doi: 10.1037/1076-8971.11.1.42.

Marczyk, G., DeMatteo, D., Kutinsky, J., & Heilbrun, K. (2008). Training in forensic assessment and intervention: Implications for principles-based models. In R. Jackson (Ed.), *Learning forensic assessment* (pp. 3–31). New York: Routledge.

McAuliff, B. D. & Bornstein, B. H. (2012). Beliefs and expectancies in legal decision making: An introduction to the special issue. *Psychology, Crime & Law, 18,* 1–10. doi: 10.1080/1068316X.2011.641557.

Miranda v. Arizona, 384 U.S. 436 (1966). Retrieved from http://laws.findlaw.com/us/384/436.html.

Morey, L. C. (1991). *Personality assessment inventory*. Odessa, FL: Psychological Assessment Resources, Inc.

Morey, L. C. (1998). Teaching and learning the personality assessment inventory (PAI). In L. Handler & M. J. Hilsenroth (Eds.), *Teaching and learning personality assessment* (pp. 191–214). Hillsdale, NJ: Lawrence Erlbaum Associates.

Nederlands Instituut van Psychologen (2008). *Beroepscode voor psychologen* [Professional code for psychologists]. www.psynip.nl/website-openbaar-documenten-nip-algemeen/beroepscode-voor-psychologen.pdf.

Nijboer, J. F. (2000). The significance of comparative legal studies. In J. F. Nijboer & W. J. J. M. Sprangers (Eds.), *Harmonization in forensic expertise: An inquiry into the desirability of and opportunities for international standards* (pp. 399–410). Amsterdam: Thela Thesis.

Otto, R. K. & Douglas, K. S. (2010). *Handbook of violence risk assessment*. New York: Taylor & Francis.

Packer, I. K. (2009). *Evaluation of criminal responsibility*. New York: Oxford University Press.

Panovits v. Cyprus, ECHR, 4268/04 (2008). http://hudoc.echr.coe.int/sites/eng/pages/search.aspx?i=001–90244.

Rogers, R. (1984). *Rogers criminal responsibility assessment scales (R-CRAS) and test manual*. Odessa, FL: Psychological Assessment Resources.

Rogers, R. (1992). *Structured interview of reported symptoms*. Odessa, FL: Psychological Assessment Resources.

Rogers, R. (Ed.) (2008). *Clinical assessment of malingering and deception* (3rd ed.). New York: Guilford.

Rogers, R., Bagby, R. M., & Dickens, S. E. (1992). *Structured interview of reported symptoms (SIRS) and professional manual*. Odessa, FL: Psychological Assessment Resources.

de Ruiter, C. (2011). Het NRGD: Een gemiste kans [Netherlands Registry of Expert Witnesses for the Court: A missed opportunity]. *Nieuwsbrief Sectie Forensische Psychologie NIP*. www.psynip.nl.

de Ruiter, C. & Greeven, P. G. J. (2000). Personality disorders in a Dutch forensic psychiatric sample: Convergence of interview and self-report measures. *Journal of Personality Disorders*, 14, 162–170. doi: 10.1521/pedi.2000.14.2.162.

Salduz v. Turkey, ECHR 36391/02 (2008). http://hudoc.echr.coe.int/sites/eng/pages/search.aspx?i=001–89893.

Sewell, K. W. (2008). Dissimulation on projective measures. In R. Rogers (Ed.), *Clinical assessment of malingering and deception* (3rd ed., pp. 207–217). New York: Guilford.

Swart, B. (1999). The European Convention as an invigorator of domestic law in The Netherlands. *Journal of Law and Society*, 26, 38–53. www.jstor.org/stable/1410577.

Unterpertinger v. Austria, ECHR 9120/80 (1986). http://hudoc.echr.coe.int/sites/eng/pages/search.aspx?i=001–57588.

Webster, C. D., Douglas, K. S., Eaves, D., & Hart, S. D. (1997). *HCR-20: Assessing the risk of violence* (version 2). Burnaby, BC: Mental Health, Law, and Policy Institute, Simon Fraser University.

Widows, M. & Smith, G. P. (2005). *Structured inventory of malingered symptomatology (SIMS) and professional manual*. Odessa, FL: Psychological Assessment Resources.

2

DOMESTIC ESTRANGEMENT AND FAMILICIDE[1]

Corine de Ruiter

There are cases in forensic psychological practice that stay in one's mind long after having submitted the forensic mental health report and the court has given its final verdict. The case I present here is one of them.

Media Reports on "the Zoetermeer Case"

On Monday, April 11, 2005 the Dutch national evening news reported a wife and her two daughters were missing from their middle-class home in the suburb of Zoetermeer, not far from The Hague. The wife, Karen, was a kindergarten teacher who purportedly had called in sick that Monday. The daughters (Marian, 5 years old and Charlene, 3 years old) had not appeared at their elementary school on Monday morning. Their father Richard H., a 33-year-old computer programmer, had reported the three as missing at the local police station that Monday evening.[2] He told the police he had no idea why his wife would run away because "I can assure you our relationship is good" (p. 15, police report, April 16, 2005).

The police investigation started with the checking of Richard's claims that he had spent the morning of Saturday, April 9 with his family at the Tropicana swimming pool in Rotterdam. However, neither Richard nor his wife and children are seen on video footage entering the swimming pool. In the subsequent weeks, reports on the "disappearance" trickled down in the media, and what started as a tale of a sorrowful husband who claimed his family had been kidnapped, ended in a story that included marital estrangement, an extramarital affair with a Polish girlfriend, and the brutal killing of his wife and daughters at the hands of their husband and father. Richard was charged with murder/manslaughter on Thursday, April 21. He confessed to having killed his wife and children in the night from Wednesday, April 6 to Thursday, April 7. Upon directions from Richard, the police dug up the three corpses on Friday, April 22 in a forest in the Southern province of North-Brabant, about 75 miles from the family home. The girls' favorite stuffed animal was buried beside them. How could a loving father, as colleagues and friends had known Richard, suddenly have turned into a seemingly cold-blooded murderer? Had they missed something during all those years of their acquaintance with him?

Richard was put on trial before the regional criminal court of the city of The Hague. Two mental health experts, a psychologist (V.) and a psychiatrist (M.), were appointed by the court to conduct an assessment of criminal responsibility and future violence risk, including advice on the possible need for psychiatric treatment to diminish the latter risk, if present. The media's reports on the contents of these assessment reports were rather sketchy, but what they did make clear was that the two experts did not agree on Richard's diagnosis. The psychiatrist saw nothing mentally wrong with Richard and considered him criminally responsible. However, the psychologist classified Richard with a Personality Disorder Not Otherwise Specified, with borderline and dependent features, and considered him as having diminished criminal responsibility. This left the court with two opposing expert opinions, which led to a decision to admit Richard to the Psychiatric Observation Clinic (POC) of the Department of Justice.

The POC is a special remand prison, where suspects can be held for a period of 7 weeks with the goal of performing a thorough mental health evaluation, including personality, neuropsychological, and neurological (EEG, MRI) assessments. Suspects are housed in small living groups where they are observed by group workers. They attend sports and work activities inside the POC. A social worker from the POC conducts a social network investigation, including interviews with family members, friends, colleagues, former employers, etc. The social worker also collects relevant collateral information, including school records, records from possible previous mental health contacts, and medical records. Police and criminal records are already available as part of the current criminal file. The outcome of the POC evaluation was somewhat equivocal. According to the evaluating team, Richard was suffering from a defective development of the personality. However, this could not be classified as a personality disorder, as the symptoms were not severe enough according to the team.

All experts, the first two and the ones from the POC, were heard at the criminal court in The Hague. Prosecution officer Beliën demanded a life sentence for Richard because, according to him, Richard had acted out of pure self-interest, and had killed his wife and children in a planned, premeditated manner in order to be able to receive his Polish girlfriend at his home. The defense pleaded for a time-limited prison sentence with or without a mandated treatment order on the basis of psychologist V.'s opinion who stated Richard was suffering from serious personality pathology, including lack of ego strength and problem-solving skills, and identity diffusion, which could be related to the offence. On March 31, 2006,

Richard was sentenced to life imprisonment on three counts of murder and hiding corpses. It is important to note that a life sentence is very unusual in The Netherlands in the case of a first offender such as Richard. Life sentences are mainly given to repeat violent offenders, for whom previous prison sentences or judicial treatment orders have not helped to deter them from new violent offences.

A Call from Richard's Defense Attorney

Richard and his defense attorney appealed against the life sentence verdict. In the summer of 2006, I received a telephone call from Richard's defense counsel, Jacqueline van den Bosch, LL.M. She explained to me that neither Richard nor she recognized Richard's psychological problems as expressed in the different available mental health reports. Both felt Richard was represented as a cunning, manipulative person, who planned the killings in advance. This was not her impression. She wanted an independent psychological evaluation, and asked if I was willing to conduct this at the request of the Court of Appeals in The Hague. It is common in The Netherlands that expert witnesses are court-appointed. This is in line with the inquisitorial justice system (de Ruiter & Hildebrand, 2003). A defense counsel can submit a request for an independent evaluation to the court, explaining why she considers this necessary in relation to the case at hand. Subsequently, the court makes an argued decision to honor the request or to refuse it. If the court refuses the request, the defense attorney can still enlist their own expert, but then the suspect would need to have the financial means to pay the expert's fee. Also, because The Netherlands has an inquisitorial system, some courts tend to be somewhat biased against "defense experts," assuming they are the proverbial "hired guns." This bias, of course, does not concur with the fact that experts are held to their professional ethics code (in the US: American Psychology-Law Society, 1991; 2013; in The Netherlands: NIP, 2007).

In Richard's case, the Appeals Court refused the request of the defense for a new mental health evaluation. Thus, I was appointed by the defense counsel and received her list of questions by letter at the end of August 2006:

- To what extent are the Diagnostic and Statistical Manual (DSM-IV) criteria for a personality disorder absolute?
- Is it possible for a personality disorder to "slumber" during adolescence, but for one reason or another not reveal itself clearly in contacts with other people?
- Mr. Richard H. stated during the trial and also during police interrogation that the idea to kill his wife came to him as an obsessional idea, which kept returning and became stronger over time. Is there literature about such obsessional thoughts (even in the absence of personality disorder, but possibly in cases of high levels of stress)?

The defense attorney sent me a copy of all collateral information she had at her disposition. This included:

- police file number PL1551/2005/6508 (pp. 1–837), among others containing verbatim reports of the interrogations of the suspect;
- consultation report by psychiatrist A., May 3, 2005;
- expert report *Pro Justitia*, by psychiatrist M., September 6, 2005;
- expert report *Pro Justitia*, by psychologist V., September 6, 2006;
- social network report by probation officer, September 6, 2006;
- report POC, February 10, 2006;
- answers of psychiatrist M., psychologist V., and POC experts to questions from the court, February 27, 2006;
- notes from the prosecution in the case against Mr. R. H., March 3, 2006;
- notes from defense attorneys C.W. Noorduyn, LL.M. and J.A. van den Bosch, LL.M., March 3, 2006;
- process notes from the court sessions of the Regional Criminal Court of The Hague, on September 26, 27, and 30, 2006.

Approach to the Case: What I Learned from the File Information

First, I studied the police files and the previous mental health reports to gain an initial impression of Richard's and others' statements to the police about his life and his offence, and to also obtain information on the type of test instruments previous experts had used. With this information in mind, I conducted a first interview with Richard, who was detained at the remand prison in The Hague. I met a somewhat skinny man, who looked young for his years. He was wearing jeans and a sweatshirt and his hair was short. Quite remarkable was his modest and insecure way of making contact. He offered a sweaty hand and was particularly grateful for this opportunity for a new evaluation. He came across as submissive and dependent. He stated he was experiencing a lot of guilt and shame over the offence and would like to understand why his life took this turn.

The file documentation I read resulted in a mixed picture of Richard's behavior before and after the alleged offence. During the first interviews with police, when he is not a suspect yet, he claims nothing is wrong in his life. But rather quickly, the police discover this rosy picture is not true: Richard has serious debts because he spends more money than he earns; he has had a number of extramarital affairs over the course of his relationship with Karen, the last one with a Polish woman, Joanna. He has visited her several times in Poland since the start of their affair in 2003, under the pretext of work obligations.

Richard states to the police that he came home from a side job around 11.45 p.m. on April 6. Karen was already in bed. He remembers lying in bed ruminating, and the thought to kill Karen as a solution to all his problems keeps entering his head. He starts hitting her with a heavy object (he claims it was a metal baseball bat, but the object was never found). When Karen stops making noises, he suffocates her. He says he burst out into tears after the killing. Subsequently, he goes to the girls' bedrooms, and suffocates them, claiming they "should be reunited with their mother in heaven." He puts the corpses into garbage bags and uses tape to keep their extremities together. With the three bodies in the trunk of his car, he drives to a forest near Alphen-Chaam, where he used to go camping with his parents when he was a child. He digs a grave and buries the dead bodies, including Charlene's favorite stuffed animal. After the drive home to Zoetermeer, he takes a shower, walks the dog, and notifies his daughters' school that they are sick. He goes to work and his colleagues don't notice anything unusual about him.

After returning from work, he tries to clean the blood traces from the parental bedroom. He cuts a bloodstain out of the mattress. The next morning, April 8, he picks up Joanna from the train station, and they spend the weekend together, making love in the same bed where the homicide took place. Joanna departs to Poland on the evening of April 10. The next day, Richard reports his wife and children as missing.

During the police interrogations, Richard appears distraught and overwhelmed. He keeps posing questions to himself: "I still cannot believe that I was able to do this . . . taking three lives" (p. 621).

Previous Mental Health Reports

The mental health experts' reports in the file are mixed and contrary. According to the first psychologist who examined him, V., Richard was suffering from a personality disorder with borderline and dependent features. V. describes Richard as an overcontrolled, inhibited, avoidant, dependent, egocentric, anxious, hyper-sensitive but also a submissive, docile, and servile man who lacks contact with his inner feelings (p. 24, report). Just like his mother, Richard suffers from immense separation anxiety; he called or texted Karen several times a day, and was also afraid to lose Joanna or his children. Richard seems to need the love affairs with women to feel that he is "somebody."

The first psychiatrist, M., concludes that Richard does not have a mental disorder: "he is a man tending towards dependency, who is hungry for attention" (p. 22, report). M. states explicitly that "the profiles of perpetrators of uxoricide and familicide described in the literature show little agreement with the personality and behaviors of the examinee" (p. 23). According to the psychiatrist, Richard was fully criminally responsible at the time he killed his family.

The next experts (psychiatrist and psychologist) of the POC do not find evidence of a mental disorder, although they do report the presence of a number of remarkable personality traits, such as dependency, conflict avoidance, ego-centrism, deficient problem-solving skills, and a negative self-image (p. 49–50, report). Nevertheless, they advise the court to consider Richard legally responsible for the alleged offences.

A Second Opinion Forensic Psychological Assessment

After the first brief interview, I conducted a full forensic psychological assessment, using the standard set of instruments I use in most pretrial cases. These include: the Psychopathy Checklist-Revised (PCL-R; Hare, 2003), the Minnesota Multiphasic Personality Inventory-2 (MMPI-2; Butcher, Dahlstrom, Graham, Tellegen, & Kaemmer, 1989), the Rorschach Inkblot Method (RIM) using the Comprehensive System (Exner, 2003), and a semi-structured interview for Axis II disorders (SIDP-IV; Pfohl, Blum, & Zimmerman, 1994). Intelligence testing was not performed because this seemed superfluous as the two previous psychologists had already done this and Richard was of average intelligence. However, none of the previous experts had used a semi-structured interview for psychiatric classification on Axis II. This seemed an omission because reliability, and thus validity, of psychiatric classification is seriously compromised when experts use unstructured clinical interviews to arrive at a psychiatric diagnosis (Heilbrun, Grisso, & Goldstein, 2008). Since there is so much at stake for a suspect who is being evaluated as part of a criminal procedure, reliability of diagnosis is even more important than in the case of a clinical referral (Slobogin, 2007). I also decided to conduct a literature review on male perpetrators of uxoricide (i.e., the killing of a wife by her husband) and familicide, in order to examine whether such perpetrators are characterized by a specific personality profile. This would allow comparison of the findings from the present forensic mental health evaluation with what is known more generally about the personality and/or psychological characteristics of perpetrators of similar offences.

Literature Review: Perpetrators of Uxoricide and Familicide

This literature review was performed with the purpose of learning what is known about the personality characteristics and psychopathology of men who commit uxoricide/familicide, to examine if this literature could shed light on Richard's case. Uxoricide is the term used for the killing of one's female spouse and familicide is a homicide in which the perpetrator kills a spouse and one or more children. Although Richard's offence was technically a familicide, it seemed that the killing of his wife was the main offence in the sense that he was highly emotionally motivated to kill her. Killing the children seemed to be a more secondary, subsequent act that Richard saw as an act of altruism because he wanted to reunite the children with their mother. Notwithstanding, he may have felt pressured into killing the girls too because his Polish girlfriend was soon arriving. For all these reasons, we will consider the research literature on both uxoricide and familicide.

A search was performed using the search engines PsycInfo, PubMed, and Web of Science, with the following search terms: uxoricide, familicide, spousal homicide and personality, psychopathology.

Summary of the Familicide Literature

When a familicide occurs, it is most likely that the perpetrator is male (Liem & Koenraadt, 2008; Wilson, Daly, & Daniele, 1995). With regard to the motives underlying familicides, previous studies have shown that perpetrators are motivated by a sense of loss of control over their spouse as well as over family life (Ewing, 1997; Wilson et al., 1995). The wife's (threat of) actual abandonment or psychological estrangement constitutes a threat to the male partner, and the lethal violence is an attempt to regain control. From this perspective, familicides resemble intimate partner homicides, as the primary object of aggression constitutes the spouse rather than the children.

Other studies (e.g., Ewing, 1997; Fox & Levin, 2005; Polk, 1994) found financial losses to be an important factor in familicide. Faced with an overwhelming threat to their role as provider for their family, these men become desperate, homicidal, and suicidal (Marzuk, Tardiff, & Hirsch, 1992). Liem and Koenraadt (2008) conducted the most recent study on familicide perpetrators (N = 23), comparing them to uxoricide perpetrators (N = 380), assessed in the Department of Justice Psychiatric Observation Clinic in The Netherlands. They found that familicidal perpetrators were significantly more likely to suffer from a personality disorder (65 percent), particularly dependent and narcissistic, in comparison to uxoricide perpetrators (33 percent). The motives for familicides largely corresponded to the motives reported for uxoricides (most prevalent were fear of abandonment and narcissistic rage), although among familicides, killing out of a psychotic motive appeared more prevalent. However, the accuracy of determining a perpetrator's motive merely from file information, as was performed in this file-based study (Liem & Koenraadt, 2008), cannot be determined. Previous research has indeed shown that motives derived from file material do not correspond one-on-one to perpetrators' self-reported motives (Thijssen & de Ruiter, 2011). It should also be noted that the familicide sample was rather small compared with the uxoricide sample; thus, just a few cases may have determined prevalence rates.

Summary of the Uxoricide Literature

Empirical research on the psychological profiles of perpetrators of uxoricide is more extensive compared to studies on familicide offenders. Dutton and Kerry (1999) found that Cluster C personality disorders were overrepresented in a sample of male incarcerated spousal killers (N = 90) in Canada. Passive-aggressive personality disorder, avoidant personality disorder, self-defeating personality disorder, and dependent personality disorder were common. Individuals with these personality disorders are generally assumed to suppress rage and are termed "over-controlled" personality types. A remarkable feature of the *modus operandi* of the partner killers was the degree of "overkill": these men had used much more violence than was "necessary" to kill their victim. Overkill points to rage.

An earlier study by Showalter, Bonnie, and Roddy (1980) found similar results: their work highlights that the personality disorders in men who kill their spouses are most likely to be dependent and passive-aggressive. They concluded that "especially significant was the fact that most of these men [spousal killers, CdR] lacked recorded histories of assaultive or other socially disturbing behaviour" (Showalter et al., 1980, p. 125). Belfrage and Rying (2004) also found personality disorders common in a study of 164 male spousal homicide perpetrators from Sweden. They found that 38 percent of their sample fulfilled diagnostic criteria for a personality disorder, with depressive and borderline features most prevalent. These authors noted a strikingly low prevalence rate of psychopathic personality disorder (7 percent) in their spousal killers.

Dobash and Dobash (2011) examined 104 case files of British men who had murdered (all the convictions were for murder, not manslaughter) their intimate partner, using qualitative analysis of their cognitions in relation to the offence. Their findings indicated that the majority of the men who murdered an intimate partner had problems in intimate relationships and a history of serious, repeated violent abuse of the woman they killed. The relationships were characterized by conflict, abuse, and controlling behavior as well as jealousy and possessiveness in which the men used violence to enforce rigid standards based on their beliefs about relationships between intimate partners. They denied agency and responsibility, often by placing blame elsewhere. The offender profile reported in this recent study did not seem to fit Richard's case, as he was not controlling and abusing, but rather submissive and avoidant in his relationship with Karen.

Dutton and Kerry (1999) report how an overcontrolled personality type can come to the point of killing his wife. They describe how emotional overcontrol may culminate in a so-called catathymic crisis, characterized by a seemingly unsolvable psychic state of tension. The person projects responsibility for this tension state onto an external situation, in this case the spouse. Their perception is that killing is the only way out of this state. After ruminating and obsessing over it and an extended period of internal conflict, the act is carried out. When the act is completed, the perpetrator feels emotional relief and calmness.

Catathymia was first identified as a motivation for homicide by Wertham (1937; Meloy, 1992, 2010). In a forensic context, the term refers to a motivational pattern of homicide wherein a fixed idea, often rather obsessional, grows in intensity over the course of time (from hours to days, weeks, months, or even years) until the person feels compelled to kill to alleviate such psychic tension. In chronic catathymia, there are three identifiable stages: an incubation period during which the idea, initially unwelcome, becomes fixed in the mind of the person; a sudden, homicidal act, usually in the absence of any history of violence; and a post-offence period of relief during which memory of the event is fully preserved (Meloy, 2010).

Forensic Assessment Findings

Richard was assessed on three separate occasions in a visitors' room at the prison in October and November 2007. The evaluation started with the administration of the semi-structured biographical interview, which belongs to the PCL-R. This interview is very well suited for pretrial assessments because, in addition to more general biographical information on domains such as education, work, family history, relationships, and mental health and substance use issues, it focuses on a number of domains highly relevant to forensic assessment, such as (early) history of antisocial behavior, and an in-depth interview about the index-offence (including what led up to it, what the subject was feeling and thinking during the offence, and the psychological aftermath of the offence). This extensive discussion of the index-offence is obviously necessary to estimate the nature and degree of the possible relationship between behaviors expressed during the index-offence and symptoms/traits of mental disorder (if present), as needs to be performed for a judgment on the degree of criminal responsibility (Rogers & Shuman, 2000). After this interview, the MMPI-2 and RIM were administered, and the last session was spent going through the questions of the SIDP-IV. In order to be able to code the SIDP-IV, a separate, 2-hour interview with Richard's parents was conducted at the author's office. This allowed for concurrent validation of statements made by Richard about his personality traits, with the observations made by his parents. Research (de Ruiter & Greeven, 2000) has shown that sole reliance on self-report of personality in forensic assessments may lead to an underestimation of certain DSM-IV-TR Cluster B personality traits (e.g., narcissistic, antisocial, sadistic). Use of collateral sources (including interviews with significant others of the subject, information from other records) is of paramount importance in forensic psychological assessment because Cluster B personality disorders have high prevalence rates among subjects in forensic settings (Hildebrand & de Ruiter, 2004).

Clinical Impressions

Richard seemed motivated to do his best during the evaluation. He tried to formulate his answers to the questions carefully and completely. In contrast to previous experts V. and M., I did not observe a manipulative or defensive attitude. On the contrary, Richard seemed quite forthcoming and did not seem to want to hide or embellish the facts. When we discussed the actual killings, Richard showed a lot of grief and shame. At these times, he was trembling and crying, and it took time for him to recover. There was no callousness or flattened affect during the interviews; his mood seemed subdued and down.

Self-reported Biography

Family of Origin

Richard was born the second of two children. His sister Angela was born 2.5 years earlier. Richard's mother lost her only sister while she was pregnant with Richard. This sister was her favorite sibling, but she said she still enjoyed Richard's baby years, despite the loss. She was an active mother who took her children on outings and she frequently helped out at school.

When I asked his parents what type of child Richard was, his mother answered: "A very sweet boy, but extremely closed off." As a child, he would often play alone in his room, first with Lego, later with electronics stuff. Richard was also extremely shy according to both parents. For example, when they were camping in Italy one summer, an Italian boy approached Richard, but he became so scared he escaped to the rest rooms and remained there for a long time, until his mother found him. Their daughter Angela was more like her mother, much more extroverted and wore her heart on her sleeve.

When Richard was 13 years of age, his parents divorced. There were a lot of conflicts before the separation. His mother was panicky about being alone in the house. On the day her husband left, her new partner immediately moved in. During nights their mother was at home alone, the children had to sleep in the bed with her. From the stories Richard told about this period, it appears that his mother was suffering from a panic disorder.

Richard had friends during his childhood, but he did not belong with the really popular guys. He described himself as very shy. In a group, he kept in the background, afraid to say the wrong thing. At parties, people often said to him: "Oh, you are here, too?!" because he was so quiet. Presentations in front of class were "a complete disaster"; he always obtained a bad grade for these. He said he would nearly explode from nervousness, stammering and not daring to look into the classroom.

Intimate Relationships

Before Richard met his wife Karen, he had a number of short-lasting relationships. Sometimes, these relationships overlapped, for instance during vacations. He thought these "conquests" were quite cool because they did not fit his insecure, shy self-image. When he met Karen, he became more serious. When asked what attracted him to her, he said: "Her appearance, her eyes, her long hair and her spontaneity; she was everything I am not." In the beginning of their relationship, Richard tried to please Karen as much as possible. He gave up a group of friends that he had been going on vacations with. Richard reported that Karen believed these friends had a bad influence on him, and she did not feel comfortable around them. Richard now says that he chose her over his friends, even though he missed them. Karen seems to have had the upper hand in their relationship, partly because Richard was not standing up for himself. Richard's parents had also noticed this.

The birth of the girls seems to have resulted in estrangement of the couple. Karen focused her attention on the children and Richard did not feel as if he had a place anymore. Being a kindergarten teacher, Karen seemed to be much more confident taking care of the girls; in her presence Richard felt an inadequate parent. However, when he was alone with the girls he enjoyed fatherhood; he taught them how to ride a bicycle and went on small outings with them. Richard's parents stated that Karen seemed overly strict with the girls, who were quite clinging with her. The grandparents would let the girls jump on the bed and things like that, which were forbidden by their mother.

After the birth of the children, the family had considerable financial problems. Karen started to work fewer hours, and expenses increased (for the children, but also on health insurance and a new car). The couple accumulated financial debts, which were "covered" with new debts. Asked why they did not start to spend less money as a family, Richard said he tends to make impulsive buys, "to fill the void and to forget my problems." When he saw audio or computer equipment he liked on the Internet, he would go to the store and buy it. According to Richard this happened when he "wasn't feeling well." After a new purchase, he would feel a little better for a while. In hindsight, he thought this was irresponsible behavior. He also binged on sweets and other junk food, to soothe feelings of emptiness and distress.

Their already strained relationship arrived at a new low after New Year's Eve 2001–2002, when Karen shared an intimate kiss with a male friend. This incident seems to have functioned as the last drop that made the bucket overflow. At least, this is how Richard viewed it, in hindsight. They kept getting into fights over the kissing incident, but never resolved it. During the course of 2002, Richard got into a relationship with an intern at his work. He said that the need for attention and affection, which he did not get from Karen, was the driving force behind the affair. Also, the kick of secret appointments gave him a pleasant feeling of thrill. One of his colleagues was notoriously unfaithful, and Richard was actually quite surprised when he found out how easy it was to have a secret affair. He fell in love with the intern, but she decided to stay with her boyfriend in the end.

Somewhat later, Richard got into a relationship with another colleague, Viola, and again a bit later, he started a (simultaneous) relationship with a Polish woman named Joanna. His feelings for Viola were only superficial, but Richard said he "was really crazy about Joanna." Thus, for almost 2 years of his marriage to Karen, Richard was having an affair with both Viola and Joanna. Asked how he kept all these relationships secret, Richard answered that he did this "through a web of lies and deceit." His contact with Karen was minimal; they did not have sex for at least a year, they did not go out together anymore, and personal conversations were virtually absent. Richard's parents also noticed something was wrong. For instance, his mother had organized a Christmas party for the grandchildren in 2004, which Karen cancelled at the last moment.

In answer to my question, if Richard ever discussed the option of divorce with Karen, he said: "I was too scared to do that. I started once, but it was off limits for her. And I also did not dare to reveal all my problems to my parents or my sister. I was very afraid of losing face." Richard seems to have avoided conflict in his relationship with Karen to an extreme extent: "She was in power, I did everything to keep things at peace." This resulted in Richard running the household (cooking, cleaning) and in his spare free time, he would go out with friends or people from work; Karen never came along. His colleagues and other friends used to make comments about his marital situation, but Richard always defended Karen, even though he knew deep down that the analysis his friends made was accurate.

School and Work

Richard had to repeat a grade twice during his school career. He said this was because he was easily distracted in elementary school. Also, he preferred to spend time at home playing with his Lego, instead of doing his homework. At the lower vocational school (in Dutch: LTS; Electronics) he failed his exam the first time. He failed subjects such as Math, English, and Physics because he preferred to "work with his hands." The second time, he did manage to obtain his diploma. He skipped classes sometimes, but not very often.

He went into military service after high school, where his technical background was useful. However, after 4 months, he got increasingly bored, and called in sick for a couple of weeks. Later, he was sentenced to extra chores and a fine of 2,500 guilders for unlawful absence from military service. During this unlawful absence, Richard stayed in his parents' home while they were vacationing. His parents did not know about this until many years later.

Over the course of the years, Richard worked for several electronics companies (software and hardware). His last job, before his arrest, was at a community college in The Hague. Richard considered himself a hardworking employee but he claimed his bosses and colleagues called him a workaholic. During the last few years, he took on a lot of extra work, next to his regular job, partly as a way to earn some extra money.

Medical History

Richard did not have any major physical problems during his life. Also, he had never sought psychological help.

Test Findings

MMPI-2

Richard's profile is valid. He responded in a consistent manner (VRIN) but his TRIN raw score of 12 (T-score of 73) could indicate a yes-saying response style, however, the other scale scores do not suggest over-reporting. The F scale score of 64 reflects a level of distress and disturbance common in psychiatric populations. His score on the L scale is low, reflecting candor about revealing minor faults and failings, which could translate into a frank and open response to other content areas. The K score is low (T = 42); this suggests limited resources for coping with the stresses and demands of daily life. Thus, his MMPI-2 profile can be interpreted.

Richard's profile is a 62 profile with clinical elevations on scales 7 (Psychasthenia), 5 (Masculinity/Femininity), and 0 (Social Introversion) also. Individuals with this MMPI-2 profile have difficulties expressing anger, and collect psychological grievances. The person retreats in bitter silence to cope with their anger. Individuals with this profile type are extremely rational, having great difficulty letting go emotionally for fear of criticism or rejection. Depressive symptoms in the form of rumination, feelings of inadequacy, and fatigue are often present. Coping skills to handle problems effectively are lacking.

The other clinically elevated scales (7, 5, and 0) point to a lack of self-confidence and assertiveness, combined with a dependent stance in interpersonal relationships. The person has difficulty saying "No" to requests and overburdens himself with responsibilities. He is shy and insecure and places himself in a submissive position towards others.

Rorschach Inkblot Method according to the Comprehensive System

Richard provided 37 responses to the RIM. He has elevations on two of the instrument's clinical indices: the Depression Index and the Hypervigilance Index. Interestingly, this finding concurs with the result on the MMPI-2, where the Depression and the Paranoia scales were the highest in the profile. When different test methods (in this case, self-report and a performance-based test) provide corroborating evidence, diagnostic conclusions can be drawn with a higher degree of certainty compared with cases where different test methods do not converge as well (Meyer et al., 2001).

The elevated Depression Index indicates that Richard is vulnerable to the development of symptoms of depression. Because he is so extremely overcontrolled, his emotional distress will not be immediately apparent to people in his environment. The elevation on the Hypervigilance Index points to an increased interpersonal sensitivity and marked reservation in contact with others. His fear of criticism and rejection dominates his social encounters in general, but it also compromises his capacity for intimacy in a relationship with a partner.

Richard's coping skills are underdeveloped. He tends towards simple solutions in response to complex problems. He avoids thinking about a problem, which results in errors of judgment. He also suppresses his feelings by rationalization and intellectualization. These automatic defensive operations take energy and limit his capacity to act adequately. Like the MMPI-2, the Rorschach provides evidence of a tendency to build up resentment.

Inferiority feelings and a lack of self-confidence are compensated by (secondary) narcissistic features. This can be seen in Richard's history of his extramarital affairs and the impulsive buying of too many, expensive commodities. These compensatory acts seem to fill his empty, inadequate self, at least for the time being. Of note on the positive side of his personality is Richard's openness to self-reflection. This is a prognostic factor for motivation to change.

Psychopathy Checklist-Revised

The coding of the PCL-R resulted in a total score below 10. Thus, Richard does not have psychopathic traits.

SIDP-IV Interview

The outcome of the SIDP-IV interview was based on the interview with Richard, the collateral file information, and the interview with Richard's parents. Richard fulfills the following diagnostic criteria for both Dependent and Avoidant Personality Disorder.

Dependent Personality Disorder

- Criterion 1: *finds it hard to take everyday decisions without an excessive amount of advice and reassurance from others.* Richard reports leaving many decisions to his wife, for instance, booking a vacation, getting a mortgage on the house, selecting a school for the children. He prefers it when others take decisions for him.
- Criterion 3: *finds it difficult to express a different opinion out of anxiety about losing support or approval.* Richard says that he often pretends to agree with something because he is too afraid to give his opinion. He is afraid of being "talked back to." At his work, he was too afraid of failing, so he did not talk about certain issues.
- Criterion 4: *finds it hard to start something by himself (more a consequence of a lack of confidence in own abilities than a lack of motivation).* For example, Richard

does not dare to go into a realtors' office by himself: "People are watching me then." He is afraid of doing something wrong. This is why he doesn't do these kinds of things alone.

- Criterion 5: *will go out of his way to receive care and support from others, can even offer to voluntarily do unpleasant things.* Richard always says "yes" to a request for assistance, even if he doesn't have the time for it. This tendency, too, was a source of conflict between him and Karen.
- Criterion 6: *feels uncomfortable or helpless when he is alone because of the excessive fear of not being able to take care of himself.* Richard finds being alone hard to tolerate. When Karen left him emotionally, he immediately sought refuge with other women. In detention now, he has a penfriend, a woman who is detained at another facility. He is afraid she will ultimately drop him: "It is the fear that the emptiness, which she fills at this moment, will return."
- Criterion 7: *looks tenaciously for another relationship to be taken care of and as a source of support when an intimate relationship ends.* Richard says he is completely devastated when a relationship ends. To feel good again, he starts a new relationship. Being single is unbearable. See also above under Criterion 6.

Avoidant Personality Disorder

- Criterion 1: *avoids professional activities that involve important interpersonal contact because of his fear of being criticized, disapproved of, or rejected.* Richard prefers to work alone. He cannot handle criticism. He says he was offered to become department manager but he did not dare apply for the job because it would have involved chairing meetings, which he was too afraid of.
- Criterion 2: *is unwilling to get involved with people unless it is certain that they will like him/her.* Richard acknowledges that he always feels inhibited about revealing what he thinks/feels in contact with others (also in relationships which are not new). He is shy and quiet in social situations and envies people who are not shy.
- Criterion 3: *is reserved in intimate relationships out of fear of being humiliated or laughed at.* Richard hardly dares to express his feelings, out of shame. He experiences this with family and friends to the same degree as with strangers. In his relationship with Karen, he put his feelings aside and avoided conflicts by submissive behavior.
- Criterion 4: *is preoccupied with the thought of being criticized and rejected in social situations.* Richard finds accepting criticism very difficult, he "shuts off." He keeps thinking about the criticism, but doesn't use it and doesn't talk about it.
- Criterion 5: *is inhibited in new interpersonal situations because of the feeling of coming up short.* Richard is afraid to take up contact with other people because of fear of rejection.

Psychiatric Classification according to DSM-IV-TR

Axis I: no diagnosis (V71.09)
Axis II: Avoidant Personality Disorder (301.82) and Dependent Personality Disorder (301.6)
Axis III: no diagnosis
Axis IV: problems in the primary support group; he killed his wife and children. Problems related to the social environment; he is in prison with a life sentence. Problems with justice/police; he is incarcerated, awaiting appeal in his trial
Axis V: Global Assessment of Functioning = 51–60.

The Offense

The account the assessee provides of what happened before, during, and after the offense needs to be compared with all the available collateral information provided in the criminal file. In the present case, the statements Richard made in the interview with me could also be compared with the experiences his parents reported to me. In the following, I will first summarize the account Richard gave of the events, along with observations his parents made in the days after the supposed "disappearance" of Karen and the children. Subsequently, I will discuss relevant information from the police file in order to gain a complete picture of what happened. Important incongruities will be noted.

Richard acknowledges he started to lose grip on his complicated life in January of 2005. He says this was when he had decided to continue with Joanna. He had visited her several times during weekends in Poland in the previous year under the pretext of work projects. He also had Joanna come over for a couple of days to The Netherlands once, when they stayed in a cottage in a state park. Richard visited Joanna in Poland that January and had resolved to finally admit to her he was married. But he was afraid of losing her. She had previously told him she had been terribly disappointed when a man she had been dating in the past told her later that he was married. She had told Richard she never wanted to be in such a situation again. Richard decided to tell her a "cover-up story" claiming his wife and children had been missing for years. Joanna seemed to believe the story, but kept insisting she wanted to come and visit his home. Richard felt he could no longer refuse and they set a date: on April 8 she would arrive by bus from Poland. The day Joanna would arrive kept coming closer and closer, and the tension inside Richard was building. He did not talk to Karen, or to his parents, friends, and colleagues about any of this.

Richard reports that the thought to kill Karen suddenly arose in his mind when he was lying next to her in bed on the night of April 6. He was ruminating about the predicament he had got himself into. The arrival of Joanna was impending. The thought of killing Karen overtook him more and more. At first, he says, it scared him. But the thought became stronger and stronger; he could not think of anything else: "You have to do it, if Karen is gone, you are free!"

He started hitting the sleeping Karen with a baseball bat, which he claims they kept in the bedroom; all the while the above-mentioned thought kept running through his head. He was experiencing anger and fear; he reports having heart palpitations and sweating excessively. Richard says he could not stop beating, he thinks he beat her five or six times: "It felt like an immense relief," he reports. While Richard is remembering all this, he is crying. He says he is angry with himself and feels ashamed to talk about this. According to him, the thought of killing his daughters arose only after he had killed Karen. He reports he "realized children belong with their mother, even if that is in heaven." Richard walked into the girls' bedroom where they were sleeping and killed them through suffocation. He says he did not feel any anger while doing this.

That same night, he put the three corpses in his car, and drove to a spot he remembered from his childhood. He says it felt as though he was acting like a maniac, displacing all the dirt as in a frenzy. He arrived back home early the next morning. In the afternoon, neighbors witnessed him vacuuming and cleaning his car, but this was not unusual behavior for him. The next morning, he picked up Joanna at the bus station.

Subsequently, we discuss the period after the offense. Why did he not report himself to the police, but instead make up so many lies and pretend not to know anything, in front of his family and his in-laws? Richard says he was too afraid of the consequences, and felt very ashamed of what he had done. He postponed confronting the real issue, just like he had done in the many years before the offense. Ultimately, police investigators started to doubt the cover-up story Richard told them and they targeted Richard as a suspect. They found Karen's blood on the bedroom wall and soon after that Richard confessed.

At the time of my assessment of Richard, over a year and a half had passed since the crime. He still does not understand what got into him on that fatal night. He was never an aggressive man. He realizes now he avoided his problems, but he cannot relate this horrendous crime to himself. He has been looking for answers in books in the prison library, but has not found them yet.

When asked what he thinks he should change in himself, he says he wants to become less shy and anxious. He wants to learn to solve problems instead of avoiding them. He thinks he also has to learn to experience and express feelings, so he can manage them better. Richard's parents noted that Richard was very emotional during the 10 days after (what later appeared to be) the offense, in contrast to his usual, walled-off personality. His father slept in his home during this time and his mother often visited during the day. His parents have not abandoned their son. Since he has been detained, they visit him every 3 weeks. His mother has noted her son is showing his emotions more now. He cries in her presence sometimes. Richard believes his contact with his parents has improved and has become more personal since he was detained.

Integration and Conclusions

Relationship between Mental Disorder and Offense

The present forensic psychological assessment employed a semi-structured interview for DSM-IV personality disorders, the SIDP-IV, in contrast to the four previous evaluations, which used only unstructured clinical interviews. The SIDP-IV was coded on the basis of all available data, including an interview with his parents, and confirmed that Richard is suffering from a personality disorder. He fulfills diagnostic criteria for both Dependent and Avoidant Personality Disorder. Moreover, test findings from two independent instruments, the MMPI-2 and the RIM, are in line with the psychiatric classification derived from the SIDP-IV.

Is Richard's mental disorder relevant in understanding his offense? I think it is. Richard is a shy, socially anxious man who avoids conflicts to an extreme extent because he is afraid of humiliation, criticism, and rejection. This avoidant interpersonal style is fueled by his inferior self-image, and expressed itself in all of his social contacts: at work, with friends and family, and to an even greater extent in his relationship with his wife Karen. In order to keep arguments with her at bay, he gave up his male friendships, took care of most of the household chores, and swallowed his anger over all of this. Upon the arrival of his daughters, his feelings of inadequacy intensified because Karen wanted to take care of them herself. Further estrangement set in, and the so-called kissing incident on New Year's Eve 2001–2002 is followed by the start of Richard's extramarital affairs. These affairs seem to fulfill a compensatory function: they provided the warmth and attention he missed at home. His negative self-image found temporary boosts in impulsive purchases of luxury items and the thrill of dates with his extramarital affairs.

The affair with the Polish woman, Joanna, seems to have developed a kind of obsessive character over time, as the increasing frequency of their contact over the Internet and via text messages shows. Richard's inability to discuss his feelings about this relationship with Karen and his possible wish for a divorce seem to be rooted in his personality pathology. His fear of criticism and his inability to share negative emotions such as anxiety, shame, and particularly anger with others took such extreme forms that it started to limit his critical judgment. He did not deal with his problems; he let them get out of hand. Extramarital affairs and spending sprees functioned as temporary escapes.

Ultimately, Richard ended up ruminating in the spousal bed about the quite imminent arrival of Joanna, on the evening of April 6, 2005—worries he had been able to keep at bay thus far. The thought to kill Karen arose in his mind as an obsession: "You have to do it, then you are free." The thought became stronger and stronger; Richard could not get it out of his mind. The weapon, the baseball bat, was readily available. Karen was killed in a sudden outburst of devastating rage; the police records testify to the "overkill." The subsequent sense of relief is what struck Richard the most. The motive for the killing of his daughters seems to lie in their reunion with their mother in death. Perhaps his own dependent personality is a factor here: Richard could not imagine his daughters being without their mother, just as he could not imagine being without a female partner.

The above sequence of events demonstrates a marked resemblance to cases of violent catathymia described in the scientific literature. The sense of calm Richard experienced after the offense is corroborated by reports from individuals who encountered Richard during the subsequent days. After he had been with Joanna over the weekend, he seemingly continued his collected composure by spreading lies to hide what had actually occurred. Richard says that in this period, shame over what he had done overruled his preparedness to confess his crime. But he also says he always knew he would get caught in the end. His careless removal of traces of the crime in the home supports this.

Richard's personality pathology can be logically associated with his behavior before, during, and after the offense, as shown in the previous paragraphs. Furthermore, this association is confirmed by empirical findings from the existing research literature on male spousal killers, who suffer from similar dependent, avoidant and overcontrolled personality pathology. On the basis of these two sources of evidence (i.e., findings of the present forensic mental health evaluation and the research literature), there seems to be a logical relationship between disorder and offense in Richard's case.

In the Dutch Criminal Code, any mental disorder (including a personality disorder) can be reason for diminished criminal responsibility. In the case of Richard, the Court of Appeals was advised that there was a strong relationship between disorder and offense. This, of course, was contrary to what three of the previous mental health experts had advised.

Conclusion and Answers to the Attorney's Questions

- *To what extent are the DSM-IV criteria for a personality disorder absolute?*

  The DSM-IV criteria are part of a consensus-based classification system, that is, psychiatrists and psychologists have agreed on a set of diagnostic criteria and on the number of criteria that must be met in order to diagnose an individual with a specific disorder. In principle, these criteria are absolute in the sense that a person does or does not meet a specific criterion. In practice, assessors may differ in terms of the threshold they use to consider a criterion met. These inter-assessor discrepancies can be limited by using semi-structured interviews for the assessment of personality disorders, such as the SIDP-IV, as was done in the present evaluation.

- *Is it possible for a personality disorder to "slumber" during adolescence, but for one reason or another not reveal itself clearly in contacts with other people?*

Personality disorders, by definition, do not reveal themselves until late adolescence, early adulthood. Before then, personality is still developing and less "crystallized." Thus, it may very well be that a youngster who is deemed shy (as Richard was) but still functioning adaptively may reveal maladaptive behaviors only in early/middle adulthood.

- *Mr. Richard H. stated during the trial and also during police interrogation that the idea to kill his wife came to him as an obsessional idea, which kept returning and became stronger over time. Is there literature about such obsessional thoughts (even in the absence of personality disorder, but possibly in cases of high levels of stress)?*

The sudden occurrence of obsessional violent ideation has been previously reported in the literature, as part of catathymic homicide, as already noted above. Often, the sudden outburst of violence follows years of suppressed rage and resentment. Meloy (2002) reported on the spousal homicide case of Mr. A., with remarkable similarities to the Richard H. case, also in terms of the MMPI-2 findings. He concluded that

> the paradox in this case is that the complete absence of conscious anger in Mr. A, his inability to recognize and discuss his negative feelings, his lack of insight into his past, and his complete avoidance of all conflict, were important risk factors for a singular event of deregulated fury.
>
> (Meloy, 2002, p. 397)

Epilogue

Richard was convicted and sentenced to 20 years imprisonment and a mandatory psychiatric treatment order called TBS (Terbeschikkingstelling) (Dutch Entrustment Act, see Chapter 4), on April 13, 2007. My report was excluded as evidence, even though I had been heard as an expert by the Court of Appeals on March 13, 2007. The Court ruled that because my report was requested by the defense and not by a justice authority and because I answered the defense's questions, my report could not be considered equal to those of the four previous court-appointed experts. Also, the Court stated in its verdict that my use of the semi-structured interview SIDP-IV did not render the outcome of the others' unstructured clinical interviews invalid (p. 3, verdict Court of Appeals; LJN: BA2902 Court of Appeals The Hague).

Despite the Court's contempt for my diagnostic efforts in the case, they opted to follow the expert opinion of psychologist V., which was surprisingly close to my conclusions on the case. Psychologist V. considered Richard H. to have diminished responsibility for the offenses and advised mandated treatment in a forensic psychiatric hospital. Thus, Richard's life imprisonment was overturned, and he was hopeful that he would be able to receive the psychological treatment he needs during the period of his treatment order.

I learned a lot from my work on this case. It alerted me to a number of very important issues in forensic psychological assessment. First and foremost is the need to keep a neutral, objective stance, and to not be led astray by the nature of the crime. Seemingly "normal," law-abiding individuals do commit heinous crimes. This point is particularly relevant if numerous media reports have already appeared and painted a particular portrait of the suspect's psyche. Prejudice and cognitive bias are always at bay (Miller, 2004). Second, this case was evaluated by many different mental health experts, who could not agree on a diagnosis. This could be avoided by employing semi-structured interviews for DSM Axis I and II diagnoses, as suggested by different scholars in the field (Heilbrun et al., 2008; Slobogin, 2007). And finally, the case illustrated that integration of empirical evidence with the findings from forensic psychological assessment of the individual increases our understanding of the perpetrator and his offence. This ultimately resulted in helping the offender gain insight into his offending behavior and the acceptance of his verdict.

Every year since this verdict, Richard has been sending me a Christmas card from prison, to express his gratitude for my evaluation in his case. He is eager to start treatment, but the law requires him to fulfill at least two-thirds of his prison term before he can be transferred to a forensic psychiatric hospital. From a psychological treatment perspective, this is obviously an awkward arrangement, which can lead to demotivation and demoralization in individuals who should first and foremost be considered (forensic) psychiatric patients.

During his time in prison, other trials have crossed Richard's path. Family members of his deceased wife were interviewed for a book (Fijen, 2010) and a related documentary entitled *The family drama of Zoetermeer*. The film was broadcast on Dutch national television on April 5, 2010, the fifth anniversary of the events. Both works paint a one-sided, all-bad picture of Richard's personality. Richard felt unfairly treated by the documentary maker, who only spoke with the victim's blood relatives and not with anyone of his relatives. By not practicing ethical journalism, which entails working according to the principle of impartiality, the public was not presented with the real story. For the actual story, one needs to dig beneath the surface of violence.

Notes

1   This chapter was also published as: de Ruiter, C. (2013). Domestic estrangement and familicide: Nothing is as it seems. Invited paper. *Journal of Forensic Practice, 15,* 5–20. doi: 10.1108/14636641311299040.

2   The Wikipedia page (in Dutch) on this case uses the actual first and last names of the family members. See: http://nl.wikipedia.org/wiki/Zoetermeers_familiedrama [accessed on January 23, 2012]. Richard H. provided written informed consent to use his case, including the test results and information provided by his parents, for publication. In the current publication, the names of the three victims are not their real names.

References

American Psychological Association (1991). Specialty guidelines for forensic psychologists. *Law and Human Behavior, 15*, 655–665. doi: 10.1007/BF01065858.

American Psychological Association (2013). Specialty guidelines for forensic psychologists. *American Psychologist, 68*, 7–19. doi: 10.1037/a0029889.

Belfrage, H. & Rying, M. (2004). Characteristics of spousal homicide perpetrators: A study of all cases of spousal homicide in Sweden 1990–1999. *Criminal Behaviour and Mental Health, 14*, 121–133. doi: 10.1002/cbm.577.

Butcher, J. N., Dahlstrom, W. G., Graham, J. R., Tellegen, A., & Kaemmer, B. (1989). *Minnesota multiphasic personality inventory-2 (MMPI-2): Manual for administration and scoring.* Minneapolis, MN: University of Minnesota Press.

Dobash, R. E. & Dobash, R. P. (2011). What were they thinking? Men who murder their intimate partner. *Violence Against Women, 17*, 111–134. doi: 10.1177/107780121039 1219.

Dutton, D. G. & Kerry, G. (1999). Modus operandi and personality disorder in incarcerated spousal killers. *International Journal of Law and Psychiatry, 22*, 287–299. doi: 10.1016/ S0160–2527(99)00010–2.

Ewing, C. P. (1997). *Fatal families: The dynamics of intrafamilial homicide.* London: Sage.

Exner, J. E. (2003). *The Rorschach: A comprehensive system—Basic foundations and principles of interpretation* (4th ed.). Hoboken, NJ: Wiley.

Fijen, L. (2010). *Het familiedrama van Zoetermeer: Karen, Marian en Charlene moesten dood* [The Zoetermeer family drama: Karen, Marian and Charlene had to be killed]. Baarn: Ten Have.

Fox, J. A. & Levin, J. (2005). *Extreme killing: Understanding serial and mass murder.* London: Sage.

Hare, R. D. (2003). *The Hare psychopathy checklist-revised* (2nd ed.). Toronto, ON: Multi-Health Systems.

Heilbrun, K., Grisso, T., & Goldstein, A. M. (2008). *Foundations of forensic mental health assessment.* Oxford: Oxford University Press.

Hildebrand, M. & de Ruiter, C. (2004). PCL-R psychopathy and its relation to DSM-IV Axis I and Axis II disorders in a sample of male forensic psychiatric patients in The Netherlands. *International Journal of Law and Psychiatry, 27*, 233–248. doi: 10.1016/ j.ijlp.2004.03.005.

Liem, M. & Koenraadt, F. (2008). Familicide: A comparison with spousal and child homicide by mentally disordered perpetrators. *Criminal Behaviour and Mental Health, 18*, 306–318. doi: 10.1002/cbm.710.

Marzuk, P. M., Tardiff, K., & Hirsch, C. S. (1992). The epidemiology of murder-suicide. *Journal of the American Medical Association, 267*, 3179–3183. doi: 10.1001/jama.1992. 03480230071031.

Meloy, J. R. (1992). *Violent attachments.* Northvale, NJ: Jason Aronson.

Meloy, J. R. (2002). Spousal homicide and the subsequent staging of a sexual homicide at a distant location. *Journal of Forensic Sciences, 47*, 395–397.

Meloy, J. R. (2010). A catathymic infanticide. *Journal of Forensic Sciences, 55*, 1393–1396. doi: 10.1111/j.1556–4029.2010.01414.x.

Meyer, G. J., Finn, S. E., Eyde, L. D., Kay, G. G., Moreland, K. L., Dies, R. R., & Reed, G. M. (2001). Psychological testing and psychological assessment: A review of evidence and issues. *American Psychologist, 56*, 128–165. doi: 10.1037//0003–066X.56.2.128.

Miller, A. G. (Ed.). (2004). *The social psychology of good and evil.* New York: Guilford.

Nederlands Instituut van Psychologen (NIP) (2007). *Beroepscode voor Psychologen* [Professional code for psychologists]. www.psynip.nl/wat-doet-het-nip/tuchtrecht-en-klachten/beroepscode.html.

Pfohl, B., Blum, N., & Zimmerman, M. (1994). *Structured Interview for DSM-IV Personality (DSM-IV).* Iowa City, IA: Department of Psychiatry, University of Iowa.

Polk, K. (1994). *When men kill: Scenarios of masculine violence.* Cambridge, UK: Cambridge University Press.

Rogers, R. & Shuman, D. W. (2000). *Conducting insanity evaluations* (2nd ed.). New York: Guilford.

de Ruiter, C. & Greeven, P. G. J. (2000). Personality disorders in a Dutch forensic psychiatric sample: Convergence of interview and self-report measures. *Journal of Personality Disorders, 14,* 162–170. doi: 10.1521/pedi.2000.14.2.162.

de Ruiter, C. & Hildebrand, M. (2003). The dual nature of forensic psychiatric practice: Risk assessment and management under the Dutch TBS-order. In P. J. van Koppen & S. D. Penrod (Eds.), *Adversarial vs. inquisitorial justice: Psychological perspectives on criminal justice systems* (pp. 91–106). New York: Plenum Press.

Showalter, C. R., Bonnie, R. J., & Roddy, V. (1980). The spousal-homicide syndrome. *International Journal of Law and Psychiatry, 3,* 117–141. doi: 10.1016/0160-2527(80) 90034-5.

Slobogin, C. (2007). *Proving the unprovable: The role of law, science and speculation in adjudicating culpability and dangerousness.* New York: Oxford University Press.

Thijssen, J. & de Ruiter, C. (2011). Instrumental and expressive violence in Belgian homicide perpetrators. *Journal of Investigative Psychology and Offender Profiling, 8,* 73–83. doi: 10.1002/jip.130.

Wertham, F. (1937). The catathymic crisis: A clinical entity. *Archives of Neurology and Psychiatry, 37,* 974–977. doi: 10.1001/archneurpsyc.1937.02260160274023.

Wilson, M., Daly, M., & Daniele, A. (1995). Familicide: The killing of spouse and children. *Aggressive Behavior, 21,* 275–291. doi: 10.1002/1098-2337.

3

NEONATICIDE IN A YOUNG IMMIGRANT WOMAN

Nancy Kaser-Boyd

Jane arrived in the United States from a Pacific Island at the age of 16, some 2 years before she became the focus of a criminal investigation. Her father had immigrated several years before and wished to give his youngest children the educational opportunities that the US provides. Jane grew up in a rural village, far from a city. She only began to learn English when she arrived in the US. She had been attending high school in the Los Angeles area, where she met a boy and fell in love. Her father was her sponsor for immigration, but he had remarried and his new wife did not want his two children living in their crowded apartment. Jane's father rented a room in a boarding house some 15 miles away. She and her brother were to share one room in the house full of immigrants from their country. The bathroom was down the hall. Jane had little access to her mother, who had stayed behind in their home country. She could text her, and she could call home about twice a month.

No one in Jane's family knew that she and her boyfriend had begun a sexual relationship, and in her culture this was a violation of religious and social norms. Within months, Jane became pregnant. She told her boyfriend of the pregnancy, and together they began to discuss what they would do when the baby came. Jane thought of names for the baby, and talked excitedly to her boyfriend and to one girlfriend, but she did not get prenatal care. Fearful of her father's reaction, she hid the pregnancy, wearing big shirts and ignoring questions about why she seemed to be gaining weight.

On a school day at 5 a.m., Jane awoke with excruciating pain in her abdomen. She called her boyfriend, crying. He told her he thought she was having the baby. She said that couldn't be the case because it wasn't time. She went to the bathroom and got in the shower. Suddenly she saw the baby's head emerge from her body.

The whole story of what transpired in that bathroom would not emerge until the forensic evaluation. Jane came to the attention of authorities after her boyfriend's mother rushed her to the hospital. Her boyfriend had found Jane on the bus, headed toward school, bleeding heavily. He could see she was no longer pregnant, but she seemed too distraught and too weak to answer questions. Once at the hospital, it was quickly apparent to doctors that she had been pregnant and had given birth. Jane was interrogated while still in her hospital bed. The search for the baby then began.

There are many teen pregnancies with children who are unplanned and for whom the mother is ill prepared. However, neonaticide—the killing of a newborn—is quite rare. Neonaticide should be distinguished from *infanticide* and the killing of older children. Neonaticide is the killing of a child within 24 hours of birth, whereas infanticide is the killing of a child up to 18 months of age. *Filicide* is all other child-killing. Neonaticide can be further divided into two categories: active neonaticide, or the killing of a newborn as a direct result of violence; and passive neonaticide, the result of negligence directly following the birth (Bonnet, 1993). The incidence of neonaticide is estimated, as there are likely cases that are never discovered. In the United States its prevalence is estimated to be less than 8.0 per 100,000. The incidence is somewhat lower in Europe (Porter & Gavin, 2010). The dynamics of neonaticide are different from those of other forms of child-killing. The typical mother who kills her newborn is young, single, and is a person for whom the pregnancy and birth is shameful or unacceptable (Meyer & Oberman, 2001). This implies that the killing is the result of a *purposeful plan*. This may not necessarily be the case.

The forensic mental health examination is a necessary step in understanding the specific mental state of a woman who kills her newborn. The first section of this chapter will walk the reader through the forensic examination. The second section will present the prosecution's case. Although it is presented out of sequence here, it is crucial to hear the challenges to a defense expert's opinion. The final section will address the issues that became crucial at trial.

The Forensic Psychological Examination

The forensic psychological examination begins with knowledge of forensic psychology ethics. Division 41 of the American Psychological Association has codified rules regarding informed consent, data collection, the weighing of arguments for and against an opinion, and the communication of results and limitations of opinions (Heilbrun, Grisso, & Goldstein, 2009; Heilbrun, Marczyk, & DeMatteo, 2002). The process of data collection starts with a review of the materials accumulated in the police investigation. This usually includes the first call to authorities, the investigation at the scene, the doctors' reports, and, if the woman allowed herself to be interviewed, a taped interview. Relatives or housemates of the woman may also be interviewed. A review of this information indicated that Jane had told her boyfriend that the baby was born dead. He noted that she was crying, pale, and bleeding heavily. Jane told doctors at the hospital that the baby was born dead. The intake nurse described Jane as very emotional, crying, scared, and impaired. Her emotions seemed labile; she would cry at times, but also smiled and laughed at times with her boyfriend at her bedside.

Police investigators conducted their first interview of Jane from her bedside. They interviewed her in English. She was not given a Miranda Warning because she was not formally "in custody," a regular practice in the United States. In broken English, Jane told the police that she had not told her father about the pregnancy and that she felt scared about being pregnant. As soon as the coroner completed his examination of the dead baby and told investigators that the baby had died from asphyxia, the police returned to the hospital and questioned her more vigorously, again in English. The interviews are taped, and the forensic psychologist can hear the extent to which Jane can communicate in English. In the second interview with police, Jane admitted that she smothered the baby by putting her hand on the baby's face. She believed the baby was dead, wrapped it in several plastic bags, and threw it in a dumpster at her residence. The following is the entire section from the police interview that led to her indictment:

Detective:	Was she going to start crying?
Jane:	I was just looking at her. I didn't know what I'm going to do, and I'm still studying [that is, she is still in school].
Detective:	You have a report to do?
Jane:	No. I can't care for her.
Detective:	You still have to go to school and you can't care for her?
Jane:	Yeah, and my dad is going to kick me out, and then what am I going to do?
Detective:	You didn't think she was going to come that soon, did you?
Jane:	No.
Detective:	Did you put your hand over her mouth?
Jane:	Yeah.
Detective:	So, after the baby was born, you put the hand. How long you think you sat there in the bathtub?
Jane:	I don't remember because I take [sic] a shower. I don't know what coming [sic]. I'm trying to stand up, but it very hurts. When I see the baby's going go out, I sit like just kind of go out and then I see the baby's just going out, and then I pull it out.
Detective:	And then you started holding her? And then you started thinking about how you're going to take care of her and that you can't take care of her?
Jane:	Yeah.
Detective:	And then you put your hand over her mouth?
Jane:	Yeah.

Detective: Did you think about doing that before she came out?

Jane: No, I did not. When the baby was going out I was happy. Then I think "What am I going to do? I can't care her."

Detective: Did you know you could bring her to a hospital and just leave her?

Jane: I can't, 'cause I'm still in the bathroom with the blood.

Jane also said that she thought she was only 4 months along in her pregnancy and felt shocked when she saw the baby's head emerging from her body. Jane was charged with first degree murder.

A competent forensic psychologist in this case would need two or three bodies of knowledge. She should know the empirical literature on neonaticide. Not all neonaticides are the result of an unwanted baby, deliberately tossed in the trash. The evaluator should know what the research says about the mental state of mothers who have committed neonaticide who have been carefully evaluated. She should know, or learn about, the Island culture from which this woman came. Why is this important? There may be cultural factors that are relevant to her mental state, her ability to make a decision, or to her behavior at the hospital, or with the police. The evaluator must know the legal standards for various exculpatory mental states. While Jane's account to the police sounded like a deliberate act, even a planned act, this isn't a "given" until a defendant has participated in a more in-depth psychological examination. If Jane provides information that indicates she had a mental disorder, or a relevant mental state at the time of the act, the forensic evaluator will also need to be proficient at evaluating the possibility of malingering.

Interviewing Jane with an interpreter would be critical. Though Jane had resided in America for 2 years and had been learning English, her English was not good. A criminal conviction can turn on the use of a word. Also, it is often the case that some cultural experiences are not easily described in English, and the native language may have specific words for certain experiences. For example, "running *amok*" has a very specific meaning that is hard to translate. The interpreter said, at the end of the interview: "Her English is not that good. Also, she can hardly say a whole sentence in Cebuano (her native language). There were quite a few words she would ask me. Simple conversation in English she can do."

The full forensic mental health assessment of this case included:

(1) multiple interviews of Jane;
(2) interviews of her boyfriend [the baby's father], her father, her brother, and her mother and sister;
(3) a review of the Discovery in the case. "Discovery" includes materials that rise from the investigation and which are available to both prosecution and defense. In this case, the following were relevant to the forensic mental health examination:

(a) two police interviews of Jane at the hospital, both conducted in English;

(b) police interview with the doctor treating Jane;

(c) police interview with Jane's high school health teacher;

(d) police interview with Jane's best friend;

(e) police interview with Jane's boyfriend;

(f) police interviews with medical personnel at the hospital.

(4) a review of the literature on neonaticide;

(5) a review of the literature on Acute Stress Disorder;

(6) consultation with an expert on the cultural values and beliefs of individuals from Jane's culture;

(7) an analysis of the question of malingering.

The last item proved to be the most challenging because Jane could not be given psychological tests that are of significant assistance in evaluating possible malingering. She did not speak and read English, nor possess the degree of acculturation that is necessary to generate a valid Minnesota Multiphasic Personality Inventory-2 (MMPI-2; Butcher, Dahlstrom, Graham, Tellegen, & Kaemmer, 1989), Personality Assessment Inventory (PAI; Morey, 1991), Millon Clinical Multiaxial Inventory (MCMI; Millon, Millon, & Davis, 1994), or other standardized test instruments. Interpreting the items of the Structured Interview of Reported Symptoms (SIRS; Rogers, 1992) into Jane's native language is not acceptable in a forensic case as an interpreter might lose the intended meaning of the questions and skew the results. An equally important issue was the lack of research with any of these instruments with individuals from her cultural background. This meant that the issue of malingering had to be examined from a rational and practical perspective.

Assessment Data

Unfortunately, for the first jail visit to Jane, the interpreter cancelled. It seemed reasonable to make an introduction to Jane and determine the extent to which she could communicate in English. Jane was very glad to speak to a female psychologist, and she spoke readily about the pregnancy, her fear, and what happened in the bathroom that night. The forensic psychological interview was some 3 months after the police interrogation. Jane's English was sometimes incomprehensible. In the first forensic psychological interview, she provided an account that was similar to the one she had given the police. She said:

> I wake up early, hurting a lot. I wanted to put baby back. I touched head and went "Oh!" I pull. A lot of blood. I'm so scared because people don't know I'm pregnant. I said "I'm sorry." About 10 minutes and she is dead. I stand up. I got pads. I put the baby in the plastic. I left, walking slowly because it's very hurt.

Because it is poor practice, if not unethical, to ask a defendant to give crucial information in a language that is not their own, I resolved to return with the interpreter. At the second visit, Jane started her account again. She now gave a much more detailed account of the pregnancy and the sudden delivery of the baby. Using her native language, suddenly important facts emerged. She said:

> During my pregnancy, something was telling me, not a real person, but something in my ears, like a devil or an angel, telling me very softly, not to go to the doctor. . . . Then that morning, I felt shocked to see the baby's head. I was in a lot of pain and I was very scared. I tried to push the baby back inside. The baby wouldn't go back in. I couldn't stand up. I was so scared. I pulled the baby out by the shoulders. I looked at her and she was crying and she opened her left eye. When I saw her, I was happy and not sad. Then I looked at her and it got dark, and the voice told me "Is that your baby?" I said "Yes, that's my baby." Then the voice was saying "No, that's not your baby. That's not your boyfriend's baby. Kill that baby!" I was talking to the voice and I didn't realize my hand was on her mouth. Then the voice was gone and I looked at my baby and she was so pale. I called her. I tried to wake her up. Her crying had stopped.

Jane then realized the baby was dead. Slowly she cleaned herself and the bathroom. She was still in a lot of pain. She put the baby in plastic bags and placed them in the large outside trash bin. In this state, she believed she could still go to school. She got on the bus and met her boyfriend, who noticed that she was hemorrhaging and insisted she go to the hospital. Why had she not told the police about a dialogue and struggle with a "voice"? This became a central focus in the trial and the cause of accusations that she was malingering. I admit that I was surprised when Jane began to describe a voice, in her second interview. In that interview, she also told me that her mother's Island house was built on top of an old cemetery. She said:

> In my home, I slept in a room that had been my parents' bedroom. When the house was built, no one knew that there were dead people there. It was a landfill. A lady said that there was a baby that died in that bathroom. When I took a shower, I could hear a baby crying. I told my mother about this and she told me there was a good woman there. I saw her once— she was a White woman with long hair. Now I feel she is with me, but it is male now. Even in the boarding house I heard him because I was always by myself.

It was not clear why Jane felt "shocked" when she began to deliver the baby on that morning. Further inquiry revealed that Jane believed she was only 4 months pregnant because she dated the beginning of her pregnancy to the day she *discovered* she was pregnant, reflecting her rather illogical thought process surrounding the baby. This false belief resulted in a complete lack of preparation for the baby. It did not appear that Jane planned to keep the pregnancy secret from everyone and then simply kill and hide the baby, a dynamic often implied in some neonaticide studies (d'Orban, 1979; Friedman, Horwitz, & Resnick, 2005; Friedman & Resnick, 2009; Saunders, 1989).[1] While she seemed to fit the common characteristics of neonaticide mothers, such as being young, unmarried, and without financial resources, there were remarkable ways in which she did not match these characteristics. For example, she had a loving boyfriend and they had named the baby and had talked about raising her. It seemed likely that it was Jane's shock, fear, and pain as she began to deliver her baby that explained the killing.

Interviews with Collateral Informants

Collateral interviews can be a helpful way to gather additional information about the defendant's mental state at the time of a crime, to attempt to address motive, and to understand the defendant's general personality. In this case, it would prove important in ruling out malingering[2] or distortion.

Jane's Father

Jane's father was a serious and very polite man whose demeanor was deferential to authority. It was clear that his daughter's act had shamed him and he put energy into trying to show that she was from "a good family." He explained that he brought his daughter and son to the United States "for a better life" and said that he had strict rules for her. However, his new wife did not want the children living with them, as their home already contained their young child and her parents. As a result, he rented a room for his son and daughter in a boarding house, which was some 15 miles from his apartment. The house was inhabited by other immigrants from their country. The room was shared by Jane and her brother. Jane's father saw the children on the weekends. Jane's father confirmed that he would have sent her back to their country if he learned she was pregnant. He said that in his country, her out-of-wedlock pregnancy would have brought intense shame to their family. He reminded her of this, he said, soon after she arrived in the US when she was helping him with his job as a janitor at an abortion clinic. Jane's father said she had always been a "very good girl," and he didn't understand how she could now be charged with murder.

Jane's Brother

Jane's brother was 2 years older, and his English was difficult to understand but better than Jane's. The boarding house had been near his job. It was noteworthy that, while his father had helped him and Jane immigrate to the US for a better life, he had to go straight to work after high school. He worked a night shift, which meant that he was not at home when his sister got out of school. This gave her the freedom to spend time after school with her boyfriend. Though they shared the same room, Jane's brother had had no idea that she was pregnant. He said he did notice that she was gaining weight, but he thought "she was just eating too much rice." He said that he would have "yelled at her" and been very mad if he had learned she was pregnant. Jane's brother was at work when she began labor at 4 a.m.

Jane's Mother

Jane's mother was interviewed telephonically with the use of an interpreter. She said that Jane was "a very good girl, very quiet and timid." She said,

> she was sleeping in a room where she saw an apparition of a lady. She and her sister can hear a voice and also a baby crying, a newborn baby, a clear voice, a female voice, but I don't know what was said. I have had prayers said[3] to get the spirit away.

She said one of her sons saw an apparition of a female ghost one night when going to the bathroom outside. Jane's mother said she herself heard a voice "calling the names of my children." Asked if she spoke to the voice, she laughed and said, "That would be crazy!"

Jane's mother was asked her thoughts about why her daughter would not confide in her about the pregnancy. She explained that they could only afford to talk on the telephone about once a month, and her father would usually be nearby. The rest of the time they sent text messages. She didn't see how her daughter could discuss such a difficult topic with her under these circumstances. If she had known, however, she would have asked Jane's father to send her back home. She said that while this would be shameful for their family, she would have helped Jane with the baby.

Jane's Sister

Jane's sister was 4 years older and she had left their village to study nursing in a larger city in their country, then returned and was living with their mother. She was also interviewed by telephone. She said that Jane told her, before they both left home, that she heard a baby crying in the bedroom where she slept. She said that the house had been built on land that had been a garbage dump "and someone threw a baby there." She had heard a baby crying, as well. Also, she said she herself saw an apparition of a "white woman" and that she, in addition, had "spells" where she lost time. These sounded like a form of epilepsy but had not been diagnosed as such. Like her mother and sister Jane, she felt convinced that there were ghosts on their property. However, like her mother, she laughed when asked whether she ever tried to communicate with them, stating, "That would be crazy."

Jane's Boyfriend

Jane's boyfriend was a self-effacing but handsome young man who had emigrated with his family from Central America when he was 12. He was 1 year younger than Jane. He recounted tearfully how they met in high school and fell in love. He said that Jane was "pretty and very sweet." Neither spoke very good English, but he said: "We could communicate." They spent time together after school, when Jane's brother and father were at work. They had been having a sexual relationship for a short time when he learned that Jane had not had a period. He thought she should go to a doctor, and even arranged an appointment for her and walked her there, but he said she had been afraid to go in, afraid that the doctor would call her father. He confirmed that she was quite fearful of her father and also of her brother. He said, however, that he and Jane were quite excited to be having a baby, and they even decided on a name. They spent many afternoons at the park after school, discussing the life they would have when the baby came. He said he realized he would have to quit school and go to work, but this was alright with him. He said he believed that his mother would help them care for the baby.

Jane's boyfriend cried as he described the morning of the baby's birth. He said that Jane had called him twice, early in the morning. She told him that her stomach hurt a lot and he told her that maybe the baby was coming. She told him she thought "it isn't time." She hung up. He wanted to go to find her but because she hid their relationship from her brother, he had never been to her boarding house. She called him again and said she would meet him at the bus stop. He said, "When I saw Jane, her eyes were all red, like she had been crying. She was very pale and she was bleeding a lot." He said that she told him that she had delivered the baby and the baby was dead. He thought she was too distraught at the time to answer more questions. He called his mother, who insisted that Jane be taken to the hospital and joined them for the trip.

Jane's boyfriend stayed by her bedside at the hospital, trying to comfort her. The fact of his loving relationship with Jane, and their discussions about the baby—even naming the baby—makes this case different from many neonaticides where the pregnancy is denied and the baby's father is unaware or uninterested.

Jane's Girlfriends

Jane also discussed the pregnancy with two of her girlfriends. The first girl said that Jane "was happy and really wanted the baby." Jane told her she talked to the baby at night. Jane wanted her to put her hand on her stomach to see if she could feel the baby kick. She said Jane's stomach "was big but not too big." The second girlfriend said that Jane told her she was pregnant and she wanted to have the baby. She said she had been scared to go to the doctor, afraid that the doctor would tell her father she was pregnant. Again, this is not like neonaticide cases where the pregnancy is completely hidden or denied. This raises the question whether some other dynamic was at play.

The Literature on Neonaticide

The first day of life has the greatest risk of death by homicide, with rates at least ten times greater than any other time of life (Overpeck, Brenner, Trumble, & Trifilliti, 1998). Yet neonaticide seems a low base-rate offense, as far as we know, because these crimes can easily go undetected. This means that there is not a large amount of literature and there is no opportunity to do case-controlled studies. The literature that exists, however, is still informative. In attempting to fully understand the mental state of this defendant, two bodies of literature are important: (1) studies on mothers who have committed neonaticide, and (2) studies on childbirth pain and distress. We will be asking questions such as "Does Jane fit the characteristics of other mothers who committed neonaticide?"; "What is the mental state of such mothers during the pregnancy and during the delivery?"; "What is the typical mental state of a woman who goes into labor and delivers a baby at home, by herself?" Published studies draw from different populations. Friedman and Resnick (2009) note that cultural, economic, and legal differences across nations may result in women from one jurisdiction being more likely to appear in the criminal justice system and in another jurisdiction in the mental health system.

The literature is in agreement on the following: neonaticide appears to occur across many ethnic groups and countries. Mothers who kill their newborns are often young with poor coping skills. They have often been left by the baby's father, or the pregnancy was the result of a short-term sexual liaison. Typically, they live with their families or they lack financial resources for independence (Riley, 2006). They may have other reasons to fear authority, such as illegal immigrant status. The pregnancy is often hidden from others. Very few are married or involved in a committed romantic relationship. Most of the young women neither have a criminal record nor a record of a psychiatric illness. The woman uses some form of denial throughout the pregnancy, and when the delivery begins is surprised and unprepared (Meyer & Oberman, 2001; Spinelli, 2001, 2003). Neonaticide is typically not a premeditated act, but rather an act committed in the midst of strong emotions (fear, shame) or shock (Pitt & Bale, 1995).

The most common way babies die after denied pregnancies is by being delivered into toilets and drowning (Green & Manohar, 1990; Kellett, 1992; Milstein & Milstein, 1983; Mitchell & Davis, 1984). The second is falling to the floor and sustaining a skull fracture (Kellett, 1992). Shelton, Corey, Donaldson, and Dennison (2011), in their sample of 55 cases, found that 80 percent of the babies suffered asphyxia-related deaths: 62 percent were due to suffocation; 30 percent due to drowning; and 8 percent due to strangulation.

The earliest work to understand the dynamics of neonaticide was published by Resnick (1970), and he coined the term neonaticide. Meyer and Oberman (2001) note that Resnick had culled his research sample from having read 37 case reports of neonaticide from many countries, which had occurred between 1751 and 1967; none of the cases were cases where he conducted interviews or directly reviewed criminal files. They note that his understanding of this phenomenon was limited by the weakness of his research methodology. They set out to improve on his methods and focused on a United States sample, reviewing documents of 37 cases of neonaticide. Twenty-six of the babies died from being smothered after being put in the trash or left in a closet under clothes. Four left the babies outside to die of exposure. Five drowned in either a bathtub or a toilet. Only three were killed by violent means. Almost all of the births occurred in bathrooms, bedrooms, or other non-medical settings. Thirty-six of the women were single; they were typically no longer involved with the men by whom they had become pregnant. Fourteen of the women had other children. Typically, pregnancies were not revealed because of fear. Some were conscious of their pregnancies but unable to make decisions about how to proceed. Instead, they put off deciding, day after day, throughout the long months of their pregnancies. Some moved into a complete denial of their pregnancies. Even those who had acknowledged that they were pregnant were surprised by and unprepared for the onset of labor. The authors characterize the mental state of these women, at the time of birth, as a mixture of shock, fear, shame, and guilt.

Few of these women were found to be mentally ill in the traditional sense (Brezinka, Huter, Biebl, & Kinzl, 1994; Meyer & Oberman, 2001). Many were quite young, although the age range was from 15 to 39. Their personalities were said to be marked by immaturity and impulsivity. They typically lacked education, and received little or no prenatal care. Many were described as socially isolated. Some had many people around them but did not feel any of them would be supportive. In many cases, the dread of being pregnant is associated with growing up in families, cultures, or religious contexts that stigmatize out-of-wedlock conceptions. This may be so intense that prenuptial pregnancy becomes literally unthinkable. Seeking an abortion would require acceptance of the situation and prompt decision making, which are not characteristic of the problem-solving of these women (Meyer & Oberman, 2001).

When delivery began, many women interviewed said they thought labor pains were menstrual cramps or that their stomach discomfort was associated with defecation and felt shocked when a baby appeared (Schwartz & Isser, 2000). Pitt and Bale (1995) indicate that the actual act of neonaticide, when it occurs, is likely not premeditated but a reaction to fear, shock, and guilt. Marks (2009) indicates that many neonaticides are more the result of inaction than a violent act.

Spinelli's work (2001, 2003) is more directly related to forensic assessments, as she actually conducted forensic evaluations on women who had been charged with neonaticide. Her sample consisted of 17 women. She reports many common features among these women. They presented in a childlike manner or with *la belle indifférence*. They lacked insight, had poor judgment, and did not have good coping skills. All of them described "watching" themselves during the birth. Eleven denied any pain and five described the pain as "not bad." Fourteen of the women experienced dissociative hallucinations, and some described an internal commentary of argumentative voices. Fourteen women experienced brief amnesia, and nine of the women described psychotic symptoms at the sight of the infant. Upon reintegration, the women could not account for the dead infant. Spinelli (2001, 2003) employed the Dissociative Experiences Scale (DES) to further study the women's reports of dissociation and found that ten women had DES scores greater than 15, the cutting score for dissociative disorders. Spinelli's description of dissociative hallucinations is particularly instructive. She indicates that 14 of the women experienced dissociative hallucinations as a commentary of internalized voices distinct from psychotic hallucinations, which are heard outside the head. She writes, "One woman recalled, 'It was like I was a third party. They had control over my decisions'." Spinelli opined that the symptoms of depersonalization accounted for the low level of reported pain. She describes cases of women who went through labor quietly in the family home while others were in adjacent rooms. Fourteen of the women experienced amnesia for various aspects of the birth. In terms of the pregnancies with these infants, most of the women showed some level of denial, but this was on a spectrum. Some, she said, described intermittent awareness of what was experienced as an intolerable reality, but this was subsequently pushed out of awareness. She comments that the women in her sample were likely vulnerable to "ego disruption," that is, individuals whose reality testing breaks down under overwhelming circumstances.

Spinelli was not the first to describe dissociative-like experiences. Atkins, Grimes, Joseph, and Liebman (1999), Riley (2006), and Shelton and colleagues (2011) indicate that women sampled reported dissociative-like experiences characterized by the inability for complete recall, blacking out, or viewing themselves outside their bodies.

Friedman, Heneghan, and Rosenthal (2007) note that there are several subtypes of both denial and concealment of pregnancy. Some women deny their pregnancy throughout its course, while others consciously conceal their pregnancy. Miller (2003) examined the role of denial in neonaticide, beginning with the pregnancy itself. She notes that there are different levels of denial, from the complete denial of the pregnancy, to brief recognition and then suppression of the knowledge.

She found that the presence and severity of denial can vary at different times during a pregnancy. Some women were described as exhibiting "psychotic denial"; they differed in that they did not hide the pregnancy. Denial was found to be especially common in women with a passive behavioral style. Many of the women were limited in intellectual functioning and problem-solving; however, pregnancy denial was also seen in women with above-average IQ scores and good school performance. Denial was especially common in adolescents. Studies of pregnant adolescents coming to emergency rooms (Causey, Seago, Wahl, & Voelker, 1997) have found that less than 10 percent requested a pregnancy test or mentioned the possibility of being pregnant. About 10 percent denied being sexually active. Some persisted in denying the possibility of pregnancy after being informed of positive pregnancy test results.

Denial may even affect the symptoms of pregnancy. Brezinka and colleagues (1994) found in a sample of 27 women denying pregnancy, 7 were amenorrheic, 12 had irregular spotting, 4 reported regular menstrual periods, and 15 gained little or no weight. This demonstrates the complexity of the psychological mechanism of denial. Forchuk and Westwell (1987) clarify the connection between denial and neonaticide. They note that denial is an emotion-focused rather than a problem-focused strategy. Threatening information is actively excluded from conscious awareness. Denial reduces anxiety, but it also decreases access to useful information and prevents adaptive action. Thus, when the delivery begins, the woman is shocked and unprepared, and she enters the delivery forced to manage the pain and fear on her own. Pregnancy denial often leads to obstetric complications, such as higher incidence of pre-term labor; precipitous, unassisted delivery; perinatal mortality, and low birth-weight (Joyce, Diffenbacher, & Greene, 1984).

Riley (2006) summarizes the behavioral and psychological responses integral to the act of neonaticide as (1) fear; (2) concealment; (3) emotional isolation; (4) denial; (5) panic; (6) dissociation; and (7) homicide.

Acute Stress Disorder

Women who commit neonaticide often experience labor and delivery alone, often at home on the toilet while others are also home, making little or no noise, followed by either exhaustion or panic (Meyer & Oberman, 2001). The high level of fear and of pain that accompanies most childbirth raises the likelihood of Acute Stress Disorder. Many women report pain at the onset of delivery but appear to have no memory of pain during the delivery, which is postulated to result from dissociation (Spinelli, 2001, 2003).

Acute Stress Disorder is defined by the Diagnostic and Statistical Manual of Mental Disorders (DSM-IV-TR; American Psychiatric Association, 2000).[4] To begin with, the person must have experienced, witnessed, or been confronted with an event or events that involved actual or threatened death or serious injury, or a threat to the physical integrity of self or others; and their response must have involved intense fear, helplessness, or horror. While experiencing or after experiencing the event, the individual has three or more dissociative symptoms, including (1) a subjective sense of numbing, detachment, or absence of emotional responsiveness; (2) a reduction in awareness of their surroundings; (3) derealization; (4) depersonalization; (5) dissociative amnesia. Afterwards, the event is re-experienced in recurrent images, thoughts, dreams, illusions, flashback episodes, or a sense of reliving the experience. Also, there is marked avoidance of stimuli that arouse recollections of the trauma, and marked symptoms of anxiety or increased arousal. The disturbance lasts for a minimum of 2 days and a maximum of 4 weeks and occurs within 4 weeks of the traumatic event. It also causes clinically significant impairment or impairment.

While childbirth is a "normal" event for women, it is now recognized that some deliveries are traumatic (Soet, Brack, & DiIorio, 2003). Research has shown that some women develop Acute Stress Disorder (ASD) or Posttraumatic Stress Disorder (PTSD) following childbirth. Creedy, Shochet, and Horsfall (2000) examined 499 women, 4 to 6 weeks postpartum. Thirty-three percent identified a traumatic birth event, and 5.6 percent met criteria for Acute Stress Disorder. The stressful events associated with ASD were: the experience of extreme pain, fear for her life, fear for the baby's life, and perceived lack of care. Olde et al. (2005) in an article entitled "Peritraumatic Dissociation and Emotion as Predictors of PTSD" describe dissociation in childbirth as the result of fear, helplessness, loss of control, pain, and horror. They examined 140 Dutch women, 8 days postpartum, and used several assessment measures to assess somatoform dissociation,[5] peritraumatic emotions, and concomitant symptoms. Twenty-one percent of their sample reported a traumatic childbirth experience. They described delivery experiences including derealization, amnesia, out-of-body experiences, altered time perception, and depersonalization. Eleven percent of the women met criteria for PTSD. Boudou, Sejourne, and Chabrol (2007) examined 117 French women and found that pain was a significant predictor of peritraumatic dissociation.

Cultural Consultation

No forensic psychologist can be knowledgeable about the culture of every defendant they may see. When evaluating a person from a culture that is not one's own, seeking consultation is important. It can address questions such as "Is the defendant accurately depicting his/her culture?"; "Is the defendant's experience normal for the culture, or abnormal?"; "Would others from this culture respond to this situation in a similar way?" One might also consult published studies of individuals from the culture, or particular cultural practices.

The cultural consultant indicated that it is common for individuals from rural parts of Jane's country to believe in ghosts and spirits. He said that many people share these beliefs and, for this reason, money is paid to exorcists to cast out spirits. Also, there are cultural practices still in place to "appease" such spirits; for example, with special offerings. He said, however, that it is not typical to "dialogue" with spirits. He thought the hallucination of a baby crying was very unusual, but he said that many people from the culture would consider it very unfortunate to have one's house built on a garbage dump.

Expert Opinion

After reviewing the data collected, as described, the expert for the defense formed the following opinions. Jane did not closely match the psychosocial characteristics of the typical neonaticide. She hid her pregnancy primarily from her father and brother but not from the baby's father or her girlfriends. She was not abandoned by the baby's father, and, in fact, they continued to see each other, they talked about the baby, and even selected a name. Jane's hesitation to get prenatal care and her inability to face the imminent birth was the result of the fear of her father. She was caught in a conundrum of wanting her baby but fearing her father. This is different from most neonaticides where there is a complete denial of the pregnancy and a lack of affect about the baby. Her anxiety caused Jane to put off dealing with this conflict, and in this way, she is like the other cases of neonaticide, as she put decisions off until it was too late and the birth was imminent. Then, in the dark, early hours of the morning, she went into labor. The fear and pain precipitated peritraumatic dissociation. Jane manifested the dissociative features of derealization ("That's not your baby"). The voice of the ghost from her village appeared as a hallucination. Unlike others from her village, however, she began to dialogue with the "ghost." The voice said: "That is not your baby. That is not your boyfriend's baby. Kill that baby!" She argued with the voice— "Yes, this is my baby!" During the dialogue she unknowingly placed her hand on the baby's mouth. Then she noticed the voice was gone and she looked down and saw that her baby was not breathing. She told her baby she was sorry. She had been responding to the command hallucination without full awareness that she was responding. Shawyer et al. (2008) studied 56 patients with command hallucinations and found that only 21 percent reported that they did not comply with the command. They were more likely to comply if the commanding voice felt threatening. Those who complied did so within an hour of hearing the command hallucination. Jane did experience the "voice" as threatening and, in fact, it was challenging the very identity of the baby.

It was the expert's opinion that Jane was psychotic at the time she killed her baby, in the throws of peritraumatic dissociation as a part of an Acute Stress Disorder. She was dialoguing with the "voice" and responding to a command hallucination. Her psychotic state impaired her capacity to form the mental state required for premeditation or deliberation and she acted without malice. Furthermore, because of mental disease, she was not able to distinguish between right and wrong and was thus Not Guilty by Reason of Insanity, under the California Insanity Standard of McNaught'n (Kaser-Boyd & Maloney, 1985).

In California, as in many US states, once the insanity issue is raised, the Court appoints two additional experts, one chosen by the prosecution and one chosen by the defense. In this case, the prosecution also had its own retained expert. This meant that four experts examined Jane. Two came forth with a finding of insanity but they seemed to know little about traumatic births and Acute Stress Disorder, citing only her psychotic symptoms.

Court Proceedings

As the trial began, the defense attorney decided to call the defense expert [the author] at both the guilt phase and the sanity phase of Jane's trial. I outlined my opinions as stated above, and the data and reasoning that formed the basis of my opinion. Jane was convicted of second degree murder. The sanity phase then began, and the defense expert plus the two court-appointed experts testified at the sanity phase.

The Prosecution's Case

The prosecution's rebuttal expert, a psychologist, interviewed Jane in English and testified that she could speak English "just fine." This was misleading, as it implied that she could speak English just fine with the police, which was 2 years before his interview with her. He put her various interviews side by side on a spreadsheet to illustrate how her story had developed over time, and especially after spending months in the county jail where he felt she had ample time to hear from other women how to create an exculpatory story. He dismissed the possibility that language played a role in the longer, more detailed interviews where Jane disclosed hearing a voice and having a dialogue with that voice.

The prosecution expert said that people who believe in spirits and ghosts are not mentally ill, that this is a "culture-bound" syndrome like those described in DSM-IV-TR, though he could not name the syndrome.[6] In other words, he implied that people from her culture "have these beliefs in ghosts and spirits" and she would be normal for her culture. He did not dig deeper to ask whether individuals from her culture who believe in ghosts and spirits actually have conversations with such beings. He said she had no mental disorder but was very much like the research on the young girls who kill their unwanted babies—poor, alone, and shamed by the pregnancy. This was akin to "profile" evidence, which is often rejected in court. In reality, the prosecution psychologist provided expert opinion that laid the groundwork for the prosecution argument that this was an intentional, practical act of getting rid of a problem.

To summarize, the prosecution expert said (1) there was no mental disorder at all, as individuals from this culture regularly believe in spirits and ghosts; (2) she was malingering a mental disorder, as her account of the voice of a spirit emerged well after she was interviewed by the police; and (3) she had very practical and realistic reasons for killing this unwanted baby.

The Defense Expert's Response

The prosecution expert's response to the issue of language and culture was both surprising and disturbing. The American Psychological Association has been a leader in the concept of "cultural competence." The California Board of Psychology has also been rigorous in its attempts to communicate to young psychologists that it is unethical to make important decisions about individuals without considering culture and language. Even the DSM-IV-TR, which the prosecution expert quoted, includes Culture-Bound Syndromes by emphasizing the importance of language and culture. For example, the DSM-IV-TR states that the evaluation

> indicates differences in culture and social status between the individual and the clinician and problems that these differences may cause in diagnosis and treatment; for example, difficulty in communicating in the individual's first language, in eliciting symptoms or understanding their cultural significance [. . .] in determining whether the behavior is normative or pathological.
>
> (p. 898)

Individuals from non-Western cultures, or rural parts of industrialized countries, often have a strong belief in a spirit world. In many cultures the spirits have formal names and specific functions. Jane's mother and sister validated Jane's belief in ghosts and spirits. They, however, didn't have conversations with such apparitions. Jane's behavior during the delivery of the infant was abnormal even considering her cultural belief in spirits and ghosts. When she experienced severe peritraumatic distress, her cultural beliefs shaped the content of her hallucinations.

The Issue of Malingering

While the forensic mental health (FMH) evaluation will often include standardized psychological tests with published research on malingerers compared to genuine psychiatric patients, there is a greater challenge to evaluating malingering when the individual is not fluent in English. Nowadays, in many urban areas in America and all over the Western world, the influx of immigrants means that many FMH practitioners will be presented with this difficulty. Our confidence level in diagnostic decision making on the issue of malingering rises when we can rely on the SIRS, or the psychometrically-derived indices of the PAI, or the standard cutting scores of the MMPI-2 validity scales. However, malingering can also be addressed in a rational/practical manner. The defense expert listed the rational/practical reasons she had employed to rule out malingering:

(1) *Jane did not want to be considered "crazy."* This was the reason she gave for not telling the police about hearing a voice. She retained the fear of being labeled "crazy" all through the trial. She had not told jail staff about hearing voices, although she continued to hear voices throughout her 2-year stay at Los Angeles County Jail. She had a good deal of shame regarding the pregnancy, the death of the baby, and the criminal charges. Being labeled insane would add one more shameful label, and she greatly wished to avoid this.

(2) *Was it logical or reasonable that she would not tell about hearing a voice until much later, when she was interviewed in her native language?* Jane's fear that she would be labeled "crazy" is not at all uncommon in individuals from other countries who know that their culture holds beliefs that are considered "crazy" in America. She could have reasonably feared that she would not be able to adequately explain her phenomenological experiences in English. It was highly significant that her complete account of the voice, and her dialogue with the voice, did not come out until she was interviewed in her native language. There is one additional feature of being interviewed in one's native language, and this is the presence of the interpreter himself/herself. In this case, it was a motherly and kind woman, who likely added to the comfort level of this petite, 20-year-old from the provinces of her country.

(3) *Is her account of what happened clinically possible, or likely?* Here, the work of Spinelli (2001, 2003) is highly relevant. There is ample evidence that women giving birth alone, in fear and pain, do experience hallucinations or dissociative symptoms. As noted in the review of the research above, even a portion of the women giving birth in a hospital develop symptoms of Acute Stress Disorder. Jane is not reporting symptoms that simply do not occur in real life, as is mostly the case when individuals are malingering symptomatology.

(4) *Does her presentation of symptoms fit the likely pattern of symptoms?* While the cultural aspects of Jane's clinical presentation are unusual in American society, they are not unusual in individuals from non-industrialized, spiritually-oriented, animistic countries or regions. They would certainly be considered hallucinations, and they are command hallucinations like those of any other person experiencing a psychotic break.

(5) *If she is faking, where would she get the information she would need in order to fake?* It is extremely unlikely that Jane could have obtained information to "fake" such a unique set of experiences. To begin with, many professionals are

unaware of the incidence of Acute Stress Disorder with its derealization and sometimes psychotic symptoms. None of the three other psychiatric/ psychological experts appeared to know this literature, and they theoretically had the ability to search the literature on the Internet, unlike Jane as an incarcerated person. The county jail library is not stocked with medical or psychological textbooks but with novels and the occasional dictionary. It is very unlikely that Jane could have been coached so accurately by another inmate. Jail-informed fakers typically give preposterous symptoms, such as seeing elves or having amnesia for an entire day.

(6)   *If she is faking, why doesn't her account completely take away her responsibility?* Jane has not said she had amnesia for the whole morning, which would have represented a more concerted effort to deny responsibility. Instead, she reported brief episodes of amnesia and these are seen in other women who give birth alone, with a high level of fear and pain (Atkins, Grimes, Joseph, & Liebman, 1999; Riley, 2006; Shelton, Muirhead, & Canning, 2010; Spinelli, 2001, 2003). Her account includes an admission that she put her hand over the baby's mouth.

Trial Outcome

The jury was hung on the issue of insanity. The prosecution chose a different expert for the retrial of the sanity phase. This expert opined that she was sane at the time of the act, because she concealed the baby in a trashcan and initially lied to authorities. The defense expert and one of the court-appointed experts testified as they had in the original sanity hearing. The jury came back with a verdict of Not Guilty by Reason of Insanity. Jane has undergone more than 2 years of treatment at the State Psychiatric Hospital, and she was recently recommended for release into the Community Psychiatric Treatment Program.

Notes

1   Some studies inappropriately refer to these cases as "murder," which is a legal term that implies a conviction for murder. Preferable terms are "death" or "unexplained death."
2   DSM-IV-TR defines malingering as "gross exaggeration" for secondary gain. It is not simple lying, nor is it mild exaggeration to obtain sympathy.
3   This was by an exorcist who came to her home to "cast out" spirits.
4   Posttraumatic Stress Disorders (PTSD) have undergone some major changes in DSM-5 (American Psychiatric Association, 2013). Mostly, criteria have become somewhat more lenient. For instance, language stipulating an individual's response to the traumatic event—intense fear, helplessness or horror, according to DSM-IV—has been deleted because that criterion proved to have no utility in predicting the onset of PTSD. For Acute Stress Disorder (ASD) in DSM-5 this means individuals may meet diagnostic criteria if they exhibit any 9 of 14 listed symptoms in these categories: intrusion, negative mood, dissociation, avoidance, and arousal.

5   This was defined as the lack of pain perception and the experience of numbness.

6   Culture-bound syndromes are defined as locality-specific patterns of aberrant behavior and troubling experience that may or may not be linked to a particular DSM-IV diagnostic category. Many of these patterns are indigenously considered to be "illnesses," or at least afflictions, and most have local names. Culture-bound syndromes are generally limited to specific societies or cultural areas and are localized, folk-diagnostic categories that frame coherent meanings for certain repetitive, patterned, and troubling sets of experiences and observations. An example is "Ataque de nervios," which is principally reported among Latinos from the Caribbean and is marked by uncontrollable shouting, attacks of crying, trembling, heat in the chest, and verbal or physical aggression.

References

American Psychiatric Association (2000). *Diagnostic and statistical manual of mental disorders* (4th ed.). Arlington, VA: American Psychiatric Association.

Atkins, E. L., Grimes, J. P., Joseph, G. W., & Liebman, J. (1999). Denial of pregnancy and neonaticide during adolescence: Forensic and clinical issues. *American Journal of Forensic Psychology, 17*, 5–33.

Bonnet, C. (1993). Adoption at birth: Prevention against abandonment or neonaticide. *Child Abuse and Neglect, 17*, 501–513. doi: 10.1016/0145-2134(93)90025-Z.

Boudou, M., Sejourne, N., & Chabrol, H. (2007). Childbirth pain, perinatal dissociation and perinatal distress as predictors of posttraumatic stress symptoms. *Gynecology Obstetrics and Fertility, 7*, 179. doi: 10.1016/j.gyobfe.2007.09.014.

Brezinka, O., Huter, W., Biebl, W., & Kinzl, J. (1994). Denial of pregnancy: Obstetrical aspects. *Journal of Psychosomatic Obstetrics and Gynecology, 15*, 1–8. doi: 10.3109/01674829409025623.

Butcher, J. N., Dahlstrom, W. G., Graham, J. R., Tellegen, A., & Kaemmer, B. (1989). *MMPI-2: Manual for administration and scoring*. Minneapolis, MN: University of Minnesota Press.

Causey, A. L., Seago, K., Wahl, N. G., & Voelker, C. L. (1997). Pregnant adolescents in the emergency department: Diagnosed and not diagnosed. *American Journal of Emergency Medicine, 15*, 125–130. doi: 10.1016/S0735-6757(97)90081-4.

Creedy, D., Shochet, I., & Horsfall, J. (2000). Childbirth and the development of acute trauma symptoms: Incidence and contributing factors. *Birth, 27*, 104–111. doi: 10.1046/j.1523-536x.2000.00104.x.

d'Orban, P. T. (1979). Women who kill their children. *British Journal of Psychiatry, 134*, 560–71. doi: 10.1192/bjp.134.6.560.

Forchuk, C. & Westwell, J. (1987). Denial. *Journal of Psychosocial Nursing and Mental Health Sciences, 25*, 9–13.

Friedman, S. H., Heneghan, A. M., & Rosenthal, M. D. (2007). Characteristics of women with denial of pregnancy and concealment of pregnancy. *Psychosomatics, 48*, 117–122. doi: 10.1111/j.1552–6909.2009.01004.x.

Friedman, S. H., Horwitz, S. M., & Resnick, P. J. (2005). Child murder by mothers: A critical analysis of the current state of knowledge and a research agenda. *American Journal of Psychiatry, 162*, 1578–1587. doi: 10.1176/appi.ajp.162.9.1578.

Friedman, S. H. & Resnick, P. J. (2009). Neonaticide: Phenomenology and considerations for prevention. *International Journal of Law and Psychiatry, 32*, 43–47. doi: 10.1016/j.ijlp.2008.11.006.

Green, C. M. & Manohar, V. (1990). Neonaticide and hysterical denial of pregnancy. *British Journal of Psychiatry, 156*, 121–123. doi: 10.1192/bjp.156.1.121.

Heilbrun, K., Grisso, T., & Goldstein, A. M. (2009). *Foundations of forensic mental health assessment.* New York: Oxford University Press.

Heilbrun, K., Marczyk, G. R., & DeMatteo, D. (2002). *Forensic mental health assessment: A casebook.* New York: Oxford University Press.

Joyce, K., Diffenbacher, G., & Greene, J. (1984). Internal and external barriers to obtaining prenatal care. *Social Work in Health Care, 9*, 89–96. doi: 10.1300/J010v09n02_09.

Kaser-Boyd, N. & Maloney, M. (1985). Standards for legal insanity. In M. P. Maloney (Ed.), *Psychological assessment of civil and criminal issues* (pp. 17–41). New York: Macmillan-Free Press.

Kellett, R. J. (1992). Infanticide and child destruction—the historical, legal and pathological aspects. *Forensic Science International, 53*, 1–28. doi: 10.1016/0379–0738(92)90129-K.

Marks, M. (2009). Disorders and their context: Infanticide. *Psychiatry, 8*, 10–12. doi: 10.1016/j.mppsy.2008.10.017.

Meyer, C. L. & Oberman, M. (2001). *Mothers who kill their children: Understanding the acts of moms from Susan Smith to the "Prom Mom."* New York: New York University Press.

Miller, L. J. (2003). Denial of pregnancy. In M. G. Spinelli (Ed.), *Infanticide: Psychosocial and legal perspectives on mothers who kill.* Washington, DC: American Psychiatric Press.

Millon, T., Millon, C., & Davis, R. (1994). *The Millon Clinical Multiaxial Inventory III manual.* Minneapolis, MN: National Computer Systems.

Milstein, K. K. & Milstein, P. S. (1983). Psychophysiologic aspects of denial in pregnancy: Case report. *Journal of Clinical Psychiatry, 44*, 189–190.

Mitchell, E. K. & Davis, J. H. (1984). Spontaneous births into toilets. *Journal of Forensic Science, 29*, 591–596. doi: 10.1520/JFS11708J.

Morey, L. C. (1991). *Personality assessment inventory professional manual.* Odessa, FL: Psychological Assessment Resources.

Olde, E., van der Hart, O., Kleber, R. J., van Son, M. J. M., Wijnen, H. A. A., & Pop, V. J. (2005). Peritraumatic dissociation and emotions as predictors of PTSD symptoms following childbirth. *Journal of Trauma & Dissociation, 6*(3), 125–142. doi: 10.1300/J229v06n03_06.

Overpeck, M., Brenner, R. A., Trumble, A. C., & Trifilliti, L. B. (1998). Risk factors for infant homicide in the United States. *New England Journal of Medicine, 339*, 1211–1216. doi: 10.1056/NEJM199810223391706.

Pitt, S. E. & Bale, E. M. (1995). Neonaticide, infanticide, and filicide: A review of the literature. *Bulletin of the American Academy of Psychiatry & the Law, 23*, 375–386. www.jaapl.org.

Porter, T. & Gavin, H. (2010). Infanticide and neonaticide: A review of 40 years of research literature on incidence and causes. *Trauma, Violence & Abuse, 11*(3), 99–112. doi: 10.1177/1524838010371950.

Resnick, P. J. (1970). Murder of the newborn: A psychiatric review of neonaticide. *American Journal of Psychiatry, 126*, 1414–1420.

Riley, L. (2006). Neonaticide: A grounded theory study. *Journal of Human Behavior in the Social Environment, 12*, 1–42. doi: 10.1300/J137v12n04_01.

Rogers, R. (1992). *Structured interview of reported symptoms.* Odessa, FL: Psychological Assessment Resources.

Saunders, E. (1989). Neonaticide following "secret pregnancy": Seven case reports. *Public Health Reports, 4*, 368–372.

Schwartz, L. & Isser, N. (2000). *Endangered children: Neonaticide, infanticide and filicide*. Boca Raton, LA: CRC Press.

Shawyer, F., Mackinnon, A., Farhall, J., Sim, E., Blaney, S., Yardley, P., Daly, M., Mullen, P., & Copolov, D. (2008). Acting on harmful command hallucinations in psychotic disorder. *Journal of Nervous & Mental Disease, 196*(5), 390–398. doi: 10.1097/NMD.0b013e318171093b.

Shelton, J. L., Corey, T., Donaldson, W. H., & Dennison, E. H. (2011). Neonaticide: A comprehensive review of investigative and pathological aspects of 55 cases. *Journal of Family Violence, 26*, 263–276. doi: 10.1007/s10896–011-9362–8.

Shelton, J. L., Muirhead, Y., & Canning, K. (2010). Ambivalence toward mothers who kill: Examination of 45 U.S. cases of maternal neonaticide. *Behavioral Sciences & the Law, 28*, 812–831. doi: 10.1002/bsl.937.

Soet, J. E., Brack, G. A., & DiIorio, C. (2003). Prevalence and predictors of women's experience of psychological trauma during childbirth. *Birth, 30*, 36–46. doi: 10.1046/j.1523–536X.2003.00215.x.

Spinelli, M. G. (2001). A systematic investigation of 16 cases of neonaticide. *American Journal of Psychiatry, 158*, 811–813. doi: 10.1176/appi.ajp.158.5.811

Spinelli, M. G. (2003). *Infanticide: Psychosocial and legal perspectives on mothers who kill*. Washington, DC: American Psychiatric Press.

4

A FIRESETTER IN LONGSTAY FORENSIC CARE

Corine de Ruiter

Like most Western societies, The Netherlands has special legal provisions for mentally disordered individuals who are deemed guilty of a serious offense. The Dutch Entrustment Act or TBS (in Dutch: *Terbeschikkingstelling*) Act, was enacted in 1928. Its goal is to protect society from individuals who have committed a serious crime on account of a serious mental disorder or defective development (including a personality disorder or severe intellectual disability), and who are believed to constitute a continuing danger to society (de Ruiter & Hildebrand, 2003). Generally, a TBS order is combined with a mandatory treatment order when the individual is considered to be a danger to people (Art. 37b, Section 1 Dutch Code of Criminal Law; CCL).

For some TBS patients, a safe return to society is not considered a realistic option. For patients who are judged to pose a permanent risk to society, long-term forensic care facilities were opened in the late 1990s (RSJ, 2008). In 1999, the Forensic Psychiatric Center Veldzicht was the first to open a longstay ward with 20 beds; at present there are around 250 forensic longstay beds in different hospitals. The Dutch Council for the Administration of Justice and Juvenile Protection (in Dutch: *Raad voor Strafrechtstoepassing en Jeugdbescherming*; RSJ) was quite critical of the legal protection afforded to TBS patients in the event of placement in a longstay forensic care facility in a report published in February 2008. Furthermore, the Council also raised concern about the lack of transparent criteria for admission to longstay forensic care and the delay in the implementation of the legally required tri-annual reviews of these cases.

In the course of my work as an expert witness, I have been asked to perform second opinion forensic mental health assessments (FMHA) on patients staying at longstay facilities. In some of these cases, the outcome of the FMHA in terms of diagnosis and risk level was in accord with the assessment of the forensic care facility, but in others it was not. The present chapter provides an example of the latter type of case, and illustrates the importance of objective FMHA by independent experts in cases where a patient has been assigned the label "permanently at risk" (see also McSherry & Keyzer, 2011 for a compilation of papers on the legal, psychological, and policy issues pertaining to individuals deemed "dangerous" to society).

The Case of Thomas

Thomas'[1] legal counsel called me in January 2007 to ask if I would be willing to conduct a second opinion forensic mental health evaluation on his client. Before this, I had been contacted by Thomas' sister Kim, who serves as a judge in a regional court. She asked me if I would be willing to assist with my expertise in the case of her brother because she was worried about his situation. Thomas was a 51-year-old man who had been admitted to a longstay forensic care facility in December of 2005, after having spent 5 years (1995–2000) in a forensic hospital in Groningen, The Netherlands and 5 years (2000–2005) in another forensic hospital in Utrecht. Thomas disagreed with his longstay status, which basically meant that he was considered untreatable and a chronic danger to society. His attorney sent me Thomas' entire file and requested my expert opinion on the following points:

(1) Provide your expert opinion on the course of treatment in the different forensic hospitals.
(2) Give a judgment on the diagnoses assigned to my client.
(3) Give an assessment of recidivism risk.

In this chapter, I will present my approach to the Thomas case and a summary of the assessment findings. But first, I will provide an overview of the Dutch forensic mental health system, to put the present case into context.

TBS and the Dutch Forensic Mental Health System

The number of people detained under the TBS Act has increased dramatically over the past decade. There were 650 TBS beds in 2001, but by May 2011 this number had increased to 1,977 TBS detainees. The percentage of TBS patients with a psychotic disorder is currently around 25–30 percent; more than 60 percent have a history of substance abuse, and around 13 percent have an IQ below 80 (Raes, 2008). The vast majority of patients in Dutch TBS hospitals have an Axis II Personality Disorder (PD), either stand-alone or comorbid with other mental disorders, with Cluster B PDs being the most prevalent (Hildebrand & de Ruiter, 2004; Timmerman & Emmelkamp, 2005).

The median length of treatment under the TBS order has increased over the past decade. For the cohort for whom the TBS started in 1990, the median duration is 7.3 years. For the 1999 cohort this has already increased to 10.2 years. Of the cohort that entered in the year 2000, a median could not yet be determined because by 2010 less than 50 percent had been released. All 13 Dutch forensic psychiatric hospitals that admit TBS patients use a cognitive-behavioral approach to treatment within a therapeutic living environment. Patients reside in a maximum-secure facility, with a number of living units housing around 12 patients. Within the first 8 weeks after admission, a structured violence risk assessment is conducted for every patient, using validated risk assessment tools, such as the Historical Clinical Risk Management-20 (HCR-20; Webster, Douglas, Eaves, & Hart, 1997) and Sexual Violence Risk-20 (SVR-20; Boer, Hart, Kropp, & Webster, 1997; de Ruiter & Hildebrand, 2007). A treatment and risk management plan is formulated, which focuses on diminishing dynamic risk factors for violence. For patients with personality disorders, these factors may include impulsivity, lack of empathy, deficient coping skills, low frustration tolerance, and hostile and/or antisocial attitudes. For patients with psychotic disorders, risk factors may include delusions and hallucinations, lack of insight into their illness and vulnerability to substance abuse. In recent years, the goal of risk management has been extended from the mere reduction of risk factors to the strengthening of protective factors (de Ruiter & Nicholls, 2011) using structured tools such as the Structured Assessment of Protective Factors for violence risk (SAPROF; de Vogel, de Ruiter, Bouman, & de Vries Robbé, 2009) and the Short Term Assessment of Risk and Treatability (START; Webster, Martin, Brink, Nicholls, & Middleton, 2004; Webster, Martin, Brink, Nicholls, & Desmarais, 2009).

Depending on their disorder and individual risk management plan, patients are offered different treatment modules. Examples of treatment modules are: sex offender treatment (van Nieuwenhuizen, 2005), Dialectical Behavior Therapy (van den Bosch, Hysaj, & Jacobs, 2012), Aggression Replacement Training (Hornsveld, Nijman, Hollin, & Kraaimaat, 2009), and Schema Therapy (Bernstein, Arntz, & de Vos, 2007). Psychopharmacological agents are used in the treatment of different types of disorders, including psychotic disorders, affective disorders, paraphilias and personality disorders. In addition to individual and group psychological interventions, patients participate in vocational training, educational activities, creative arts, and sports. Vocational training takes place in several workshops within the hospital, where patients can practice carpentry, welding, gardening, cooking, cleaning, etc.

Leave or furlough plays an important role in the TBS treatment. When staff conclude that there is no immediate danger of escape, escorted leave is implemented in order to avoid hospitalization effects, to encourage patients to take responsibility, and to test whether a patient can apply the skills learned (de Boer, Whyte, & Maden, 2008). The Department of Justice must approve all proposals for leave. Typical progression is from escorted to unescorted leave and finally to the "transmural" phase. During transmural leave, the patient lives outside the hospital, but is still closely supervised by hospital staff. Structured risk assessments are conducted when an extension of the patient's liberties is contemplated and independent of these moments at least every half year. If the patient breaches a condition, he or she can be recalled to the hospital. Re-integration into the community takes places gradually and the patient is supported in finding work, leisure activities, and a social network (de Boer et al., 2008). The usual avenue to termination of the TBS order is via conditional discharge, with supervision from the probation service. Conditions vary from patient to patient, and may include, for instance, continued outpatient forensic treatment, random urine checks for substance use, and/or sheltered living arrangements.

Thomas' Index Offenses

In 1993, Thomas was sentenced to 4 years' imprisonment and TBS with mandatory treatment because of deliberate firesetting in two residential dwellings and in a mobile home, i.e., an unlawful fire started or allowed to spread in violation of the law. More specifically, Thomas had thrown a self-made firebomb into the bedroom of a house where people were sleeping in October 1988. In April 1990, he had thrown a firebomb into a mobile home. Finally, in September 1990, he had intentionally set fire to another home by similar means. None of these offenses had resulted in harm to persons but there was some material damage in the two homes and the mobile home was burned down completely.

The first home was owned by a former boyfriend (Frank) of his wife Jane. When Jane and Thomas began dating, this former boyfriend had said to Thomas that Jane "was easy to get in bed," which had angered Thomas. To him, this was no way to talk about a woman. In the years prior to the arson offenses, Thomas owned his own cafeteria but business was getting slow because another snack bar opened close by. Even though he worked 80 hours a week, his income dropped from 2,400 to 1,400 guilders a month. Thomas closed himself off and was unable to discuss his business problems with his wife Jane. He had serious sleeping problems and his family physician referred him for mental health treatment in April 1988. According to information from mental health care, Thomas had been offered several types of treatment (cognitive-behavior therapy, medication, couples counseling) but he was not motivated to enter treatment. When his mother-in-law made a remark to Jane that Frank had been such a nice person, Thomas snapped and yelled at his mother-in-law. Her remark seems to have refueled the old resentment he held against Frank and he thought about throwing a firebomb into his home, which he did in October 1988.

The trailer and the second home were owned by Lee. He was angry with Lee because he had read in Jane's diary that Lee had once sexually molested her. Thomas claimed he made sure there was nobody in the mobile home before throwing the firebomb. Similarly, he said he knew Lee was sleeping upstairs so he threw the bomb into the living room downstairs. Thomas found out only after these facts that he had actually targeted the wrong person. Thomas believed the main reason for his offenses was a nervous breakdown from all those years of stress: "The throwing of firebombs was a failed attempt to deal with my frustrations. During that period I was burnt out, I could not sleep, I was very tense and anxious." There was an accumulation of stressful events and disillusions: the failure of his own company and related financial problems, strained relations with his wife, and—uncorroborated—threats by a former employee. His inability to talk about this situation with others or handle these problems led to increasing isolation. His fourth and last arson offense (for which he was never convicted) took place in 1991. Thomas could not find a stable job, while Jane was working. He felt like a failure, spending his days taking care of the children at home. The marital relationship continued to be strained, with little intimacy. After a burglary in their home, Thomas felt overwhelmed. He went to his former cafeteria and threw a firebomb inside. Why? The new owner had said to him earlier that he had done a bad job running his business there.

During the pretrial mental health assessment in 1993, Thomas seemed to realize that his offenses could have resulted in serious injuries to other people. He said: "It is terrible, I have been incredibly lucky that no one got hurt." In hindsight, he considered the firesetting as "odd behavior," but not at the time. He had shown other strange behaviors too, such as drowning the family cats, because he was worried he could not pay the vet.

Biography as Reported in File Information

Thomas is the younger of two children. He has a sister who is 4 years older. His mother is described by him as caring, his father as authoritarian and moody. There is no evidence of serious domestic violence, although his father would use physical punishment on occasion. The parents earn their living with hard work in a dairy store. Thomas is the problem child of the two. His sister is smart and well-behaved; Thomas is held back a grade in elementary school and then follows vocational training. However, he stops without a diploma. He regularly gets into conflict with authorities, such as employers, the police, and his father. At the age of 17, he is first sentenced for violation of the Firearms Act. In the following 6 years, he gets convicted for bicycle theft several times. At age 20, Thomas meets his future wife Jane. He works for various employers, but his dream is to have his own business. At the age of 26, he starts his own cafeteria, which earns the family a good living. In this period, the couple have two children, a boy and a girl.

A Potpourri of Diagnoses

During my examination of the case file of Thomas, it soon became apparent that in the course of his time in the forensic psychiatric system, he had been assigned many different psychiatric diagnoses. We know from research that comorbidity among mental disorders is high (Henderson, 2012). If a person meets the criteria for a particular mental disorder, chances are high that he/she also meets the criteria for another disorder, for instance an affective disorder and an anxiety disorder. This applies even more to the personality disorders because the criteria for some of these disorders show a large degree of overlap (for example, borderline and antisocial personality disorder). However, it is the range of disorders that Thomas has been given that is remarkable, and they are listed in Table 4.1.

Over the years, Thomas has been diagnosed with quite different and also mutually contradictory diagnoses. A character neurosis, a Narcissistic Personality Disorder with psychopathic traits, and a Psychotic Disorder Not Otherwise Specified (NOS) are so far apart that serious doubts arose in my mind about the accuracy of these diagnostic conclusions. This doubt was reinforced by the fact that few of these diagnoses in the mental health reports were supported by objective evidence in the form of symptoms, information from collateral sources, specific behavioral observations, and findings from objective psychodiagnostic tests. Needless to say that, especially in forensic mental health evaluations, which often play a weighty role in the decision of the judge, verifiable and transparent methods are crucial (Slobogin, 2007).

Second Opinion FMHA

When I meet Thomas at the longstay department of his third forensic psychiatric hospital in May of 2007, I see a tall, thin man who is a bit shy at first. He disagrees with his longstay placement, however, that does not mean his judgment on his years under the TBS order is entirely negative. He believes he was too cynical about the treatment from the beginning and that this attitude has been self-destructive. He speaks quite positively about his treatment in the first forensic hospital, and about his good relationship with the cognitive-behavior therapist there. He thinks he learned a lot in this therapy, especially how to take better care of himself: "I overcommitted myself to exhaustion, worked 80 hours a week during the period the offenses occurred. It is important for me to seek relaxation in the form of running, painting, and music." The "life rules" he drafted together with his therapist, he still keeps on a piece of paper as an "aide memoire" and he claims to use these on a daily basis. Thomas explains his transfer to the second hospital was motivated by a governance crisis in the first hospital, which resulted in the closing of several wards.

He says he got off to a bad start in the new hospital; he missed his former therapist and the contact with the new staff was difficult. Thomas felt hurt when, shortly after his admission, he was described as "sadistic" in advice to the court. He absolutely did not recognize himself in the report; on the contrary, according to him, he tends to support vulnerable individuals and provides some examples. In the second hospital, he says he did not receive any individual therapy focused on insight into his offense chain and relapse prevention.

TABLE 4.1 Summary of diagnoses and conclusions of mental health professionals (1993–2007) re: Thomas

Date and type of evaluation	Diagnosis	Conclusion/advice
1993 (pretrial evaluation)	• Serious hysterical character neurosis	• TBS with mandated treatment; therapy should focus on increasing resilience and coping skills
1995 (selection for specific forensic psychiatric hospital)	• Narcissistic Personality Disorder with neurotic features (psychologist's opinion) • Narcissistic Personality Disorder with antisocial features (psychiatrist's opinion)	• Stress tolerance should be increased; treatment should focus on reintegration in society
1997 (evaluation in first forensic hospital)	• Diagnosis of 1995 is repeated	• First treatment plan: social skills training (e.g., learning to express anger adequately); build self-esteem through vocational training
1999 (first forensic hospital)	• Narcissistic Personality Disorder with psychopathic and passive-aggressive features	• Treatment progress: Thomas lacks treatment motivation and it is difficult to develop a therapeutic alliance with ward staff (exception is his individual behavior therapist); hospital advises extension of TBS of 2 years
2000 (start treatment in second forensic hospital; 2001 advice to the court)	• No DSM-classification mentioned in report; personality features are: low self-esteem, passive-aggression, obsessiveness, self-aggrandizement	• Thomas should show increased assertiveness; acknowledgement of vulnerabilities; high recidivism risk and extension of TBS of 2 years is advised

Year/Source	Diagnosis	Events/Advice
2002 (second forensic hospital; advice to the court)	• No DSM-classification mentioned in report; personality features are: low self-esteem, passive-aggression, obsessiveness, self-aggrandizement, reality distortion	• Thomas complies with his treatment program, but progress is slow; extension of the TBS-order of 2 years, but the hospital thinks he might be chronically dangerous and in need of intensive care and supervision
2003 (second forensic hospital)	• No DSM-classification mentioned in report; personality features are: low self-esteem, passive-aggression, obsessiveness, self-aggrandizement, reality distortion	• Limited progress; performance at creative arts, sports, and work is good; no aggressive incidents during stay at this hospital; a proposal for transfer to longstay was sent to the Ministry at end of 2000
2005 (second forensic hospital)	• Axis I: Psychotic Disorder NOS • Axis II: Obsessive–Compulsive Personality Disorder with narcissistic, antisocial, and sadistic features	• During unsupervised leave in 2004, Thomas breaks an agreement (he visits another city than the one planned); • Hospital advises again a placement in a longstay facility
2005 (psychiatrist/ counter-expert)	• No indications for a mental disorder on Axis I or for a personality disorder on Axis II	• The psychiatrist sees no indications/signs to justify continued treatment. He states the previous psychiatric assessments are inaccurate and the reports of the hospital are lacking in terms of evidence for personality features such as narcissism, obsessive-compulsiveness, and sadism
2007 (third forensic hospital; longstay department)	• Axis I: Psychotic Disorder NOS, in remission • Axis II: Obsessive–Compulsive Personality Disorder with narcissistic and antisocial features	• This hospital adopts the conclusions of the second hospital; risk of recidivism is considered high and long term, and Thomas has longstay status; advice to extend the TBS order by 2 years

Thomas says that at this moment he is not experiencing psychological problems; he is not depressed or anxious. He also reports no hallucinations or delusions. In painting, he finds peace and satisfaction. Thomas shows a relativistic sense of humor with regard to his own personality. He says, for example, he is kind of a dreamer, "suppose I ever win the lottery . . .," only to add dryly, "but I am not participating": he admits that he likes beautiful houses, brand watches, etc. but seems less focused on this than what I read in some of the previous reports. He seems to realize that great wealth is very far away for him and he is satisfied with smaller things. Thomas still has contact with his mother and sister. He also maintains written contact with a patient who still resides in the second forensic hospital. Furthermore, he still sees two old friends.

Psychological Test Findings

For the psychological assessment, I made use of the MMPI-2 (see Figure 4.1, for Thomas' scores on the validity and clinical scales) and the Rorschach Inkblot Method. In order to establish a possible diagnosis of personality disorder, the semi-structured interview SIDP-IV was employed.

MMPI-2

The MMPI-2 has a number of validity scales that allow investigation of distortions in the assessee's response style. Thomas' answering style shows no inconsistencies (raw TRIN score = 8; raw VRIN score = 1). However, there appears to be a tendency to deny or downplay problems (T-score L-scale = 75; T-score K-scale = 75; T-score F-scale = 43). Thomas wants to leave a good impression (T-score Superlative scale = 74). The defensive response style is probably partly due to the fact that this is a forensic evaluation, where there is a lot at stake for him. Notwithstanding, the tendency to minimize psychological problems also appears to be part of his psychological make-up, as we have observed in the period leading up to his offenses.

The profile of the main clinical scales (a Spike 4 profile; T-score Scale 4 = 71) suggests a person characterized by irritation towards rules and increased risk of behavioral loss of control. The only subscale of Scale 4, which is elevated to a subclinical level, is Pd2, Authority Problems (T-score = 64).

Thomas dislikes overt conflict and may act out his anger in passive-dependent ways (see Friedman, Lewak, Nichols, & Webb, 2001, p. 451). The latter personality traits are apparent in his elevated scores on scale Hy2, Need for Affection (T-score = 70) and Hy5, Inhibition of Aggression (T-score = 68). Because he does not dare to admit anger to himself, it builds over time, resulting in resentment. This personality feature is demonstrated in the elevated score on the Overcontrolled Hostility (O-H) scale (T-score = 72). The final subscale that is elevated is Pa3, Moral Virtue (T-score = 71), which means Thomas tends to

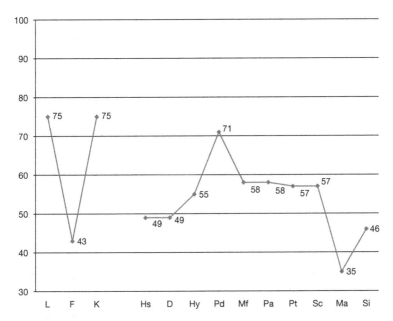

FIGURE 4.1 MMPI-2 Profile of Thomas (LFK Scales and Clinical Scales).

L = Lie scale; F = Infrequency scale; K = Correction scale; Hs = Hypochondriasis scale; D = Depression scale; Hy = Hysteria scale; Pd = Psychopathic deviate scale; Mf = Masculinity-femininity scale; Pa = Paranoia scale; Pt = Psychasthenia scale; Sc = Schizophrenia scale; Ma = Mania scale; Si = Social introversion scale.

have naïve and overly optimistic ideas about the trustworthiness of others, often resulting in disappointments and an inability to forgive.

None of the content scales of the MMPI-2 were clinically elevated. On the contrary, some of the scales showed extremely low scores, such as Antisocial Practices (T-score = 34), Cynicism (T-score = 30), and Anger (T-score = 31). The only two supplementary scales that showed clinically relevant elevations were R (T-score = 77) and the O-H scale (T = 72; see above for the interpretation). The score on the R-scale reflects his inhibition, avoidance of conflict, and tendency towards denial and repression.

Rorschach Inkblot Method Test (RIM)

Thomas provided 17 responses to the Rorschach test, which means the verbatim protocol (see Appendix 4.1 at the end of this chapter) may be interpreted. The RIM was coded and interpreted according to the Comprehensive System (CS; Exner, 2003), the best evidence-based system for RIM interpretation at the time this forensic evaluation was conducted (2007). Since then, Meyer, Viglione, Mihura, Erard, and Erdberg (2011) have developed the Rorschach Performance

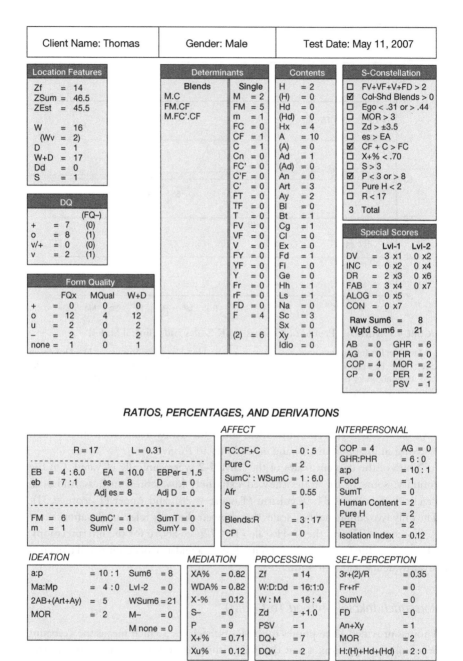

| Client Name: Thomas | Gender: Male | Test Date: May 11, 2007 |

Location Features

Zf	=	14
ZSum	=	46.5
ZEst	=	45.5
W	=	16
(Wv	=	2)
D	=	1
W+D	=	17
Dd	=	0
S	=	1

DQ

			(FQ–)
+	=	7	(0)
o	=	8	(1)
v/+	=	0	(0)
v	=	2	(1)

Form Quality

		FQx	MQual	W+D
+	=	0	0	0
o	=	12	4	12
u	=	2	0	2
–	=	2	0	2
none	=	1	0	1

Determinants

Blends	Single		
M.C	M	=	2
FM.CF	FM	=	5
M.FC'.CF	m	=	1
	FC	=	0
	CF	=	1
	C	=	1
	Cn	=	0
	FC'	=	0
	C'F	=	0
	C'	=	0
	FT	=	0
	TF	=	0
	T	=	0
	FV	=	0
	VF	=	0
	V	=	0
	FY	=	0
	YF	=	0
	Y	=	0
	Fr	=	0
	rF	=	0
	FD	=	0
	F	=	4
	(2)	=	6

Contents

H	=	2
(H)	=	0
Hd	=	0
(Hd)	=	0
Hx	=	4
A	=	10
(A)	=	0
Ad	=	1
(Ad)	=	0
An	=	0
Art	=	3
Ay	=	2
Bl	=	0
Bt	=	1
Cg	=	1
Cl	=	0
Ex	=	0
Fd	=	1
Fi	=	0
Ge	=	0
Hh	=	1
Ls	=	1
Na	=	0
Sc	=	3
Sx	=	0
Xy	=	1
Idio	=	0

S-Constellation

☐	FV+VF+V+FD > 2
☑	Col-Shd Blends > 0
☐	Ego < .31 or > .44
☐	MOR > 3
☐	Zd > ±3.5
☐	es > EA
☑	CF + C > FC
☐	X+% < .70
☐	S > 3
☑	P < 3 or > 8
☐	Pure H < 2
☐	R < 17
3	Total

Special Scores

			Lvl-1	Lvl-2
DV	=	3 x1		0 x2
INC	=	0 x2		0 x4
DR	=	2 x3		0 x6
FAB	=	3 x4		0 x7
ALOG	=	0 x5		
CON	=	0 x7		

Raw Sum6	=	8
Wgtd Sum6	=	21

AB	= 0		GHR	=	6
AG	= 0		PHR	=	0
COP	= 4		MOR	=	2
CP	= 0		PER	=	2
			PSV	=	1

RATIOS, PERCENTAGES, AND DERIVATIONS

R = 17	L = 0.31

EB	=	4 : 6.0	EA = 10.0	EBPer = 1.5	
eb	=	7 : 1	es = 8	D = 0	
			Adj es = 8	Adj D = 0	

FM	=	6	SumC' = 1	SumT = 0
m	=	1	SumV = 0	SumY = 0

AFFECT

FC:CF+C	= 0 : 5
Pure C	= 2
SumC' : WSumC	= 1 : 6.0
Afr	= 0.55
S	= 1
Blends:R	= 3 : 17
CP	= 0

INTERPERSONAL

COP = 4	AG = 0
GHR:PHR	= 6 : 0
a:p	= 10 : 1
Food	= 1
SumT	= 0
Human Content	= 2
Pure H	= 2
PER	= 2
Isolation Index	= 0.12

IDEATION

a:p	= 10 : 1	Sum6 = 8
Ma:Mp	= 4 : 0	Lvl-2 = 0
2AB+(Art+Ay)	= 5	WSum6 = 21
MOR	= 2	M– = 0
		M none = 0

MEDIATION

XA%	= 0.82
WDA%	= 0.82
X-%	= 0.12
S–	= 0
P	= 9
X+%	= 0.71
Xu%	= 0.12

PROCESSING

Zf	= 14
W:D:Dd	= 16:1:0
W : M	= 16 : 4
Zd	= +1.0
PSV	= 1
DQ+	= 7
DQv	= 2

SELF-PERCEPTION

3r+(2)/R	= 0.35
Fr+rF	= 0
SumV	= 0
FD	= 0
An+Xy	= 1
MOR	= 2
H:(H)+Hd+(Hd)	= 2 : 0

PTI = 1	☐ DEPI = 3	☐ CDI = 1	☐ S-CON = 3	☐ HVI = No	☐ OBS = No

FIGURE 4.2 RIAP™ Structural Summary.

Assessment System (R-PAS) in an attempt to ground the administration, coding, and interpretation of the RIM in its research base, improve its norms, integrate international findings, reduce examiner variability, and increase utility. The primary resource for the R-PAS research foundation is a meta-analytic review of the validity of the Comprehensive System (Exner, 2003) variables by Mihura, Meyer, Dumitrascu, and Bombel (2013). R–PAS also includes a new administration procedure to limit variation in the number of responses given by the subject, and it relies on a new normative reference group with percentile-based standard score transformations and adjustments for complexity. Finally, R–PAS also includes variables not used in the CS, including Complexity, Space Integration (SI) and Space Reversal (SR), Oral Dependency Language (ODL; previously called the Rorschach Oral Dependency scale (ROD); Bornstein & Masling, 2005; Masling, Rabie, & Blondheim, 1967), the Mutuality of Autonomy (MOA) scale (Urist, 1977), the Ego Impairment Index (EII–3; Perry & Viglione, 1991), and Aggressive Content (Gacono & Meloy, 1994).

Since I did not use the R-PAS for my forensic mental health assessment of Thomas, I will report the findings from the original CS Structural Summary (see Figure 4.2), and interpretation here. However, as Mihura et al.'s (2013) meta-analysis uncovered that the research base for some of the CS variables was quite weak, these variables will not be reported on in this chapter. Of note, the omission of these variables from the analysis did not affect the main thrust of the RIM interpretation.

The first finding on the RIM is that none of the Clinical constellations (e.g., Perceptual Thinking Index [PTI]; Depression Index [DEPI], Coping Deficit Index [CDI], Suicide-Constellation [S-CON]) are positive. Thus, there do not seem to be signs of serious psychopathology, such as psychosis or depression. Thomas' problem-solving style is extratensive (EB = 4:6.0), which means he will mostly make decisions on the basis of intuitive feelings rather than thinking through several options. This preferred coping style may be somewhat compromised because Thomas tends to be emotionally undercontrolled, resulting in overly intense and dramatic expression of emotions (FC: CF+C = 0: 5). Still, many of his Color-responses (numbers 2, 3, 4, 14 and 15) are associated with intellectualization (Art, Hx, Ay), which points to some degree of adaptation and, thus, control. Thomas demonstrates less psychological complexity (Blends: R = 3:17) than most people, which could mean he has difficulty dealing with complex and emotionally-charged situations.

Thomas appears to be less introspective than most people. As a result he is less aware of the impact he has on others and has limited ability to change his behavior. Interpersonally, Thomas shows dependent behaviors (Food = 1) and is prone to rely on others for direction and support. He may have naïve expectations which may increase his chance of experiencing disappointment in his interpersonal relationships. Thomas enjoys the company of others and likes to keep harmonious relationships (COP = 4). He is likely to be quite well-liked among the social group to which he belongs. His interpersonal behavior is generally adaptive and adequate (GHR: PHR = 6:0).

His coping abilities are sufficient to deal with stressful events in his life (EA = 10.0). One liability, however, may be his high aspiration level (W: M = 16:4) because it increases the risk of disappointment. His reality testing is good (WDA% = .82; XA% = .82; X+% = .71; X–% = .12) and he identifies with social rules and norms and tends to abide by them (P = 9). Finally, his opinions tend to be inflexible (a:p = 10:1). He also shows signs of impaired judgment (FAB = 3; WSum6 = 21). He uses intellectualization (2AB+Art+Ay = 5) as a way of dealing with unpleasant emotions.

SIDP-IV Interview

The results of the SIDP-IV are based on a semi-structured interview with Thomas and on the collateral information from his entire file. Thomas did not meet diagnostic criteria for a personality disorder as defined in the DSM-IV-TR.

Firesetting in the Scientific Literature

The findings from my counter-expertise corroborated the diagnostic conclusions the psychiatrist had drawn in 2005: there was no evidence for a mental disorder, neither on Axis I nor on Axis II. Thomas did show a number of distinct vulnerabilities, such as his interpersonal dependency and difficulty dealing adequately with anger. At the same time, Thomas' personality has some definite strengths, such as his ability to engage positively with others, his good reality testing, and his identification with generally accepted social values. The absence of a diagnosable mental disorder purely by itself undermines the basis for the TBS-order. After all, without a disorder, treatment is not needed (anymore). But Thomas resides in a forensic longstay facility, which means he is regarded by experts as difficult to treat and a "chronic risk" to society. This assessment of risk needs to be as much as possible science-based, so I reviewed the empirical literature to find out what is actually known about the risk of recidivism among arsonists. Furthermore, I was also curious to learn more about psychological theories of firesetting and to learn about effective treatments.

For a long time, arsonists were considered by psychoanalysts as very dangerous, perverted individuals with disturbed sexual urges and a very high risk of recidivism. Harris and Rice (1984) criticize this psychoanalytic literature because it is solely based on case-analysis and research has failed to support a link between firesetting and sexual disorder (Bradford, 1982; Quinsey, Chaplin, & Upfold, 1989; Prins, Tennent, & Trick, 1985). Research also showed that arsonists actually have a lower risk of recidivism in comparison with other types of violent offenders (Repo & Virkkunen, 1997). This is also confirmed by German research. Barnett and colleagues (1997) found that of a group of 87 arsonists who were declared partially insane, 10 percent recidivated over an average follow-up period of 10 years. This is a very low rate of reoffending after such a long follow-up period compared with many other violent crimes, such as sexual offenses and violent crimes. In research we conducted in The Netherlands after a follow-up period of 11.8 years on average, the sexual reoffense rate among rapists after discharge from a forensic hospital was three times higher, at 34 percent (Hildebrand, de Ruiter, & de Vogel, 2004). For violent offenders, we found an even higher recidivism rate (36 percent) after a follow-up period of only 5 years (de Vogel, de Ruiter, Hildebrand, Bos, & van de Ven, 2004).

In a comprehensive review of the literature on firesetting in adult males, Gannon and Pina (2010) start by acknowledging that given the enormous societal costs associated with intentional firesetting, it is curious that current psychological understanding of this offending behavior is relatively underdeveloped, when compared with that relating to violent or sexual offending. Similarly, the empirical evidence-base on psychopathological and personality characteristics of adult firesetters is equally limited. Still, the empirical evidence does show some consistency across studies. Many researchers have reported poor assertiveness and communication skills (Jackson, Glass, & Hope, 1987; Rice & Chaplin, 1979; Rice & Harris, 2008), low self-esteem (Smith & Short, 1995; Swaffer, Haggett, & Oxley, 2001), and impulsivity (Räsänen, Puumalainen, Janhonen, & Väisänen, 1996) in firesetters. Also, some researchers have noted a tendency for firesetters to have low frustration tolerance (Jackson, 1994), suggesting some firesetters may use fire as a method of emotional expression (Canter & Fritzon, 1998).

In terms of psychopathology, arsonists can be distinguished into those with psychotic disorders, personality disorders, intellectual disability, and pyromania (Lindberg, Holi, Tani, & Virkkunen, 2005). Of these, the most common diagnosis associated with firesetting appears to be antisocial personality disorder (American Psychiatric Association, 2000; Bradford, 1982; Repo & Virkkunen, 1997). A diagnosis of pyromania among firesetters is actually quite rare; researchers report either no pyromaniacs in their samples (Geller & Bertsch, 1985; Leong, 1992; O'Sullivan & Kelleher, 1987; Prins et al., 1985), or a very small prevalence of 3 to 10 percent (Lindberg et al., 2005; Ritchie & Huff, 1999). A diagnosis of pyromania can only be given in case of an intense fascination with and desire to associate oneself with fire and fire paraphernalia (American Psychiatric Association, 2000). Pyromania is dependent upon (a) intentional and multiple firesetting, (b) tension or arousal prior to firesetting, (c) fascination with and attraction to fire, fire paraphernalia, and the consequences of fire, and (d) pleasure, gratification, or relief upon firesetting or witnessing and participating in the consequences. Furthermore, exclusion criteria for a diagnosis of pyromania include: the firesetting must not be motivated by financial gain, sociopolitical ideology, desire to mask criminal activity, expression of anger or revenge, intention to improve living circumstances, or be the consequence of delusions, hallucinations, or any other

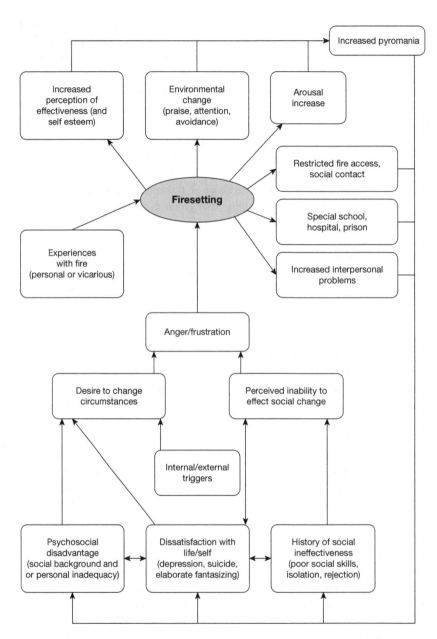

FIGURE 4.3 Overview of Jackson et al.'s (1987) Functional Analysis Theory of Firesetting.

Adapted from Gannon, T.A. & Pina, A. (2010). Firesetting: Psychopathology, theory and treatment. *Aggression and Violent Behavior*, 15, p. 232. Copyright 2010 by Elsevier. Reprinted with permission.

form of judgment impairment (e.g., intoxication, dementia, or intellectual disability). Finally, the firesetting must not be better accounted for by other psychiatric diagnoses such as mania or antisocial personality disorder.

Gannon and Pina (2010) provide a historical overview of theoretical models that have been proposed to explain firesetting: psychoanalytical, neurobiological, social learning, and functional analysis theory. The latter theory seems to be particularly useful for gaining a clinical understanding of firesetting behavior because it is multifactorial and includes a number of the abovementioned empirical findings regarding poor social skills, low frustration tolerance, and negative affect. Using a functional analysis theory framework, Jackson and colleagues (1987) present firesetting as facilitated and maintained via a complex interaction of antecedents and behavioral consequences (see Figure 4.3).

Of note, the Thomas case shows remarkable resemblance to the antecedents mentioned in Jackson's model, including personal inadequacy (losing a stable source of family income), dissatisfaction with self/life (including strained marital relationship), and poor social skills (social isolation).

Risk Assessment

The literature on the prediction of reoffending in firesetters is scarce (Gannon & Pina, 2010) and provides little specific guidance as to what are the most relevant risk factors to consider. Recidivism among personality disordered firesetters appears to be related to antisocial personality disorder and alcohol abuse (Lindberg et al., 2005; Repo, Virkkunen, Rawlings, & Linnoila, 1997). Harris and Rice (1996) found that for mentally disordered adult firesetters, predictors for reoffending tended to be fire-specific variables such as age at first firesetting incident, overall number of firesetting charges, over a mean follow-up period of 7.8 years. In a more recent study, Dickens and colleagues (2009) examined the discriminating characteristics between UK repeat and non-repeat firesetters ($N = 167$). Among other factors, Dickens et al. (2009) found that recidivist firesetters could be characterized by factors such as being young, single, having a family history of violence or substance abuse, a diagnosis of personality disorder and relationship problems.

Based on this limited empirical basis, it seems reasonable to conclude that Thomas does not fit the profile of a high-risk arsonist. Personality disorder and substance abuse are absent in his case; he did not grow up in a violent or disadvantaged home, he was married (albeit with relationship problems), and he was not young (he was 33 years old) when he first committed arson. For present-day forensic clinicians involved in clinical risk assessment in firesetters, the HCR-20 structured professional judgment guideline (Webster et al., 1997) includes arson as a "less clear" case of violence. When firesetting is motivated by anger and revenge or coupled with reckless regard for others' safety, it may be classified as violence. As is the case with Thomas, when firesetting appears to stem from intentions relating to violence, the HCR-20 may be used as a structured clinical guide for the assessment of risk for violence by means of firesetting.

Table 4.2 contains the 20 risk factors comprising the HCR-20. Coding of the HCR-20 in Thomas' case resulted in a maximum score of 2 on the historical factors H4 and H8, which means that these risk factors are clearly present. A number of risk factors are present to a lesser extent: Previous violence, Instability in relationships, Past violation of conditions. On the other four Histor-ical factors (problems with Substance abuse, Psychiatric disorder, Psychopathy, and Personality disorder), Thomas received a score of 0. On the five Clinical risk factors, which relate to current functioning, three were slightly elevated: Lack of insight, Impulsivity, and Unresponsive to treatment. There were no Active psychotic symptoms or Negative attitudes. The five Risk management factors were coded for a situation where Thomas would be rehabilitated and living in the community, because this is the crucial question in his case: is a safe return to society feasible? Three of the five Risk management factors would not be present upon a return to society: Exposure to destabilizing factors (here one must think of the factors leading up to the original arson, such as stress because of his failing business, relationship problems), Lack of personal support, and High level of experienced stress. Regarding social support, conditions are favorable: Thomas has a good relationship with his sister; they have become more open towards each other in recent years. He also has regular contact with his son. The risk factors R1 and R4 could not be coded, because to do this a detailed rehabilitation plan would need to be made.

Looking at the scoring of the HCR-20, we can conclude that the sum of the risk factors present leads to a relatively low total score, namely 12. However, a structured professional judgment based on the HCR-20 is more than a mere summation of the risk factors. We should also investigate whether there may be a combination or interaction of risk factors that could significantly increase the future risk of firesetting. This is not the case here. From the research literature we learned that recidivism among arsonists of the vengeful type is particularly associated with substance abuse and antisocial personality disorder. Both diagnoses are absent. This means that on the basis of the HCR-20 Thomas can be considered at low risk of firesetting recidivism.

Treatment

Gannon and Pina (2010) also reviewed the literature on treatment of firesetters and found out there are no standardized, manualized treatments for adult fire-setters in the UK, US, or Australasia. They suggest this state of affairs may be a consequence of our lack of knowledge concerning adult firesetters' risk factors (Palmer, Caulfield, & Hollin, 2007). What is known about the treatment of arsonists of Thomas' type—dependent, conflict avoidant, and resentful? In the cognitive-behavioral treatment program that Rice and Chaplin (1979) developed, learning

TABLE 4.2 HCR-20 coding of Thomas

	Historical items	Code (0, 1, 2)
H1	Previous violence	1
H2	Young age at first violent incident	1
H3	Relationship instability	1
H4	Employment problems	2
H5	Substance use problems	0
H6	Major mental illness	0
H7	Psychopathy	0
H8	Early maladjustment (school dropout, thievery, conflicts with father)	2
H9	Personality disorder	0
H10	Prior supervision failure (incident during TBS in 2004)	1
	Total historical items:	8/20

	Clinical items	Code (0, 1, 2)
C1	Lack of insight	1
C2	Negative attitudes	0
C3	Active symptoms of major mental illness	0
C4	Impulsivity	1
C5	Unresponsive to treatment (however, also did not receive appropriate treatment)	1
	Total clinical items:	3/10

	Risk management items ☐ in ☑ out	Code (0, 1, 2)
R1	Plans lack feasibility (no plan available)	X
R2	Exposure to destabilizers	0
R3	Lack of personal support	0
R4	Noncompliance with remediation attempts	X
R5	Stress (the transfer to society would be stressful for anyone)	1
	Total risk management items:	1/10
	HCR-20 Total score	12/40

Final risk judgement ☑ *low* ☐ *moderate* ☐ *high*

to express anger, making and refusing requests, and handling criticism are central. The effects of treatment of arsonists are not reported in the literature, however. Swaffer and colleagues (2001) described a group-based intervention program for mentally disordered firesetters comprising 62 group sessions, covering (1) education regarding fire danger, (2) coping skills (including social skills, assertiveness, conflict resolution, and problem-solving), (3) reflective insight (including self-esteem and self-concept work), and (4) relapse prevention. Although Swaffer et al. describe a detailed case study outlining the apparent effectiveness of their program, they do not report any data on clinical change at a group level, nor do they report on a control group. Plinsinga, Colon, and de Jong (1996) recommend a pragmatic and symptom-oriented approach, with a special focus on increasing frustration tolerance, changing coping mechanisms and learning social skills. Looking back at the treatment Thomas received in the context of the TBS order, the therapy in the first forensic hospital seems to have come close to the state of the art.

Return to the Attorney's Questions

What is striking about the diagnostic conclusions in the previous expert reports and in the reports to the court from the hospitals is the lack of clear justification. This applies most to the diagnosis in the first report, the hysterical character neurosis, which is not even listed in DSM-IV. But it is, for example, also true for the diagnosis of Psychotic Disorder NOS, which was presented by the second hospital a few years after Thomas was admitted there. This psychosis seems to suddenly arrive "out of thin air"; nowhere in the report are specific psychotic symptoms mentioned. Even if we suppose this diagnosis is correct (which I seriously doubt), this would mean that the psychological condition of Thomas actually worsened rather than improved during the course of his treatment under the TBS order. My evaluation, which included the use of standardized, objective tools for psychological and risk assessment, revealed the absence of serious mental disorder and high recidivism risk.

The treatment plans from the first hospital, such as learning to express anger, and social skills training seem to fit well with the vulnerable aspects of his personality. Also, these treatment goals are consistent with those found in the international literature on key elements of arsonist treatment (e.g., Gannon & Pina, 2010; Jackson et al., 1987; Rice & Chaplin, 1979). However, nowhere in the documents I received did it become clear whether these treatment targets (such as learning to express anger adequately) were actually met. Thomas himself tells me his treatment in the first hospital mainly focused on means to avoid stress. The documents produced by the second forensic hospital do not contain clear formulations of treatment goals, neither could I infer if the treatment worked.

On the whole, I arrived at the conclusion that although Thomas had been treated under the TBS measure in different hospitals, this had not involved a suitable treatment that focused on the vulnerable aspects of his personality.

The fact that Thomas had managed to reside in maximum secure hospitals for over 10 years and had clearly been frustrated, without ever having an aggressive outburst, seemed quite remarkable.

Epilogue

Independent of my report as a counter-expert for the defense, the court that had to decide on the extension of the TBS measure ordered another psychologist and a psychiatrist to perform a forensic evaluation of Thomas in 2007. The questions of the court involved an assessment of recidivism risk, suggestions for risk management, and advice on the need to extend the TBS. The psychologist diagnosed a personality disorder with narcissistic, dependent, and obsessive features. However, he did not agree with the previous diagnosis of sadistic and antisocial features. He also saw no justification for a classification of Psychotic Disorder NOS. The psychologist also expressed his doubts regarding the decision of the second forensic hospital to stop all reintegration attempts when Thomas did not comply with leave agreements. His transgression seemed a minor incident and not actually dangerous. The psychologist did not answer the court's questions, but recommended an extensive, clinical mental health evaluation in the Psychiatric Observation Clinic of the Ministry of Justice to further examine the risk of recidivism and the possibilities of reintegration. The psychiatrist's evaluation did not offer new insights beyond those of the second and third forensic hospitals, whose diagnoses he seemed to accept without a critical analysis. According to him, Thomas had a personality disorder, but he didn't observe psychotic symptoms. The risk of recidivism outside of the secure hospital environment, was considered high: "A number of historical risk factors increase recidivism risk: early childhood conflict with his father, inadequate behavior at school, and offending behavior during adolescence" (p. 11, psychiatric report to the court of April 23, 2007).

During the summer of 2008, Thomas was admitted to the Psychiatric Observation Clinic for a period of seven weeks. The conclusions of the report dated August 28, 2008 are clearly formulated and objectified. According to the multidisciplinary team, Thomas did not fulfill diagnostic criteria for a personality disorder, nor for an Axis I disorder, such as a psychotic disorder. The team did see psychological vulnerabilities, in the form of an obsessive preoccupation with money and design and a cynical façade to hide inadequacies. The report offers the academic question that these findings may actually be a consequence of Thomas' coping with a sheer hopeless situation in the longstay facility. The experts also point to several positive aspects: Thomas demonstrated insight into the factors that cause stress for him: excessive aspirations, subassertiveness, obsessive pre-occupation with money, and vulnerability in intimate relationships. Also, the notable absence of a fascination with fire and problems with substance use were favorable. In sum, the conclusion was drawn that there were no grounds to justify the present longstay status. The team of experts advised the court to extend the TBS for 1 year, but to end the mandated treatment. This meant the way was paved for Thomas to start his reintegration into society under the supervision of a probation officer. Subsequently, the court ruled on December 16, 2008, that the mandated treatment was terminated and that he would start living with his sister and her family. He had to abide by a number of release conditions, such as probation supervision (including giving access to his financial situation), commitment towards finding (volunteer) work for no more than 32 hours a week, keeping weekends for relaxation, accepting treatment at a forensic outpatient facility, and, of course, no reoffending.

When I wanted to obtain permission to use Thomas' case for publication purposes, I contacted his sister Kim. She had kept me informed of developments in his case after I had turned in my report. In an email of December 2, 2009 she wrote:

> It has been a year since Thomas showed up on our doorstep with his belongings. He has been working for a half year at a sheltered workshop in order to get used to a work rhythm, after 16 years behind four walls. He is living in his own apartment now, enjoying his racing bicycle and his work as a postman. After reading his file over again, my hairs are raised once again. It is terrible what happened to my brother over the years, experts who plagiarize each other and in the end they even assumed psychoses for no apparent reason (except perhaps the ardent desire to keep him locked up . . .). It almost sounds like a bad movie.

My last contact with Kim was in the spring of 2012. She said Thomas was doing okay, but had to get by on a small income, because of all the years of work experience he had missed. She said he was determined to never cross any legal norm again in his life, "not even running a red light."

The case of Thomas shows the prime importance of using the evidence-base from the empirical literature in conjunction with objective instruments for forensic psychological assessment, in order to arrive at a balanced diagnostic conclusion. Even though, in the case of arsonists, the empirical evidence on recidivism risk and the factors which influence it is still limited, use of the empirically based testing resulted in a more informed risk estimate than professional judgment alone. In hindsight, one could ask the question whether cases such as Thomas should be sentenced to a mandated treatment order such as TBS in the first place, because the literature shows that arsonists generally show low recidivism rates and Thomas' risk profile did not include the most predictive risk factors. This case also illustrates the social-psychological processes that may be at work in forensic psychiatric hospitals which lead treatment providers to a one-sided subjective opinion about a patient who doesn't pose a high risk to society from a more objective standpoint. In an earlier study, we had found that clinicians' risk judgments of a patient in a TBS setting correlated significantly with their feelings towards the patient (de Vogel & de Ruiter, 2004). For instance, if the patient was experienced as helpful this was associated with a lower judgment of risk, whereas negative feelings of frustration and suspicion were related to higher risk estimates. Twenty-three percent of the variance in HCR-20 final risk judgments could be explained by feelings the staff members had towards the patients (de Vogel & de Ruiter, 2004). Previously, Dernevik, Falkheim, Holmqvist, and Sandell (2001) had also found a high correlation ($r = .66$) between nurses' scores on the HCR-20 and their feelings towards patients in a Swedish forensic psychiatric institution. Both studies remind us that we may be biased as assessors of risk when we are also very much involved in the patient's treatment. In a subsequent study, we found that a consensus risk judgment between a treatment staff member and an independent assessor actually provided the most accurate risk prediction, compared with risk judgments performed by either rater individually (de Vogel & de Ruiter, 2006; see also McNiel, Lam, & Binder, 2000 for a similar finding). In conclusion, the Thomas case shows the need for independent forensic assessment and the "risk" of mixing the roles of forensic assessor and treating clinician (Ackerman, 1999; Litwack & Schlesinger, 1999).

APPENDIX 4.1 Verbatim Rorschach Protocol of Thomas[2]

I.1. It looks like a bat flying. I don't see anything else [*W*]. [*please look some more, see if you can see anything else*] No.

> With these wings and those ears. The feet too. It is looking for something to hang on to, he wants to land so to say. He wants to sit somewhere, on a tree or a cliff.

II.2. Oh yes, I have seen this one before. Two little pigs [*D6*], heads against each other, noses towards each other. There's a party with red balloons [*D2*].

> They are kissing each other: "happy birthday." It is a birthday, since they hung up balloons. [*balloon?*] the red part.

3. [*Can you see something else?*] Two young dogs [*D6*]. Or two baby rhinoceros, with their heads against each other.

> [*baby rhinos?*] Fat heads and it looks like they have a horn on their noses. And the red blots are what they are thinking: "let's do some mischief." [*do you mean thought balloons?*] Yes, but you can also see that their hind legs are a bit red, which means that they are very lively.

III.4. These are like two ladies who cooked something in a pot [*D1*]. I think it's a birthday in Africa or something. A birthday because of the red spots [*D2*].

> Two dark ladies from Africa. They are enjoying the cooking. Cooking for the family, they are really happy. These spots are what they are thinking. The bowtie [*D3*] means that the food in the pot is really good. Rice with nuts and a tasty sauce. [*birthday?*] Someone is having a birthday and they have cooked a delicious meal.

---

continued

APPENDIX 4.1 *continued*

IV.5. This looks like a dinosaur [*W*]. He is running away, you see him from behind. An animal from 400 to 600 thousand years ago.

>   With those big feet and thick tail. The head has a crest. It is a scary animal, I am glad he is running away. [*crest?*] It is down now, like a cockscomb.

6. My other thought is a motorist who is driving away [*W*]. A Hell's Angel at age.

>   This is the rear wheel he is riding on, he doesn't have a mudguard. His feet are somewhat spread out to keep his balance, because he's just speeding away. [*Hell's Angel at age?*] Because he's kind of fat. Also his shoes, they are big, wide motorcycle boots.

V.7. A bat flying away [*W*]. I don't know what else to make of it. My fantasy is limited.

>   The same bat as in the previous image, but now it is flying away, because I don't see the feet anymore.

8. Or a bat flying towards you [*W*]. He is looking like: "who are you?" He could also come towards me, like: "how are you doing," because I see eyes here. A curious bat.

VI.9. This is a buffalo hide [*W*]. Like those hanging to dry with the Indians.

>   A pelt. [*pelt?*] On the sides, and there used to be a tail at the top. I don't find this a pleasant image, I don't like pelts.

10. A fried fish, a fish you can eat, but in reality it is brown [*W*].

>   I have seen this before, a flat, brown fish. I used to buy them in the past, they tasted good.

VII.11. These are two rabbits [*D2*] doing the twist. They are having fun together since their mouths are open. They are acting crazy.

>   They are having lots of fun dancing. [*rabbits?*] Ears, open mouths, paws. They are standing on a rock or a piece of dirt [*D4*]. [*rock?*] because it is round like this.

VIII.12. I see two animals on the sides [*D1*]. Two beavers climbing a mountain [*D6*]. I can't see a lot in here. Or two little pigs.

>   The tree is not healthy anymore. They are climbing up to see if there are any fresh leaves, health branches there. They want to build a nest. [*not healthy?*] Because there are some holes here [*points at S*].

13. It also reminds me of Cartier, the two panthers. That's my second thought, a panther wearing a necklace.

>   Cartier has a panther hanging from a necklace. I am kind of a brands freak. I always pay attention to that, on clothing. Cartier and Chanel.

IX.14. This looks like an X–ray of a smoker [*W*]. Someone who has been smoking for 20 years [*W*].

>   The upper part is still healthy. [*unhealthy?*] The upper part is still healthy, the bottom part too. In another 20 years everything will be green.

continued

APPENDIX 4.1 *continued*

---

15. My second thought is a filter from a sea aquarium [*W*]. This one is a bit dirty. It needs to be cleaned. I used to have that with my koi carp.

> This middle part is where all the dirt is. The upper and bottom parts are still clean, but in a week everything will be green. So it's okay to leave it for another week.

X.16. This looks like the bottom of the ocean [*W*]. With fossils, two scorpions and two shrimp. Shells.

> Two scorpions [*D1*]. These are shrimp [*D2 and D7*]. Seahorses [*D9*]. And this is part of a boat that has sunk, the animals are around it [*D11*]. [*boat?*] A boat propeller or an anchor. You see this often, these fish near shipwrecks.

17. Or sheet music, and these are the notes [*W*]. I've always loved music. [*points at the different elements, means musical notation*] Something from Beethoven or Mozart. Only the colors don't fit, because musical notes are not colored.

Notes

1   Thomas (not his real name) has given permission to the author to use his case material in a scientific publication. Names of persons and irrelevant details were changed. The test results and relevant information remained unchanged.
2   Questions and remarks of the assessor and locations of objects are in italics.

References

Ackerman, M. J. (1999). *Essentials of forensic psychological assessment*. New York: Wiley.

American Psychiatric Association (2000). *Diagnostic and statistical manual of mental disorders, text revision*. Washington, DC: Author.

Barnett, W., Richter, P., Sigmund, D., & Spitzer, M. (1997). Recidivism and concomitant criminality in pathological firesetters. *Journal of Forensic Science, 42*, 879–883.

Bernstein, D. P., Arntz, A., & de Vos, M. (2007). Schema focused therapy in forensic settings: Theoretical model and recommendations for best clinical practice. *International Journal of Forensic Mental Health, 6*, 169–183. doi: 10.1080/14999013.2007.10471261.

Boer, D. P., Hart, S. D., Kropp, P. R., & Webster, C. D. (1997). *Manual for the Sexual Violence Risk-20: Professional guidelines for assessing risk of sexual violence*. Vancouver, BC: Institute against Family Violence.

de Boer J., Whyte, S., & Maden, T. (2008). Compulsory treatment of dangerous offenders with severe personality disorders: A comparison of the English DSPD and Dutch TBS systems. *Journal of Forensic Psychiatry & Psychology, 19*, 148–163. doi: 10.1080/1478 9940701830726.

Bornstein, R. F. & Masling, J. M. (2005). The Rorschach Oral Dependency scale. In R. F. Bornstein & J. M. Masling (Eds.), *Scoring the Rorschach: Seven validated systems* (pp. 135–157). Mahwah, NJ: Erlbaum.

van den Bosch, L. M. C., Hysaj, M., & Jacobs, P. (2012). Dialectical behavior therapy in an outpatient forensic setting. *International Journal of Law and Psychiatry, 35*, 311–316. doi: 10.1016/j.ijlp.2012.04.009.

Bradford, J. M. (1982). Arson: A clinical study. *Canadian Journal of Psychiatry, 27,* 188–193.

Canter, D. & Fritzon, K. (1998). Differentiating arsonists: A model of firesetting actions and characteristics. *Legal and Criminological Psychology, 3,* 73–96. doi: 10.1111/j. 2044–8333.1998.tb00352.x.

Dernevik, M., Falkheim, M., Holmqvist, R., & Sandell, R. (2001). Implementing risk assessment procedures in a forensic psychiatric setting: Clinical judgement revisited. In D. P. Farrington, C. R. Hollin, & M. McMurran (Eds.). *Sex and violence: The psychology of crime and risk assessment* (pp. 83–101). London: Routledge.

Dickens, G., Sugarman, P., Ahmad, F., Edgar, S., Hofberg, K., & Tewari, S. (2009). Recidivism and dangerousness in arsonists. *Journal of Forensic Psychiatry and Psychology, 20,* 621–639. doi: 10.1080/14789940903174006.

Exner, J. E. (2003). *The Rorschach: A comprehensive system. Vol. 1: Basic foundations and principles of interpretation* (4th ed.). Hoboken, NJ: Wiley.

Friedman, A. F., Lewak, R., Nichols, D. S., & Webb, J. T. (2001). *Psychological assessment with the MMPI-2.* Mahwah, NJ: Erlbaum.

Gacono, C. B. & Meloy, J. R. (1994). *The Rorschach assessment of aggressive and psychopathic personalities.* Hillsdale, NJ: Erlbaum.

Gannon, T. A. & Pina, A. (2010). Firesetting: Psychopathology, theory and treatment. *Aggression and Violent Behavior, 15,* 224–238. doi: 10.1016/j.avb.2010.01.001.

Geller, J. L. & Bertsch, G. (1985). Fire-setting behavior in the histories of a state hospital population. *American Journal of Psychiatry, 142,* 464–468.

Harris, G. T. & Rice, M. E. (1984). Mentally disordered firesetters: Psychodynamic versus empirical approaches. *International Journal of Law and Psychiatry, 7,* 19–34.

Harris, G. T. & Rice, M. E. (1996). A typology of mentally disordered firesetters. *Journal of Interpersonal Violence, 11,* 351-363. doi: 10.1177/088626096011003003.

Henderson, A. S. (2012). Psychiatric epidemiology now: Some achievements and prospects. *Epidemiology and Psychiatric Sciences, 21,* 161–166. doi: 10.1017/S2045796 012000042.

Hildebrand, M. & de Ruiter, C. (2004). PCL-R psychopathy and its relation to DSM-IV Axis I and Axis II disorders in a sample of male forensic psychiatric patients in The Netherlands. *International Journal of Law and Psychiatry, 27,* 233–248. doi: 10.1016/ j.ijlp.2004.03.005.

Hildebrand, M., de Ruiter, C., & de Vogel, V. (2004). Psychopathy and sexual deviance in treated rapists: Association with sexual and nonsexual recidivism. *Sexual Abuse: A Journal of Research and Treatment, 16,* 1–24. doi: 10.1177/107906320401600101.

Hornsveld, R. H. J., Nijman, H. L. I., Hollin, C. R., & Kraaimaat, F. W. (2009). Aggression control therapy for violent forensic psychiatric patients: Method and clinical practice. *International Journal of Offender Therapy and Comparative Criminology, 52,* 222–233. doi: 10.1177/0306624X07303876.

Jackson, H. F. (1994). Assessment of fire-setters. In M. McMurran & J. Hodge (Eds.), *The assessment of criminal behaviours in secure settings* (pp. 94–126). London: Jessica Kingsley.

Jackson, H., Glass, C., & Hope, S. (1987). A functional analysis of recidivistic arson. *British Journal of Clinical Psychology, 26,* 175–185.

Leong, G. B. (1992). A psychiatric study of persons charged with arson. *Journal of Forensic Science, 37,* 1319–1326.

Lindberg, N., Holi, M. M., Tani, P., & Virkkunen, M. (2005). Looking for pyromania: Characteristics of a consecutive sample of Finnish male criminals with histories of recidivist fire setting between 1973 and 1993. *BMC Psychiatry, 5*, 47. www.biomedcentral.com/1471–244X/5/47.

Litwack, T. R. & Schlesinger, L. B. (1999). Dangerousness risk assessments: Research, legal, and clinical considerations. In A. K. Hess & I. B. Weiner (Eds.), *The handbook of forensic psychology* (pp. 171–217). New York: Wiley.

Masling, J. M., Rabie, L., & Blondheim, S. H. (1967). Obesity, level of aspiration, and Rorschach and TAT measures of oral dependence. *Journal of Consulting Psychology, 31*, 233–239.

McNiel, D., Lam, J., & Binder, R. (2000). Relevance of interrater agreement to violence risk assessment. *Journal of Consulting and Clinical Psychology, 68*, 1111–1115. doi: 10.1037//0022–006X.68.6.1111.

McSherry, B. & Keyzer, P. (Eds.). (2011). *Dangerous people: Policy, prediction and practice.* New York: Taylor & Francis.

Meyer, G. J., Viglione, D. J., Mihura, J. L., Erard, R. E., & Erdberg, P. (2011). *A manual for the Rorschach Performance Assessment System.* Toledo, OH: R–PAS.

Mihura, J. L., Meyer, G. J., Dumitrascu, N., & Bombel, G. (2013). The validity of individual Rorschach variables: Systematic reviews and meta-analyses of the Comprehensive System. *Psychological Bulletin, 139*, 548–605. doi: 10.1037/a0029406.

van Nieuwenhuizen, C. (2005). A treatment programme for sexually violent forensic psychiatric inpatients: Development and first results. *Psychology, Crime & Law, 11*, 467–477. doi: 10.1080/10683160500256701.

O'Sullivan, G. H. & Kelleher, M. J. (1987). A study of firesetters in the south-west of Ireland. *British Journal of Psychiatry, 151*, 818–823.

Palmer, E. J., Caulfield, L. S., & Hollin, C. R. (2007). Interventions with arsonists and young firesetters: A survey of the national picture in England and Wales. *Legal and Criminological Psychology, 12*, 101–116. doi: 10.1348/135532505X85927

Perry, W. & Viglione, D. J. (1991). The ego impairment index as a predictor of outcome in melancholic depressed patients treated with tricyclic antidepressants. *Journal of Personality Assessment, 56*, 487–501.

Plinsinga, A. E., Colon, E. J., & de Jong, S. (1996). Brandstichting is meestal geen Pyromanie [Arson is not pyromania most of the time]. *Nederlands Tijdschrift voor Geneeskunde* [Dutch Journal of Medicine], *141*, 129–131.

Prins, H., Tennent, G., & Trick, K. (1985). Motives for arson (fire raising). *Medicine, Science and the Law, 25*, 275–278.

Quinsey, V. L., Chaplin, T. C., & Upfold, D. (1989). Arsonists and sexual arousal to firesetting: Correlation unsupported. *Journal of Behavior Therapy and Experimental Psychiatry, 20*, 203–209. doi: 10.1016/0005–7916(89)90024–4.

Raes, B. C. M. (2008). 25 jaar forensische psychiatrie in Nederland: Een beknopt overzicht [25 years of forensic psychiatry in The Netherlands: A brief overview]. *Tijdschrift voor Psychiatrie, 50* [anniversary issue 1959–2008], 71–75.

Räsänen, P., Puumalainen, T., Janhonen, S., & Väisänen, E. (1996). Firesetting from the viewpoint of an arsonist. *Journal of Psychosocial Nursing and Mental Health Services, 34*, 16–21.

Repo, E. & Virkkunen, M. (1997). Outcomes in a sample of Finnish fire-setters. *Journal of Forensic Psychiatry, 8*, 127–137. doi: 10.1080/09585189708411999.

Repo, E., Virkkunen, M., Rawlings, R., & Linnoila, M. (1997). Criminal and psychiatric histories of Finnish arsonists. *Acta Psychiatrica Scandinavica, 95*, 318–323. doi: 10.1111/j.1600–0447.1997.tb09638.x.

Rice, M. E. & Chaplin, T. (1979). Social skills training for hospitalized male arsonists. *Journal of Behavior Therapy and Experimental Psychiatry, 10*, 105–108. doi: 10.1016/0005–7916(79)90083–1.

Rice, M. E. & Harris, G. T. (2008). Arson. In V. N. Parrillo (Ed.), *The encyclopedia of social problems*. Thousand Oaks, CA: Sage.

Ritchie, E. C. & Huff, T. G. (1999). Psychiatric aspects of arsonists. *Journal of Forensic Science, 44*, 733–740.

RSJ (2008). Longstay in the context of a hospital order (TBS), advice to the Minister of Justice. www.rsj.nl/english/Summaries_of_recommendations.

de Ruiter C. & Hildebrand, M. (2003). The dual nature of forensic psychiatric practice: Risk assessment and management under the Dutch TBS-order. In P. J. van Koppen & S. D. Penrod (Eds.), *Adversarial vs. inquisitorial justice: Psychological perspectives on criminal justice systems* (pp. 91–106). New York: Plenum Press.

de Ruiter, C. & Hildebrand, M. (2007). Risk assessment and treatment in Dutch forensic psychiatry. *Netherlands Journal of Psychology, 63*, 166–175.

de Ruiter, C. & Nicholls, T. L. (2011) Protective factors in forensic mental health: A new frontier. *International Journal of Forensic Mental Health, 10*, 160–170. doi: 10.1080/14999013.2011.600602.

Slobogin, C. (2007). *Proving the unprovable: The role of law, science and speculation in adjudicating culpability and dangerousness*. New York: Oxford University Press.

Smith, J. & Short, J. (1995). Mentally disordered firesetters. *British Journal of Hospital Medicine, 53*, 136–140.

Swaffer, T., Haggett, M., & Oxley, T. (2001). Mentally disordered firesetters: A structured intervention programme. *Clinical Psychology and Psychotherapy, 8*, 468–475.

Timmerman, I. G. H. & Emmelkamp, P. M. G. (2005). The effects of cognitive-behavioral treatment for forensic inpatients. *International Journal of Offender Therapy & Comparative Criminology, 49*, 590–606. doi: 10.1177/0306624X05277661.

Urist, J. (1977). The Rorschach test and the assessment of object relations. *Journal of Personality Assessment, 41*, 3–9.

de Vogel, V. & de Ruiter, C. (2004). Differences between clinicians and researchers in assessing risk of violence in forensic psychiatric patients. *Journal of Forensic Psychiatry and Psychology, 15*, 145–164. doi: 10.1080/14788940410001655916.

de Vogel., V. & de Ruiter, C. (2006). Structured professional judgment of violence risk in forensic clinical practice: A prospective study into the predictive validity of the Dutch HCR-20. *Psychology, Crime & Law, 12*, 321–336. doi: 10.1080/10683160 600569029.

de Vogel, V., de Ruiter, C., Hildebrand, M., Bos, B., & van de Ven, P. (2004). Type of discharge and risk of recidivism measured by the HCR-20: A retrospective study in a Dutch sample of treated forensic psychiatric patients. *International Journal of Forensic Mental Health, 3*, 149–165. doi: 10.1080/14999013.2004.10471204.

de Vogel, V., de Ruiter, C., Bouman, Y., & de Vries Robbé, M. (2009). SAPROF: Guidelines for the assessment of protective factors for violence risk. Utrecht, The Netherlands: Forum Educatief.

Webster, C. D., Martin, M. L., Brink, J., Nicholls, T. L., & Desmarais, S. (2009). *Manual for the short-term assessment of risk and treatability (START) (Version 1.1).* Port Coquitlam, BC: Forensic Psychiatric Services Commission and St. Joseph's Healthcare.

Webster, C. D., Martin, M. L., Brink, J., Nicholls, T. L., & Middleton, C. (2004). *Manual for the Short Term Assessment of Risk and Treatability (START) (Version 1.0 Consultation Edition).* Port Coquitlam, BC, Canada: Forensic Psychiatric Services Commission and St. Joseph's Healthcare.

5

INDECENT EXPOSURE, EXHIBITIONISM, AND OTHER PARAPHILIAS

Nancy Kaser-Boyd

This is the case of Mr. H. He was referred to me by a young public defender who initially asked whether Mr. H.'s rape in State Prison had been the cause of his recent indecent exposures. He asked whether the after-effect of rape might be that Mr. H. had a compulsion to show he was heterosexual. Mr. H. was 25 years old at the time of his arrest. He was arrested after a college counselor reported that he sat in her office, unzipped his pants and stroked his penis. When she called to a nearby colleague for help, he calmly walked out of her office.

"Indecent exposure" is a legal term referring to a specific type of legally prohibited behavior. In the United States, a person can be convicted of indecent exposure if they have intentionally shown their private parts with the intent to draw attention, either for the purpose of sexually arousing themselves or another person, or for the purpose of sexually insulting or offending another person. The legal term is often confused with "exhibitionism," which is a psychological/psychiatric term used to delineate a specific paraphilia of recurrent, intense sexually arousing fantasies, sexual urges, or behaviors, which involve exposure of one's genitals to an unsuspecting stranger (American Psychiatric Association, 2000). The public defender wished to introduce evidence that Mr. H.'s behavior was the product of a mental disorder and that he had motive or intent other than the intent(s) required for indecent exposure.

The forensic mental health evaluation was conducted at the county jail. Mr. H. was a nice-looking, baby-faced man of African-American ethnicity. He was pleasant and friendly and he seemed to be above average in intelligence. Mr. H. was 25, but he looked very young. Mr. H. understood the nature of his charges. He had already been to prison once, and he was not naïve about the seriousness of these charges. He seemed oriented and alert, and I did not detect any overt signs of thought disorder, delusions, or manic symptoms, although at times he gave an odd smile, and he voiced some unusual religious beliefs; for example, he said that he believed God talks directly to him, not through prayer, but in an actual voice. He said: "That's not crazy, is it?" He was not taking medication at the time of my evaluation, although between then and his trial, he deteriorated and ultimately was placed on psychiatric medication.

Mr. H. had a considerable history of mental disorder, which began when he was just 13 years old. He attributed his first psychiatric hospitalization, at 13, to his parents' divorce, but his symptoms went beyond a typical stress reaction. He got heavily involved with Black Magic, and he began to act-out, imitating gang members from the inner city, which was far from where he grew up. Mr. H. had a second psychiatric hospitalization shortly after graduating from high school. He said,

> I was hearing voices and seeing things, and feeling someone was out to get me. I thought I was doing a séance with another person. I put a Pentagram on the floor with a rock and was in, like, a prayer position, and was trying to pull myself closer to Satan.

Mr. H. assaulted his mother, who was trying to get him to calm down. He said, "I thought Satan was on the TV and that she was in danger and I should try to get her out of the house." Though he was clearly mentally ill during this period, he was charged with assault on his mother, and he was convicted of assault and sent to prison, where he was almost immediately seen as having a serious mental disorder. During his first incarceration in State Prison, he was diagnosed with Bipolar Disorder and prescribed Depakote (a mood stabilizer) and Risperdal (an antipsychotic). The prison records document bizarre, primitive behavior. In one interview, he told a prison doctor he heard the voice of God. He told another, "There is evil coming out of me. The Devil wants me to kill myself with a razor but I won't." He also felt people were out to get him. At another point, he felt there were spiders in his cell biting him. To combat this, he spread feces on the walls and urinated on the mattress, he said, to get rid of the spiders and "fight evil." On a subsequent occasion, he drank disinfectant because he was feeling suicidal. He was constantly prescribed mood stabilizers and antipsychotic medication, but often refused to take these. He would sometimes expose himself to female correctional officers and said that this was "because voices tell me to."

Despite his severe symptoms, at the end of his term of imprisonment for the assault against his mother, Mr. H. was released into the community and referred for outpatient treatment. He soon had a second run-in with the law when he walked near his halfway home and attempted to carjack a passing car. He ran up to the car, banged on the hood, and screamed, "This is a jack! Mafia! Get out of the car!" When apprehended, he told police, "I wanted to take a car and have a high speed chase." He said he wanted this in order to be famous and be on television. His parole conditions were violated and he was sent back to prison.

During this second sojourn in State Prison, Mr. H. said he was sexually assaulted by a male prisoner. He said: "I had a homosexual person in my cell and that person wanted sex and forced me." Asked if he thought that had an effect on him, he said: "Yes, but I gave it all to God."

Mr. H. was released again but continued to have multiple parole violations. While living with his father, an apartment manager accused him of attempted rape. His father ejected him from the apartment and he went to live at a halfway house, where another resident accused him of masturbating in front of her. Several other women in that facility complained that he had grabbed his crotch in front of them, or made lewd comments. These events caused his parole to be violated again.

The index offense occurred shortly after his most recent release from prison. He was again living in a halfway house but now he had been given funds to gain vocational training, thus his attendance at the school where he exposed himself to his counselor. Mr. H. told arresting officers that he "suffered from an illness." He said he had exposed himself several years ago and went to jail but he "continued to do it because I got away with it." He said he did it "On the street, in laundromats, and in parks" all around the city. He said he had been diagnosed Bipolar Disorder and had been prescribed Abilify (an antipsychotic medicine) "because I hear voices telling me to do it." He also stated "God tells me not to." He said he felt, however, that "God is obligated to come into my life and take it away from me." He said he prayed about this.

Mr. H. said that on the day in question, he was sitting in his counselor's office and "I just got the urge and did it." He did not think it upset her. He said he had "never done it to a woman who didn't like it." He volunteered that he believed "it helped them with their urges." He said, "These women get off on that." He said, "Only a couple didn't like it" and they were the ones that called the police. He said that he had done this "whenever I get an urge." Overall, he estimated that he had exposed himself 40–50 times, or three or four times a week. He said it had "picked up lately" because "my hormones are getting higher." He added, "It's like a fetish, you know how some men like to dress up in different attire?" He said, "It pleases me so I do it more." Mr. H. declared himself to be heterosexual. However, he had been out of prison for quite brief periods since he turned 18, and he had few social skills and thus little success in heterosexual relationships.

There was a family history of Bipolar Disorder in Mr. H.'s maternal grandmother and an uncle. Mr. H. denied ever having been sexually molested. He indicated he had a good relationship with his mother in childhood but more conflict with her in his teenage years. He had a rather distant relationship with his father, who was a long-time employee of the post office.

Is Mr. H. like those who expose themselves (exhibitionists), or is his behavior a product of his mental disorder? This is an important question because if he is the latter, treatment could substantially reduce this behavior, whereas paraphilias are more difficult to treat. Is Mr. H.'s exhibitionistic behavior the result of the hypersexuality and grandiosity of a manic phase of Bipolar Disorder, or a stand-alone diagnosis of exhibitionism, or does he have both disorders? Can he control his behavior or does he choose not to? Is the behavior done with the intent to sexually arouse himself or another, or to sexually insult or offend another person? Are there underlying psychodynamic motives? What intervention is most likely to stop this behavior?

The records were extensive. When just 19, Mr. H. was convicted of assaulting his mother, as mentioned. Mr. H. spent much of his time in an inpatient mental health setting of the State Prison system, which is unusual in California because of the cost, and this usually requires fairly extreme symptoms. I noted that he was given mood stabilizers and antipsychotic medication, which supported the existence of a mood disorder and psychotic symptoms. His diagnosis varied between Schizophreniform Disorder and Bipolar Disorder. He was frequently psychotic, with bizarre and regressed behavior. When compliant with medication, he often reconstituted rather quickly. When psychotic, however, he usually became manic. He often had bizarre, grandiose delusions such as the one involving the Mafia. He demonstrated an increase in sexual and impulsive behavior and an "excessive involvement in pleasurable activities that have a high potential for painful consequences" (American Psychiatric Association, 2000, p. 362). His belief that women enjoy seeing his penis and that it "helps them with their urges" is a sign of the grandiosity that is seen with this disorder.

Indecent Exposure and Exhibitionism: The Literature

Research on the assessment and treatment of exhibitionism is surprisingly limited given that this behavior is among the most common of sexual offenses (Morin & Levenson, 2008) and appears to be seen in a heterogeneous group that exposes their genitals for sexual satisfaction (Murphy & Page, 2008). A sample of college women in the United States (Cox & MacMahon, 1978) reported that as many as 39 percent had experienced exposure by a male perpetrator. In terms of incidence, there are several studies. In The Netherlands, one study (Frenken, Gijs, & Van Beek, 1999) found that one-third to one-half of all sex crimes reported to the police between 1980 and 1984 were for exhibitionism. It was once thought that individuals who engage in indecent exposure were harmless and too timid to engage in aggressive acts. Although an individual may be convicted for exposing himself and labeled an exhibitionist, exposing may not be his sole, or even his primary, paraphilia (Freund, 1990). Research indicates that exhibitionism is frequently seen in men who engage in an array of sexually deviant acts (Abel & Rouleau, 1990). Lang, Langevin, Checkley, and Pugh (1987) note that almost half of their sample consisted also of cross-dressers. Abel and Rouleau (1990) reported that over 90 percent of the exhibitionists in their sample had more than one paraphilic diagnosis, and 73 percent had over three paraphilic diagnoses.

Abel and Rouleau (1990) studied 142 exhibitionists from an outpatient clinic who were promised confidentiality, and found that 50 percent of the exhibitionists reported the onset of their exhibitionist inclinations before the age of 18. A number of studies explored the family background of exhibitionists to attempt to find commonalities. Surprisingly, a history of sexual abuse was not one of the factors (Finkelhor, Hotaling, Lewis, & Smith, 1990). The most frequent finding was childhood emotional abuse and family dysfunction. Exhibitionists were 3.67 times more likely to have experienced emotional abuse than the control group, but this rate was similar to that for the other paraphilic groups (e.g., pedophilia, voyeurism; Murphy & Page, 2008).

Much effort has gone towards understanding the exact psychopathology of individuals who expose themselves. For example, are they narcissists? Sociopaths? Early studies (Murphy & Page, 2008) found exhibitionists to be shy, inhibited, and non-assertive. However, the methodologies of these early studies were questioned. When standardized measures of these traits are used, exhibitionists as a group do not appear to differ from controls (Langevin, Paitich, Freeman, Mann, & Handy, 1978). Lee, Pattison, Jackson, and Ward (2001) used a number of standardized instruments measuring psychopathology thought to be relevant to paraphilias. They factor-analyzed results and created four composite variables: (1) anger and hostility; (2) sexual maladjustment and social skills deficits; (3) control of anger and sexual thoughts; and (4) interpersonal sensitivity. When exhibitionists were compared with non sex-offenders, they were significantly different on the anger and hostility variable and the sexual maladjustment and social skills deficits variable. These results were also found in the other paraphilias.

Kafka and colleagues (Kafka & Hennen, 2002, 2003; Kafka & Prentky, 1994, 1998) examined comorbid diagnoses in exhibitionists. In a group of 32 exhibitionists, they found the tendency to be hypersexual was an important variable. The most commonly observed comorbid psychiatric diagnoses in exhibitionists are Bipolar Spectrum Disorders and Depression (Kafka & Hennen, 2002). Hypersexuality was also suggested in a study by Långström and Seto (2006). They found that those individuals who had engaged in exhibitionism had more sexual partners, greater sexual excitability, higher frequency of masturbation, higher frequency of pornography use, and greater likelihood of having had a same-sex partner. Kafka and Hennen (2002) found the second-most commonly diagnosed comorbid disorders were Impulse Control Disorders, ADHD, and Obsessive-Compulsive Disorders.

Other scholars have looked at more specific features of exhibitionists. For example, Marshall, Hamilton, and Fernandez (2001) found that exhibitionists, similar to other sex offenders, engage in cognitive distortion. They hold beliefs that serve to rationalize, justify, or minimize sexual offending, and this is correlated with a lack of empathy for the victim. Underlying an exhibitionist's minimization of the impact of his act on victims are distorted beliefs and difficulty in viewing a situation from a victim's perspective. Specifically, the exhibitionist is frequently invested in the idea that because he has not attacked or made physical contact with a victim, little or no trauma has been caused (Murphy & Page, 2008).

Exhibitionism has also been discussed in the psychoanalytic literature. Meyer (1985) writes that exhibitionism and voyeurism are in many respects paired opposites. They are "showing" and "looking," which represent opposite positions along the same dimensional axis. Kernberg (1995) states that there is an intimate connection between exhibitionism and sadism: the wish to excite and frustrate the significant other. In exhibitionism, the presence and power of the penis is reasserted by watching the reaction—fright, surprise, awe, disgust—of a woman confronted with the act. Exhibitionists both identify with their victims and feel contentiously superior to them. Their sexual performance in the marital bed is usually lackadaisical, they state. Stoller (1975) indicates that more often than not, the exhibitionist reveals a flaccid penis, has trouble becoming erect, and, if he masturbates, never reaches orgasm. Meyer (1985) adds that real excitement is confined to the situation of showing or looking. The preferential objects of the perverse acts, such as young girls, women with large breasts, or brunettes, are selected because of attributes that make them adequate maternal substitutes in the reenactment of the struggle over separation and castration. Exhibitionism is supposed to serve as the expression of feminine identification and resistance to that, compulsively repeated through the constant reexamination of genitals and the reactions to seeing them (Meyer, 1985).

Stoller (1991) defines perversion as "hatred that manifests in the wish to harm the object by gaining power over it as an act of revenge" (p. 47). He postulates that the source of the hatred is childhood trauma, which is transformed through the perversion into adult triumph. The sequence, he writes, is: "I am humiliated. I discover revenge. I humiliate. I have mastered the past" (p. 49). Bach (1991) indicates that individuals involved in perversion have perverse modes of relating, and Stoller (1975, 1991) indicates that, in these individuals, it is the enactment of hostility that results in efforts to dehumanize relationships by sadistically teasing, torturing, humiliating, and controlling others while at the same time disavowing one's need of the now-degraded object. Tuch (2008), in an article entitled "Unraveling the riddle of exhibitionism," describes exhibitionism as a power tactic of perverse interpersonal relationships. Citing Stoller (1975, p. 128), he states, "The triumph comes from being in control while the other loses control." He notes that the exhibitor intends to inspire a mixture of terror and sexual excitement, to cause fear and humiliation, to inspire envy, or even embarrassment. The woman often feels "taken over by the experience, unable to think or act, merged with, or swallowed by, the experience" (Tuch, 2008, p. 149). He calls this a "perverse disregard for the rules of interpersonal engagement" (p. 147). By nature, the act ignores the victim's needs, wishes, and personhood (Cox & Maletzky, 1980).

Furthermore, Tuch (2008) notes that the exhibitionist is dismayed by indifference, and if the woman responds aggressively, by showing interest, by belittling the man, or by going on with her business, the exhibitionist fails to achieve his goal. Gittleson, Eacott, and Mehta (1978) interviewed victims of indecent exposure. One-third of the victims reported feeling "stunned." Only 10 percent were able to muster a verbal rebuke. Tuch (2008) notes that exhibitionists are looking for an unsuspecting victim, who is not only naïve and vulnerable but likely to submit long enough, under the spell of the exhibitionist's regressive behavior, for the exhibitionist to conduct his business and be gone. Tuch notes that exhibitionistic acts are usually not psychotic, but they are "clearly reality-challenged" (p. 157). He states, "The exhibitionist can simultaneously believe his victim is not a victim at all but a willing accomplice who is grateful for the chance to have a peek, awestruck by what she's been shown . . . and a woman demeaned" (p. 157). This is remarkably similar to the statements made by Mr. H.

Unfortunately for the defense side of the case, it seems the psychoanalytic theory of exhibitionism would fit quite nicely into the intent required for a conviction for indecent exposure. To repeat: the law centers around whether the defendant has intentionally shown their private parts with the intent to draw attention, either for the purpose of sexually arousing himself or another person, or for the purpose of sexually insulting or offending another person. The legal terminology of "sexually insulting or offending" could include demeaning or gaining power and control over the victim. The psychoanalytic theory of exhibitionism, however, has not been tested experimentally.

Diagnostic Issues

Exhibitionism is defined by DSM-IV-TR as "recurrent, intense sexually arousing fantasies, sexual urges, or behaviors involving the exposure of one's genitals to an unsuspecting stranger. The fantasies, urges, or behaviors must occur over a period of at least 6 months and must cause distress for the person" (American Psychiatric Association, 2000, p. 566). Exhibitionism is one of the paraphilias, including pedophilia, voyeurism, frotteurism, sadism, and masochism. A true exhibitionist has fantasies and urges around exposing his genitals expressly for the sexual excitement they derive from being seen. According to DSM, this may be the only mode of sexual excitement, may be one of several forms of sexual excitement, or may occur only during times of stress. There are often associated features. Individuals with a paraphilia may select an occupation or develop a hobby or volunteer work that brings them into contact with the desired stimulus, for example, selling ladies' shoes. They may view, read, purchase, or collect photographs, films, and textual depictions that focus on their preferred type of paraphilic stimulus. They may assert that the behavior causes them no distress, although some report extreme guilt or embarrassment. There is often impairment in the capacity for reciprocal, affectionate sexual activity. Personality disturbances may also be present and may be severe enough to warrant a diagnosis of a personality disorder. Sexual dysfunctions may also be comorbid. DSM-IV-TR clarifies that there are several "rule outs" for a diagnosis of paraphilia: a Manic episode, Schizophrenia, as well as intellectual disability, Dementia, substance intoxication, or personality change due to a general medical condition, where "there is a decrease in judgment, social skills, or impulse control that, in rare instances, leads to unusual sexual behavior" (American Psychiatric Association, 2000, p. 568). DSM notes,

> This can be distinguished from a paraphilia by the fact that the unusual sexual behavior is not the individual's preferred or obligatory pattern, the sexual symptoms occur exclusively during the course of these mental disorders, and the unusual sexual acts tend to be isolated rather than recurrent and usually have a later age of onset.
>
> (p. 568)

To diagnose a manic episode, using the DSM-IV-TR as our classification guide, the individual must have at least three of the following:

(1) inflated self-esteem or grandiosity (in our case, a belief that one is helping women by exposing one's penis);
(2) decreased need for sleep;
(3) more talkative than usual or pressure to keep talking;
(4) flight of ideas or racing thoughts;
(5) distractibility;
(6) an increase in goal-directed activity, socially or sexually, or psychomotor agitation;
(7) excessive involvement in pleasurable activities that have a high potential for painful consequences (such as sexual impropriety).

Goodwin and Jamison (1990) discuss sexual behavior in Bipolar Disorder. They describe a number of studies, which they state are all too limited in number. Beigel, Murphy, and Bunney (1971) asked nurses to judge 26 items most characteristic of manic behavior. Of those items, two—"talks about sex" and "is sexually preoccupied"—had high concordance with independent ratings on both a global mania scale completed by a psychiatrist and a nurse-rated manic symptom checklist. Hypersexuality was observed or reported in 57 percent of manic patients, averaged across seven studies, and actual nudity or sexual exposure was reported in 29 percent (Goodwin & Jamison, 1990). Jamison, Gerner, Hammen, and Padesky (1980) studied changes attributed to affective disorder in 35 bipolar and 26 unipolar patients. Twenty percent of the men and 40 percent of the women reported that sexual activity was very much increased during manic and hypomanic periods.

Winokur, Clayton, and Reich (1969) found that 65 percent of manic episodes were characterized by increased sexual drive. In one third (32 percent) of these, the increased sexuality was of a socially approved type; that is, within a marriage or long-lasting relationship. In 10 percent, it was in thought or discussion only, and in 11 percent, increased sexuality was manifested in socially disapproved behavior. This was further defined as being promiscuous and hypersexual. Allison and Wilson (1960) studied 24 manic patients using data based on physician observations or reports of relatives. In 78 percent of the patients, the frequency of sexual intercourse substantially increased while they were manic. Conversely, high rates of Bipolar Disorder have been found in sex offenders who met DSM-IV criteria for paraphilias (Galli et al., 1999; McElroy et al., 1999).

Forensic Mental Health Assessment

Forensic mental health assessment (FMHA) is a unique endeavor—not necessarily different in scope, but different in goals from assessment for treatment recommendations (Heilbrun, Marczyk, & DeMatteo, 2002). Assessment of individuals accused of indecent exposure must focus not only on the dynamics and triggers of sexual behavior, but also on its amenability to treatment, the type of treatment, and the likelihood that treatment will be effective. An FMHA should also include a risk assessment (Anderson & Hanson, 2010). Rather than focus on any one psychological test, one needs to define the domains that are important in the assessment. The Association for the Treatment of Sexual Abusers (Maletzky, 1987) surveyed over 1,500 professionals involved in sex offender treatment and research around the world. This sample, with an average of 10 years of experience treating sex offenders, identified the following domains:

(1) offense pattern and victim preference
(2) frequency of behavior
(3) compulsivity
(4) duration of behavior
(5) variety of offending behavior
(6) motivation and amenability for treatment.

Areas also judged important were: substance abuse, history of child abuse, and attachment style (Maletzky, 1997). Experts in the field emphasize the importance of understanding the need the exhibitionist is attempting to meet. As noted above, exhibitionists seek a range of reactions, from shock to amusement to sexual interest (Freund, Watson, & Rienzo, 1988).

As with other court-referred individuals, records review is considered essential to the assessment. Relevant records include police reports, victim statements, pre-sentence investigation reports, criminal records of prior sexual and non-sexual offenses, prior mental health evaluations, and treatment progress assessments. Morin and Levenson (2008) indicate that one should not imagine that anything resembling a true picture of the client's sexual issues will be elicited by even the most thorough initial interview(s). Standard psychological tests do not have uniform acceptance as useful tools for evaluating sex offenders, nor the more specific target in this case, a person who has committed indecent exposure. Psychological tests are considered potentially useful in identifying comorbid disorders and the domains identified above. What FMHA strategies might be useful to evaluate the relevant domains for Mr. H.?

For this referral, where time was limited, the Personality Assessment Inventory (PAI; Morey, 1991, 1998), the Psychopathy Checklist-Revised (PCL-R; Hare, 1991, 2003), the Psychopathic Personality Inventory-Revised (PPI-R; Lilienfeld & Widows, 2005), and the Static-99 (Hanson & Thornton, 1999, 2000) were used, and this section will illustrate how the data from these instruments, combined with the extensive criminal and mental health records available, resulted in a complete forensic mental health evaluation. There is, admittedly, some criticism regarding the use of objective personality inventories, such as the Personality Assessment Inventory, with sex offenders (Davis & Archer, 2010). There is not a great deal of research on the PAI in sex offenders, although it has been admitted repeatedly into legal proceedings involving sex offenders (Mullen & Edens, 2008). The inclusion of a general personality inventory in this test battery was to test for general mental health symptoms rather than to identify specific characteristics of a sex offender.

The Personality Assessment Inventory

The Personality Assessment Inventory is a 344-item self-report inventory comprising 22 non-overlapping scales that cover a wide range of diagnostic possibilities (e.g., Axis I disorders such as Schizophrenia, and Axis II disorders such as Antisocial Personality Disorder and Borderline Personality Disorder). It offers actuarially-derived indices to evaluate malingering and defensiveness, as well as Violence Potential and Treatment Amenability. The PAI was developed with a construct validation approach, rather than the empirical correlate method of the Minnesota Multiphasic Personality Inventory (MMPI; Morey, 2003). The internal consistency coefficients range between .81 (normative sample) and .86 (clinical sample) and the test-retest reliability correlations for a 4-week interval were .86 for the 11 full clinical scales (Morey, 1991, 1998). The PAI has scales that are highly relevant to the assessment questions raised in this evaluation: (1) Does Mr. H. have test results similar to persons with bipolar or manic features? (2) Does he have other personality features that could be relevant to sexual acting out? (3) Is he elevated on the aggression scale? How does he score on the violence potential index? (4) Is he likely to cooperate with treatment? All of these questions can be answered with the PAI scales. It can also provide information about the risk for alcohol or drug problems. The PAI, in addition, is easier to read than the long MMPI-2 (reading level of fourth grade), compared with the MMPI (reading level of eighth grade), without sacrificing good psychometric quality.

At the time Mr. H. was tested, he was not on medication, and he was housed in the general population. He said he did not want to have a mental disorder. The validity indices of the PAI were somewhat elevated. He was elevated on "Infrequency," suggesting he may have had trouble attending to or interpreting item content, perhaps interpreting items idiosyncratically. He did not score elevated on "Negative Impression Management," a scale associated with malingering, nor on "Positive Impression Management," i.e., he was not trying to present himself in a particularly positive manner, also called "faking good." Thus, Mr. H. appears to have been relatively honest in responding to the items of this test.

On the clinical scales of the PAI, Mr. H. obtained two highly significant elevations (on Mania and on Antisocial Personality Disorder). He obtained lesser but still high elevations on the scales Borderline Personality Disorder and Schizophrenia. Finally, he was elevated at two standard deviations above the mean on the Paranoia and the Aggression scales. One significant advantage of the PAI is the provision of subscales for each clinical scale. Similar to the Harris-Lingoes scales of the MMPI and MMPI-2, the subscales make it possible to determine which item clusters were responsible for the clinical scale elevation. In the case of the Mania scale elevation, Mr. H. scored particularly high on Activity Level and Irritability. He was not elevated on Grandiosity. This finding is significant and points towards racing thoughts, pressured behavior, and a likely intensity of sex drive, such as is often seen in Mania. Not surprisingly, Mr. H. was also elevated on the scale Antisocial Personality Disorder. His highest subscale score was on Stimulus-seeking, and he was also elevated on the subscale Egocentricity. The lowest of the three subscales was on Antisocial Behavior, even though his history showed a number of seemingly antisocial behaviors, but all of these appear to have happened when he was manic.

Mr. H.'s lower but clinically significant score on the Borderline Personality Disorder scale and on Schizophrenia probably reflect a deviation from "normal" in emotional control and clear thinking, rather than the existence of the full symptom range of these disorders. This is supported by his moderate elevations on the subscales Psychotic Experiences, Affective Instability, Negative Relationships, and Self-Harm. Taken as a whole, Mr. H.'s highest overall PAI subscales were Activity Level and Stimulus-Seeking, two scales which are highly relevant to level of sex drive. Mr. H. did not score elevated on the two substance abuse scales, but his risk for substance abuse was considered increased given the other features of his profile, notably stimulus-seeking and antisocial tendencies.

As noted, one of the advantages of the PAI is its actuarially-derived Violence Potential Index (VPI). The VPI is taken from 20 configural features of the PAI profile involving information from 24 different scales and subscales related to risk factors for violence. The highest correlates of the VPI are the scales Borderline, Antisocial, and Aggression. Mr. H. scored very high on the VPI, with a T-score of 93. At this level, in his current state, he has a clear risk of repeating the index behavior, and perhaps other violent acting-out.

Turning to the potential for treatment, it seems clear, given that mania is a neurobiologically driven state, that Mr. H. might be different if he was on medication and if he complied with a treatment regimen. The PAI offers two ways to look at amenability to treatment: (1) openness to treatment and interest in change (the scale RXR); and (2) the difficulty of treatment, given the diagnosis (the Treatment Process Index; TPI). Mr. H.'s RXR score indicated that he has an interest in and motivation for therapy. He acknowledges important problems and believes he has a need for help. Furthermore, he endorses the importance of personal responsibility. The TPI, however, indicates that Mr. H. will be a difficult patient. The TPI-score of 91 shows that there may be many and varied obstacles to a smooth treatment process. This is most likely due to his mood instability and pressured, impulsive behavior.

PCL-R and PPI-R

The diagnostic label psychopathic personality disorder or psychopathy, for short, is generally reserved for individuals who do not have an Axis I disorder. However, if psychopathic personality traits are present, research has shown these individuals are at higher risk of reoffending and more difficult to treat (Chakhssi, de Ruiter, & Bernstein, 2010), also if they have concomitant Axis I disorders (Leistico, Salekin, DeCosta, & Rogers, 2008; Salekin, Rogers, & Sewell, 1996; Stadtland, Kleindienst, Kröner, Eidt, & Nedopil, 2005). The PCL-R Manual (Hare, 2003) acknowledges the issue of Axis I disorders, stating, "some forensic patients with Bipolar Disorders or psychoses may have dramatically different presentations at different times." While the manual encourages clinicians to "score PCL-R items according to the person's typical functioning" (p. 20), this doesn't adequately address the issue. Several of the PCL-R items could easily be related to an illness with manic symptoms (such as impulsivity, poor behavioral controls, need for stimulation/proneness to boredom, or grandiose sense of self-worth). Recently, Hare himself (Spiegel, 2011) has expressed reservations about the overuse of this tool, which was designed essentially as a research instrument. Lilienfeld and Widows (2005) have noted that the PCL-R will be impractical in some cases due to the need for extensive formal training and time and labor intensity for accurate and reliable ratings and the necessity of extensive criminal records. For the current FMHA, I used the self-report questionnaire PPI-R.

The PPI-R (Lilienfeld & Widows, 2005) was chosen to evaluate Mr. H. because rather than focusing exclusively on antisocial or criminal behavior, it was constructed so that it provides scales for separate lower-order facets of psychopathy in addition to a global score. The PPI-R is a 154-item self-report measure that requires a fourth grade reading level and can be given to people aged 18 to 86. It has both offender and community norms. The PPI-R total score displays good convergent and discriminant validity with self-report, interview, and observer-rated measures of psychopathy, antisocial behavior, DSM personality disorders, and normal-range personality traits (Lilienfeld & Fowler, 2006). PPI-R Factor 1 (Fearless Dominance) correlates moderately to highly with PCL-R Factor 1; PPI-R Factor 2 (Self-Centered Impulsivity) correlates moderately to highly with PCL-R Factor 2 (Lilienfeld & Fowler, 2006).

Mr. H. scored clinically elevated on the following content scales: Blame Externalization, Carefree Non-Planfulness, and Coldheartedness. On the factor scales, his highest score was on Self-Centered Impulsivity (T = 89), which correlates with PCL-R Factor 2, the antisocial behavior and lifestyle indicator. What stands out most from the PPI-R findings is not the constellation of affective and interpersonal features, but Mr. H.'s tendency to be impulsive. He has additional problematic features including a lack of empathy and a tendency to externalize blame. It is unclear whether these would improve if the core symptoms of his mental illness (mania) were treated.

Risk Assessment

While the attorney in Mr. H.'s case did not ask for an evaluation of future risk, and this was not a subject of the direct examination, such an evaluation would be a common request in a case such as Mr. H.'s. Exhibitionism is generally considered to be a highly compulsive and repetitive behavior (Murphy & Page, 2008). In the exhibitionist group of individuals, future risk for both sexual and non-sexual offenses is present. Firestone, Kingston, Wexler, and Bradford (2006) conducted a 13-year follow up of over 200 exhibitionists, and found that approximately 15 percent reoffended non-sexually, and 23.6 percent reoffended sexually. Among those with paraphilias, exhibitionists have one of the highest recidivism rates. Rabinowitz Greenberg, Firestone, Bradford, and Greenberg (2002) conducted a long-term follow-up of a group of exhibitionists and found that those who reoffended were less educated, had a greater likelihood of substance abuse, and higher scores on the PCL-R.

To evaluate Mr. H.'s risk of reoffending, I used the Static-99 (Hanson & Thornton, 1999, 2000), which is commonly used in sex offender risk assessment. The Static-99 was developed from the Rapid Risk Assessment for Sexual Offense Recidivism (RRASOR; Hanson, 1997) and the RRASOR's items were derived from Hanson and Bussière's (1998) meta-analytic study of factors related to sexual offense recidivism. They found that the factors most strongly correlated with sexual reoffending were: prior sexual offenses, stranger victims, prior offenses of any type, young age, never married, non-related victims of sex offenses, and male victims of sex offenses. The Static-99 was developed by adding several additional variables that demonstrated an empirical relationship with recidivism. The Static-99 items include: young age (defined as 18 to 24.99), never cohabited, convictions for non-violence, prior sex offenses, prior sentencing dates, convictions for non-contact sex offenses, unrelated victims, stranger victims, and male victims. The "prior sex offenses" item is the only item that is not scored 0 or 1 (absent/present); for this item a score of up to 3 is possible with an increasing number of charges or convictions. Antisocial traits are indicated by non-sexual violence and number of previous sentencing dates.

The Static-99 has received a fair amount of research interest. The original validation samples included men from four different prisons in Canada, numbering over 1,200 convicted sex offenders, with follow-up data on recidivism from 4 to 23 years (Anderson & Hanson, 2010). There have been at least 42 studies (n = 13,288) examining the extent to which the Static-99 accurately rank orders the offenders in terms of relative risk to reoffend in independent replication studies (Hanson & Morton-Bourgon, 2004). When results are presented as AUC scores (Rice & Harris, 2005), AUCs are typically around .70 (Anderson & Hanson, 2010). Of note, however, in a study directly comparing the Static-99 with the Sexual Violence Risk-20 (SVR-20; Boer, Hart, Kropp, & Webster, 1997), a risk assessment instrument that comprises both historical and dynamic, changeable risk factors, in a sample of sexual offenders (N = 122), de Vogel, de Ruiter, van Beek, and Mead (2004) found the SVR-20 predicted new sexual offenses over a follow-up of 140 months significantly better than the Static-99: AUC_{SVR-20} = .83 vs. $AUC_{Static-99}$ = .66, respectively. Furthermore, the SVR-20 also significantly predicted violent and general reoffending, whereas the Static-99 did not (de Vogel et al., 2004).

We must bear in mind the ethical standards of the American Psychological Association (2002), which state that psychologists need to be aware of the limits to the certainty with which diagnoses, judgments, or predictions can be made about individuals. Campbell (2003) discusses the problem of false positives and false negatives and the varying rates of these which depend on base rates and cut-off scores. Often, a high sensitivity comes with a high false positive (or low specificity) rate. For example, Campbell (2003) notes that using a Static-99 cut-off score > 1 results in a sensitivity of .92, i.e., accurately identifies 322 of 350 of actual recidivists in a target sample, but has a high false positive rate of 55 percent. The correlation of an actuarial instrument such as the Static-99 with sex offender recidivism is .33 (Hanson & Thornton, 2000), which is a modest correlation. As noted by de Vogel et al. (2004), the Static-99 also relies on factors considered static (such as number of prior sex offenses) rather than dynamic (such as situational stressors, social support). Much less is known about dynamic factors when assessing the recidivism rate of sex offenders (Campbell, 2003). Finally, Vess (2011) notes that the Static-99 was normed on very specific criminal offender groups and its accuracy for a given offender would depend on the degree to which that offender is similar to the research sample on which the cut-off score was tested. For example, Craig and Hutchinson (2005) found that sexual reconviction rates of sex offenders with learning disabilities were found to be considerably greater than those of non-learning disabled sex offenders at 2-year and 4-year follow up, but learning disability is obviously not one of the characteristics considered in the Static-99. Despite these methodological and ethical issues, the Static-99 is mandated as a risk assessment tool by the California Department of Rehabilitation and Corrections; it is the most widely used measure for the assessment of risk of recidivism among sex offenders in Canada and the United States, and it is used in jurisdictions as diverse as Taiwan, Israel, Finland, and Singapore (Anderson & Hanson, 2010).

Mr. H. obtained a total of 6 points on the Static-99, which places him in the High Risk category. However, it is important to note that his prior convictions for both sexual and non-sexual violence were for crimes committed while he was also in a manic episode. Also, the Static-99 doesn't allow rating amenability for treatment, which is a dynamic factor that is included in structured professional judgment risk assessment tools such as the SVR-20. The forensic report and later expert testimony mentioned his PAI Treatment Process Index—his openness to treatment, willingness to acknowledge he had a problem for which he needed help, and his belief in personal responsibility. Whether these positive indicators would translate into compliance with medication remained to be seen.

Psycholegal Opinions

It is clear from the DSM-IV-TR diagnostic criteria that in the manic phase of the disorder, there is an increase in sexual and impulsive behavior and an excessive involvement in pleasurable activities that have a high potential for painful consequences. Mr. H.'s psychological test results strongly support a diagnosis of Bipolar Disorder. Mr. H.'s episodes of indecent exposure were very much tied to the manic phase of his mental disorder. When he does not take his medication, he decompensates and the full manifestation of his manic and psychotic symptoms emerges. His belief that women enjoy seeing his penis and that it "helps them with their urges" is the grandiosity that is often seen with this disorder. Mr. H. is also a stimulus-seeking man and this, plus his irritability, resulted in an elevation on the Antisocial Personality scale of the PAI as well. His potential for acting out, especially when not on medication and perhaps only when not on medication, is clear. Still, he does not show an elevation on the personality scale Aggression, which could indicate that in the absence of manic impulsivity, he does not have personality traits in common with trait-aggressive individuals.

The Static-99 rating does result in a judgment of "high-risk," although it is important to note that the rating does not take into account the reality that both his sexual and non-sexual offenses occurred when he was manic, nor does it take into account his current strong professed interest in treatment and the fact that for men with sex offenses, the manic phase of their Bipolar Disorder is shown to be successfully managed by means of psychopharmacological agents (for Lithium, see Kafka (1991) and Ward (1975); for Depakote, see Nelson et al., 2001)).

California criminal law centers on whether the defendant has shown their private parts with the intent to draw attention, either for the purpose of sexually arousing himself or another person, or for the purpose of sexually insulting or offending another person. The young public defender was an energetic advocate for Mr. H., but his original notion—that the indecent exposure was a reaction to having been raped, rather than the intent to sexually arouse—was not realistic, because Mr. H. had engaged in indecent exposure well before he was raped in prison. What seemed to be a more viable defense was that Mr. H. had manic episodes during which he was hypersexual and showed very poor judgment and impulse control. When Mr. H. was on medication his exhibitionism, as well as other impulsive behaviors, were well controlled. Most exhibitionists do not have bipolar or manic symptoms, certainly not the bizarre psychotic symptoms that Mr. H. exhibited in his non-medicated state. Unfortunately, Mr. H. frequently did not take his medication when left to his own devices. In the trial, there was no opposing expert, but the District Attorney was a modest, likeable guy who had years of experience doing sex crimes, and he was very convincing. Two factors were in his favor: (1) the law requires a fairly simple "intent"; (2) it seemed clear that Mr. H. was frequently non-compliant with medication, so the jury could predict that he would become psychotic and sexually inappropriate again. Therefore, it was no surprise that Mr. H. was convicted, even though the defense made a good case for Bipolar Disorder and not a Paraphilia.

Conclusion

Exhibitionism is the most common of the paraphilias, and research now shows that many who engage in indecent exposure may be at risk to commit more "hands-on" sexual offenses (Firestone et al., 2006; Rabinowitz Greenberg et al., 2002). It is likely that a forensic examiner will happen upon more than a few exhibitionists in her career and it is important to conduct a thorough forensic mental health evaluation which (1) results in an understanding of the dynamics of the behavior and makes an accurate diagnosis; (2) can specify the risk of future offending; and (3) can outline a treatment program. This chapter has not discussed in detail the features of an evidence-based treatment program for Mr. H., as he was convicted and sent to California State Prison, where the likelihood of entering such a program is low. However, when Mr. H. seeks parole, a new FMHA can prescribe such a program to assist in reducing his risk upon re-entry to the community.

References

Abel, G. G. & Rouleau, J. L. (1990). The nature and extent of sexual assault. In W. L. Marshall, D. R. Laws, & H. Barbaree (Eds.), *Handbook of sexual assault: Issues, theories, and treatment of the offender* (pp. 9–21). New York: Plenum Press.

Allison, J. B. & Wilson, W. P. (1960). Sexual behaviors of manic patients: A preliminary report. *Southern Medical Journal, 53*, 870–874. http://journals.lww.com/smajournal online/pages/default.aspx.

American Psychiatric Association (2000). *Diagnostic and statistical manual of mental disorders* (4th ed., text revision). Washington, DC: Author.

American Psychological Association (2002). Ethical principles of psychologists and code of conduct. *American Psychologist, 57*, 1597–1611. www.apa.org/ethics/code/code.pdf.

Anderson, D. & Hanson, K. (2010). An actuarial tool to assess risk of sexual and violent recidivism among sexual offenders. In R. K. Otto & K. S. Douglas (Eds.), *Handbook of violence risk assessment* (pp. 251–268). New York: Routledge.

Bach, S. (1991). On sadomasochistic object relations. In G. Fogel & W. Myers (Eds.), *Perversions and near-perversions in clinical practice* (pp. 75–92). New Haven, CT: Yale University Press.

Beigel, A., Murphy, D. L., & Bunney, W.E. (1971). The Manic-State Rating Scale: Scale construction, reliability, and validity. *Archives of General Psychiatry, 25*, 256–262. doi: 10.1001/archpsyc.1971.01750150064009.

Boer, D. P., Hart, S. D., Kropp, P. R., & Webster, C. D. (1997). *Manual for the Sexual Violence Risk-20: Professional guidelines for assessing risk of sexual violence.* Vancouver, British Columbia: Institute against Family Violence.

Campbell, T. W. (2003). Sex offenders and actuarial risk assessments: Ethical considerations. *Behavioral Sciences and the Law, 21*, 269–279. doi: 10.1002/bsl.530.

Chakhssi, F., de Ruiter, C., & Bernstein, D. (2010). Change during forensic treatment in psychopathic versus nonpsychopathic offenders. *Journal of Forensic Psychiatry and Psychology, 21*, 660–682. doi: 10.1080/14789949.2010.48328.

Cox, D. J. & MacMahon, B. (1978). Incidence of male exhibitionism in the United States as reported by victimized female college students. *International Journal of Law and Psychiatry, 1*, 453–457. doi: 10.1016/0160–2527(78)90008–0.

Cox, D. J. & Maletzky, B. (1980). Victims of exhibitionism. In D. J. Cox & R. J. Daitzman (Eds.), *Exhibitionism: Description, assessment, and treatment* (pp. 289–293). New York: Garland Press.

Craig, L. A. & Hutchinson, R. (2005). Sexual offenders with learning disabilities: Risk, recidivism and treatment. *Journal of Sexual Aggression, 11*, 289–304. doi: 10.1080/13552600500273919.

Davis, K. M. & Archer, R. P. (2010). A critical review of objective personality inventories with sex offenders. *Journal of Clinical Psychology, 66*, 1254–1280. doi: 10.1002/jclp.20722.

Finkelhor, D., Hotaling, G., Lewis, I. A., & Smith, C. (1990). Sexual abuse in a national study of adult men and women: Prevalence, characteristics, and risk factors. *Child Abuse and Neglect, 14*, 19–28. doi: 10.1016/0145–2134(90)90077–7.

Firestone, P., Kingston, D. A., Wexler, A., & Bradford, J. M. (2006). Long-term follow-up of exhibitionists: Psychological, phallometric, and offense characteristics. *Journal of the American Academy of Psychiatry and the Law, 34*, 349–359. Retrieved from www.jaapl.org.

Frenken, J., Gijs, L., & Van Beek, D. (1999). Sexual offender research and treatment in The Netherlands. *Journal of Interpersonal Violence, 14*, 347–371. doi: 10.1177/0886 26099014004001.

Freund, K. (1990). Courtship disorder. In W. L. Marshall, D. R. Laws, & H. E. Barbaree (Eds.), *Handbook of sexual assault: Issues, theories, and treatment of the offender* (pp. 221–342). New York: Plenum Press.

Freund, K., Watson, R., & Rienzo, D. (1988). The value of self-reports in the study of voyeurism and exhibitionism. *Sexual Abuse: A Journal of Research and Treatment, 1*, 243–262. doi: 10.1177/107906328800100205.

Galli, V., McElroy, S., Soutullo, C., Kizer, D., Raute, N., Keck, P., & McConville, B. (1999). The psychiatric diagnosis of twenty-two adolescents who have sexually molested other children. *Comprehensive Psychiatry, 40*, 85–88. doi: 10.1016/S0010–440X(99) 90110–4.

Gittleson, H., Eacott, S., & Mehta, B. (1978). Victims of indecent exposure. *British Journal of Psychiatry, 132*, 61–66.

Goodwin, F. K. & Jamison, K. R. (1990). *Manic-depressive illness* (1st ed.). New York: Oxford University Press.

Hanson, R. K. (1997). *The development of a brief actuarial risk scale for sexual offense recidivism* (User Report 97–04). Ottawa, ON, Canada: Department of the Solicitor General of Canada.

Hanson, R. K. & Bussière, M. T. (1998). Predicting relapse: A meta-analysis of sexual offender recidivism studies. *Journal of Consulting and Clinical Psychology, 66*, 348–362. doi: 10.1037/0022-006X.66.2.348.

Hanson, R. K. & Morton-Bourgon, K. (2004). *Predictors of sexual recidivism: An updated meta-analysis* (Corrections User Report No. 2004–02). Ottawa, ON: Public Safety and Emergency Preparedness.

Hanson, R. K. & Thornton, D. (1999). *Static-99: Improving actuarial risk assessments for sex offenders* (User Report 99–02). Ottawa, ON: Department of the Solicitor General of Canada.

Hanson, R. K. & Thornton, D. (2000). Improving risk assessments for sex offenders: A comparison of three actuarial scales. *Law and Human Behavior, 24*, 119–136. doi: 10.1023/A:1005482921333.

Hare, R. D. (1991). *Hare psychopathy checklist-revised* (PCL-R). Toronto, ON: Multi-Health Systems.

Hare, R. D. (2003). *Hare psychopathy checklist-revised technical manual* (2nd ed.). Toronto, ON: Multi-Health Systems, Inc.

Heilbrun, K., Marczyk, G. R., & DeMatteo, D. (2002). *Forensic mental health assessment: A casebook*. New York: Oxford University Press.

Jamison, K. R., Gerner, R. H., Hammen, C., & Padesky, C. (1980). Clouds and silver linings: Positive experiences associated with primary affective disorders. *American Journal of Psychiatry, 137*, 198–202. http://ajp.psychiatryonline.org/journal.aspx?journalid=13.

Kafka, M. (1991). Successful antidepressant treatment of nonparaphilic sexual addictions and paraphilias in men. *Journal of Clinical Psychiatry, 52*, 60–65.

Kafka, M. P. & Hennen, J. (2002). A DSM-IV Axis I comorbidity study of males (N = 120) with paraphilias and paraphilia-related disorders. *Sexual Abuse: A Journal of Research and Treatment, 14*, 349–366. doi: 10.1023/A:1020007004436.

Kafka, M. P. & Hennen, J. (2003). Hypersexual desire in males: Are males with paraphilias different from males with paraphilia-related disorders? *Sexual Abuse: A Journal of Research and Treatment, 15*, 307–321. doi: 10.1023/A:1025000227956.

Kafka, M. P. & Prentky, R. (1994). Preliminary observations of DSM III-R Axis I comorbidity in men with paraphilias and paraphilia-related disorders. *Journal of Clinical Psychiatry*, 55, 481–487.

Kafka, M. P. & Prentky, R. (1998). Attention-deficit/hyperactivity disorder in males with paraphilias and paraphilia-related disorders: A comorbidity study. *Journal of Clinical Psychiatry*, 59, 388–396. www.psychiatrist.com/default2.asp.

Kernberg, O. F. (1995). *Love relations: Normality and pathology.* New Haven, CT: Yale University Press.

Lang, R. A., Langevin, R., Checkley, K. L., & Pugh, G. (1987). Genital exhibitionism: Courtship disorder or narcissism? *Canadian Journal of Behavioral Science*, 19, 216–232. doi: 10.1037/h0080011.

Langevin, R., Paitich, D., Freeman, R., Mann, K., & Handy, L. (1978). Personality characteristics and sexual anomalies in males. *Canadian Journal of Behavioral Science*, 10, 222–238. doi: 10.1037/h0081551.

Långström, N. & Seto, M. C. (2006). Exhibitionistic and voyeuristic behavior in a Swedish national population survey. *Archives of Sexual Behavior*, 35, 427–435. doi: 10.1007/s10508–006–9042–6.

Lee, J. K., Pattison, P., Jackson, H. J., & Ward, T. (2001). The general, common, and specific features of psychopathology for different types of paraphilias. *Criminal Justice and Behavior*, 28, 227–256. doi: 10.1177/0093854801028002005.

Leistico, A. M. R., Salekin, R. T., DeCosta, J., & Rogers, R. (2008). A large-scale meta-analysis relating the Hare measures of psychopathy to antisocial conduct. *Law and Human Behavior*, 32, 28–45. doi: 10.1007/s10979–007–9096–6.

Lilienfeld, S. O. & Fowler, K.A. (2006). The self-report assessment of psychopathy: Problems, pitfalls, and promises. In C. J. Patrick (Ed.), *Handbook of psychopathy* (pp. 107–132). New York: Guilford.

Lilienfeld, S. O. & Widows, M. R. (2005). *Psychopathic Personality Inventory-Revised professional manual.* Lutz, FL: Psychological Assessment Resources.

Maletzky, B. M. (1987). *Treating the sexual offender.* Newbury Park, CA: Sage.

Maletzky, B. M. (1997). Exhibitionism: Assessment and treatment. In D. R. Laws & W. T. O'Donahue (Eds.), *Sexual deviance* (pp. 40–74). New York: Guilford.

Marshall, W. L., Hamilton, K., & Fernandez, Y. (2001). Empathy deficits and cognitive distortions in child molesters. *Sexual Abuse: A Journal of Research and Treatment*, 7, 205–219. doi: 10.1023/A:1026652321327.

McElroy, S., Soutullo, C., Taylor, P., Nelson, E., Beckman, D., Strakowski, S., & Keck, P. (1999). Psychiatric features of 36 persons convicted of sexual offenses. *Journal of Clinical Psychiatry*, 60, 414–420. www.psychiatrist.com/default2.asp.

Meyer, K. (1985). Paraphilias. In H. I. Kaplan & B. J. Sadock (Eds.), *Comprehensive textbook of psychiatry* (4th ed., pp. 1075–1072). Baltimore: Williams & Wilkins.

Morey, L. C. (1991). *Personality Assessment Inventory.* Odessa, FL: Psychological Assessment Resources.

Morey, L. C. (1998). Teaching and learning the Personality Assessment Inventory (PAI). In L. Handler & M. J. Hilsenroth (Eds.), *Teaching and learning personality assessment* (pp. 191–214). Hillsdale, NJ: Lawrence Erlbaum Associates.

Morey, L. C. (2003). *Essentials of PAI assessment.* New York: Wiley.

Morin, J. W. & Levenson, J. S. (2002). *The road to freedom.* Oklahoma City, OK: Wood & Barnes Publishing.

Morin, J. W. & Levenson, J. S. (2008). Exhibitionism: Assessment and treatment. In D. R. Laws & W. T. O'Donohue (Eds.), *Sexual deviance: Theory, assessment, and treatment* (2nd ed., pp. 76–107). New York: Guilford.

Mullen, K. L. & Edens, J. F. (2008). A case law survey of the Personality Assessment Inventory: Examining its role in civil and criminal trials. *Journal of Personality Assessment, 90*, 300–303. doi: 10.1080/00223890701885084.

Murphy, W. D. & Page, I. J. (2008). Exhibitionism: Psychopathology and theory. In D. R. Laws & W. T. O'Donohue (Eds.), *Sexual deviance: Theory, assessment, and treatment* (2nd ed., pp. 61–75). New York: Guilford.

Nelson, E., Brusman, L., Holcomb, J., Soutullo, C., Beckman, D., Welge, J. A., Kupili, N., & McElroy, S. L. (2001). Divalproex sodium in sex offenders with Bipolar Disorders and comorbid paraphilias: An open retrospective study. *Journal of Affective Disorders, 64*, 249–255. doi: 10.1016/S0165-0327(00)00255-X.

Rabinowitz Greenberg, S. R., Firestone, P., Bradford, J. M., & Greenberg, D. M. (2002). Prediction of recidivism in exhibitionists: Psychological, phallometric, and offense factors. *Sexual Abuse: A Journal of Research and Treatment, 14*, 329–347 doi: 10.1023/A:1019921720366.

Rice, M. E. & Harris, G. T. (2005). Comparing effect sizes in follow-up studies: ROC area, Cohen's d, and r. *Law and Human Behavior, 29*, 615–620. doi: 10.1007/s10979–005–6832–7.

Salekin, R. T., Rogers, R., & Sewell, K. W. (1996). A review and meta-analysis of the psychopathy checklist and psychopathy checklist–revised: Predictive validity of dangerousness. *Clinical Psychology: Science and Practice, 3*, 203–215. doi: 10.1111/j.1468–2850.1996.tb00071.x.

Spiegel, A. (2011, May 27). *Creator of psychopathy test worries about its use* [Audio podcast]. www.npr.org/2011/05/27/136723357/creator-of-psychopathy-test-worries-about-its-use.

Stadtland, C., Kleindienst, N., Kröner, C., Eidt, M., & Nedopil, N. (2005). Psychopathic traits and risk of criminal recidivism in offenders with and without mental disorders. *International Journal of Forensic Mental Health, 4*, 89–97. doi: 10.1080/14999013.2005.10471215.

Stoller, R. (1975). *Perversion: The erotic form of hatred.* New York: Pantheon.

Stoller, R. (1991). The term perversion. In G. Gofel & W. Myers (Eds.), *Perversions and near-perversions in clinical practice* (pp. 36–56). New Haven, CT: Yale University Press.

Tuch, R. H. (2008). Unraveling the riddle of exhibitionism: A lesson in the tactics of perverse interpersonal relationships. *International Journal of Psychoanalysis, 89*, 143–160. doi: 10.1111/j.1745–8315.2007.00006.x.

Vess, J. (2011). Ethical practice in sex offender assessment: Consideration of actuarial and polygraph methods. *Sexual Abuse: A Journal of Research and Treatment, 23*, 381–396. doi: 10.1177/1079063210382045.

de Vogel, V., de Ruiter, C., van Beek, D., & Mead, G. (2004). Predictive validity of the SVR-20 and Static-99 in a Dutch sample of treated sex offenders. *Law and Human Behavior, 28*, 235–251. doi: 10.1023/B:LAHU.0000029137.41974.eb.

Ward, N. G. (1975). Successful lithium treatment of transvestism associated with manic-depression. *The Journal of Nervous and Mental Disease, 161*, 204–206. http://journals.lww.com/jonmd/toc/1975/09000.

Winokur, G., Clayton, P. J., & Reich, T. (1969). *Manic depressive illness.* St. Louis, MI: Mosby.

6

FILICIDE OR FALSE CONFESSION?

Corine de Ruiter

Around 2.50 a.m. on Wednesday June 14, 2006, then 21-year-old Kim V.[1] calls 112 (the equivalent of 911 in The Netherlands). The following conversation ensues:[2]

O = Operator at the ambulance service
K = Kim V.

O: Ambulance service.
K: Yes, you have to (*come/hope??, unintelligible*)
O: Hey, what's going on?
K: I had a conflict with a young man.
O: What are you saying?
K: I had a conflict with a man, but I . . . (*sobbing*)
O: What happened?
K: He has taken my children, he grabbed a knife and he has slashed my kids.
O: What did he do? Slashed your kids?
K: Yes, and me once (*pause*) you have to help them.
O: Hey, where do you live?
K: Overlander Street.
O: In P.?
K: Yes.
O: What number?
K: Uh . . . Uh . . . 324.
O: Okay.
K: Please, because there's blood all over the place.
O: Yes, we are coming over, what is your telephone number? 0299 . . . ?
K: No, I have a mobile phone.

O: What is your mobile number?

K: It is uh . . . 2 . . . 26.

O: Yes.

K: 408.

O: 408.

K: . . . 58.

O: 58?

K: 658.

O: Okay, hey listen, how are the children doing?

K: I don't know, I am afraid to look.

O: Okay, we'll come to you with emergency.

K: Yes . . . (*unintelligible and call is disconnected*)

In her home at Overlander Street, five policemen find the lifeless bodies of a 2-year-old girl Roxanne and her 6-month-old brother Don. The two children have apparently been stabbed to death multiple times in their own beds. They encounter Kim, who is intensely emotional. She talks in a confused way about a man who had been in her apartment. She is wearing a blue T-shirt and jogging pants and is barefooted. The police notice blood on her left underarm and on the left side of her neck is a scratch of about 13 centimeters. One of the officers notices a blood stain on the left upper leg of her jogging pants. On the floor in the hallway lies a kitchen knife with blood traces on it.

When the police inform her upon arrival at the police station that her children are dead, Kim starts to cry hard. At 3.10 a.m., Kim's clothing is taken from her for trace evidence, and she is provided with other clothing. At 3.48 a.m., the assistant public prosecutor decides that Kim will be arrested and taken into custody, on grounds of Articles 287 (murder) and 289 (manslaughter) of the Dutch Code of Criminal Procedure. While he is conducting his investigation, the technical police investigator presents her with the caution[3] and asks Kim what had happened that night. She answers that a young man came to her door and that she let him in. She also said the man had hit her on the head.

All of the above information was part of the official police documentation in the case file I received from the Regional Court of the city of Haarlem in May 2007, when I was requested to conduct a second opinion forensic mental health assessment (FMHA) of Kim. Cases such as this are hard to stomach emotionally, even for an experienced clinical-forensic psychologist. Almost immediately, it also becomes apparent that different scenarios are operating simultaneously. In one scenario, Kim is the culprit, she was found at the crime scene. This is obviously the scenario the police believed to be true as they arrested her almost immediately. In the other scenario, a man who came to Kim's door in the middle of the night is the person who killed her young children. For the clinical-forensic psychologist who is asked to examine the defendant's mental state at the time of the offense, objectivity and openness to both scenarios is essential.

Appointment as an Expert by the Court

As is customary in The Netherlands in cases of serious crime, an independent psychiatrist (J. de Man) is also appointed to evaluate Kim at the same time. Kim is detained in one of the two women's prisons in The Netherlands. The investigating judge is asking for an FMHA because the defense attorney and the defendant are displeased with the forensic mental health report that has been produced by the Justice Department's Psychiatric Observation Clinic (POC). The defense counsel had asked an independent legal psychologist, prof. Harald Merckelbach, to review the POC report, and he had noted several shortcomings. After legal counsel presented these shortcomings to the investigating judge, the latter decided another independent forensic mental health evaluation was needed.

During a telephone call, the investigating judge asks me which parts of the criminal file I need for my evaluation. We decide jointly that I will not gain access to the content of the previous mental health report by the POC, in order to limit bias. However, the judge does send me the social network analysis prepared by the social worker of the Observation Clinic. This is a standard part of POC mental health evaluation procedure and in this case it contained information from interviews with Kim's parents, her two half-sisters (from her father's previous marriage), her best friend Dorothy, her ex-partner (father of her children), and her current partner. Also, medical records of Kim and her children, Kim's school records (both elementary and high school), and criminal record were part of the case file. The medical records included information on the health status, vaccinations, and growth curves of Kim's children from Public Youth Health Care services, a service that is provided to all parents in The Netherlands, and the medical record of Kim from the family doctor. Having access to the social network analysis report provided me with the necessary information from collateral sources and made further interviews with collaterals on my part superfluous.

The questions for my examination of Kim consisted of the standard set of questions posed by Dutch courts in criminal cases. They relate to the issues of criminal responsibility, risk of recidivism, and treatment advice. The specific questions are:

(1) Is the individual suffering from a mental disorder and/or defective development of his/her mental capacities, and if so, how can this be classified in terms of diagnosis?
(2) In case the answer to the first question is affirmative: would the current diagnosis also apply at the time of the alleged offense?
(3) Did the mental disorder or defective development of mental capacities affect the behavioral choices, *casu quo* behaviors at the time of committing the alleged offense?
(4) If yes, can the expert explain:
    (a) in what way this happened;
    (b) to what degree this happened;

(c) which conclusion in terms of criminal responsibility should be drawn based on this.

(5) (a) Which factors resulting from the disorder could be relevant for the risk of recidivism?

(b) Which other factors and conditions should be considered in relation to this?

(c) Can anything be said about a possible mutual influence of these factors and conditions?

(6) Which interventions of a behavioral or other nature are advisable to reduce the risk of recidivism and within which legal framework could this be realized?

Kim in the Women's Prison

In September 2007, I meet a 22-year-old woman who looks much younger than her chronological age. She appears nervous, depressed, and exhausted. She says she feels restless inside and has difficulty concentrating. Also, she reports nightmares with fragments of the events surrounding the death of her children. She expresses guilt; she says she feels like a failure as a mother because she did not manage to protect her children: "If I had done better, perhaps my children would still be here. You can never know. But I get up every morning with that feeling." The past few weeks she has been suffering from anxiety, coupled with chest pain. She says she does not have suicidal thoughts. For 2 months she has been taking an antidepressant.

Notwithstanding her depressed mood and fatigue, she cooperates well during the evaluation. She tells in detail about her childhood, which has certainly not left her unscarred. Revealing some self-insight, she looks back on her rebellious attitude during adolescence, during which she hung out with the wrong friends and neglected her school work by truancy. The death of her children, the arrest, and subsequent detention have made her angry but also combative. She thinks that before these events, she was led too much by circumstances and showed little self-determination. Her past relationships speak of this fact.

When Kim got to know Richard, the father of her two children, she was 17. She says she was in love and they could communicate well in the beginning. He had a steady job as a road worker at a company. Before Richard, she had other boyfriends but these were not really serious relationships according to her. The relationship with Richard became more and more unstable over time; they had lots of conflicts, according to Kim about the smallest things. The relationship ended. Then it turned out Kim was expecting a baby. Richard first said he would help out with the baby but he was not present at the delivery and only showed interest when Roxanne was 4 months old. The relationship was resumed, although they no longer lived together. Again, there were a lot of fights mostly about Roxanne. Kim put an end to the relationship because Roxanne began to become afraid of Richard. He yelled and threw things.

Richard had a second life: he dealt in drugs, mainly cocaine and ecstasy. When they were still living together he did this from their joint home. Kim started using cocaine shortly after she got into a relationship with Richard. She says she tried it out of curiosity. It was always available because Richard was dealing it. There was a period when she was addicted to cocaine; she used it from morning to evening. She started losing a lot of weight. She says she did not use drugs during her pregnancies, except one or two times when she was pregnant with Roxanne. This statement, however, cannot be verified, and the pregnancy was unplanned. According to Kim, cocaine makes her feel relaxed inside, although on the outside she becomes quite talkative. On the night the alleged offense took place, Kim had used cocaine together with a friend named Bob. She says that since her son Don's birth around 6 months ago, she has used cocaine twice (once on the fateful night). According to Kim, the cocaine she consumed that night had no special or different effect on her than usual.

In order to be able to answer the questions posed by the court in a reliable and valid manner, a psychological test battery needs to be selected. Naturally, an examination of the possible presence of an Axis I and/or Axis II disorder is necessary in a case like this. Subsequently, criminal responsibility needs to be determined,

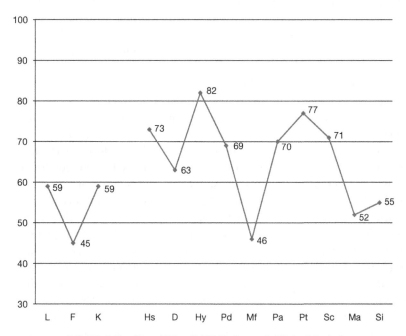

FIGURE 6.1 MMPI-2 Profile of Kim (LFK Scales and Clinical Scales).

L = Lie scale; F = Infrequency scale; K = Correction scale; Hs = Hypochondriasis scale; D = Depression scale; Hy = Hysteria scale; Pd = Psychopathic deviate scale; Mf = Masculinity-femininity scale; Pa = Paranoia scale; Pt = Psychasthenia scale; Sc = Schizophrenia scale; Ma = Mania scale; Si = Social introversion scale.

obviously dependent on the presence of mental disorder. A structured, research-based risk assessment would be the last step in the evaluation. However, as we will see in what follows, during my evaluation of Kim I had to change this original plan.

Forensic Mental Health Assessment

For the forensic mental health evaluation, I made use of the MMPI-2 (see Figure 6.1, for Kim's scores on the primary validity and clinical scales) and a clinical interview to check for the presence of a symptom disorder on Axis I of DSM-IV. The semi-structured interview SIDP-IV was used to determine the presence/absence of personality disorder (Axis II).

MMPI-2

Inspection of Kim's scores on the MMPI-2 validity scales did not reveal evidence of distorted response styles. Her TRIN raw score of 9 shows there is no evidence for excessive nay-saying or yea-saying. There is also no evidence for inconsistent responding (VRIN = 52T). Her T-score of 45 on the F-scale suggests some, but not overwhelming psychological distress. Problems may also be chronic and/or ego-syntonic. The L-scale (T-score = 59) indicates some defensiveness, but this may be context-related since the stakes of the present forensic evaluation were high for Kim. Her K-scale score (T = 59), together with her elevated profile on the clinical scales, indicates an adequate degree of behavioral control and a likely ability to cope despite her underlying problems.

Six of the 10 clinical scales show an elevation above a T-score of 65. The three-code type that fits the profile is 371. Friedman, Lewak, Nichols, and Webb (2001) describe these individuals as "constantly on edge, fearing abandonment, emotional letdown, or anger" (p. 290). They are afraid of confrontation or conflict, and try hard to please others. They go through life seeking reassurance and approval, fearful of independence and self-assertion. Somatic complaints are also common, as is reflected by the elevation on the Hypochondriasis scale (T-score = 73). More specifically, Friedman et al. (2001) suggest people with this profile type are suggestible and easily upset by intense emotions.

Kim's scores on the Harris-Lingoes subscales suggest physical complaints (D3 = 70; Hy4 = 66), a high need for affection (Hy2 = 70), and feelings of weakness and tiredness (Hy3 = 73). Scale Pd2 (Authority Problems) has a T-score of 70 and the content scale ASP2 is also elevated (T-score = 73), signifying that Kim has a tendency towards unconventional and socially disinhibited conduct. Her substance dependence and her truancy are historical markers for these scores. Sc5 is elevated (T-score = 73) and reflects fear of loss of control. Restlessness and periods of uncontrollable laughing/crying may be present. Since the content scales Anger (T = 44) and Type A Personality (T = 37) are not elevated, it is not likely that her deficient inhibition will be expressed in uncontrollable rage. Of note, Kim has a subclinical T-score of 62 on the subscale Si1 (Shyness) which points to social anxiety and low self-esteem.

Only one of the content scales on Kim's MMPI-2 has a score in the clinical range (T ≥ 65): Health Concerns (T = 72). Kim reports gastrointestinal symptoms, sensory and motor problems and headaches, and general worries about her health. Her second-highest content scale score is a 62 on the DEP (Depression) scale.

On inspection of the supplementary scales, it is noteworthy that the Addiction Acknowledgement Scale (AAS) is elevated (T = 67), but the Addiction Potential Scale (APS) and the MacAndrew Alcoholism Scale (MAC-R) are not (T = 46 and 42, respectively). This combination of scores indicates that the substance abuse may be largely situational and therefore has a highly favorable prognosis (Friedman et al., 2001, p. 324). Kim also scores in the clinical range on the Overcontrolled-Hostility scale (O-H; T = 69). However, this scale has only been validated for use in male correctional populations and there is some evidence to suggest that women may score somewhat higher on the O-H scale. Thus, we refrain from making interpretive statements based on the O-H scale score. Two supplementary scales reveal a T-score below 35, signifying a clinically relevant lowering. Kim got a T-score of 33 on both the Ego-strength (Es) and the Dominance (Do) scales. The low Es score indicates lower than average stress tolerance and a tendency to overreact to life stressors with slow physiological recovery. A low Do score pertains to an absence of self-direction. Graham, Butcher and McNulty (1997) report that psychiatric outpatients with Do T-scores < 40 often have histories of abuse and a broad range of symptoms.

Biographical Information from the Social Network Analysis

For both Kim's parents, their marriage was their second one. Both had two children from a previous marriage. They started living together with the mother's two children (4 and 6 years old at the time) in the home; Kim was their love baby. While her mother was pregnant with Kim, her former husband still visited her regularly and even assaulted her several times. She says she was afraid of him and the thought of refusing him entry to their home did not seem to even occur to her. At a certain point, she had had enough and chased her ex away with a frying pan. After that, he did not return. Kim's father's two children visited regularly and all five (step)children got along well.

The parents said they shared household duties. It was a busy life, taking care of three—and often five—children. When Kim was 12, she was the only child still living at home. Over time, the marriage got into a rut. Her mother wanted to go on outings at the weekends. Her father said he worked very hard at this time, and was often very tired and just wanted to relax. There were many arguments and finally her mother filed for divorce. Both parents kept in good contact with each other, except for the first years after the separation. Kim lived with both parents alternately.

Kim had a vivid imagination as a child, according to her parents. When the lights went out for the night, she told her sisters endless stories about her own horse that she wished to have. If something was bothering Kim, she talked about it with her parents, according to them. Nevertheless, Kim told the social worker of the POC she had been sexually abused between the ages of 3 and 7 by one of her mother's brothers, where she sometimes stayed for the weekend. Showing emotional distress during the conversation about this abuse, she said she felt ashamed and dirty, and therefore did not want to look at herself in the mirror as a child. Out of shame she told nothing about the abuse to her parents. According to Kim, the abuse stopped after she told her parents she no longer wanted to stay at her uncle's house. She did not want to tell the social worker exactly what her uncle had done to her.

Kim remembers that, as a child, her parents would quarrel and shout at each other. She would cry, put her fingers in her ears, or go to her room. Information from mental health services, where Kim sought help nearly 9 months before the alleged offense, reveals that her brother, in response to the relationship problems between the parents, often hit and kicked Kim and once threatened her with a knife.

Her primary school years were uneventful. According to the school records, she was an unremarkable student. Kim was quite talkative and a social butterfly. She had an eye for the more vulnerable children: a boy who wasn't welcome anywhere because he was not housebroken yet and a girl with a skin condition came to her home to play. Because she spent time with them, they were subsequently accepted by her classmates. Kim loved animals, she had rabbits, mice, and guinea pigs and when her animals died, they were buried with a ritual.

According to her parents and sisters, Kim went through a major behavior change during the transition to secondary school. Her parents said they worried about her and said that Kim changed into someone they did not know and with whom contact got increasingly difficult. Kim herself said that from about the age of 12 years she had eating problems and often vomited to prevent herself from gaining weight.

Kim finished secondary vocational school with a diploma, and continued taking courses in caring for the elderly at a community college. According to her father, this period was "a real drama." Kim did not abide by the house rules, stayed away from home at night, and started to skip classes. Both parents said Kim manipulated them with lies. When Kim was confronted with this by the DOC social worker, she said she did not know what to do with her father's grief about the divorce and chose to avoid him as much as possible.

Collateral information from the community college shows that at the time she attended school there, Kim was not doing well. She made a dysphoric, lethargic impression, was socially isolated, and needed plenty of encouragement. She neglected her appearance. Her level of concentration seemed to depend on her mood. She worked meticulously. Kim was initially indifferent to her mentor, but as she made clear she wished to help her, she appreciated this and became more open.

The school had frequent contact with her father about his daughter, but not with her mother.

When her father entered a new relationship about 4 years after the divorce, Kim had difficulty adjusting. She resisted the "mothering," as she called it, of her father's new partner. During this period, she started to have intimate relationships herself. At 17, she met Richard. He was a drug dealer and Kim started to use drugs herself. Her older half-sister describes Kim as a two-faced person: one side of her is social, interested, and helpful, but often, she also seems not to be herself and starts to believe in her own stories: "She was attracted to bad boys, to intense relationships and boyfriends who are on drugs. Kim was drawn to guys who give her attention, she used drugs to fit in and she adapted to the person with whom she was."

When Kim was 19, her daughter Roxanne was born. At the time, Richard was on holiday. He was angry with Kim and said he didn't want to have anything to do with her. Her half-sister reports that Kim took "okay" care of the baby, but she needed a lot of help from her parents. She was inept at cooking and mainly ate junk food. A few months after Roxanne's birth, Kim and Richard met during an evening out on the town. The next day, after Kim got Roxanne from where she had spent the night, they went to Richard's flat. Kim said that Richard had sworn that he had changed a lot, but she soon found out that this was not true. The relationship between Kim and Richard remained highly unstable; sometimes he stayed with her and Roxanne in Kim's apartment; sometimes he was gone for weeks or months. Kim reported that Richard ignored Roxanne, yelled at her and scared her with the vacuum cleaner. Kim's best friend Dorothy also noted that Richard hardly paid attention to his daughter.

Information from the family doctor reveals that about half a year after giving birth, Kim made a visit to him because she felt depressed and restless. She was not sleeping well and felt exhausted. She was having financial difficulties because she was spending more money than she could afford on the basis of her monthly welfare check. Her parents used to help out with buying baby clothes.

When Roxanne was almost 1 year old, Kim met another man, Kevin, and she fell in love for the first time in her life. At a certain point she noticed she was pregnant by Richard, but kept it silent out of fear of losing Kevin. In this same period, Kim told her sisters that she was being threatened by Richard, who wanted custody of Roxanne with his new girlfriend and harassed her numerous times by telephone. Both parents had a talk with Richard, after which this behavior stopped.

The preventive child health care worker reports that Roxanne showed a healthy development over the first 2 years of her life. Still, Kim kept feeling depressed and the family doctor's notes show she reported difficulty feeling love for her daughter. The doctor decided to refer her to a community mental health center. During the intake there, Kim said she was still suffering from nightmares and depression, related to the sexual abuse during her childhood. She also explained she was really sorry she had not consciously experienced the delivery of Roxanne, because she had been so anxious that they had to give her a lot of tranquillizers. Community mental health referred her to a support group for young mothers, but this advice did not concur at all with her wishes, so she never contacted the support organization. Her symptoms remained unaltered.

A couple of months later, Don was born. The delivery went very fast, so together Kim and Kevin brought the baby into the world. According to Kim's mother, also present at the delivery, Kevin immediately fell in love with the baby. All collateral sources state that Roxanne and Don were sweet, easy children. Kim sometimes acted indifferently and left her children in the care of others, but she was also often caring and patient. Kevin said that there were difficulties in their relationship. Kim would respond with defensive movements to sudden arm movements of Kevin and was startled when he stood behind her. She told him she had been beaten a lot by Richard. Also, Kim had problems with intimacy. Kim says that Kevin was the first person who was interested in what she wanted and considered her feelings. Over time and with patience, their sexual relationship got better.

During the months prior to the fatal night, Kim and Kevin started to make plans for the future. They were talking about buying a larger house, but then Kim would have needed to get a job, so she started to send out job applications. According to most of the collateral informants, in the last weeks before the alleged offense, Kim seemed to flourish in her relationship and the children were also doing very well. Whereas she would mostly remain inside with them before, she now started taking them for walks in the park.

Criminal History

Kim has never been convicted for any crime, according to an official excerpt from the Judicial Documentation Registry.

SIDP-IV

The results of the SIDP-IV interview are based on a semi-structured interview with Kim and on the information from her file. She did not meet diagnostic criteria for a personality disorder as defined in the DSM-IV-TR. She does have a number of dependent and borderline personality traits.

DSM-IV Classification

Axis I: Posttraumatic Stress Disorder (at present); Dysthymic Disorder (presently and also at time of offense); cocaine abuse (in remission); bulimia nervosa (in remission)
Axis II: no disorder.

Psychiatrist de Man independently arrived at a similar diagnostic classification.

Benny and the Police Interrogation

An important component of any FMHA in a criminal case is, of course, the conversation with the defendant about the alleged offense. In Kim's case, the interview takes a remarkable turn, as Kim denies the killing of her children. She says her friend Bob came over to visit that evening; he brought cocaine, which they used together. After Bob had left her apartment, the doorbell rang and a man named Benny was on her doorstep. According to Kim, he came to the door to claim money that Richard still owed him. Kim replied that she did not have money and she wanted Benny to leave her home, but he did not:

> And he kept on going and I got a big push from him. I went to the kitchen and I threatened him with a knife. That he had to get out of my house. But he did not. Thus, at a given moment there was a struggle, and he got the knife out of my hands. But I was with him in the living room and at one point I heard my son Don cry. And from that moment on, it really is a black hole. Because always when there were tensions in the home or too much noise, he would wake up. Don is just very sensitive. And from that time on, I wanted to go and see him. I actually don't remember what happened, I ended up on the floor. Only when I wanted to get up, he was there with a smile on his face and said: "Your kids will sleep forever."

I asked Kim how long she thought the period that she doesn't recall lasted. She could not tell. In the process notes from the official police interrogation, I read that during one of the sessions she admitted to having slain her children. During the conversation with me, she says this was a false confession, given under great psychological pressure from the police. She says the investigating police officers did not believe her Benny story. Her actual confession is quite meager in terms of detail and she retracted it later. Possibly, there is a serious problem here, and I decide to examine the video footage of the interrogations in detail.

Superintendent J. Bond

In the literature on police interrogation, a distinction is made between an information-gathering ("investigative") and an accusatory ("confrontational") questioning style (Hasel & Kassin, 2012). In the investigative style, the primary purpose is obtaining detailed information from the suspect, using open questions such as: "Where were you between 3 and 4 o'clock in the afternoon?" The accusatory interviewing confronts the suspect with allegations, such as: "Your comments make me think you are hiding something from me." The primary objective of this approach is elicitation of a confession (Vrij, Mann, Kristen, & Fisher, 2007).

In the interrogation interviews with Kim, we encounter both interviewing styles. During the first interviews, the police work primarily with an information-gathering style. Kim provides a lot of information about herself. During the first five interrogations, she basically tells the story she told me, in more or less detail. The sixth interviewing session, 8 days after the alleged offense, however, is different for a number of reasons. First, it lasts a very long time. It starts at 1.19 p.m. and finishes at 8.05 p.m. In the process notes, it is stated that the session is interrupted at 7.08 p.m. for a break. Gradually, during this sixth session, the interviewing style becomes (very) accusatory. Kim is accused of lying. Kim admits that she cannot remember certain things, such as whether she heard water running down the toilet or in the kitchen, but the interrogators consider this (and many other things) as a sign of lying. Then Superintendent J. Bond, who has not participated in the interrogations thus far, enters the room. He says Kim will soon be allowed to say farewell to her children in the morgue. Bond uses a very suggestive and accusatory interviewing style, for example: "You should put a letter in the coffin there, saying you regret it." Between the sixth and the seventh interrogation, when she says goodbye to her children, she changes position. She then says that she must have been the person who killed her children. During the seventh and eighth interrogation, the police question her about more details. She then withdraws the confession.

In the conversation I have with her in the prison, she states the following (literal translation; CdR refers to Corine de Ruiter, K refers to Kim):

CdR: And what does the police say you did?
K: Police say that I killed my children.
CdR: And how did they draw that conclusion?
K: Because I was alone in my house when they arrived. And because I was in a panic in the hallway, waiting for them. And they said they had found my fingerprints on the knife. And the DNA, the blood of my children under my fingernails.[4] From that, they said: you did it. But even before they had done all this investigation, they immediately said it was me. They never listened to me, to anything I said. Also, I sat down in the little cell there and I was told: Kim, if you start talking, then we can see if you can say farewell to your children. And then you might be able to attend the funeral. Then at a certain point I just thought: to hell with it, because I had continuously been asking them: can I go to my children, may I please go to my children. And each time they refused. And then during one such interrogation, some other detective came into the room; he was very threatening because he started to scream at me and I was really scared he was going to give me a blow. And then I thought: you know, never mind, I'll confess it. And then I said I had done it and 10 minutes later we were in a car to say goodbye to my children. So yes . . .
CdR: Is that on video, Kim?

K: No idea. I have never thought about it, frankly.

CdR: But what you are telling me now, then . . . You are telling me actually, well, you just confessed, because you wanted to see your children.

K: Yes, otherwise I could not. Otherwise, I would stay in full limitations and then I could not attend the cremation of my own children. And I thought to myself: they may not do this to me. I was so sad and I wanted to share that with my boyfriend and my family. And they would not let me. And that hurt so much because they were also grieving.

CdR: And Benny, you said that he said . . . or . . . what did you say? I will make sure that your children will sleep forever?

K: No, he said, your children will sleep forever. This he said with a smile on his face.

CdR: And uhm . . . you knew then what he was going to do? Were you scared?

K: No, it had already happened. But I did not realize that at the time. And you're also not thinking, what does this mean or what will happen now? The only thing you try to do at such a moment is to survive, because he comes at you with a knife. That's all you try. You try to defend yourself with all the power that is in you, no matter how strong the other is. And thanks to one kick on my part, the knife fell, and he just slowly walked away. He did not even run. And this . . . I experience every night . . . again. Especially his words that my children will sleep forever.

CdR: Did you also tell this to the police?

K: They did not listen. They never listened to anything I said. I have told them where they could find him. Then the next day, they came back to say: we did not find him. You can't tell me, with so many places that you know that in one day, you will not find anybody. That is just impossible. So they have just never done anything with it. Nothing at all. Things, which have been found, they did nothing with it. Afterwards, I thought, and I still think about it this way, that people simply make mistakes by thinking: oh, that's a young mother, she must have gotten crazy with these small children, because she is single. I think in cases like this, they conclude too easy that the mother did it. There are also mothers who have a lot of love for their children who . . . the worst thing I ever did to my daughter, was that I gave her a tap on her fingers, because she held her hands above a burning candle. That's the worst that I did to my daughter. The worst thing I did to my son is that I left him crying for a quarter or a half hour, because he would not go to sleep. But hey, does that make me a bad mother. I don't think so.

Research on False Confessions

The myth that people do not confess to crimes they did not commit is quite persistent. In fact, this myth is probably one of the reasons it is considered such a potent piece of evidence in criminal cases. With the advent of DNA exonerations, we now know that false confessions have been a contributing factor in 25 percent of wrongful convictions (Garrett, 2008; www.innocenceproject.org). The last few decades of psychological research on false confessions have documented the presence of dispositional and situational factors that put innocent people at risk of confessing to a crime they did not commit (Gudjonsson, 2003; Kassin et al., 2010).

There are three types of false confession. The first type is the *voluntary false confession*, in which a person claims responsibility for a crime without pressure from the police. Examples of reasons why people voluntarily confess are: a pathological need for attention (often in high-profile cases), the desire to protect someone else, and delusions of their own guilt (Hasel & Kassin, 2012). *Coerced-compliant false confessions* are elicited due to pressure during the interrogation process. This pressure may result from social pressure from police staff to confess, but also from the mere interrogation situation itself, which is aversive because it often involves isolation from loved ones, lack of sleep, fatigue and hunger. Research has demonstrated that people make choices that maximize comfort, given a specific situation, which means they prefer delayed punishment to immediate aversive stimulation (Herrnstein, Rachlin, & Laibson, 1997). The third type is the *coerced-internalized false confession*, in which an individual not only confesses but also comes to believe that he/she committed the crime, sometimes even offering pseudo-memories. This type occurs when vulnerable suspects are exposed to highly suggestive interrogation techniques, such as guided imagery or misinformation.

Proven false confessions have been documented in a large number of countries (Kassin et al., 2010). In the UK, Professor Gisli Gudjonsson's expert testimony was the basis for the overturning of the convictions of the Birmingham Six and Guildford Four (Gudjonsson, 2003). The Netherlands also has a number of cases of wrongful convictions, in which false confession evidence formed the basis for the conviction: the cases of Ina Post (Israëls, 2004) and Putten.[5] Ina Post was a Dutch nurse who worked in a home for the elderly. In 1987 she was convicted and sentenced to 6 years' imprisonment for manslaughter of one of her patients. She confessed twice to the homicide, according to her because of pressure by the investigating officers. She served part of her sentence, being released in 1990 because of good behavior. Ina Post made several requests to reopen her case. After four failed attempts, the High Court ruled in 2009, 22 years after her conviction, that the case had to go back to trial. This new trial was carried out by the Court of Appeals of Den Bosch. On October 6, 2010 she was finally acquitted. On July 7, 2010, the documentary "The nightmare of Ina Post: Reconstruction of a confession" was broadcast, in which she shared her experience.[6] Most recently, the Prosecutor's Office at the High Court of The Netherlands asked the Court to order a reopening of the case of three men and three women convicted of the murder of a 56-year-old woman in 1994. The conviction was based almost exclusively on the confessions of the three women, who were put under undue pressure and given information by police during the interrogations.[7] As Hasel and Kassin (2012) note, known cases of false confession represent only "the tip of an iceberg" (p. 55).

Laboratory research, case studies, and observational studies into false confessions have resulted in a body of psychological knowledge that can and should be applied in actual cases. A thorough review of this literature is beyond the scope of this chapter, but readers are encouraged to read Gudjonsson's (2003) work for striking and illuminating case descriptions and Cutler's (2012) edited volume for an up-to-date review of the empirical literature on false confessions. In summary, false confessions seem more likely to occur in some individuals (disposition) and under some conditions (situations) (Hasel & Kassin, 2012; Kassin & Gudjonsson, 2004). In terms of dispositional characteristics, suggestibility and compliance in social situations are traits that make people vulnerable to confess under interrogation (Gudjonsson, 2003). People with mental health problems including depression, anxiety, and delusions are at heightened risk to falsely confess (Redlich, 2007). Other vulnerable suspects include those with intellectual disability and adolescents; both are more compliant and suggestible than normally gifted adults (Drizin & Leo, 2004; Gudjonsson, 2003).

The situational components of the interrogative process that render an individual vulnerable to falsely confess are manifold. Hasel and Kassin (2012) divide them into three aspects: (1) isolation, (2) confrontation, and (3) minimization. The first aspect of isolation is inherent to any police interrogation process which is specifically designed to increase anxiety and the desire to escape the situation. The isolating experience can be reinforced by allowing only limited contact with the outside world (e.g., no access to loved ones), sleep deprivation, and other hardship. Confrontation is a common tactic used by interrogators, and includes assertions of guilt and presentation of false evidence (e.g., pretending to have the person's fingerprints or blood on an object from the crime scene).[8] Decades of social psychological research have demonstrated how easy it is to alter people's visual perceptions (Asch, 1956) and memories (Loftus, 2005) by means of misleading information. The famous computer crash paradigm (Kassin & Kiechel, 1996) revealed how easy it is to get innocent subjects to sign a confession to an outcome they did not cause, even when a confession would result in a financial penalty (Horselenberg et al., 2006). Minimization is a technique used by interrogators after they have used confrontation tactics to make the person feel trapped. The crux of minimization is the suggestion that a confession will save the suspect's face. In laboratory research, minimization (promising leniency) led to a threefold increase in the rate of false confessions (Russano, Meissner, Narchet, & Kassin, 2005).

Several other components of the criminal investigative process bias towards false confessions. First, police are biased towards a presumption of guilt, which is frequently in error (Garrido, Masip, & Herrero, 2004; Meissner & Kassin, 2002). Second, police are overconfident in their ability to detect deception whereas their actual ability to detect deception is no better than that of lay individuals (Leach, Talwar, Lee, Bala, & Lindsay, 2004). Thus, inaccurate guilt assumptions may result in tunnel vision and harsh interrogations, with the risk of a false confession. Subsequently, the prosecutor takes on the guilt presumption, which is often maintained even after contrary forensic evidence (Findley & Scott, 2006). Empirical research has shown that people tend to see confessions as highly incriminating evidence (Hasel & Kassin, 2012; Kassin & Neumann, 1997) and most people believe they would never confess to a crime they did not commit. This tendency to attribute the behaviors of others to dispositional traits while neglecting the role of situational factors is called the fundamental attribution error (Gilbert, Pelham, & Krull, 1988; Kassin & Gudjonsson, 2004; Ross, 1977).

Forensic Report and Legal Outcome at First Trial

I wrote the report to the court based on the FMHA of Kim. My diagnostic conclusion was that she showed symptoms of Posttraumatic Stress Disorder (PTSD) and depression at the time of my assessment of her. She had shown symptoms of depression for a number of years prior to the alleged offense, but they seemed to have exacerbated during the period of incarceration. I also noted in my report that she claimed to be innocent of the alleged offense and that she did not remember killing her children. Therefore, I was unable to provide an answer to the questions regarding the relationship between her disorder and the alleged offense (questions 3 to 6 of the court, see pp. 114–115 of this chapter).

I reported on my observations of the extreme interrogative pressure that was put on her, the use of isolation (interrogation sessions lasting long hours; sleep deprivation, hunger), confrontation (not believing her innocence, accusing her of lying), and minimization (she would be allowed to see her children if she confessed). Furthermore, she was presented with misinformation/false evidence. I also noted that Kim's assessment results revealed a number of psychological vulnerabilities that would increase the risk of a false confession. These vulnerabilities included: long-standing mental health symptoms (depression, anxiety), sub-assertiveness, low self-esteem, suggestibility, need for reassurance, and a relatively young age. Finally, the fact that Kim had withdrawn her confession was also a possible indication that it was false (Gudjonsson, 2003).

Providing a forensic mental health report on denying suspects can be a precarious undertaking, as I have reported previously (de Ruiter, 2007; see also Chapter 10). Especially in a criminal justice system such as the Dutch which does not have separate phases for the determination of guilty/not guilty and the sentencing decision, the forensic mental health report may unintentionally influence the judges' decision on the guilt issue. For instance, if the behavioral expert concludes the defendant is "mentally disturbed" but claiming innocence, this may lead the court to use the supposed "mental disturbance" as additional proof that the person is guilty.

My advice to the court in Kim's case was: "Given the fact that Ms. V. denies having committed the alleged and indicates to have no memory of it, no statements can be made about a possible relationship between the observed mental disorder and the alleged offense." I also recommended the following: "The findings from my limited analysis of the interrogation of the suspect in this case constitute grounds to advise the court to carry out a further investigation into the possible existence of a false confession."

I was not called to testify at the trial in Kim's case. The decision to call on the expert to testify at the trial is at the discretion of the court. On November 9, 2007, the court ruled, without further investigation into the possibility of a false confession (LJN: BB7483, Court Haarlem, 15/630471–06).[9] Kim was acquitted of double homicide. The court reached this conclusion based on the fact that in the opinion of the court: (1) the confessions were unlawfully obtained (June 22, 2006) and obtained with insufficient reliability (June 29, 2006); (2) the technical forensic investigation provided insufficient evidence that the defendant had slain her children; and (3) the statement of the defendant that [the unknown person; Benny] had killed the children could not be ruled out. The court was quite harsh in its judgment of Superintendent J. Bond's behavior: in the opinion of the court he had presented the suspect as established facts information that was yet unconfirmed by the technical forensic investigation, or was manifestly contrary to the ultimate investigative findings. The prosecution went into appeal against this verdict and Kim could await the second trial at the Amsterdam Court of Appeal as a free citizen.

Benny was never found. But from all I read in the case file, I did not get the impression that the investigating police team made a serious attempt to locate him. However, this cannot be ascertained definitively, because the file that is submitted to the court by the prosecution in an inquisitorial system is prepared with the aim of supporting a presumption of guilt (see Chapter 1). Because the Dutch legal system does not have separate phases for the determination of guilt and the sentencing, the forensic-psychologist/expert is confronted with having to deal with the guilty/not guilty issue to some extent, in particular in cases where the defendant is claiming to be innocent.

Appellate Court Trial and Final Outcome

In the Appeal phase, the court ordered three new experts to examine Kim's statements during the interrogation process. These three experts differed in terms of their professional expertise. One was a cognitive psychologist and an expert in lie detection, one was a cognitive psychologist specialized in human memory and its failings, and the third was a legal psychologist and expert in false confessions. All three experts were sent the 12 DVDs with video footage of the interrogations and the transcripts of these. No other parts (e.g., forensic technical evidence, mental health evaluation reports) of the file were given to these experts.

This, obviously, was a grave omission on the court's part, because the latter information is crucial to be able to conduct a thorough assessment of the quality of confession evidence. For instance, without access to the technical evidence, it cannot be determined whether the police interrogators have presented the defendant with misleading information. Also, without information on the suspect's mental health status, it is impossible to provide a judgment on possible psychological vulnerabilities in the suspect. Only the legal psychologist, Dr. Robert Horselenberg (Horselenberg, Merckelbach, & Josephs, 2003; Horselenberg et al., 2006), made a request to the court on June 19, 2009 to gain access to the technical part of the police file and to the mental health experts' reports. This request was refused by the court on July 17, 2009.[10] The other two experts did not request this additional information. All three experts received the same set of questions from the court:

(1) Can you give an opinion based on your expertise on how the interrogations were carried out (e.g., technique of questioning, information provided to the suspect during the interrogations)?
(2) Can you give an opinion about the circumstances in which the interrogations took place?
(3) Can you give an opinion on the questions of the officers?
(4) Is it your opinion (or not) that there has been subjective pressure and coloring of the scenarios that were presented?
(5) If so, to what extent?
(6) Do you have any other comments based on your profession that you consider important in the context of this assignment?

Having read all three expert reports, it is quite striking how dissimilar their conclusions are. The two cognitive psychologists limited themselves to an assessment of the content of Kim's statements during the interrogations, focusing on their consistency and credibility in terms of details, and a comparison with other information from the file (which, as noted above, was quite limited). Both cognitive psychologists concluded that Kim's statements showed evidence of unreliability and might contain lies. One of the cognitive psychologists contended that Kim easily changed her story when confronted with contradictory facts. The legal psychologist considered this same behavior as evidence of her compliance. It is also quite striking that the two cognitive psychologists did not see anything wrong with the way the interrogations were conducted: ". . . the interrogations were conducted in a correct manner" is the conclusion of one of them. One of the cognitive psychologists also stated that the suspect was "relaxed and alert during all interrogations," which is in stark contrast to the crying spells Kim showed during some of the interrogations I observed. The legal psychologist came to a completely different conclusion on the basis of the exact same information:

Repeated questioning about certain subjects, the insertion of information from others and suggestive questions about this, leads Kim to adjust her story to what she is told. Thus, it can not be ruled out that Kim is suggestible. [. . .] In addition to these characteristics (during one of the interrogations Kim shares her IQ score of 70 as observed by the POC), this would indicate Kim has an intellectual disability that makes her vulnerable to making a false confession. [. . .] Also, the loss of her children plays a role. The mental state associated with this loss may also have made her vulnerable. During the interrogations the officers repeatedly referred to this loss.

There is one conclusion on which the three experts agree more or less, and that is that Kim revealed no verifiable perpetrator information during the interrogations. The legal psychologist concluded that the probability that Kim's confession is false should be seriously considered. The cognitive psychologists, on the contrary, concluded that the confession was not false. Still, one of them adds the following caution: "a confession should only be accepted as evidence if the suspect demonstrates verifiable perpetrator knowledge that does not come from other sources."

The trial at the Court of Appeal took place on February 9, 10, and 12, 2010. The main strategy of the defense was that the police acted out of obvious *tunnel vision*, i.e., "the compendium of common heuristics and logical fallacies" to which all humans are susceptible, that lead key players in the criminal justice system to "focus on a suspect, select and filter the evidence that will 'build a case' for conviction, while ignoring or suppressing evidence that points away from guilt" (Martin, 2002, p. 848; Findley, 2012). Counsel tried to convince the court that the defendant had confessed under subjective and excessive pressure (LJN: BL5731, Amsterdam Court of Appeal, 02–26–2010 via www.rechtspraak.nl). The defense requested the court to let Drs. Horselenberg, de Ruiter, and de Man testify at trial. However, according to the court, these experts' reports were sufficiently clear; it was deemed not necessary to hear them in person. In an inquisitorial justice system, it is the court that ultimately decides who will be heard at the trial (see Chapter 1). In Kim's case, the appellate court only asked to hear the two experts from the POC who had reported on Kim's mental health in 2007.

It is beyond the scope of this paper to present all the details of the technical forensic investigation in this case. Of note, several forensic DNA labs examined objects taken from the scene of the crime. One of these labs determined that there were a few traces of DNA from an unknown donor, i.e., not Kim, her children, her boyfriend, her father, or her friend Bob who visited earlier that night. The experts from this lab contended it could not be ruled out that a more extensive Y-chromosomal study of samples from, for instance, the handle of the knife and blood found in the sink, whether or not in combination with a larger number of reference samples, would have led to more clarity. Thus, it appears that more extensive sampling from the crime scene would have been desirable. While this argument was used by the Haarlem Court to acquit Kim, this evidence did not convince the Court of Appeal. The latter opted to follow the reasoning of two other DNA experts, who claimed there was no indication for the consistent presence of Y-chromosomal DNA-material originating from an unknown man.

On Appeal, the psychiatrist and the psychologist from the POC testified about their reports from 2007. From the verdict, it can be gathered that the POC experts assigned Kim a diagnosis on both Axis I and Axis II:

> The examinee is suffering from Borderline Personality Disorder with avoidant features. She has a vulnerable personality structure with limited psychological resources in which negative feelings and impulses are kept from conscious experience. Nevertheless, she experiences a diffuse sense of restlessness, depression and gnawing emptiness (borderline traits) that she labels herself as depression. She has a very weak identity and there are problems in aggression regulation. By superficial consent and avoiding conflict, she tries to cope (avoidant traits). Based on the test material, it is reasonable to assume that she is suffering from complex Posttraumatic Stress Disorder (PTSD), which developed from an early age and has not been integrated and processed. Finally, there is abuse of cocaine, which matches the personality.

These experts also provided an explanation for the supposed relationship between Kim's mental disorder and the alleged offense, as stated in the Court of Appeal's verdict:

> If the alleged facts are proven, the explanation for this can be thought of primarily as a combination of chronic overload [. . .], a state of depersonalization (probably also related to the borderline personality features) and cocaine use. In this condition, it is likely that relatively small internal stimuli or frustrations or seemingly minor external causes (e.g., a crying child) can have very serious consequences, one should think particularly of a decreased level of consciousness associated with a breakthrough of impulses.

The experts make one reservation: "The cocaine use does not explain the gravity and timing of the examinee's explosion of violence towards her children, which also cannot—at least not entirely—be accounted for by her personality disorder." Still, they end their report with the conclusion that Kim had diminished responsibility for the alleged offense and they recommend the court to sentence her to a TBS-order with mandatory treatment (see Chapter 1), because of a serious risk of recurrence of a violent crime. As explained previously, the Court of Appeal did not hear the other experts (de Ruiter, de Man, Merckelbach). In the verdict it is stated as follows:

> Unlike the defense argued, the court sees no reason to doubt the quality
> of the evaluation and the accuracy of the contents of the report as well as
> the explanation given by the experts from the POC at the trial. The findings
> of the experts De Ruiter, De Man and Merckelbach have not led the court
> to a different judgment.

In the end Kim is sentenced to 4 years' imprisonment and mental health treatment under the TBS-order.

Epilogue

At present, Kim V. is staying in one of two Dutch forensic psychiatric hospitals that admit women. She still claims she is innocent (personal communication, Dr. V. de Vogel, May 14, 2012). This poses a problem for the hospital staff, because all patients receive therapy, which focuses on their individual risk factors for reoffending by means of the so-called offense scenario and development of a relapse prevention plan (Greeven & de Ruiter, 2004).

One aspect that has not been discussed yet is the role the media played in Kim V.'s case. Already on the day the children were found dead, the media were reporting this as a case of a "family drama." Like the police investigators, the media seemed to have assumed from the very beginning that Kim, as the mother of the children, was the culprit. It is well known that highly publicized crimes increase pressures on police to "solve the case," thus stimulating tunnel vision (Findley, 2012). In the fall of 2009, before the case came before the Appellate Court, Kim and her parents decided to seek media publicity. Crime reporter Peter R. de Vries obtained parts of the video footage from the "Bond interrogation" from Kim's legal counsel, and spent an hour analyzing the case in his TV show.[11] Kim was interviewed while walking along the beach and repeated her Benny story. Peter de Vries is well known for his "tough-on-crime" attitude. He presented some excerpts from Kim's statements to the police which, placed out of context, could easily have led the uninformed television viewer to believe she was guilty after all. Obviously, "framing" is a craft the media is quite good at. Kim and her family were displeased with the crime reporter's program because his take on the case led to only one conclusion: that Kim had taken cocaine and lost it. My guess is that this media adventure did Kim's case more harm than good. After the case was tried at the Court of Appeal her legal counsel, Esther Vroegh, reiterated Kim's statement in court on camera before the regional TV station North-Holland: that she was innocent and that the alternative scenario with Benny as the possible culprit was never pursued.[12]

After the conviction in the appeal phase, Kim's legal counsel appealed at the Supreme Court of The Netherlands. This appeal process is limited to procedural rather than factual errors in a case. On October 11, 2011, the Supreme Court[13] ruled that the verdict of the Appellate Court should be upheld, with one minor amendment, that is a lessening of the sentence by 2 months, because the Court had exceeded the so-called reasonable time period before arriving at the verdict.

I am not reassured that no miscarriage of justice was committed in this case. All the necessary ingredients for tunnel vision seemed present; the technical forensic evidence was of limited quality; and the possible false confession was the main piece of evidence used by the Court of Appeal. Moreover, the forensic mental health evaluation by the experts from the POC was biased towards a presumption of guilt.

Notes

1 The names of Kim's children are fictitious. The name of Kim is not fictitious because her legal counsel Esther Vroegh previously published on the case and consistency in terms of names avoids confusion. Moreover, documentary maker Michiel van Erp made a film on Kim's case in the series *Murder stories*, see www.how2ask.nl/2011/12/moord verhalen-over-de-kindermoorden-in-purmerend/.

2 This conversation is translated literally from the police file (pp. 21-22, definitive file investigation 'Dokter', file number 06-001911, Police region Zaanstreek-Waterland).

3 The Dutch caution entails informing the accused that he/she has the right to remain silent. Thus, it serves the same purpose as Miranda rights warnings in the US, but is less comprehensive (see van Koppen & Penrod, 2003).

4 This is in fact not true; in the final verdict of the Court of Appeal in Kim's case, it is explicitly stated that there were no traces of blood with DNA of her children under her fingernails.

5 See http://nl.wikipedia.org/wiki/Puttense_moordzaak for a brief summary of this case.

6 www.human.nl/inapost/ep-32979-de-nachtmerrie-van-ina-post.

7 See www.nrc.nl/nieuws/2012/06/05/bredase-moordzaak-leidt-tot-grootste-gerechtelijke-dwaling-in-nederland-ooit/ [Breda murder case leads to largest wrongful conviction ever in The Netherlands].

8 Note that in Kim's case, the police confronted her with the fingerprints found on the knife, but this finding seems quite innocent since the knife came from her own kitchen.

9 Downloadable via www.rechtspraak.nl.

10 As stated on p. 2 of Dr. Horselenberg's report to the court.

11 See www.misdaadjournalist.nl/2009/11/zondag-22-11-de/. Peter R. de Vries ended his crime reporter TV-shows (July 2012).

12 www.rtvnh.nl/nieuws/38284/Opnieuw+8+jaar+in+zaak-kindermoord.

13 www.dichtbij.nl/waterland/regio/artikel/2163378/celstraf-kim-v-voor-kindermoord-definitief.aspx.

References

Asch, S. E. (1956). Studies of independence and conformity: A minority of one against a unanimous majority. *Psychological Monographs, 70,* 1–70. doi: 10.1037/h0093718.

Cutler, B. L. (Ed.) (2012). *Conviction of the innocent: Lessons from psychological research.* Washington, DC: American Psychological Association.

Drizin, S. A. & Leo, R. A. (2004). The problems of false confessions in the post-DNA world. *North Carolina Law Review, 82,* 891–1007.

Findley, K. A. (2012). Tunnel vision. In B. L. Cutler (Ed.), *Conviction of the innocent: Lessons from psychological research* (pp. 303–323). Washington, DC: American Psychological Association.

Findley, K. A. & Scott, M. S. (2006). The multiple dimensions of tunnel vision in criminal cases. *Wisconsin Law Review, 291*, 291–397.

Friedman, A. F., Lewak, R., Nichols, D. S., & Webb, J. T. (2001). *Psychological assessment with the MMPI-2*. Mahwah, NJ: Lawrence Erlbaum Associates.

Garrett, B. (2008). Judging innocence. *Columbia Law Review, 108*, 55–142.

Garrido, E., Masip, J., & Herrero, C. (2004). Police officers' credibility judgments: Accuracy and estimated ability. *International Journal of Psychology, 39*, 254–275. doi: 10.1080/00207590344000411.

Gilbert, D. T., Pelham, B. W., & Krull, D. S. (1988). On cognitive busyness: When person perceivers meet person perceived. *Journal of Personality and Social Psychology, 54*, 733–744.

Graham, J. R., Butcher, J. N., & McNulty, J. L. (1997). Empirical correlates of low scores on MMPI-2 scales in an outpatient mental health setting. *Psychological Assessment, 9*, 386–391. doi: 10.1037/1040–3590.9.4.386.

Greeven, P. G. J. & de Ruiter, C. (2004). Personality disorders in a Dutch forensic psychiatric sample: Changes with treatment. *Criminal Behaviour and Mental Health, 14*, 280–290. doi: 10.1002/cbm.594.

Gudjonsson, G. H. (2003). *The psychology of interrogations and confessions: A handbook*. New York: Wiley.

Hasel, L. E. & Kassin, S. M. (2012). False confessions. In B. L. Cutler (Ed.), *Conviction of the innocent: Lessons from psychological research* (pp. 53–77). Washington, DC: American Psychological Association.

Herrnstein, R. J., Rachlin, H., & Laibson, D. I. (1997). *The matching law: Papers in psychology and economics*. New York: Russell Sage.

Horselenberg, R., Merckelbach, H. L. G. J., & Josephs, S. (2003). Individual differences and false confessions: A conceptual replication of Kassin and Kiechel. *Psychology, Crime & Law, 9*, 1–8. doi: 10.1080/10683160308141.

Horselenberg, R., Merckelbach, H., Smeets, T., Franssens, D., Peters, G.-J., & Zeles, G. (2006). False confessions in the lab: Do plausibility and consequences matter? *Psychology, Crime & Law, 12*, 61–75. doi: 10.1080/1068310042000303076.

Israëls, H. (2004). *De bekentenissen van Ina Post* [The confessions of Ina Post]. Alphen aan den Rijn, The Netherlands: Kluwer.

Kassin, S. M., Drizin, S. A., Grisso, T., Gudjonsson, G. H., Leo, R. A., & Redlich, A. D. (2010). Police-induced confessions: Risk factors and recommendations. *Law and Human Behavior, 34*, 49–52. doi: 10.1007/s10979–009–9188–6.

Kassin, S. M. & Gudjonsson, G. H. (2004). The psychology of confession evidence: A review of the literature and issues. *Psychological Science in the Public Interest, 5*, 33–67.

Kassin, S. M. & Kiechel, K. L. (1996). The social psychology of false confessions: Compliance, internalization, and confabulation. *Psychological Science, 7*, 125-128. doi: 10.1111/j.1467–9280.1996.tb00344.x.

Kassin, S. M. & Neumann, K. (1997). On the power of confession evidence: An experimental test of the fundamental difference hypothesis. *Law and Human Behavior, 21*, 469–483. doi: 10.1023/A:1024871622490.

van Koppen, P. J. & Penrod, S. D. (2003). Adversarial or inquisitorial: Comparing systems. In P. J. van Koppen & S. D. Penrod (Eds.), *Adversarial versus inquisitorial justice:*

Psychological perspectives on criminal justice systems (pp. 1–19). New York: Kluwer Academic/Plenum.

Leach, A-M., Talwar, V., Lee, K., Bala, N. C., & Lindsay, R. C. L. (2004). "Intuitive" lie detection of children's deception by law enforcement officials and university students. *Law and Human Behavior, 28*, 661–685. doi: 10.1007/s10979–004-0793–0.

Loftus, E. F. (2005). Planting misinformation in the human mind: A 30-year investigation of the malleability of memory. *Learning & Memory, 12*, 361–366. doi: 10.1101/lm.94705.

Martin, D. L. (2002). Lessons about justice from the "laboratory of wrongful convictions": Tunnel conviction, the construction of guilt and informer evidence. *University of Missouri-Kansas City Law Review, 70*, 847–864.

Meissner, C. A. & Kassin, S. M. (2002). "He's guilty": Investigator bias in judgments of truth and deception. *Law and Human Behavior, 26*, 469–480. doi: 10.1023/A: 1020278620751.

Redlich, A. D. (2007). Double jeopardy in the interrogation room: Young age and mental illness. *American Psychologist, 62*, 609–611. doi: 10.1037/0003–066X62.6.611.

Ross, L. (1977). The intuitive psychologist and his shortcomings: Distortions in the attribution process. In L. Berkowitz (Ed.), *Advances in experimental social psychology* (Vol. 10, pp. 173–220). New York: Academic Press.

de Ruiter, C. (2007). Een dubieuze gedragskundige rapportage bij een ontkennende verdachte. De casus van de Anjummer pensionmoorden [A dubious mental health report of a denying suspect: The case of the Anjum hostel murders]. *Proces: Tijdschrift voor Strafrechtspleging, 86*, 136–145.

Russano, M. B., Meissner, C. A., Narchet, F. M., & Kassin, S. M. (2005). Investigating true and false confessions within a novel experimental paradigm. *Psychological Science, 16*, 481–486. doi: 10.1111/j.0956–7976.2005.01560.x.

Vrij, A., Mann, S., Kristen, S., & Fisher, R. P. (2007). Cues to deception and ability to detect lies as a function of police interview styles. *Law and Human Behavior, 31*, 499–518. doi: 10.1007/s10979–006–9066–4.

7

DOMESTIC VIOLENCE

Evaluating the Effects of Intimate Partner Battering

Nancy Kaser-Boyd

Rosa, a 28-year-old woman of Hispanic ethnicity,[1] was charged with capital murder. The charges resulted from the death of her niece. The criminal complaint listed multiple charges, including torture.

The defendant and her husband were the parents of five biological children, and they had taken in the niece, who was 4 years old, after the child was removed from the defendant's sister by the Dependency Court, with allegations of drug addiction. After approximately 4 months in Rosa's home, the child was found with multiple injuries that indicated a history of severe physical punishments, which resulted in the charge of torture. The child died from her injuries, and there was no indication that the couple sought any medical care for the child while she lay dying. Rosa was charged with first-degree murder, and also "aiding and abetting" murder and felony-murder. In the United States, a person can be charged with murder if the intent to commit the felony, which led to the death, can be shown. If a jury failed to convict her of murder charges, or of felony child endangering, they could also consider a charge of "failure to protect" the child. Rosa's husband was charged with capital murder as well.

When questioned by the police, Rosa and her husband gave conflicting stories. Each claimed that they had been battered by the other, and that they had not sought help for the child, or stopped the horrible abuse, because they were afraid of the other adult. The husband claimed that he was a battered man, and presented witnesses who described Rosa as the dominant partner and as an aggressive person. Rosa stuck to her claim that her husband had been abusive to her and she was afraid of him. When she was told that he had implicated her in his statement to the police, she became angry and blamed him for the serious injuries that led to the child's death. Rosa's defense attorney presented a report from a psychologist that concluded that she was a battered woman.

The prosecution wanted a second opinion, and the judge permitted a reevaluation of Rosa. In the United States, in most jurisdictions, if a defendant puts her mental state at issue in a defense, the prosecution has the right to have its own expert conduct an evaluation. This evaluation was therefore conducted for the prosecution.

In the United States, Battered Woman Syndrome (BWS) is now, for several reasons, referred to as the effects of Intimate Partner Battering.[2] In 1996, a report by the US Department of Health and Human Services (Tjaden & Thoennes, 2000), resulting from a survey of judges and attorneys, concluded that the term Battered Woman Syndrome did not adequately reflect the breadth or nature of the empirical knowledge about battering and its effects, and that it portrayed a stereotypical image of battered women as helpless, passive, or psychologically impaired, and battering relationships as matching a single pattern. As a result, the more widely used term now is Intimate Partner Battering (IPB), and the psychological symptoms that appear to come from IPB are called the effects of Intimate Partner Battering. Also, it is important to acknowledge that men can be battered as well, although statistically this is not as common. The term Intimate Partner Battering makes the syndrome more gender-neutral. Many mental health professionals and lawyers still use the term Battered Woman Syndrome and it conveys a certain constellation of clinical and social features of individuals who are abused in relationships. When it is used in this chapter, the reader should bear in mind that men who are abused by a partner can have the same or similar features and effects. Battered Woman Syndrome can be read as Battered Person Syndrome, or as the effects of Intimate Partner Battering/Violence.

In this case, the prosecutor asked the following questions about this female defendant:

(1) Can Battered Woman Syndrome/IPB be malingered or exaggerated?
(2) Does Rosa have Battered Woman Syndrome/IPB?
(3) Does she have any other mental disorder?
(4) Is "learned helplessness" a given in Battered Woman Syndrome/IPB?
(5) Would such "learned helplessness" or any other aspects of Battered Woman Syndrome/IPB explain a woman's failure to stop extreme violence on a child?
(6) Would Battered Woman Syndrome/IPB explain the defendant's confession, wherein she blamed her husband for the violent acts that led to the child's death and admitted she had committed some abusive acts?

Battered Woman Syndrome/Intimate Partner Battering

Battered Woman Syndrome or Intimate Partner Battering is a broad term for a variety of types of abuse including physical beating, sexual abuse and coercion, and emotional abuse. Battering and its effects were first described in the 1970s by Pizzy (1974), working in the UK, and Martin (1976) and Walker (1979), working in the US. The literature in the beginning consisted of clinical descriptions of intimate partner violence and its impact on the battered woman. Research literature on the topic mushroomed, and the clinical and research literature was considered scientifically credible as early as 1983 (*Hawthorne v. State of Florida*, Amicus Brief, 1983). Follingstad (2003, 2009) has summarized the legal history of Battered Woman Syndrome/IPB and its applications to legal cases. The following is an integration of the author's clinical experiences, hundreds of interviews with battered women, and many research studies, including the author's previous work on BWS/IPB (Kaser-Boyd, 2004).

There is some debate in the literature about whether intimate partner violence is committed mostly by men or is gender symmetrical (Straus, 2010). This can be explained by very different methods of collecting data (Winstok, 2011). Studies which conclude that interpartner violence is roughly symmetrical tend to be the result of voluntary samples from the general population, where there is a rate of non-response of questionnaires of up to 40 percent. In contrast, studies which conclude that intimate partner violence is largely male-perpetrated draw from service samples such as law enforcement, courts, hospitals, and shelters (Winstok, 2011). However, there is no argument about the fact that injuries resulting from violence are more common in women (Archer, 2000). Interviews with thousands of people (mostly women) who have been subjected to IPB, published and described in peer-reviewed journals, document that such women are subjected to: (1) physical and sexual assaults; (2) psychological manipulation and verbal threat and abuse; (3) economic deprivation; (4) coerced social isolation; (5) physical or sexual abuse of children and abuse of pets; and (6) destruction of valued property. Since this forensic case asks whether the female defendant has the effects of Intimate Partner Battering, this chapter will focus on the effects of IPB in women.

The World Health Organization studied data about domestic violence against women in ten countries (Bangladesh, Brazil, Ethiopia, Japan, Namibia, Peru, Samoa, Serbia, Thailand, and Tanzania) and found the proportion of women who had ever suffered physical violence by a male intimate partner ranged from 13 percent in Japan to 61 percent in Peru, with most sites falling between 23 percent and 49 percent. The prevalence of severe physical violence (a woman hit with a fist, kicked, dragged, choked, burnt, threatened with a weapon, or attacked with a weapon) ranged from 4 percent in Japan to 49 percent in Peru. The vast majority of women physically abused by partners experience acts of violence more than once (Garcia-Moreno, Jansen, Ellsbert, Heise, & Watts, 2005). A national survey in America of the prevalence of domestic violence found that 22.1 percent of women compared with 7.5 percent of surveyed men reported they were physically assaulted by a current or former spouse, cohabiting partner, boyfriend or girlfriend, or date, in their lifetime. Approximately 1.3 million women and 835,000 men reported an assault by an intimate partner in a calendar year (Tjaden & Thoennes, 2000).

Male violence against women takes many forms. Violent men use verbal threats, including threats to repeat past acts, threats to harm the woman's family, pets, or children. They isolate their partner and use mental manipulation to make the woman feel powerless and worthless. They coerce the woman into acts and behaviors they wouldn't ordinarily do and blame the woman for causing bad things to happen. They manipulate the woman's psychological weaknesses. A batterer at the more extreme end of pathology is intimidating, controlling, and frightening.

To understand IPB, it is important to understand the dynamics of a person who engages in intimate partner violence. The earliest studies of batterers indicated that they came from homes where the male role model(s) used violence in family disputes and had little regard for women's needs or rights. The earliest literature on batterers consisted of clinical studies which described batterers in terms of common features. Batterers were described as controlling, jealous, angry, blaming, suspicious, and markedly self-centered. They were said to have poor tolerance for frustration of their needs, and poor empathy for the distress they caused in others. Some batterers seemed to enjoy the suffering of others. For some, physical and psychological abuse appeared to compensate for inferiority feelings. For others, the suffering of a partner appeared to be sexually exciting; batterers with this sadistic response are among the most disturbed and dangerous. A number of studies now indicate that batterers are not all the same and can be classified into subtypes. Holtzworth-Munroe and Stuart (1994) examined existing male batterer typologies to determine the subtypes that consistently appear across typological models and to identify underlying descriptive dimensions, including (a) severity and frequency of spousal physical violence, (b) generality of violence, that is family vs. extrafamilial violence, and (c) the batterer's psychopathology or personality disorder. On the basis of this review, they suggested three major subtypes of batters, which were labeled family only, dysphoric/borderline, and generally violent/antisocial. In a more recent study, Thijssen and de Ruiter (2011) examined 146 cases of individuals (mostly men) arrested for spousal assault but not yet convicted. Using the Brief Spousal Assault Form for the Evaluation of Risk (B-SAFER; (Kropp, Hart, & Belfrage, 2005), they identified four subtypes of interpartner assaulters: family only, generally violent/antisocial, low-level antisocial, and psychopathology.

Living in a violent relationship creates strong emotions, such as fear, helplessness, anger, or intense ambivalence. Intimate partner battering may be responded to with extreme methods of coping (such as avoidance, denial, emotional numbing, and/or substance abuse). These may be difficult for the layperson to understand. IPB creates a distinct set of behavioral (i.e., observable) and psychological (i.e., less observable) effects or symptoms (Campbell, 2002; Golding, 1999; Kaser-Boyd, 2004; Silva, McFarlane, Socken, Parker, & Reel, 1997).

Regarding observable behavior, battered women have been shown to hide or minimize the symptoms, fail to follow through on criminal charges, leave and return to the relationship, become passive or immobilized, develop low self-esteem, become chronically depressed, and so on. These responses are observed in women from a variety of backgrounds. Symptoms not readily observable by a layperson embody the biological and psychological changes associated with trauma and include symptoms such as: heightened sense of threat, hyperarousal and hypervigilance, (re)experiencing intense emotions of fear and vulnerability, as well as emotional numbing, denial, and dissociation (Silva et al., 1997). Individuals who are chronically fearful and who have developed other effects of battering often "self-medicate" with drugs or alcohol, which facilitates numbness (Kilpatrick, Acierno, Resnick, Saunders, & Best, 1997). Individuals who have suffered IPB often have a number of physical symptoms related to chronic stress, such as migraine headaches, lower back pain, chronic fatigue, or irritable bowels (Campbell, 2002; Koss, Koss, & Woodruff, 1991). The high levels of anxiety and the unpredictable quality of their lives is associated with chronic fatigue and with impaired immune system function (Campbell, 2002).

Some of the effects of IPB are often misunderstood and require further explanation. Battered women are frequently reported to deny the violence and coercion to which they are subjected. Denial consists of denying the battering or recanting the report made at the time of the battering. Battered women deny the abuse to others, including family and friends, police, the court, and sometimes their treatment providers or lawyers. Denial is also a psychological defense mechanism that is at least partly unconscious, and it protects the person from the painful reality of their situation. Denial is one of the Posttraumatic Stress Disorder "avoidance" symptoms—that is, in the time between domestic violence incidents, a battered woman may use denial to avoid painful reminders and emotionally "constrict" so that she can function. Battered women, when interviewed, use words like "I just tried not to think about it," "I wanted to believe it would never happen again," or "I just blocked it out of my mind." The blocking or numbing may be so extreme that the memories and feelings are "dissociated" or split off from conscious awareness. Experts in trauma and dissociation explain this as the development of a separate trauma-based memory, stored in a different part of the brain (Brewin, 2005; Brown, Scheflin, & Hammond, 1998; LeDoux, 1996).

When "blocking" occurs, memory of the traumatic event might be poor. Women subjected to IPB report that they worked hard to "forget" painful memories. This is a universal phenomenon for women and men who have experienced trauma. It protects the trauma survivor from being constantly flooded with painful memories and the anxiety and fear that are associated with them. Having a poor memory and a wish to avoid remembering may make interviews (police interviews, lawyer interviews, forensic clinical interviews) challenging. Time sequences may be unclear and history becomes fragmented.

The effects of IPB are not accessible via a simple checklist. A battered woman can have some but not all of the effects or symptoms, and she may also be so emotionally constricted that the effects of the battering are hidden. The more extreme the physical and psychological abuse, the more severe the effects of battering (Golding, 1999; Silva et al., 1997). This means more fear and hyper-vigilance to threat, more desperation and helplessness, more exhaustion, and more extreme psychological defense mechanisms. There may be other symptoms or behaviors not discussed here that are unique to the violence a woman has endured. For example, a woman subjected to repetitive sexual abuse in the context of a violent relationship may experience shame and reluctance to disclose. She may have tell-tale gynecological symptoms.

Does Rosa show the commonly reported effects of IPB? How can these be measured? With such a substantial potential for reducing her culpability for the child's death, could she be malingering the effects of IPB? How should this question be addressed?

Admissibility in Court

In the early 1970s in the US, there was no automatic admissibility of expert testimony on spousal battering and its effects. To mount a self-defense claim, a battered woman had to fit herself into a legal standard that was more suited to men because the classic example of self-defense was two men in a bar fight. A battered woman, attacked by the man she lived with, faced numerous myths about battered women, such as "She could have just left." Thus began the move by battered women's advocates to seek admission of expert testimony about battered women that dispelled myths and described the impact of interpartner violence on women's psychological functioning. In most states, a trial in which BWS was offered as a defense included a pretrial hearing, called a Kelly-Frye hearing, to determine whether BWS was "beyond the ken" of the jury, i.e., whether it was beyond their knowledge and beyond common sense, and also whether the content of the testimony reflected the current state of science. By the mid-1990s one-third of the states in America had explicitly noted that testimony about battering and its effects was admissible to rebut common myths and misconceptions about battered women (Hempel, 2004; Parrish, 1996). Such testimony might include the following points, depending on the relevance to the case:

- why a battered woman might lie about the existence of the abuse, or use denial when questioned by others;
- why she may be unable to leave the relationship;
- why she may not call the police to report abuse, or seek medical care for her injuries;
- why she may self-medicate with alcohol or drugs;
- why she may be angry, assaultive, or have poor emotional control;
- why she may be afraid of Child Protective Services;
- why she may have a poor memory of events, or be cognitively scattered or tangential.

In California, the legislature adopted Evidence Code (EC) Section 1107 in 1994. EC 1107 makes expert testimony regarding intimate partner battering and its effects, including the nature and effect of physical, emotional, or sexual abuse on the beliefs, perceptions, or behavior of victims, admissible in a criminal action to the extent that its relevance is established. Such evidence originally was recognized as potentially relevant in a murder case to a claim of self-defense. However, it can be applied as a defense to failure to protect a child or to a charge of aiding and abetting the murder of a child. California law holds that a parent has a duty to protect his or her young child and may be criminally culpable as an aider and abettor for an assault causing death, and on an implied malice theory for (second degree) murder where the parent fails to take reasonably necessary steps for the child's protection (*People v. Rolon*, 2008). The parent must have intended to aid the perpetrator of the crime; however, intent can be assumed from presence at the scene, the duty to protect, and the failure to do so. In *People v. Rolon*, in trial court, evidence was presented that the defendant did not cry out, ask a neighbor for help, call 911, or do anything else to prevent the violence against her 1-year-old child. Evidence regarding a history of battering by the co-defendant could have explained why she did little to oppose him. Generally, a battered woman has to provide evidence of a level of violence and fear that immobilized her.

For a detailed comparison between the United States and The Netherlands of the admissibility and acceptability of expert testimony on BWS/IPB, see Römkens (2001). Römkens notes that in the United States, in trials of women who kill an abuser, knowledge about battering and its effects is allowed in some form in most states, whereas in Dutch criminal legal practice and doctrine, battered women are not yet the subject of a specific and elaborate psycholegal discourse or doctrine. Abuse is usually addressed in the context of existing criminal law doctrine (i.e., self-defense, insanity, or diminished responsibility).

Battered Women and Abused Children

When a child is abused in a home with interpartner violence, is the abuse more likely to come from the man or the woman? This would become a critical question in this case. It is clear that some abused children are in homes where the mother is being battered (Edelson, 1999). Ross (1996) analyzed data from a 1985 survey of 6,000 American families and found that 22.8 percent of men who had battered their partner had also battered their child. Of women who were physically violent in the relationship, 23.9 percent had battered their child. Walker (1984), in a study of 400 women, reported that 53 percent of the batterers also physically abused the children, and 28 percent of the battered women admitted abusing their children. It seems that children are at risk of abuse by either parent.

Most families involved in child fatalities were two-person caretaker situations where the majority of the perpetrators were the father of the child or the boyfriend of the mother (Pecora, Whittaker, Maluccio, Barth, & Plotnick, 1992).

One large study, the Oregon Child Fatality Project, reported that domestic violence was present in 41 percent of the families experiencing critical injuries or deaths due to child abuse and neglect. This study found that abuse-related child fatalities were most often committed by male perpetrators (Oregon Children's Services Division, 1993). Stiffman, Schnitzer, and Adam (2002) found that children living in a household with an unrelated adult were 27 times more likely to die of inflicted injury than children living with one or two biological parents.

One study, in particular, addressed the dynamics involved when a battered woman abuses a child (Coohey, 2004). A case-control design was used to compare two groups of women who battered their children (battered women, $N = 53$, and non-battered women, $N = 41$) with two groups of mothers who did not physically abuse their children (battered women, $N = 33$, and non-battered women, $N = 57$). The purpose of the study was to understand why some battered women physically abuse their children and some do not. The study examined the woman's relationship with her own parents. More important than the experience of having been battered by their husband was having been abused by their own mother (Odds Ratio = 16.70). Having been severely assaulted by her mother and rating her mother as critical both substantially increased the odds that the mother would be both battered herself and physically abuse her children (Odds Ratio = 19.01), and mothers who were severely assaulted by their own mothers tended to physically abuse their children regardless of whether they were battered by their partner.

Substance abuse is a clear risk factor for child maltreatment (Wells, 2009). Children whose parents were abusing substances were found to be 2.7 times more likely to be abused than children whose parents were not substance abusers (Health and Human Services, 1996; Kelleher, Chaffin, & Hollenberg, 1994). Substance abuse was one of the two leading problems exhibited by families reported for child maltreatment, with poverty being the other most frequently reported (Wang & Harding, 1999). Substance abuse by caregivers is associated with as many as two-thirds of all cases of child maltreatment fatalities (Reid, Macchetto, & Foster, 1999). Many substances of abuse make adult caregivers violent, paranoid, and angry, creating a situation where the caregiver is more prone to injure or neglect their children (Bays, 1990).

The Psycholegal Issues

A finding that Rosa was a battered woman with Battered Woman Syndrome (or the effects of Intimate Partner Battering) is legally relevant to the accusation that she failed to protect her young niece as well as the charge of aiding and abetting the child's death. It might also be applied to the "intent" required for criminal conviction, i.e., if she was abusing the child, did she have the intent to kill? Would her own psychological suffering and other effects of IPB have caused her to be unable to form the necessary intent for a conviction of first-degree murder?[3]

To address the "failure to protect" charge, Rosa would need more than BWS, but a level of violence from her husband that caused her to be extremely fearful of him, actually immobilized by fear. In other words, there are two steps to addressing the psycholegal issues: (1) was Rosa a battered woman suffering from the effects of Intimate Partner Battering?; (2) was she battered to such an extent that she was immobilized by fear and unable to take action to protect the child? If Rosa was shown to be the adult who abused the child, at a level of severity to cause death, a presentation of the effects of IPB or abuse as a child would not likely be helpful in the trial in chief, where a defendant can be convicted of murder under the felony murder rule, that is, that they had the intent to commit the underlying felony (child abuse). It might be presented as mitigation in a penalty phase.

The Forensic Mental Health Assessment

The FMHA begins from a position of objectivity (Heilbrun, 2001). This means, among other things, examining the case from several different perspectives. To begin with, the evaluator retained by the prosecution would ask questions raised by the prosecutor, but she would also ask questions raised by the defense. An evaluation about Intimate Partner Battering requires expertise in interviewing victims and considerable knowledge about the effects of IPB. Some of the effects of IPB defy logic; for example, why wouldn't a battered woman remember each and every time she was beaten? Why wouldn't she try to flee or call the police? How could she be immobilized when her own life was threatened? In cases like the present, it would also be important to learn about what type of information is widely available to the average person, through television or the Internet, and what symptoms are less well known. This information would be important in the evaluation of malingering IPB.

Heilbrun, Grisso, and Goldstein (2009) outline the basic principles of an FMHA. In practice, the formal FMHA always begins with a review of background documents. These are fundamental to forming questions for the clinical interviews because they provide perspectives other than the battered woman's and alert the evaluator to facts that may be presented in court. Background materials may include the following:

- any videotapes or audiotapes that were collected at the time of the investigation;
- statements of the defendant to investigators;
- witness statements;
- photographs of the crime scene;
- the autopsy report and other reports of the physical evidence;
- preliminary hearing transcripts;
- police reports from past incidents of domestic violence;
- mental health records, if any;

- any other pertinent health records;
- diaries, journals, or letters that reveal the client's mental state or the nature of the relationship;
- any correspondence received from the partner after arrest.

The forensic clinical interview incorporates facts from the various collateral sources, and utilizes these to take perspective on the defendant's account and to formulate questions. An FMHA with a battered woman, or any person with a possible post-trauma disorder, requires training and clinical experience with trauma survivors. A defendant who has this syndrome may present in unexpected ways. A severely traumatized woman may be unable to provide history in a logical, coherent fashion. Memory difficulties in traumatized individuals have been well documented in the literature (e.g., Brown, Scheflin, & Hammond, 1998; Schacter, 1996; Vasterling & Brewin, 2005). Alternatively, the emotional constriction, avoidance, and numbing of Posttraumatic Stress Disorder (PTSD) may cause the defendant to avoid discussing traumatic incidents or experiences that were particularly shameful or terrifying. One woman seen by the author who had assaulted her boyfriend with a baseball bat was interviewed for over 30 hours before she disclosed that her boyfriend had been sodomizing her. Memory difficulties, avoidance, and the fragmentation that sometimes comes with trauma may leave the individual mentally fragmented, making their statements jumbled and confusing.

It is unusual, however, for a battered person to be *unable*, with encouragement and support, to provide detailed accounts of specific violent incidents, or threats of violence. Typically these are accompanied by the intense emotion that comes with traumatic experiences. A victim of IPB can be calm and controlled when discussing neutral aspects of her history, then begin to sob and tremble as traumatic incidents are discussed. In clinical terms, when interviewed about traumatic incidents, she may be re-experiencing them, including the overwhelming feelings of fear she had at those times.

Skeptics point out that it can be relatively easy to claim that one has been battered and was afraid. This case is a clear example, since both Rosa and her husband made this claim. Can the effects of Intimate Partner Battering (IPB) be faked? In the author's experience, having interviewed over 1,000 battered women, as well as some women faking IPB, individuals "faking" trauma syndromes are not able to generate the detailed account of traumatic incidents, nor the distraught emotion that accompanies them (Kaser-Boyd, 1995). Their accounts are vague and don't become richer when support is provided for the telling of upsetting details. Despite beliefs to the contrary, there is no single method or instrument that is universally recognized as being the best tool to detect malingering in PTSD claimants (Guriel & Fremouw, 2003).

FMHA often includes psychological testing. The tests chosen for the battery should meet psychometric standards for reliability and validity and should have published research on the diagnostic group(s) in question (Heilbrun et al., 2009). They should also be able to rule out malingering. One test that has been proven particularly useful with battered women is the Millon Clinical Multiaxial Inventory (MCMI; Kaser-Boyd, 2004; Millon, 2009). The MCMI (now in its third edition, Millon, 2009) has the ability to capture some of Walker's clinical descriptions of battered women as well as the diagnostic criteria for PTSD. Collecting MCMI data on a group of consecutive non-criminal cases of battered women, I found they had significant mean elevations on the scales Avoidant, Dependent, Self-Defeating (Masochistic), and on Axis I disorders of Anxiety and Depression. I conducted a research study (Kaser-Boyd, 2001, 2004) comparing battered women with charges of neglect or abuse to children (25 Dependency Court cases) to battered women charged with murder (20 women, all of whom were charged with killing a battering partner). The control group ($N = 23$) was a sample of non-battered mothers from Dependency Court. There were no significant differences between groups in age, ethnicity, religion, or education. The two groups of battered women were significantly elevated on scales Dependent ($F = 17.55$, $p = .000$), Avoidant ($F = 23.92$, $p = .000$), and Self-Defeating ($F = 34.37$, $p = .000$) compared with the non-battered women. Battered women who had killed their batterer had a significantly greater mean elevation on the scale Schizoid ($F = 8.34$, $p = .0005$) which captures the emotional numbness and constriction that is seen in severe cases of PTSD.

Next, I examined whether "fakers" achieve the same elevations on the MCMI, and furthermore, whether "faked" profiles could be detected (Kaser-Boyd, 2001, 2004). I selected a group of graduate students in psychology—presumably a smart group of people—and instructed them about BWS and also about the MCMI. I then asked them to "complete the MCMI as if you are on trial for killing your husband and wish to present a defense of Battered Woman Syndrome." Nineteen graduate students completed the study. Their mean MCMI-II scores were computed and compared with the results of the women on trial from the prior study. The "fakers" achieved elevations on the scales previously found elevated in battered women, as well as other scales that assess acute distress and emotional instability, but their elevations were much higher than those of the real battered women. Fakers scored significantly higher than bona fide battered women on Debasement, Schizoid, Avoidant, Dependent, Self-Defeating, Borderline, Anxiety, Somatoform, Dysthymia, and Major Depression (all significant findings with p < .01).

The data were further analyzed to determine whether validity scale cut-off scores could maximize accurate classification as "battered" or "faking." The MCMI Disclosure scale was not significantly elevated in fakers. The Debasement scale, on the other hand, was significantly different between groups. A cut-off score of 85 on Debasement correctly classified 75 percent of fakers and 85 percent of battered women. A cut-off score of 92 identified the same number of fakers while improving the hit rate for battered women to 95 percent—that is, only one real battered woman was misclassified (Kaser-Boyd, 2001, 2004).

In an actual forensic case, no one should be diagnosed as a malingerer based on a single psychological test. In a typical FMHA for criminal court, I would add other instruments to the battery, i.e., those that have published research with trauma survivors, preferably battered women. There is research on battered women using the MMPI-2 (Butcher, Dahlstrom, Graham, Tellegen, & Kaemmer, 1989). Rosewater and Walker (1985) reported that battered women in their sample had elevations on scales 6 (Paranoia) and 8 (Schizophrenia). They noted that it was not surprising that women who had been battered would be fearful or feel threatened (scale 6) or that they would have some disruptions in their reality testing (scale 8) because of the destabilizing and fragmenting effect of trauma. Kahn, Welch, and Zillmer (1993) examined a group of battered women at a shelter and also found elevations on scales 6 and 8. The women also scored significantly higher on scale 4, likely because they endorsed many of the Harris-Lingoes items about family discord. Rhodes (1992) found that her sample of 46 battered women, compared with a matched control group of 46 non-battered women, showed elevations on the Harris-Lingoes subscale Pd1 Family Discord.

There are many MMPI studies with individuals who have PTSD from varying types of trauma, and these yield consistent findings on scales 2, 4, 6, 7, and 8 (Wilson & Walker, 1990). MMPI research also indicates that individuals with histories of trauma, such as battered women, may score elevated on the F and Fback scales which measure the endorsement of rare symptoms (Rogers, Sewell, Martin, & Vitacco, 2003).

The author has also used the Rorschach Inkblot Method to evaluate battered women. When women are tested shortly after leaving a battering relationship, they tend to deliver Rorschach protocols flooded with images of harm and danger, with formal Rorschach scores (m and Y) that suggest helplessness and a preoccupation with morbid and aggressive content (Kaser-Boyd, 2007). When time has elapsed (e.g., months or years later), Rorschach protocols tend to become more constricted (Kaser-Boyd, 2007). Battered women in the "avoidant" phase of BWS/PTSD give shorter, less complicated Rorschach records and seem to avoid the more provocative images on the blots.

Van der Kolk (1987) was one of the first to describe two phases of response to trauma—a flooded phase and a constricted phase. Psychological test results can follow a similar pattern. Thus, a battered woman in the constricted or avoidant phase of the post-trauma disorder will have a test profile with validity indicators indicating guardedness, and a relatively flat clinical profile, while in the flooded state, she will typically have a profile with a greater number of infrequent items endorsed (e.g., higher MMPI-2 F scale), and an elevated set of clinical scales. Typically, all of the tests in the battery would follow this phasic pattern—which is not the case with Rosa, as we will see.

An FMHA with a question concerning malingering might also employ the Structured Inventory of Reported Symptoms (SIRS-2; Rogers, Sewell, & Gillard,

2010). The SIRS-2 asks a series of questions about plausible and implausible symptoms, and provides a profile which classifies the individual as either similar to those individuals who report genuine symptoms or not (with three sub-classifications: interdeterminate, probably feigning, or definite feigning). Using common sense, if a defendant has already shown a pattern of malingering, such as a very elevated Fp scale on the MMPI-2, or a very high elevation on the Debasement scale of the MCMI-III, administering a SIRS-2 may be unnecessary but could be a useful measure for cross-validation. However, individuals with a history of childhood abuse and serious trauma have more complex symptoms and have been shown to score higher on the SIRS, due to their endorsements of a broad array of symptoms (Rogers et al., 2010; Rogers, Payne, Correa, Gillard, & Ross, 2009). It remains to be seen how individuals with more recent trauma histories will score on the SIRS-2.

Forensic Psychological Test Data

Rosa was evaluated in the county jail. The evaluation spanned 2 days. She was subjected to forensic clinical interviews on both days. The test battery that was chosen included the Minnesota Multiphasic Personality Inventory (MMPI-2), the Millon Clinical Multiaxial Inventory (MCMI-III) and the Rorschach. Rosa was also asked to complete the Spousal Assault Violent Acts Continuum (Kaser-Boyd, 2004), a rating scale of acts of domestic violence, and the Child Abuse Potential Inventory (CAPI; Milner, 1986).[4] The SIRS was considered for use in the case of ambiguous data about symptom-reporting on the MMPI-2 and MCMI. In reviewing the Discovery materials provided by the district attorney, I learned that the defense expert had given Rosa the MMPI-2 on two occasions. He testified that the first MMPI-2 was invalid and the defendant's "responses were characteristic of a subject who is lying." He had given the test again 18 months later and testified that the profile "reflected a high score for falsity, but not so high as to automatically invalidate the test results." It seemed important to obtain his raw data and to rescore and reinterpret the results. This is routinely done when forming an opinion on another forensic expert's data collection, to rule out scoring errors and determine whether the other expert has provided accurate interpretations (see Chapter 10 for examples of scoring and interpretation errors).

At the time of the evaluation, Rosa was 26 years old. She had attended school up to the eleventh grade. Her vocabulary, abstract thinking, and understanding of the legal issues seemed good and her intelligence appeared to be average. She did not seem intimidated by the evaluation or evaluator. She seemed comfortable making requests and verbalizing needs or feelings. She became irritable when pressed for clarifications about events surrounding the injuries to her niece and complained that the evaluator was going to make her miss her shower if the interview lasted any longer.

Rosa indicated that she was raised by her mother and stepfather, both of whom were physically abusive. Rosa said her mother "hit me a lot . . . abused me physically, emotionally." She said,

> They would both hit me with whatever they had around. They would drink and beat me. They'd take turns to beat me. My stepfather has pulled knives out on me, hit me with irons. My mom has hit me with fly swatters and branches and shoes and belts. Mainly with whatever they could get their hands on.

Rosa's description of the abuse in her childhood was corroborated by documents from the Department of Children and Family Services, which is the child protection agency in the state. They indicated that Rosa's mother would also make her stand in the hot sun, holding bricks, and Rosa at one time admitted this but denied it in the present interview. In addition to physical and verbal abuse, Rosa reported that her stepfather had sexually molested her, beginning when she was just 5 years old. When the Department of Children and Family Services was looking for a home for Rosa's niece, after they removed the child from her sister, they considered the home of Rosa's mother and stepfather, and at that time, Rosa recanted her earlier allegations of physical abuse by her mother and sexual abuse by her father. In the present interview, she said that she recanted so that her niece could stay in the family. She said her original reports of abuse were true, except for her descriptions of holding bricks. This confusing pattern of admissions and denials is sometimes seen in survivors of abuse, but it obviously raises issues about credibility.

Rosa said that she began abusing substances in the eighth grade: "smoking weed" and drinking. She said she drank up to a pint of alcohol a day. She said that she did this to "stay numb." She reported that she decreased her alcohol and drug use when she met her husband and became pregnant with their first child; however, by the time her niece died, she said that both she and her husband had been using methamphetamine. This may have contributed to the abuse of her niece, as it is well-known that substance abuse and child maltreatment are strongly related (Wells, 2009).

Rosa and her husband went on to have five children. One important issue for battered women is whether they feel they have control over their bodies, and, in particular, over conception. Many battered women report that they had no "say-so" in whether they had sexual intercourse, or used birth control (Campbell, 2002; Kaser-Boyd, 2004). Rosa volunteered that she was "not into birth control." She never maintained that her husband forced sex or interfered with using birth control. She said that she kept having children "because I felt if I gave him more children, he would love me more."

Rosa readily admitted that after the first three children, she had a brief affair with a man who came to her house while her husband was at work. She speculated that her fourth child was the product of that union, and she maintained that she had told her husband this and he accepted the child as his own. Battered women are often repeatedly accused of being unfaithful by their jealous husbands but it is quite rare for them to actually be unfaithful since they know that this often is their husband's "hot point." When asked whether she hadn't been afraid to have sex with another man, she said it happened "real quick" and "wasn't planned." Ultimately, Rosa took the bold step of having her tubes tied and she told her husband after the fact. Overall, this story did not seem characteristic of a woman who was cowed by a frightening husband.

An evaluation for BWS/IPB centers on the actual acts of physical, sexual, and emotional abuse, the injuries, and psychological effects. Asked to describe the physical abuse, Rosa said:

> He started abusing me when I was pregnant with our first child. He would start hitting me, pulling my hair, hitting me in the sides of the stomach, or on the back, and kicking me. He would kick my legs. I'd be sitting on the couch and he would kick at me.

Rosa said that what scared her was that her husband would threaten to hurt himself. She said, "If he doesn't love himself, how is he going to love my kids?" She said he sometimes would tell her that he would "hurt the ones you love." She thought he was threatening her family, and possibly their children. She was somewhat equivocal about whether he was as abusive to the children as he was to her. Asked to describe his abuse of the children, she said that on one occasion, in a rage, he kicked a toy across the room and it hit one of the children in the face. She said he would yell a lot at the children, insult them, and "tell them things like he doesn't love them." These things seemed a far cry from what was done to her niece. Rosa said that there was also sexual abuse in the relationship. She said that as the relationship wore on, "it wasn't love, it was just sex." She said, "If I didn't give him what he wanted, he was mad." However, it did not seem that this led to a battering.

The Discovery materials[5] contained interviews with several people who knew the couple. There were reports that Rosa was the more dominant partner. Both family members and acquaintances said that Rosa "ran the show." When her husband was evaluated, he said that she had attacked him with a knife on at least two occasions; on one of the occasions, he had told her he had been seeing another woman, and she became enraged. Rosa said she only recalled one incident where she picked up a knife and this was because he "was beating me and he backed me into the sink." Protective violence is seen in battered women, so her use of a knife, if feeling threatened, would not rule out the possibility that she was a battered woman.

The last time Rosa was battered, as far as she could recall, was several months prior to the death of the little girl. At the time of her arrest, she did not have physical injuries. Her own physical injuries across the relationship seemed like one measure of the severity of domestic violence. I used an injury severity scale from Walker's National Institute of Mental Heath funded study (Walker, 1984). Rosa said "no" or "I don't remember" to lost teeth, joint injury, spinal injury, permanent eye injury, broken bones, severe cuts, broken eardrums, or other permanent injury. She endorsed the following items, with the accompanying description:

-   *Concussion*: "I would be knocked out and would be on the floor and wake up and he would be over there doing something different." She was not medically examined and doesn't know whether she actually had concussion.
-   *Back injury*: Rosa said that she believes she may have permanent injuries to her head and back. She said, "I didn't have a good back anyway, and he would kick my back a lot." There were no medical records to support this complaint.
-   *Black eyes*: "I had black eyes nine or eleven times." There was no corroboration of black eyes.
-   *Bruises*: "I would have bruises on my legs, back, chest, and arms."
-   *Burns*: "He would hold the lighter at my hair, like light my hair on fire, quickly." Asked whether her hair would catch on fire, she said it didn't.
-   *Clothes ripped*: "He would cut my underwear and bras when I was wearing them and when I was not wearing them. He would rip them off of me sometimes. Sometimes when I was asleep or passed out on Crystal, he would cut my clothes off of me."
-   *Head injury*: Rosa said that her husband would hit her head against the wall and she would get blurred vision and want to throw up. She said she gets "a lot of bad headaches and gets dizzy a lot." She said she had not reported this to a doctor.
-   *Internal injuries*: Rosa said that one time her husband kicked her in the private parts and this caused her to bleed.
-   *Lost hair*: Rosa said that her husband would snatch out batches of hair. She said she never reported this to a doctor.

Next, in the interview, I reviewed a list of the things done to her niece and asked if any of these things had been done to her. She did not indicate that she or the couple's natural children had suffered any of the abusive acts done to her niece. Rosa said that she never sought medical attention for any of the injuries described above. She was never hospitalized during the relationship, other than to give birth, and she never informed any doctor she saw while delivering her children that she was being abused. There were no police calls for domestic violence to the residence. It is entirely possible that a woman can be physically, sexually, and/or emotionally abused and never report this to an outside source; this, by itself, wouldn't invalidate her claim. Rosa's husband had also never been arrested for violence of any sort, and family and acquaintances described him as a passive man.

The couple's children were interviewed after their cousin died, and they told authorities that both of their parents hit them. They said that their mother hit them with some kind of metal rod that was near the window, and also with a plastic bat. Two of the children described the abuse to their cousin, and one of these, a boy, said he believed he would be "the second one dead." Rosa denied that she physically abused her own children.

Rosa was interviewed at length about the various injuries to her niece. The medical examiner opined that these had been inflicted over an extended period of time. Some injuries were healing and some appeared fresh, such as the injuries that led to her death. There were indications that she had been burned as apparent punishment, and she had ligature marks, which indicated she had had ties around her hands. The cause of death was an immersion burn. The medical examiner opined that the little girl had been held in very hot water. He said that this was not necessarily fatal, but she went into shock and the couple did not seek medical treatment, so she died within hours of that burn. Rosa's responses to questions about the girl's injuries consisted largely of denials of her culpability. This differed from her statement to the police, where she admitted that both her and her husband engaged in some of the abusive acts, while her husband was solely responsible for holding the girl down in hot water.

Test Results

The testing began with an analysis of the MMPI-2 collected by the defense psychologist, who actually gave her the MMPI-2 twice, once shortly after she was arrested, and again because the first test was invalid. He said he could not find the original answer sheet from the first administration. The profile sheet, however, indicated that the raw score on F was 28, which is extremely elevated with a T-score of > 120, and F-K was 25. The answer sheet for the second administration was available, and I subjected it to computer scoring, which the defense expert had not done. The F scale was high again (T = 85), but not as high as at the first administration. An examination of the VRIN-scale (T = 58) ruled out problems with reading and understanding the items.[6] On the clinical scales, she showed remarkable elevations on scale 4 (T = 94), and on scale 8 (T = 87). She also had an elevated score on the PTSD scale PK (T = 75).

The computer-generated narrative (National Computer Systems, 1989) stated:

> The MMPI-2 profile should be interpreted with caution [. . .]. She omitted from 10 to 15 percent of the items on Scales TRIN, Pa, D5, Pd2, Pa1, Pa2, and DEP3. She omitted 16 to 25 percent on the items on Scales DEP2 and ASP2.

In addition:

> There is some possibility that the clinical report is an exaggerated picture of the client's present situation and problems. She is presenting an unusual number of psychological symptoms [. . .]. Her test-taking attitudes should be evaluated for the possibility that she has produced an invalid profile. She may be showing a lack of cooperation with testing, or she may be malingering by attempting to present a false claim of mental illness. She endorsed items at the end of the booklet in an extreme or exaggerated manner [. . .].

Moving to the clinical profile, the computer-generated narrative read:

> Individuals with this extreme MMPI-2 clinical profile tend to be quite disturbed psychologically. The client appears to be extremely alienated and nonconforming, with long-standing antisocial and sometimes bizarre behavioral patterns. She is quite immature and irresponsible, and she may engage in antisocial behavior or aberrant sexual practices for the thrill of it. She is likely to appear very uncooperative, hostile, and aggressive, but she denies responsibility for her behavior and tends to blame others for her problems. [. . .] She endorsed a number of extreme and bizarre thoughts, suggesting the presence of delusions and/or hallucinations.

Battered women tend to show high scores on MMPI-2 scale 4 (Pd), but when the Harris-Lingoes scales are inspected, they mostly tend to have elevations on "Family Problems," whereas Rosa's highest elevations were on "Authority Problems" and "Social Alienation." The "Authority Problems" (Pd2) scale correlates most strongly of all Pd subscales with antisocial tendencies. Since I had the original answer sheet and the print-out of "Critical Items," I questioned Rosa about some of her more surprising endorsements. In the present court-ordered forensic evaluation, she denied that she had the symptoms which she had endorsed. She said she "didn't understand" them, but she said that the defense psychologist was sitting in a cubicle near her reading the paper, and she could have asked him, but she didn't.

Perhaps the most relevant question is whether a battered woman would show the type and extent of score elevations as observed in Rosa. When battered women are tested they tend to obtain highly elevated profiles only in the early phase of their life away from the batterer. Subsequently, their profiles tend to look more constricted. The scales that are elevated are also different. The classic profile is 2–4–6–8 (Kahn et al.,1993), or 4–6–8. The overall level of elevation in battered women is not typically as high as Rosa's, particularly not on scale 4. Battered women rarely exhibit the 4–8/8–4 profile. This profile type is typically associated with individuals who have shown acts of bizarre violence. For example, Lachar (1974) offers the following interpretive narrative for the 4–8/8–4 profile:

> These are people, who, as children, acquired a set to perceive other people as hostile, rejecting, and dangerous. They also learned, however, that they could protect themselves and alleviate to some degree their painful anticipations of hurt by striking out in anger and rebellion. This pattern is continued into adulthood, the person being so rebellious and angry that their social behavior continually reinforces alienation. This is usually an aggressive, punitive individual who is most comfortable when inspiring anxiety and guilt in others. The behaviors expected range all the way from stern, punitive, cold disapproval to clinical sadism.
>
> (p. 85)

The MCMIs (MCMI-II and MCMI-III) were also very elevated. I gave the MCMI-II to allow a comparison between Rosa and my research sample on the MCMI-II with battered women. I gave her the MCMI-III so that she could be compared to the revised standardization sample. On both tests, her Debasement score was a BR of 85 or above. On the MCMI-II, her profile was more complicated than the battered women's profiles in my research. She was at BR scores of over 100 on Major Depression, Dysthymic Disorder, Anxiety Disorder, and the personality scales Self-Defeating and Dependent. Elevations this high were not seen in actual battered women but were seen in "malingerers" in the research study (Kaser-Boyd, 2001; 2004). The profile suggested that malingering was possible. On the MCMI-III, Rosa again showed a very elevated profile. She was at BR 100 or above on Major Depression and Anxiety Disorder and the personality scales Dependent and Depressive. Again, these are very high scores for confirmed battered women. She was also elevated on Posttraumatic Stress Disorder (BR 93), Dysthymic Disorder, Somatoform Disorder, and Self-Defeating Personality Disorder. Of note, the present evaluation occurred almost 3 years after Rosa's arrest. Many battered women by this time would obtain constricted MCMI profiles after the passage of time in custody. This was another way her test profile didn't concur with expectation.

It was on the Rorschach, however, that the malingering stance seemed most clear. Rosa was very guarded. Early on in the administration of the 10 cards, she rejected cards, stating that she "didn't know." I gave the standard encouraging statements, such as "Take your time, there are no wrong answers." This prompt seemed to make her angry and she retorted, "Well, I come from a disadvantaged background!" The language she used here suggested a smart, even sophisticated person. Overall, Rosa gave 16 responses (which is significantly below average), and most of them were very simple (pure Form) and Popular. This stood in marked contrast to her highly elevated responses on the MMPI-2 and MCMI-III. I began to think that she wanted to exaggerate her distress and could do so given the structure of the objective tests, but when it came to the Rorschach, she did not know how to do this, and she shut down. Her angry and oppositional behavior during the Rorschach administration was quite atypical of battered women.

When the Rorschach responses of battered women are examined (Kaser-Boyd, 2007), they are noteworthy for "breakthrough" trauma images (Armstrong & Kaser-Boyd, 2003) at various points in the record. For example, a woman who had been badly battered by her husband gave the following responses to the Rorschach:

Card II

A broken chest, somebody busted 'em in the chest, broken, bleeding. It's like this is your chest here and they hit you here in the heart, the heart exploded from the top because they hit you there, and then part of your lungs or kidneys or whatever would be down here. It would be like an x-ray of the chest where somebody just punched it and there's blood spots just where it's bruised [*Bruised?*] The color. [*Exploded?*] The burst of the fingers, but the splatter going out from it.

Card III

Two ovaries here, the hip bones, and this could possibly be the womb for a baby or something and they got hit in the stomach and busted it up. Two bloodstains coming down. Looks like they coulda been pinned against the wall and whoever had 'em there just put their hand up and then the blood was running down the wall, all the extra blood was, off their hands.

We might expect a woman who has seen a child so badly injured to report traumatic imagery in response to (some of) the cards. Rosa also did not obtain Rorschach scores associated with feelings of helplessness (m, Y), which have been well-validated as measures of anxiety and helplessness in trauma populations (Mihura, Meyer, Dumitrascu, & Bombel, 2013).[7]

The Testimony

Testimony stemming from this evaluation was presented in the rebuttal phase of Rosa's guilt phase trial.[8] When the expert witness is serving as a rebuttal witness and the defense expert has testified in depth about psychological findings, the prosecution may conduct a similarly detailed rebuttal or simply hit the most important points. In reality, jurors can become confused or exhausted with detailed and technical testimony. The prosecution used the results of the present forensic mental health evaluation to argue that: (1) the behavior and test results from this evaluation were inconsistent with those usually obtained from battered women; (2) the defendant appeared to be exaggerating her symptoms and was likely malingering Battered Woman Syndrome/IPB; and (3) the violence which Rosa reported did not approach the level of violence at which women are immobilized by fear and unable to come to the aid of a child. As an expert in interpartner violence as well as in child abuse, I testified that the type of violence suffered by Rosa at the hands of her own mother and her stepfather could have caused Post-traumatic Stress Disorder. Findings from the Coohey (2004) study were mentioned in testimony. More specifically, a childhood history of abuse by one's mother, although less proximate than other factors, such as recent life stressors, drug abuse, and a poor marital relationship, was found to exert a powerful influence on a mother's propensity to physically abuse her children regardless of whether she is battered. This meant that Rosa may have abused her niece mainly because of the way she was raised herself and the abuse may have had little to do with the nature of her marital relationship.

An expert in American courts is not allowed to state an "ultimate opinion" such as "the defendant was unable to form the intent to kill because . . . ." Once testimony about a mental state is presented to a jury, the jury must make the connection between an impaired mental state, the actual behavior, and the defendant's culpability. As Rosa's case drew to an end, the following had been established:

(1)   She may have been a badly battered child, but she had recanted several times.
(2)   She may have been battered by her husband, but evidence of exaggeration/malingering on psychological tests made it hard to trust this part of her story.

Was she an abused child who went on to become an abusive adult? Was she a battered woman who also joined in battering her niece? In the end, it appeared that Rosa's depiction of the abuse she suffered at the hands of her husband, if believed, fell far short of the horrible trauma inflicted on Rosa's niece. She was convicted of first degree murder with special circumstances (torture) and sentenced to death. Her husband's case had the same outcome.

There are, of course, other cases of child fatalities in a violent home where a battered woman was too terrified and immobilized to take action to protect an abused child. If this is paired with an absence of evidence that the woman participated willingly in the abuse, the outcome of the case might be quite different.

Notes

1   The case name has been changed.
2   See the discussion of these terms in Hempel (2004).
3   If her case proceeded to the Death Penalty phase, would she be able to show that battering and its effects mitigated her abusive conduct with her niece, or her failure to

protect the child from abuse? In a Death Penalty hearing, the level of violence could theoretically be less than that which would immobilize. In a Death Penalty hearing, her own childhood history might also be presented as mitigation for the crime.

4   The Child Abuse Potential Inventory is often used in Dependency Courts in California to evaluate violence risk to children. Standardized on several groups of parents who had been found by a court to be physically abusive to their children, it measures the childhood history, familial experiences of the assessee, her feelings about others, her stress level and self-esteem, and whether she tends to externalize blame to others. Prior to testimony, the Court in Rosa's case ruled that the CAPI results were like "profile" evidence, i.e., that she "fit the profile of an abusive parent." The judge ruled that this was inadmissible. The results are therefore not discussed here.

5   The "Discovery" is the term used to include all of the case materials "discovered" to both sides of a case.

6   Butcher, Dahlstrom, Graham, Tellegen, & Kaemmer (1989) note: "in the case of high F and low VRIN, carelessness (confusion, etc.) can be ruled out and a high F score can be interpreted in terms of actual content" (p. 28).

7   See Kaser-Boyd (2008) for a more in-depth discussion of battered women and the Rorschach.

8   In the United States, when a state has a death penalty, there are two phases of a trial: a guilt phase and a penalty phase.

References

Archer, J. (2000). Sex differences in aggression between heterosexual partners: A meta-analytic review. *Psychological Bulletin, 126,* 651–680.

Armstrong, J. & Kaser-Boyd, N. (2003). Projective assessment of trauma. In M. Hilsenroth & D. Segal (Eds.), *Objective and projective assessment of personality and psychopathology* (pp. 500–512). New York: Wiley.

Bays, J. (1990). Substance abuse and child abuse: Impact of addiction on the child. *Pediatric Clinics of North America, 37,* 881–904.

Brewin, C. R. (2005). Encoding and retrieval of traumatic memories. In J. J. Vasterling & C. R. Brewin (Eds.), *Neuropsychology of PTSD: Biological, cognitive, and clinical perspectives* (pp. 131–150). New York: Guilford.

Brown, D., Scheflin, A. W., & Hammond, D. C. (1998). *Memory, trauma, treatment, and the law.* New York: W. W. Norton.

Butcher, N., Dahlstrom, W. G., Graham, J. R., Tellegen, A., & Kaemmer, B. (1989). *Minnesota multiphasic personality inventory-2 (MMPI-2): Manual for administration and scoring.* Minneapolis, MN: University of Minnesota Press.

Campbell, J. C. (2002). Health consequences of intimate partner violence. *The Lancet, 359,* 1331–1336.

Coohey, C. (2004). Battered mothers who physically abuse their children. *Journal of Interpersonal Violence, 19,* 943–952. doi: 10.1177/0886260504266886.

Edelson, J. L. (1999). The overlap between child maltreatment and woman battering. *Violence Against Women, 5,* 134–154. doi: 10.1177/107780129952003.

Follingstad, D. R. (2003). Battered woman syndrome in the courts: Issues and application. In A. Goldstein (Ed.). *Handbook of Psychology* (Vol. 11—Forensic Psychology, pp. 485–507). Hoboken, NJ: Wiley.

Follingstad, D. R. (2009). The impact of psychological aggression on women's mental health and behavior. *Trauma, Violence, & Abuse, 10,* 271–289. doi: 10.1177/1524838009 334453.

Garcia-Moreno, C., Jansen, H. A. F. M., Ellsbert, M., Heise, L., & Watts, C. (2005). *WHO multicountry study on women's health and domestic violence against women*. Geneva, Switzerland: World Health Organization.

Golding, J. M. (1999). Intimate partner violence as a risk factor for mental disorders: A meta-analysis. *Journal of Family Violence, 14*, 99–132. doi: 10.1023/A:1022079418229.

Guriel, J. & Fremouw, W. (2003). Assessing malingered posttraumatic stress disorder: A critical review. *Clinical Psychology Review, 23*, 881–904. doi: 10.1016/j.cpr.2003.07.001.

Hawthorne v. State of Florida, Brief of Amicus Curiae, American Psychological Association in Support of Appellant, February 11, 1983.

Health and Human Services, Public Health Service, Substance Abuse and Mental Health Services Administration & Office of Applied Studies (1996). *National household survey on drug abuse: Main findings*. Rockville, MD: US Department of Justice.

Heilbrun, K. (2001). *Principles of forensic mental health assessment*. New York: Kluwer Academic/Plenum.

Heilbrun, K., Grisso, T., & Goldstein, A. M. (2009). *Foundations of forensic mental health assessment*. New York: Oxford University Press.

Hempel, C. (2004). Battered women who strike back. In B. J. Cling (Ed.), *Sexualized violence against women and children* (pp. 71–150). New York: Guilford.

Holtzworth-Munroe, A. & Stuart, G. L. (1994). Typologies of male batters: Three subtypes and the differences among them. *Psychological Bulletin, 116*, 476–497.

Kahn, F.I., Welch, L., & Zillmer, E. A. (1993). MMPI-2 profiles of battered women in transition. *Journal of Personality Assessment, 60*, 100–111. doi: 10.1207/s15327752jpa 6001_7.

Kaser-Boyd, N. (1995). Detecting malingering in criminal defendants. *Prosecutor's Brief, 18*, 19–22.

Kaser-Boyd, N. (2001). *Can battered woman syndrome be malingered?* Poster presented at the Sixth International Conference on Family Violence, San Diego, CA.

Kaser-Boyd, N. (2004). Battered woman syndrome: Clinical features, evaluation, and expert testimony. In B. J. Cling (Ed.), *Sexualized violence against women and children* (pp. 41–70). New York: Guilford.

Kaser-Boyd, N. (2008). Battered woman syndrome: Assessment-based expert testimony. In C. B. Gacono, B. F. Evans, N. Kaser-Boyd, & C. Gacono (Eds.), *Handbook of forensic Rorschach assessment* (pp. 467–487). New York: Wiley.

Kelleher, K., Chaffin, M., & Hollenberg, J. (1994). Alcohol and drug disorders among physically abusive and neglectful parents in a community-based sample. *American Journal of Public Health, 84*, 1586–1590.

Kilpatrick, D. G., Acierno, R., Resnick, H.S., Saunders, B. E., & Best, C. I. (1997). A two-year longitudinal analysis of the relationships between violent assault and substance use in women. *Journal of Consulting and Clinical Psychology, 65*, 834–847.

van der Kolk, B. A. (1987). *Psychological trauma*. Washington, DC: American Psychiatric Press.

Koss, M. P., Koss, P. G., & Woodruff, W. (1991). Deleterious effects of criminal victimization on women's health and medical utilization. *Archives of Internal Medicine, 151*, 342–347.

Kropp, P. R., Hart, S. D., & Belfrage, H. (2005). *The Brief Spousal Assault Form for the Evaluation of Risk (B-SAFER): User manual*. Vancouver, British Columbia, Canada: ProActive ReSolutions.

Lachar, D. (1974). *The MMPI: Clinical assessment and automated interpretation*. Los Angeles: Western Psychological Services.

LeDoux, J. (1996). *The emotional brain*. New York: Simon and Schuster.

Martin, D. (1976). *Battered wives*. San Francisco: Glide Publications.

Mihura, J. L., Meyer, G. J., Dumitrascu, N., & Bombel, G. (2013). The validity of individual Rorschach variables: Systematic reviews and meta-analyses of the comprehensive system. *Psychological Bulletin, 139*, 548–605. doi: 10.1037/a0029406.

Millon, T. (2009). *MCMI-III: Manual* (4th ed.). Minneapolis, MN: Pearson.

Milner, J. S. (1986). *The Child Abuse Potential Inventory: Manual* (2nd ed.). Webster, NC: Psytec.

National Computer Systems (1989). *The Minnesota report, adult clinical system-revised interpretive report*. Minneapolis, MN: National Computer Systems.

Oregon Children's Services Division (1993). *Task force on child fatalities and critical injuries due to abuse and neglect*. Salem, OR: Oregon Department of Human Resources.

Parrish, J. (1996). Trend analysis: Expert testimony on battering and its effects in criminal cases. *Wisconsin Women's Law Journal, 11*, 75–131.

Pecora, P. J., Whittaker, J. K., Maluccio, A. N., Barth, R. P., & Plotnick, R. D. (1992). *The child welfare challenge: Policy, practice, and research* (pp. 102–125). New York: Aldine de Gruyter.

People v. Rolon, 160 Cal. App. 4th 1206 (2008).

Pizzy, E. (1974). *Scream quietly or the neighbors will hear*. London: If Books.

Reid, J., Macchetto, P., & Foster, S. (1999). *No safe haven: Children of substance-abusing parents*. New York: National Center on Addiction and Substance Abuse at Columbia University.

Rhodes, N. R. (1992). Comparison of MMPI psychopathic deviate scores of battered and non-battered woman. *Journal of Family Violence, 7*, 297–307.

Rogers, R., Payne, J. W., Correa, A. A., Gillard, N. D., & Ross, C. A. (2009). A study of the SIRS with severely traumatized patients. *Journal of Personality Assessment, 91*, 429–438.

Rogers, R., Sewell, K. W., & Gillard, N. D. (2010). *Structured interview of reported symptoms: Professional manual* (2nd ed.). Lutz, FL: Psychological Assessment Resources.

Rogers, R., Sewell, K. W., Martin, M. A., & Vitacco, M. J. (2003). Detection of feigned mental disorders: A meta-analysis of the MMPI-2 and malingering. *Assessment, 10*, 160–177.

Römkens, R. (2001). Ambiguous responsibilities: Law and conflicting expert testimony on the abused woman who shot her sleeping husband. *Law & Social Inquiry, 25*, 355–391. doi: 10.1111/j.1747–4469.2000.tb00965.x.

Rosewater, L. B. & Walker, L. E. (1985). *Handbook of feminist therapy: Women's issues in psychotherapy*. New York: Springer.

Ross, S. M. (1996). Risk of physical abuse to children of spouse abusing parents. *Child Abuse and Neglect, 20*, 589–598. doi: 10.1016/0145–2134(96)00046–4.

Schacter, D. L. (1996). *Searching for memory*. New York: Basic Books.

Silva, C., McFarlane, J., Socken, K., Parker, B., & Reel, S. (1997). Symptoms of post-traumatic stress disorder in abused women in a primary care setting. *Journal of Women's Health, 6*, 543–552.

Stiffman, M. N., Schnitzer, P. G., & Adam, P. (2002). Household composition and risk of fatal child maltreatment. *Pediatrics, 109*, 615–621.

Straus, M. A. (2010). Thirty years of denying the evidence on gender symmetry in partner violence: Implications for prevention and treatment. *Partner Abuse, 1*, 332–362. doi: 10.1891/1946–6560.1.3.332.

Thijssen, J. & de Ruiter, C. (2011). Identifying subtypes of spousal assaulters using the B-SAFER. *Journal of Interpersonal Violence, 26*, 1307–1321. doi: 10.1177/08862605 10369129.

Tjaden, P. & Thoennes, N. (2000). *Full report of the prevalence, incidence, and consequences of violence against women: Findings from the National Violence Against Women survey.* Washington, DC, and Atlanta, GA: U.S. Department of Justice, National Institute of Justice, and U.S. Department of Health and Human Services, Centers for Disease Control and Prevention, NCJ 18378.

Vasterling, J. J. & Brewin, C. R. (Eds.), *Neuropsychology of PTSD: Biological, cognitive, and clinical perspectives.* New York: Guilford.

Walker, L. (1979). *The battered woman.* New York: Harper & Row.

Walker, L. (1984). *The battered woman syndrome.* New York: Springer.

Wang, C. T. & Harding, K. (1999). *Current trends in child abuse reporting and fatalities: The results of the 1998 annual fifty state survey.* Chicago: National Committee to Prevent Child Abuse.

Wells, K. (2009). Substance abuse and child maltreatment. *Pediatric Clinics of North America, 56*, 345–362.

Wilson, J. P. & Walker, A. J. (1990). Towards an MMPI trauma profile. *Journal of Traumatic Stress, 3*, 151–168.

Winstok, Z. (2011). The paradigmatic cleavage on gender differences in partner violence perpetration and victimization. *Aggression and Violent Behavior, 16*, 303–311. doi: 10.1016/j.avb.2011.04.004.

8

AN ADOLESCENT VIOLENT OFFENDER

Avoiding Premature Labeling

Corine de Ruiter

Two months before Samir[1] turned 18, he committed a number of armed robberies with two boys of similar age, within a period of a few weeks in January 2009. They robbed fast-food restaurants and video stores, wearing dark clothing and their faces covered. The victims were extorted with fake firearms and knives to obtain their money and other goods. Samir and his comrades also robbed and held a 16-year-old boy captive for a number of hours in his home. Samir was tried in the Regional Court of Den Bosch. On the basis of two expert reports (one by a psychologist, one by a psychiatrist), the court decided to apply adult criminal law to his case. On November 30, 2009, Samir was sentenced to 6 years' imprisonment and payment of compensation to the injured parties. The Public Prosecutor's Office appealed because it claimed the defendant should receive treatment under the TBS-order (see Chapter 4, for an explanation) because of diminished responsibility, which was not part of the verdict.

This chapter describes the forensic mental health assessment (FHMA) of Samir, a young man born in Morocco, who moved to The Netherlands with his family when he was a teenager. I will report on the use of two forensic assessment tools for adolescents: the Psychopathy Checklist: Youth Version (PCL:YV; Forth, Kosson, & Hare, 2003; authorized Dutch version: de Ruiter & Hildebrand, 2010) and the Structured Assessment of Violence Risk in Youth (SAVRY; Borum, Bartel, & Forth, 2006; authorized Dutch version: Lodewijks, Doreleijers, de Ruiter, & de Wit-Grouls, 2006), with a special focus on the ethics of classifying adolescents as psychopathic and/or dangerous, since their personality is still in development. The chapter will also demonstrate the importance of transcultural sensitivity in the forensic assessor, and how this is helpful to avoid ethnic, religious, and cultural bias.

Second Opinion on the Request of the Court of Appeal

In Samir's case, the Appeals Court granted the request of the defense for a new forensic mental health evaluation. Thus, I was appointed by the investigating judge of the Appeals Court of Den Bosch and received the entire criminal file. The questions posed by the Court consisted of the standard set of questions posed by Dutch courts in criminal cases. They relate to the psycholegal issues of criminal responsibility, risk of recidivism, and treatment advice (see Chapter 6, pp. 114–115 for a listing of these questions).

First, I studied the police files that included the statements the three defendants made to the police. At first, all of them denied their involvement in the robberies, but soon after confrontation with the available evidence (from camera surveillance footage to eyewitness testimony), they all confessed. Samir explains he was living in supervised housing for young people at the time and because the others did not have a place to live, he invited them in. The three of them did not have any income. Samir had conflicts with his parents and wasn't allowed in the home anymore. The three of them thought of ways to obtain money, and the idea of the robberies came up. They first stole a car, and used it to commit the offenses, with Samir behind the steering wheel since he was the only one who knew how to drive. During the offenses, one of them remained in the car, while the other two went inside.

The conviction also contained one robbery inside a private dwelling. This crime started as a burglary, but when the three boys discovered a 16-year-old boy had locked himself in the bathroom, they forced him out of this room, assaulted, threatened, and bound him. The offenders took numerous objects from the house and left the victim strapped and helpless. The police file contains a victim statement written by the mother of the 16-year-old, explaining the grave emotional and practical impact the incident has had on her and her son. A brief excerpt serves as an illustration:

> Not a day passes without thinking about the robbery. You three are the reason my son and I are seeing fewer and fewer people; you are the reason why I am still afraid to open the door when the doorbell rings; you are the reason for my financial problems and the reason why we are so stressed out.

Previous Mental Health Reports

There were two mental health reports in the file, one by a psychologist and one by a psychiatrist. According to the psychologist who examined him, Samir is suffering from Conduct Disorder (DSM-IV code 312.8). She also notes features of psychopathy, including egocentric and narcissistic traits, lack of empathy and remorse, and emotional shallowness. His WAIS-III IQ scores are 89 (verbal) and

107 (performance). The psychologist concludes that Samir is developing in the direction of Antisocial Personality Disorder. She concludes there is a direct causal relationship between the disorder and the alleged offenses and she estimates Samir is at high risk to recidivate, both in the short and the long term. The psychologist considers Samir's lacunar conscience as a reason not to advise the court to impose a treatment order: "In accordance with the seriousness of the facts, when proven, a prison sentence seems sufficient. [. . .] A sanction can serve a healing function when considering his level of conscience development" (p. 26, psychologist's report). She also advises an extended period of probation, to assist Samir in finding housing and a job.

The psychologist was also requested by the court to answer the following question: "Are there arguments in relation to the defendant's personality that give reason to apply adult criminal law?" Article 77b of the Dutch Criminal Code allows the judge discretion to apply adult criminal law, instead of juvenile law, for defendants who were 16 or 17 years old at the time they committed the offense. Under Dutch law, every child between the ages of 12 and 18 will appear before a juvenile court, even if the defendant has turned 18 by the time of the trial. Youths under the age of 16 can get a maximum prison term of 1 year, those between 16 and 18 a maximum of 2 years. Besides a prison sentence, there is the option of a mandated treatment order for juveniles, similar to a TBS-order for adults. In recent years, The Netherlands has seen an upsurge in the societal debate against the more rehabilitation-focused juvenile system; those who see proportionality and retribution as equally (or more) legitimate goals that must be achieved when dealing with serious juvenile crime are gaining support. A parallel development took place in the US in the 1990s and early 2000s, with more and more states adopting statutes which both widened the eligibility criteria for transfer to adult court and broadened the range of mechanisms by which transfer could be accomplished (Zimring, 2000). Currently, in the US there are legal standards for transfer to adult court that differ by state. Different jurisdictions consider one or more of three standards: "danger to others," "amenability to rehabilitation," and "the best interests of the juvenile" (see Salekin & Grimes, 2008 for a comprehensive review of the research literature on this topic).

The psychologist who assessed Samir advised that Samir be treated as an adult in view of: "the seriousness and the number of offenses, his leading role in them, and Samir's personality. He is psychologically an adult, he shows little dependency on and/or attachment to his family, and he demonstrates autonomy in thinking and feeling" (p. 27, psychologist's report). The psychiatrist arrived at the same diagnostic conclusions. In the US, prominent scholars advise against the provision of advice to the court on whether the legal standard has been met or what the legal decision ought to be (Heilbrun, 2001; Salekin & Grimes, 2008).

The psychiatrist used an unstructured clinical interview to arrive at a diagnosis. The psychologist stated that she used the PCL:YV and the SAVRY in her assessment. What is noteworthy, however, is that the findings from these structured assessment tools are summarized in less than a page, and do not contain specific examples of the psychopathic traits or the risk factors which are deemed present. A statement such as: "Samir knows how to create an impression and shows superficial charm" begs further explanation and illustration.

Besides the two previous mental health evaluation reports, there was information from the detention center and from Samir's designated probation officer in the file. The detention center reported that Samir had adequately adapted to the regimen. He was communicative with staff and fellow-inmates, and he abided by the institutional rules. He is helpful and stimulates the group to do the household chores. He was also a member of the youth detention council. Samir's probation officer contended that she believed he had learned from the present verdict. She thought he was serious now about working towards a positive change and she saw the robberies as the result of a group process which Samir would not have committed on his own.

After studying the file, I made an appointment for the assessment of Samir. He was detained in a juvenile justice institution in the city of Breda in the south of The Netherlands.

A New Forensic Mental Health Assessment

I conducted a complete forensic psychological assessment in February 2010, using the standard set of instruments I use in most pretrial cases. In this case, these included: the PCL:YV, the SAVRY, and the MMPI-2 (Butcher, Dahlstrom, Graham, Tellegen, & Kaemmer, 1989). Intelligence testing was not performed because Samir had been tested during the first psychological evaluation (in 2009) and also 1 year prior to that (2008). I used the collateral information that was already in the extensive file, including witness statements, technical forensic findings, mental health, and criminal history data.

Samir was assessed on 2 days in a visitors' room at the juvenile justice institution. The semi-structured biographical interview, which belongs to the PCL:YV, was administered. The PCL:YV was selected, as opposed to the PCL-R, even though Samir was 19 at this point in time. The PCL:YV was considered more appropriate in this case because although the instrument is meant for adolescents between 12 and 18 it can also be used with somewhat older individuals, particularly when they have not led an independent life with opportunities to develop their own lifestyle in terms of relationships, work, and leisure. After the interview, the MMPI-2 was administered. I opted for the MMPI-2, instead of the MMPI-A, because the Dutch MMPI-2 has more extensive validation research than the MMPI-A. Finally, the SAVRY was coded on the basis of all available data.

Clinical Impressions

Samir was cooperative and friendly during the evaluation. On the second day of the assessment, he entered the room with a cup of tea for me, since he remembered

I drank tea the previous day. Samir seemed to thrive when you showed an interest in him. At the end of the second session, he spontaneously offered to conduct the assessment feedback session by telephone, because he wanted to save me the long travel time. This appeared to me as genuine concern, not as a sign of superficial charm.

Self-reported Biography

Family of Origin

Samir was born in The Netherlands, but spent the first 10 years of his life living in a medium-size city on the Moroccan coast. He is the middle son of five children, with an older brother, an older sister, and two younger sisters. He was raised in an extended family, and calls his aunt his second Mom. His father worked in The Netherlands during his childhood. He used to come to Morocco during the Christmas season and the family visited The Netherlands during the summer.

When Samir was 11 the entire family moved to The Netherlands, following the father's plan. He believed his children would have more opportunities in Europe. Samir did not speak Dutch. He reports he was very homesick and had crying spells, unlike his siblings, who seemed to enjoy the move. When Samir talks about his childhood in Morocco, he starts to beam. He says he wants to return in a few years, because most of his family is still there.

Samir's father is an Imam who works at different mosques and also for the Dutch correctional service. According to him, his father is a scholar: sociable, quiet, and smart, and sometimes "a little cocky and irritable." He provides the example that his father never wanted a navigation system for his car, but stuck to reading maps, but now that he finally got the navigation he is very pleased with it. His father has high expectations of Samir, who feels a lot of pressure to succeed. On the other hand, his father doesn't spend much time with him and there seems to be hardly an emotional connection between father and son. His mother is a homemaker. She sometimes assists her friends who make some money cooking for Moroccan weddings.

Education and Work

Samir attended one elementary school in Morocco. In The Netherlands, he enrolled in an elementary school for non-Dutch speaking children, together with his younger sisters. Samir had difficulty adjusting. He was a quiet boy, but he had difficulty concentrating. At times, he reacted in an oppositional and verbally aggressive way. He did not skip school. He received help with his homework, but the problems remained, and he was sent to a boarding school by his father.

Samir started vocational training to become a plasterer, which he really enjoyed. Unfortunately, he had to stop his internship at a plastering company because he had to enter a supported living program for adolescents in a town that was too far away from the company. Samir had been sentenced to 18 days' juvenile detention for embezzlement in 2007 (see below under Criminal History), and his entry into supported living was one of the conditions set by the probation service. As a consequence, he did not obtain his diploma. Over many years, Samir has been actively playing in a soccer team, and practicing Thai boxing and fitness training.

Samir said he started looking for work in January 2009. He was living in with one friend (21 years old), and another friend (19). He said they did not have any income and Samir started looking for work as a plasterer. The three of them came up with the idea of the robberies during this period and put this idea into action.

During his present period in detention, Samir has continued his education. In the future, he would like to work as a sports instructor at a fitness center, to gain experience. His ultimate dream is to own his own fitness school in Morocco. He knows it will be challenging to reach this goal, and he does expect some setbacks.

Intimate Relationships and Friendships

Samir reported he'd had several girlfriends, the first one when he was 15. This relationship with a 15-year-old Indonesian girl lasted 4 months. Recently, he had ended his relationship of 3 years with a Dutch girl, because he felt he could not ask her to wait until he had served his sentence.

Samir says he has two good friends, boys he has known from his parents' neighborhood for 7 years. They are 21 and 22 years old now and they are successful athletes. He says they come and visit him in the detention facility.

Criminal History

According to the official criminal justice register, Samir has had two prior contacts with the justice system. In 2006, the prosecution imposed a transaction in connection with a burglary. In connection with embezzlement in 2007, he got 18 days' juvenile detention with a probation period of 2 years and a special condition of undergoing counseling at a mental health care agency. Samir reported the following on the 2007 offense:

> A friend of mine was having a conflict with a guy on a moped. My friend hit the guy, and I rode away on the moped. I wasn't thinking at all, I was just riding in circles in the neighborhood. The police knew me and they had called my parents. Then I went to the police station and I was arrested.

Samir served his detention in a juvenile justice center in the south of The Netherlands "Het Keerpunt" ("The Turning Point"), about 85 miles from his parents' home. He says his parents were very angry with him and did not come to visit him while he was there. He says he didn't really think about the consequences when he rode away on the moped, he just wanted to see what it was like.

Medication Use and Substance Use History

Samir says he uses Advil (ibuprofen) regularly because he has frequent headaches. He reports stiff neck muscles as the cause for this and he has made an appointment with a physical therapist.

Samir has been drinking alcohol since the age of 16, which is the legal drinking age in The Netherlands.[2] He says he used to go out on the town at weekends, but also on Thursdays (the "students' night" in big cities). His parents do not approve of his alcohol consumption, as alcohol is forbidden by Islam. Samir says he has never used drugs. He smokes cigarettes, around 6 or 7 a day, he says.

The Offenses

Samir and I discussed the offenses he committed together with the other boys/ men. He reported that he had committed and confessed to 13 criminal offenses, including robberies, burglaries, and car theft. All of the crimes were committed with others and he says lack of money was their motive. According to the statements of the other boys, Samir had the leading role, but he does not agree with this. The first robbery was at a video store: "We had a fake gun and a knife. I held the knife in my hand. The booty was almost 600 euros. We used the car. Afterwards we went back to the apartment. I was thinking: 'Is this really necessary?'"

Subsequently, they committed the burglary of a house, where they did not take much. "What is the most serious offense you ever committed?" I ask Samir. He answers: "A robbery in a private home. There was a boy who got an asthma attack. The boy was assaulted and tied up by my two friends. I gave him his inhaler, but we did take all sorts of stuff." Samir thinks his present verdict will have a large impact on his life. He says he has realized through his personal therapy the type of traumas people suffer when they are robbed like this. He says he is learning to talk about his feelings more now. My final question is why he didn't seek help from his parents in January 2009 when he had no money left. He says he didn't want to hurt his mother, and didn't want to admit that he was doing badly.

Test Findings

MMPI-2

Samir completed the MMPI-2 in a consistent manner. He responded in a consistent way (VRIN T score = 54) and there is no evidence of a yes- or no-saying response style (TRIN T score = 59). More problematic are the elevated

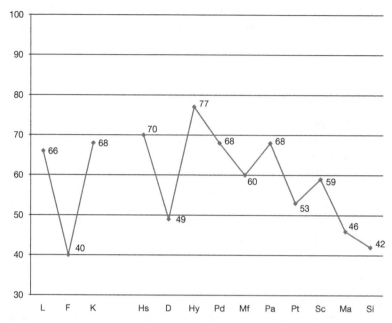

FIGURE 8.1 MMPI-2 Profile of Samir (LFK Scales and Clinical Scales).

L = Lie scale; F = Infrequency scale; K = Correction scale; Hs = Hypochondriasis scale; D = Depression scale; Hy = Hysteria scale; Pd = Psychopathic deviate scale; Mf = Masculinity-femininity scale; Pa = Paranoia scale; Pt = Psychasthenia scale; Sc = Schizophrenia scale; Ma = Mania scale; Si = Social introversion scale.

scores on the L- (T = 66) and the K-scales (T = 68) and his slightly low scores on the F-scale (T = 40) and the Fb-scale (T = 54). This combination of scores suggests that he may be attempting to present himself in a favorable light by minimizing or denying problems and unacceptable feelings. In line with this is the slightly elevated score on the Superlative scale (T = 67), which suggests that Samir's claims of good adjustment might be exaggerated. In general, the more elevated above a T-score of 65 the L- and K-scales are, the higher the likelihood that the profile may be invalid. However, in Samir's case, the L- and K-scales are only slightly elevated, and this level of elevation is not unusual for assessments taking place in a forensic context (Friedman, Lewak, Nichols, & Webb, 2001). Furthermore, Moroccan culture places a lot of emphasis on conformity and conventionality, which might also lead to L- and K-scale elevations.

Samir shows a 3–1 profile with additional elevations on scales 4 (Psychopathic deviate) and 6 (Paranoia). The main clinical scales (31 profile; T-score scale 3 = 77; T-score scale 1 = 70) draw the picture of a psychologically immature individual whose primary defense mechanisms are repression and denial. Samir tends to express his emotional issues in an indirect way via somatization, and he indeed reports frequent headaches. Additionally, Samir has a high need for social approval and presents himself as very considerate and cooperative during the assessment by, for example, bringing tea for the evaluator. He has a strong need for social approval, affection, and sympathy, and fears being judged by others. As a result he tends to avoid interpersonal conflict, as indicated by the elevated score on the Hy2 (Need for affection: T = 70) scale. Although he tends to be sociable and outgoing, social relationships are often superficial (Scale 0 is below T = 50). Elevations on the K-scale in combination with this profile suggest difficulties in expressing negative feelings, and the elevation on scale 4 predicts anger and its expression in occasional outbursts or in a passive-aggressive way. The elevation on the O-H (Overcontrolled Hostility: T = 80) scale reflects the overcontrol of feelings, and the elevated score on the Hy5 scale (Inhibition of aggression: T = 68) adds specifically the inhibition of aggression.

Adding scale 6 to the 3–1 profile, with scale 3 at least 8 points higher than scale 6, argues against overt distrust. However, behind a veneer of socially conventional behaviour, there is extreme sensitivity to criticism and judgment. The elevation on the Pd2 (Authority problems: T = 71) scale indicates a lack of behavioural control, especially in the form of violations of social norms, or attitudes supporting rule-violating behavior. However, the content scale ASP1 (Antisocial attitudes: T = 35) is not elevated, indicative of an absence of antisocial attitudes and lack of empathy. ASP2 (Antisocial behavior: T = 78) is elevated, expressing Samir's admission of his antisocial conduct. In line with this is the elevated score on the supplementary scale MAC-R (MacAndrew Alcoholism: T = 68) indicating impulsivity and rebelliousness. His AAS (Addiction Acknowledgement) and APS (Addiction Potential) scales had T-scores in the normal range, rendering serious substance use problems unlikely.

Psychopathy Checklist: Youth Version

In comparison with the population of male adolescents in their probationary period (see Dutch PCL:YV manual; de Ruiter & Hildebrand, 2010), Samir's total PCL score lies in the twentieth percentile. He obtained the maximum score of 2 on two PCL criteria: Irresponsible behavior and Serious criminality.

Moroccan Adolescents in The Netherlands: Factors related to Delinquent Behavior

The case at hand raises a number of questions that need to be clarified. Cross-cultural issues seem to play a role in Samir's case. The move to The Netherlands at the beginning of his adolescent years seems to have led to adjustment problems, including internalizing and externalizing behavior problems. Also, the strained relationship with his father, including the high expectations for his (second) son, with the added stress of the shame of his first incarceration, may have been exacerbated by the strong pressure to conform in a collectivistic culture.[3]

What is known from empirical research about disruptive and antisocial behavior problems in Moroccan adolescents in The Netherlands? Are the causal and risk factors similar to those found in Dutch adolescents? What do we know about the possible influence of cultural factors in cases such as Samir's?

To find an answer to these questions, a search was performed using PsycINFO® and Web of Science© with the following search terms: "Moroccan" and "Dutch" or "Netherlands," "problem behavior," "criminality," "delinquency," "antisocial behavior," "adolescents," or "juveniles." The first part of this review will focus on the prevalence of disruptive and antisocial behavior problems in Moroccan adolescents. In the second part, I will focus on risk factors related to cultural factors.

Moroccans belong to one of the largest immigrant groups in The Netherlands. In 2012, about 363,000 Moroccans were living in The Netherlands, which is 2.2 percent of the total population. Moroccan men were recruited to work in the Dutch labor market in the 1960s. From the early 1970s many Moroccan migrants brought their families to The Netherlands. In The Netherlands, the socioeconomic position of Moroccans is unfavorable. The educational level of Moroccans is low, although it has increased since their migration to The Netherlands (Stevens, Vollebergh, Pels, & Crijnen, 2005). About 54 percent were born in The Netherlands and are considered second-generation Moroccans. Their mean age of 27.8 years suggests a group with predominantly young people. In comparison, the mean age of Dutch people is 41.4 years (Nicolaas, Loozen, & Annema, 2012). According to official crime statistics, Moroccans, especially those from the second-generation and those younger than 20, are overrepresented in the Dutch criminal justice system. Of all criminal suspects, 5.2 percent come from the Moroccan group. Also, recidivism rates are highest among Moroccans: eight out of ten juveniles and seven out of ten adult Moroccans recidivate (Jennissen & Besjes, 2012).

Despite the overrepresentation of Moroccan juveniles in official crime statistics, studies using self-report measures typically don't find significant differences in problem behavior between different ethnic groups. For example, Deković, Wissink, and Meijer (2004) found that levels of self-reported antisocial behavior did not differ between the four largest ethnic groups in The Netherlands (Dutch, Moroccan, Turkish, and Surinamese). They also didn't differ in terms of involvement with deviant peers. A possible explanation for the discrepancy between self-report and official reports may be a bias in the crime statistics. Moroccan adolescents may get caught and convicted more often than Dutch adolescents. This has been suggested by Pakes (2010), who points to a possible selective attention bias by the police. However, results could also be distorted due to a social desirability bias, which is inherent in self-report measures. It can be expected that questions, especially those about antisocial behavior, will be answered in a socially desirable and misleading way.

Parent and Teacher Ratings

Zwirs, Burger, Schulpen, and Buitelaar (2006) studied the occurrence of behavioral problems (ADHD, ODD, and CD) among 5–11-year-old Dutch, Moroccan, Turkish, and Surinamese children. They also compared the likelihood of getting treatment for behavioral problems between those ethnic groups. Based on parent and teacher ratings, they found that, compared with Dutch boys, Moroccan boys were about 70 percent more likely to display problem behavior, whereas Turkish boys were about 60 percent less likely to show problem behavior. The authors suggest that this could be caused by the wider cultural gap that Moroccans have to bridge in comparison with other ethnic groups. Another explanation they offer deals with the gender-specific parenting in Moroccan culture, which confronts Moroccan boys with a harsh authoritarian socialization in the home but with a lack of supervision from their parents outside the home. Regarding the likelihood of treatment, they found that Moroccan boys were almost 65 percent less likely than Dutch boys to be treated for behavioral problems. A possible explanation for this lower treatment rate could be ethnic differences in parental detection of behavioral disorders. Zwirs, Burger, Buitelaar, and Schulpen (2006) tested this hypothesis and found that, in comparison with Dutch parents, Moroccan parents were less likely to detect externalizing behavior disorders and ADHD in their child. In their study on ethnic differences in parental problem perception, Bevaart et al. (2012) found similar results. Moroccan parents showed low levels of problem perception: only 47 percent of the Moroccan parents recognized problem behavior in their 5–6-year-old children, in contrast with 81 percent of the Dutch parents.

The higher prevalence of problem behavior, the lack of parental detection, and the resultant lower likelihood of getting treatment are likely to be one explanation for the overrepresentation of Moroccan adolescents in the juvenile justice system. Evidence shows that ADHD and conduct problems (Oppositional Defiant Disorder and Conduct Disorder) are commonly related to criminality, especially without early intervention (Abramowitz, Kosson, & Seidenberg, 2004; Copeland, Miller-Johnson, Keeler, Angold, & Costello, 2007).

Acculturation Problems as a Risk Factor

A number of risk factors have been linked empirically to disruptive and criminal behavior. These include family problems (Mulder, Brand, Bullens, & Van Marle, 2010), involvement with criminal peers (Howell, 2009; Mulder et al., 2011), substance misuse, socioeconomic disadvantages, and poor educational attendance (Brown & Campbell, 2010). Are those risk factors similar for Moroccan immigrant children?

Stevens, Vollebergh, Pels, and Crijnen (2005) found a number of predictors of externalizing behavior problems in Moroccan adolescents in The Netherlands.

They found clear correlations between gender and externalizing problems. Boys were at a higher risk than girls of developing those problems. At the family level, high levels of conflict within the family, both between parents and especially between parents and their children, and low levels of parental monitoring, affection, and support were strong predictors of externalizing behavior. Other predictors of externalizing behavior included school problems, involvement with deviant peers, and hanging out regularly with friends, that is, without parental supervision. These findings are in line with research on risk factors in majority groups. For example, Deković, Janssens, and Van As (2003) found similar predictors of antisocial behavior in Dutch adolescents.

Only one predictor was found to distinguish between Moroccan and Dutch adolescents. The migration factor "perceived discrimination" was related to externalizing behavior, however, this association was found to be relatively weak. The authors argue that migration factors nonetheless may play an important role in externalizing behavior, though only indirectly (Stevens et al., 2005). As an example, they point to the fact that immigrant children tend to acculturate faster than their parents. This could lead to a "clash of values" which results in frequent conflicts between parents and children. This in turn is, as mentioned before, a major predictor of externalizing behavior in Moroccan adolescents.

In their study, Paalman, van Domburgh, Stevens, and Doreleijers (2011) focused on risk factors that could differentiate between different offender groups in a high-risk sample of Moroccan boys in The Netherlands. They found that many of the general risk factors for juvenile delinquency, such as financial hardship and single parenthood, predicted first-time offending and reoffending in Moroccan boys. The difference between one-time offending and reoffending was predicted by reading problems, having an older brother, and closer proximity to the Dutch culture. The explanation offered for this finding is that those who are strongly oriented toward Dutch society may feel more distressed by their disadvantaged position, with consequential feelings of frustration which enhance the risk of delinquent behavior. This finding is in line with results from a recent study by Stevens, Veen, and Vollebergh (2014) who found incarcerated Dutch-Moroccan adolescent boys to be more orientated toward Dutch society compared with a control group of non-offending Dutch-Moroccan boys.

Berry (2005) defines acculturation as "the dual process of cultural and psychological change that takes place as a result of contact between two or more cultural groups and their individual members" (p. 698). These changes occur through both group and social factors, as well as through individual changes. Acculturation also refers to one's attachment to the host culture. Paalman and colleagues (2011) report beneficial outcomes for children with strong bonds to both the ethnic and the host culture.

In summary, despite an overrepresentation of Moroccan adolescent boys in the Dutch criminal justice system, studies based on self-report do not find differences in externalizing problem behavior between Moroccan and Dutch adolescents. This could be explained by a possible selection bias by the police or by socially desirable responding on the part of Moroccan adolescents and their parents (i.e., denial of behavioral problems). Teacher ratings suggest an actual higher level of behavioral problems among Moroccan boys, compared with other minority groups and Dutch boys. Furthermore, evidence shows that ethnic differences in parental detection of behavioral disorders exist. Moroccan parents are less likely to recognize problem behavior in their children, compared with Dutch parents. Higher occurrence of problem behavior and the lack of treatment could explain why Moroccan adolescents come into contact with the justice system more frequently than other ethnic groups. Most of the risk factors that are typically associated with antisocial and criminal behavior in youth are similar for Moroccan adolescents. However, migration-related factors, such as acculturation problems, high parent-child conflict over values, and language difficulties, could play an indirect role in predicting externalizing behavior problems.

When applying these findings to the case of Samir, we note that many of these factors specific to Moroccan youth are present. As his father is an Imam it is reasonable to expect that a high significance is placed on conventional Muslim values. The low level of family acculturation, combined with the extreme pressure to succeed and the lack of warmth and an emotional bond between Samir and his father, is associated with an increased chance of internalizing problems and externalizing problem behavior (Stevens, Vollebergh, Pels, & Crijnen, 2007). Additionally, low levels of parental monitoring are linked to more externalizing problems (Stevens et al., 2007), which is applicable since Samir was no longer living with his parents at the time of the crimes. The issue of shame, which is quite characteristic of Moroccan culture, also seemed to have played an important role, because Samir did not dare share his problems with his parents when he was having major difficulties at the beginning of 2009.

Diagnostic Conclusions and Violence Risk Assessment

Psychiatric Classification According to DSM-IV-TR

On the basis of the findings derived from the current FMHA, a psychiatric classification on the five axes of DSM-IV-TR was made:

Axis I: Conduct disorder, starting in adolescence
Axis II: Problems in the father-child relationship
Axis III: Frequent tension headaches
Axis IV: Incarceration, awaiting trial in Court of Appeal, acculturation-related stress
Axis V: Global Assessment of Functioning (current = 60).

Risk Assessment

For the structured risk assessment, the SAVRY (Borum, Bartel, & Forth, 2006; Dutch version: Lodewijks et al., 2006) was used. The SAVRY belongs to the category of structured professional judgment risk assessment instruments, developed for use with adolescent violent offenders. The SAVRY is modeled after structured risk assessment instruments for adults, such as the Historical, Clinical, Risk Management–20 (HCR-20; Webster, Douglas, Eaves, & Hart, 1997); the items are factors relevant to adolescents. The SAVRY comprises 24 risk items, divided into three domains (see Table 8.1), and six protective items. The risk items are coded on a three-point scale (absent, somewhat present, and clearly present), and the protective items have a two-level structure (absent or present). The interrater reliability and the predictive validity of the Dutch version of the SAVRY have been found to be good to excellent in several different adolescent offender samples (Lodewijks, de Ruiter, & Doreleijers, 2008a; Lodewijks, Doreleijers, & de Ruiter, 2008b; Lodewijks, Doreleijers, de Ruiter, & Borum, 2008c). The SAVRY scoring and argumentation of Samir are provided in Table 8.1 below.

Risk Judgment

My final judgment on Samir's risk of recidivism, assuming that he will not receive continued treatment, is estimated to be moderate. Samir scored high (i.e., a maximum score of 2 on six of the SAVRY items, however, half of these items represent static, historical factors that will not be changed by behavioral or other types of intervention. For an adolescent who is still in development, this is actually not as problematic as for an adult. For instance, our research into the validity of the SAVRY in three independent samples of violent adolescents in The Netherlands actually revealed that the Historical scale (items H1 to H10) was not significantly related to future violent behavior, as measured by official reconvictions, police information, and institutional records (Lodewijks, de Ruiter, & Doreleijers, 2010). On the contrary, the contextual and individual items, which together form the Dynamic risk scale, did predict future violence. Note that most of Samir's high scores are found on the Historical risk scale and that the Dynamic risk scale items still allow room for further improvement. On a further positive note, Samir's scores on the Individual risk factors are generally low, indicating a certain positive foundation for refraining from delinquency. Especially the fact that Samir does not endorse antisocial attitudes, does not suffer from anger management problems/abuse substances, nor shows low commitment to school, constitutes a good basis for being able to lead a conventional life. Samir seems serious about succeeding in school and working toward his dream of moving back to Morocco. He also seems to grasp the seriousness of his current situation, and the emotional impact his previous offenses have had on his victims.

TABLE 8.1 SAVRY Risk Assessment

Item	Argumentation	Score
Historical risk factors		
H1: History of violence	In total Samir committed 15 offenses (2 prior convictions which included non-violent criminal activity, and 13 index offenses). Samir has committed "a number" of armed robberies and he participated in strapping a boy, which implies more than two incidents of violent behavior.	2
H2: History of non-violent offending	Theft and embezzlement	2
H3: Early initiation of violence	No known prior acts of violence before the age of 14	0
H4: Past supervision/ intervention failures	He was put on probation for 2 years in 2007 and committed a series of crimes in January 2009. This is a serious supervision failure.	2
H5: History of self-harm or suicide attempts	No attempts	0
H6: Exposure to violence in the home	No information	X
H7: Childhood history of maltreatment	Youth has not been physically abused or neglected	0
H8: Parental/caregiver criminality	No history of criminal acts	0
H9: Early caregiver disruption	*Argument pro*: Samir's father hardly had a care-giving role before age 11; Samir had limited contact with his parents after his first detention and was signed up for supervised living shortly before he turned 18. *Argument contra*: No disruption in continuity of care (mother mostly available).	1
H10: Poor school achievement	*Argument pro*: Samir was sent to boarding school because of concentration difficulties and general adjustment problems. *Argument contra*: Samir never skipped school; he started an internship to become a plasterer. The fact that he did not obtain his diploma was due to the loss of his internship placement.	1

TABLE 8.1 *continued*

Item	Argumentation	Score
Contextual risk factors		
C1: Peer delinquency	*Argument pro*: Samir has lived with two delinquent peers and committed all of his index offenses together with deviant peers. *Argument contra*: Samir has two close friends who are not delinquent and who visit him at the detention facility, and his former girlfriend did not seem to engage in criminal behavior.	1
C2: Peer rejection	Samir doesn't appear to have been subjected to rejection by peers.	0
C3: Stress and poor coping	Samir has experienced severe stress due to initial adjustment problems after immigrating to The Netherlands and high expectations of his father; he has shown poor coping skills which ultimately resulted in criminal behavior.	2
C4: Poor parental management	There is a significant lack of parental supervision due to the fact that Samir was not allowed in his parental home anymore shortly before he turned 18. Before his move to The Netherlands, he probably had an extended family upbringing, which got lost after his move (the loss of his aunt especially seems to have been difficult).	2
C5: Lack of personal/ social support	*Argument pro*: Parental support is missing, due to the fact that Samir has had conflicts with his family. He does not seem to have the feeling that he can come to his parents when in trouble. He also broke up with his girlfriend, who otherwise could have been another supportive factor. Nothing is known about his current relationship to his siblings. *Argument contra*: Samir reports having two good friends that visit him regularly.	1
C6: Community disorganization	Nothing is known about the neighborhood in which his family lived, neither in Morocco nor in The Netherlands.	X
Individual risk factors		
I1: Negative attitudes	Samir reports that treatment has helped him gain insight into the impact that his previous offenses have had on the victims. Furthermore, he indicates that he had moral concerns after committing the crimes ("is that really necessary?").	0 0
I2: Risk taking/ impulsivity	*Argument pro*: Although most of his offenses seemed to be planned, his previous crime of embezzlement indicates a tendency to act without	

TABLE 8.1 *continued*

Item		Argumentation	Score
		thinking about the possible consequences. He presents with numerous violations of authority and rules/laws without considering the consequences. *Argument contra*: Samir's offenses are highly planned and well-prepared. He never skipped school, never abused drugs or alcohol, and has been with his latest girlfriend for several years.	1
I3:	Substance-use difficulties	Although Samir has used alcohol in the past, he did not start before the legal drinking age and his alcohol consumption did not cause any adjustment problems.	0
I4:	Anger management problems	According to the MMPI-2 results, Samir tends to suppress anger, which may come out in undercontrolled outbursts and passive-aggression. His history doesn't reveal examples of hot-tempered anger or reactive aggression.	0
I5:	Low empathy/ remorse	*Arguments pro*: He has committed 13 offenses, and used his financial problems as a rationalization. *Arguments contra*: Samir expresses remorse for his offenses and admits to all of them (although not right away). He claims that he now understands what the emotional impact on the victims is.	1
I6:	Attention deficit/ hyperactivity difficulties	Samir is reported to have had concentration problems in school, leading to a subsequent referral to boarding school. However, these difficulties seem to have been caused by his homesickness and feelings of loneliness. There is no evidence of symptoms of hyperactivity.	0
I7:	Poor compliance	*Arguments pro*: Samir has committed criminal acts while still on probation, demonstrating poor compliance. *Arguments contra*: Samir now understands the need for intervention and demonstrates a positive attitude by stating that his treatment has helped him gain more insight. He is highly motivated to succeed and has started working toward his dream career while in the detention facility.	0
I8:	Low interest/ commitment to school	*Arguments pro*: Samir failed to obtain a diploma but this was due to his move to a supported living group so he couldn't finish the plastering internship.	0

TABLE 8.1 *continued*

Item		Argumentation	Score
		Arguments contra: Samir has never skipped school, and seems ambitious due to the fact that he is currently continuing his education and is highly motivated to pursue a career as a fitness instructor/ owner. Samir has specific plans for his future and is working on obtaining his goals.	
*Protective factors**			
P1:	Prosocial involvement	Samir has been a long-term member of a soccer club and practices Thai boxing and fitness. Structured leisure activities.	1
P2:	Strong social support	Samir does not have any parental support. He has two prosocial friends who visit him during his incarceration, but this is a rather limited network for a young man of his age.	0
P3:	Strong attach-ments and bonds	Samir does not have any parental support, and there is no evidence of the presence of another prosocial adult that supports him.	0
P4:	Positive attitude toward inter-vention and authority	Samir thinks that his treatment in the juvenile detention center is beneficial and has helped him gain more insight into the consequences of his offenses. He appreciates the seriousness of his situation and knows that it will have a big impact on his future. Furthermore, Samir is friendly and forthcoming to his assessor.	1
P5:	Strong commit-ment to school	Samir is continuing his education in the institution and plans to become a sports instructor, and later, hopefully, the owner of a fitness center. He is highly motivated to succeed and reach his ultimate goal of moving back to Morocco.	1
P6:	Resilient personality traits	*Argument pro*: Samir tends to be quiet and non-impulsive. *Argument contra*: Slow adaptability to change, poor coping skills, intellectual abilities not above average.	0

* The six protective factors are scored on a dichotomous scale: 0 = absent and 1 = present.

Lodewijks et al. (2010) also demonstrated that items from the Protective factors scale could actually buffer risk factors from the other scales. Items P2 (strong social support) and P3 (strong attachment and bonds) had significant predictive values for non-recidivism in all samples, with AUCs for P2 ranging from .32 to .36 ($p \leq .05$) and AUCs for P3 ranging from .30 to .35 ($p \leq .05$). In addition, in Sample 2 (institutional violence), items P5 (strong commitment to school or work; AUC = .28, p = .001) and P4 (positive attitude towards intervention and authority; AUC = .35, p = .04) were found to be significant protective buffers. Samir already shows positive scores on P4 and P5, and further coaching to add on positive social support and attachment bonds could help reduce his recidivism risk even further. In the past, Samir was engaged in several conventional sports clubs that not only offered structured leisure activities, but also offered him the chance to get to know conventional peers. In such an environment it is likely that Samir will be able to find friends with a more positive influence on his life. His current attitude and ambition to change and build a foundation for a career could serve as very good motivation.

In conclusion, since Samir's recidivism risk is still highly situation-dependent, a risk judgment of moderate seems to be adequate to capture the possibility of him relapsing into old behavioral patterns under a combination of adverse circumstances. It needs to be clear, though, that his criminal behavior is mainly related to peer delinquency and poor coping skills. Samir does not endorse any antisocial attitudes, he did try to find a job as a plasterer before the commission of the index crimes, and the time frame in which his delinquent behavior occurred was very brief and highly dependent on situational factors, i.e. financial problems. The two earlier offenses listed on his record are rather minor. Furthermore, the troublesome relationship with his parents is likely to improve with time if Samir succeeds at staying out of the criminal justice system. The withdrawal of his father was related to his contact with the law, and therefore might improve once his father regains trust in Samir. With potential parental support, the risk to recidivate would further decrease.

Return to the Findings from the First FMHA

After reaching my conclusions regarding Samir's formal diagnosis and recidivism risk, I reread the two previous mental health reports, and asked myself how my conclusions could be so remarkably different. How could the psychiatrist conclude that Samir was suffering from a personality disorder with narcissistic and antisocial features in development? How could the psychologist have concluded that a cluster of affective and interpersonal traits was present that pointed in the direction of psychopathy? The reasoning that seemed to make the most sense to me was that the two experts had placed an undue degree of weight on the criminal acts that Samir and his companions had committed. The many robberies were instrumental and took place with high frequency over a brief period of time. It might seem as if only a cold-blooded, unempathic individual could commit such acts. This is, of course, a serious attribution error, because a diagnosis should never be based on the type of crime a person has committed, but needs grounding in the person's behavior over the course of a lifetime. Furthermore, the experts also seemed to have overlooked the cultural aspects in Samir's case and the influence these had on his psychological functioning, and ultimately on his engagement in criminal behavior. Finally, they appear to have overlooked the now commonly held understanding that adolescents are still forming a cohesive personality and that they have features in common with adults with personality disorders (Seagrave & Grisso, 2002; Vitacco, Salekin, & Rogers, 2010). In recent years, the US Supreme Court has issued landmark opinions in three cases that involved the criminal culpability of adolescents. In the most recent ruling in *Miller v. Alabama* of 2012, states are prohibited from mandating life without parole for crimes committed by juveniles. In fact, the US Supreme Court pointed out that adolescents are more immature, more impulsive, and more susceptible to peer pressure—all of which are relevant features of Samir and the offenses. The Supreme Court cases and their argumentation were nicely summarized by Steinberg (2013; see Table 8.2).

The previous psychologist advised the court to adjucate Samir under adult criminal law because she considered him to be mature. What this maturity entailed exactly remains obscure. On the contrary, I would argue that a "maturity gap" played into his offenses as well. The motivation behind the crimes was primarily financial. Samir didn't see another way out of his financial difficulties: he didn't see it fit to alert a counselor or social worker, even though supported housing provides this kind of help. He says he couldn't tell his mother because he was afraid she'd feel hurt. He did not see that the spree of offenses would hurt her as well—and maybe even more. Retrospectively, he does remember having reservations (e.g., asking himself: "Is this really necessary?"), but was unable to act accordingly and refrain from committing the crimes. From reading his file and from his psychological assessment findings, there seem to be several reasons for this: out of fear of rejection by his companions, or because he suppressed the reservations and rationalized them. His thinking surrounding the offense illustrates many of the features of logic of the adolescent brain. From early adolescence well into early adulthood, the brain goes through an important maturation process, particularly in executive functioning (involving decision making, planning, voluntary response inhibition) and social cognition (self-awareness, theory of mind, perspective taking, etc.; Blakemore & Choudhury, 2006; Burke, 2011). During this time, decisions may be based on peer influences (committing crimes in a group) and egocentric needs, valuing short-term outcomes over long-term gains (fast money), and engaging in risky behavior more readily. This deficit in decision making ability relates to the concept of criminal responsibility and may be one of the inherent mitigating factors of adolescence (Scott & Steinberg, 2008).

Not all maturation is purely biological; it is influenced by social factors as well. The lack of an emotional bond between Samir and his father and the extended period of conflict means that his opportunities for positive social role modeling were limited.

Adolescents transferred to adult court receive harsher punishments, with longer and disproportionate sentencing (Kurlychek & Johnson, 2010). "Adult time for adult crime" does not discourage future offending, but may even promote it. Given all previous arguments, it would be reasonable to put Samir in a category of diminished responsibility, which, together with the findings from the FMHA, leaves little rationale for a transfer to adult court.

TABLE 8.2 The US Supreme Court's rationale in several cases concerning adolescents' criminal culpability

Case/ Year decided	Ruling	Rationale	Refs
Thompson v. Oklahoma, 1988	Capital punishment is found unconstitutional for individuals under the age of 16 years	"Contemporary standards of decency confirm our judgment that such a young person is not capable of acting with the degree of culpability that can justify the ultimate penalty."	8
Roper v. Simmons, 2005	Capital punishment is found unconstitutional for individuals under the age of 18 years	"As any parent knows and as the scientific and sociological studies . . . tend to confirm, [a] lack of maturity and an underdeveloped sense of responsibility are found in youth more often than in adults and are more understandable among the young."	3
Graham v. Florida, 2010	Life without parole is found unconstitutional for individuals under the age of 18 years convicted of crimes other than homicide	"No recent data provide reason to reconsider the Court's observations in Roper about the nature of juveniles. . . . Developments in psychology and brain science continue to show fundamental differences between juvenile and adult minds. For example, parts of the brain involved in behaviour control continue to mature through late adolescence."	4
Miller v. Alabama, 2012	States may not mandate life without parole for individuals under the age of 18 years, even in cases of homicide	"The evidence presented to us . . . indicates that the science and social science supporting Roper's and Graham's conclusions have become even stronger . . . It is increasingly clear that adolescent brains are not yet fully mature in regions and systems related to higher-order executive functions such as impulse control, planning ahead, and risk avoidance."	2

Discussion

The FMHA of a juvenile offender, more so than the FMHA of an adult subject, gives rise to a number of fundamental psycholegal issues, such as criminal responsibility and transfer to adult court. It also begs the question of continuity vs. discontinuity of psychopathology. It is incorrect to assume that a disorder present at time 1 is always predictive of the same disorder at time 2 (i.e., homotypic continuity). Research in developmental psychopathology has shown that a disorder may also be predicted by another disorder, so-called heterotypic continuity (Costello, Mustillo, Erklani, Keeler, & Angold, 2003). For example, in a prospective-longitudinal study, conduct and oppositional disorders in childhood showed associations not only with later addiction problems and antisocial personality disorder, but also vulnerability to subsequent depression, anxiety, eating disorders, and psychotic disorder (Kim-Cohen et al., 2003). This makes long-term predictions, such as those stated by the two previous mental health experts, quite inappropriate. In other words, if one identifies traits and behaviors consistent with psychopathy at a given point in time for a given youth (as the two previous experts did, albeit without enough basis in my opinion), these may be enduring characteristics of a future psychopathic adult. However, there is also the risk one may be observing a transient feature of a developmental process that will not be characteristic of the individual as he or she reaches adulthood (Edens, Skeem, Cruise, & Cauffman, 2001; Seagrave & Grisso, 2002). On the basis of this, scholars in the field of juvenile psychopathy advise against the use of psychopathy as a basis to justify transfer decisions (Vitacco et al., 2010, p. 387).

At the court hearing, the first two experts and I testified. The child psychiatrist who had also reported at the request of the court was also asked to testify but was prevented by illness. It was a remarkable court session. The first two experts had read my report and the report of the second psychiatrist (which came to similar conclusion as mine). The judge presiding over the court asked them if they had reconsidered their previous mental health evaluations and their conclusions. They had not. In fact, the psychiatrist, in particular, expressed a strong conviction that she saw signs of "hardening" in Samir and therefore adult criminal law had to be applied. During her testimony, she made some glaring errors. For instance, she claimed that Samir had been sent back to Morocco because of severe behavioral problems when he was still a young child. In response to this, Samir became upset and informed the court that this story of the psychiatrist was incorrect. Notwithstanding my report and my court testimony, the court decided to apply adult criminal law, and upheld the ruling of the lower court. While completing this chapter in March 2014, Samir is still imprisoned.

Notes

1   Samir (not his real name) gave written informed consent for use of the findings of the forensic mental health assessment and his file information, for teaching and publication purposes.

2   The legal drinking age was changed to 18 years as of January 1, 2014.
3   The distinction between individualistic and collectivistic cultures is seen as the most meaningful dimension in cross-cultural psychology (Heine, 2008). Collectivism emphasizes embeddedness of the individual in a social group. It encourages conformity and discourages dissenting. Individualism emphasizes personal freedom and achievement (Hofstede, 2001).

References

Abramowitz, C. S., Kosson, D. S., & Seidenberg, M. (2004). The relationship between childhood ADHD and conduct problems and adult psychopathy in male inmates. *Personality and Individual Differences, 36,* 1031–1047. doi: 10.1016/S0191–8869(03)00198–3.

Berry, J. W. (2005). Acculturation: Living successfully in two cultures. *International Journal of Intercultural Relations, 29,* 697–712.

Bevaart, F., Mieloo, C. L., Jansen, W., Raat, H., Donker, M. C. H., Verhulst, F. C., & van Oort, F. V. A. (2012). Ethnic differences in problem perception and perceived need for care for young children with problem behaviour. *Journal of Child Psychology and Psychiatry, 53,* 1063–1071. doi: 10.1111/j.1469–7610.2012.02570.x.

Blakemore, S. J. & Choudhury, S. (2006). Development of the adolescent brain: Implications for executive function and social cognition. *Journal of Child Psychology and Psychiatry, 47,* 296–312. doi: 10.1111/j.1469–7610.2006.01611.x.

Borum, R., Bartel, P., & Forth, A. (2006). *Structured assessment of violence risk in youth: Professional manual.* Sarasota, FL: PAR.

Brown, J. M. & Campbell, E. A. (2010). *The Cambridge handbook of forensic psychology.* New York: Cambridge University Press.

Burke, A. S. (2011). Under construction: Brain formation, culpability, and the criminal justice system. *International Journal of Law and Psychiatry, 34,* 381–385. doi: 10.1016/j.ijlp.2011.10.001.

Butcher, J. N., Dahlstrom, W. G., Graham, J. R., Tellegen, A., & Kaemmer, B. (1989). *Minnesota Multiphasic Personality Inventory-2 (MMPI-2): Manual for administration and scoring.* Minneapolis, MN: University of Minnesota Press.

Copeland, W. E., Miller-Johnson, S., Keeler, G., Angold, A., & Costello, E. J. (2007). Childhood psychiatric disorders and young adult crime: A prospective, population-based study. *American Journal of Psychiatry, 164,* 1668–1675. doi: 10.1176/appi.ajp.2007.06122026.

Costello, E. J., Mustillo, S., Erkanli, A., Keeler, G., & Angold, A. (2003). Prevalence and development of psychiatric disorders in childhood and adolescence. *Archives of General Psychiatry, 60,* 837–844. doi: 10.1001/archpsyc.60.8.837.

Deković, M., Janssens, J. M. A. M., & van As, N. M. C. (2003). Family predictors of antisocial behavior in adolescence. *Family Process, 42,* 223–235. doi: 10.1111/j.1545-5300.2003.42203.x.

Deković, M., Wissink, I. B., & Meijer, A. M. (2004). The role of family and peer relations in adolescent antisocial behavior: Comparison of four ethnic groups. *Journal of Adolescence, 27,* 497–514. doi: 10.1016/j.adolescence.2004.06.010.

Edens, J., Skeem, J., Cruise, K., & Cauffman, E. (2001). Assessment of "juvenile psychopathy" and its association with violence: A critical review. *Behavioral Sciences and the Law, 19,* 53–80.

Forth, A., Kosson, D., & Hare, R. D. (2003). *Psychopathy checklist: Youth version*. Toronto, ON: Multi-Health Systems.

Friedman, A. F., Lewak, R., Nichols, D. S., & Webb, J. T. (2001). *Psychological assessment with the MMPI-2*. Mahwah, NJ: Erlbaum.

Heilbrun, K. (2001). *Principles of forensic mental health assessment*. New York: Kluwer Academic/Plenum.

Heine, S. J. (2008). *Cultural psychology*. New York: W. W. Norton.

Hofstede, G. (2001). *Culture's consequences: Comparing values, behaviors, and organizations across nations* (2nd ed.). Thousand Oaks, CA: Sage.

Howell, J. C. (2009). *Preventing and reducing juvenile delinquency*. Thousand Oaks, CA: Sage.

Jennissen, R. & Besjes, G. (2012). Geregistreerde criminaliteit [Registered criminality]. In *Jaarrapport Integratie 2012*. The Hague, The Netherlands: Sociaal en Cultureel Planbureau.

Kim-Cohen, J., Caspi, A., Moffitt, T. E., Harrington, H., Milne, B. J., & Poulton, R. (2003). Prior juvenile diagnoses in adults with mental disorder: Developmental follow-back of a prospective longitudinal cohort. *Archives of General Psychiatry, 60,* 709–717. doi: 10.1001/archpsyc.60.7.709.

Kurlychek, M. C. & Johnson, B. D. (2010). Juvenility and punishment: Sentencing juveniles in adult criminal court. *Criminology, 48,* 725–758. doi: 10.1111/j.1745-9125.2010. 00200.x.

Lodewijks, H., Doreleijers, Th., de Ruiter, C., & de Wit-Grouls, H. (2006). SAVRY: *Handleiding voor de gestructureerde risicotaxatie van gewelddadig gedrag bij Jongeren* [Structured Assessment of Violence Risk in Youth: Dutch version]. Zutphen, The Netherlands: Rentray.

Lodewijks, H. P. B., de Ruiter, C., & Doreleijers, T. A. H. (2008a). Gender differences in risk assessment and violent outcome after juvenile residential treatment. *International Journal of Forensic Mental Health, 7,* 133–146. doi: 10.1080/14999013.2008.9914410.

Lodewijks, H. P. B., Doreleijers, T. A. H., & de Ruiter, C. (2008b). SAVRY risk assessment in relation to sentencing and subsequent recidivism in a Dutch sample of violent juvenile offenders. *Criminal Justice and Behavior, 35,* 696–709. doi: 10.1177/0093854808316146.

Lodewijks, H. P. B., Doreleijers, T. A. H., de Ruiter, C., & Borum, R. (2008c). Predictive validity of the Structured Assessment of Violence Risk in Youth (SAVRY) during residential treatment. *International Journal of Law and Psychiatry, 31,* 263–271. doi: 10.1016/j.ijlp.2008.04.009.

Lodewijks, H. P. B., de Ruiter, C., & Doreleijers, T. A. H. (2010). The impact of protective factors in desistance from violent reoffending: A study in three samples of adolescent offenders. *Journal of Interpersonal Violence, 25,* 568–587. doi: 10.1177/0886260509334403.

Mulder, E., Brand, E., Bullens, R., & Van Marle, H. (2010). A classification of risk factors in serious juvenile offenders and the relation between patterns of risk factors and recidivism. *Criminal Behaviour and Mental Health, 20,* 23–38. doi: 10.1002/cbm.754.

Mulder, E., Brand, E., Bullens, R., & Van Marle, H. (2011). Risk factors for overall recidivism and severity of recidivism in serious juvenile offenders. *International Journal of Offender Therapy and Comparative Criminology, 55,* 118–135. doi: 10.1177/ 0306624X09356683.

Nicolaas, H., Loozen, S., & Annema, A. (2012). Demografie [Demography]. In *Jaarrapport Integratie 2012*. The Hague, The Netherlands: Sociaal en Cultureel Planbureau.

Paalman, C. H., van Domburgh, L., Stevens, G. W. J. M., & Doreleijers, T. A. H. (2011). Individual, family and offence characteristics of high risk childhood offenders:

Comparing nonoffending, one-time offending and re-offending Dutch-Moroccan migrant children in The Netherlands. *Child and Adolescent Psychiatry and Mental Health*, 5, 33. www.capmh.com/content/5/1/33.

Pakes, F. (2010). Global forces and local effects in youth justice: The case of Moroccan youngsters in The Netherlands. *International Journal of Law, Crime and Justice*, 38, 109–119.

de Ruiter, C. & Hildebrand, M. (2010). *Hare Psychopathie Checklist: Jeugdversie (PCL:JV): Handleiding* [Psychopathy Checklist: Youth Version. Dutch manual]. Amsterdam, The Netherlands: Pearson.

Salekin, R. T. & Grimes, R. D. (2008). Clinical forensic evaluations for juvenile transfer to adult criminal court. In R. Jackson (Ed.), *Learning forensic assessment* (pp. 313–346). New York: Taylor & Francis.

Scott, E. S. & Steinberg, L. (2008). *Rethinking juvenile justice*. Cambridge, MA: Harvard University Press.

Seagrave, D. & Grisso, T. (2002). Adolescent development and the measurement of juvenile psychopathy. *Law and Human Behavior*, 26, 219–239. doi: 10.1023/A:1014 696110850.

Steinberg, L. (2013). The influence of neuroscience on US Supreme Court decisions about adolescents' criminal culpability. *Nature Reviews Neuroscience*, 14, 513–518. doi: 10.1038/nrn3509.

Stevens, G. W. J. M., Veen, V. C., & Vollebergh, W. (2014). Psychological acculturation and juvenile delinquency: Comparing Moroccan immigrant families from a general and pretrial detention population. *Cultural Diversity and Ethnic Minority Psychology*, 20, 254–265. doi: 10.1037/a0035024.

Stevens, G. W. J. M., Vollebergh, W. A. M., Pels, T. V. M., & Crijnen, A. A. M. (2005). Predicting externalizing problems in Moroccan immigrant adolescents in the Netherlands. *Social Psychiatry and Psychiatric Epidemiology*, 40, 571–579. doi: 10.1007/s00127–005–0926-x.

Stevens, G. W. J. M., Vollebergh, W. A. M., Pels, T. V. M., & Crijnen, A. A. M. (2007). Parenting and internalizing and externalizing problems in Moroccan immigrant youth in The Netherlands. *Journal of Youth and Adolescence*, 36, 685–695. doi: 10.1007/s10964–006–9112-z.

Vitacco, M. J., Salekin, R. T., & Rogers, R. (2010). Forensic issues for child and adolescent psychopathy. In R. T. Salekin & D. R. Lynam (Eds.), *Handbook of child and adolescent psychopathy* (pp. 374–397). New York: Guilford.

Webster, C. D., Douglas, K. S., Eaves, D., & Hart, S. D. (1997). *HCR-20: Assessing the risk of violence (version 2)*. Burnaby, BC: Mental Health, Law, and Policy Institute, Simon Fraser University.

Zimring, F. E. (2000). The punitive necessity of waiver. In J. Fagan & F. E. Zimring (Eds.), *The changing borders of juvenile justice: Transfer of adolescents to the criminal court* (pp. 207–224). Chicago: University of Chicago Press.

Zwirs, B. W. C., Burger, H., Buitelaar, J. K., & Schulpen, T. W. J. (2006). Ethnic differences in parental detection of externalizing disorders. *European Child and Adolescent Psychiatry*, 15, 418–426. doi: 10.1007/s00787–006–0550–7.

Zwirs, B. W. C., Burger, H., Schulpen, T. W. J., & Buitelaar, J. K. (2006). Different treatment thresholds in non-western children with behavioural problems. *Journal of the American Academy of Child and Adolescent Psychiatry*, 45, 476–483. doi: 10.1097/01.chi.0000192251.46023.5a.

9

THREAT ASSESSMENT IN HOMICIDE/SUICIDE

The Duty to Warn[1]

Nancy Kaser-Boyd

Evaluating the threat of homicide and suicide has become a critical skill for mental health practitioners because of the occurrence of so many mass shootings. Klein (2012) notes in *The Washington Post* that there have been at least 61 mass murders in the United States since 1982. Europe has had its own mass murders, while not equal in number, equal in horror. Few of the mass murderers have been seen in mental health settings and often what we know about them comes from post-mortem data-gathering. In some cases, the shooter survives and proffers a mental state defense, which affords the forensic psychologist the opportunity to come to know and understand the risk factors and their interaction and use these to assist in the assessment of violence risk. This chapter will present research findings and clinical insight about such individuals. Violence risk assessment has mostly focused on evaluating the risk of individuals in forensic psychiatric and correctional facilities, to evaluate sexually violent predators, offenders with mental illness, and offenders being considered for parole (McSherry & Keyzer, 2011; Otto & Douglas, 2010). Meloy, Hoffmann, Guldimann, and James (2011) outline the difference between violence risk assessment and threat assessment. In risk assessment, there is often a history of violent behavior and the evaluation is performed in a static setting such as a prison or hospital. In contrast, in threat assessment, there may be no history of violence. Something has caused the individual to become of concern. The evaluation is often acutely dynamic, unfolding in real time as the threat evolves toward an unidentified or possibly identified target.

This chapter is about threat assessment rather than violence risk assessment. I will use the term *violence risk*, but the population I will be discussing is different from that on which violence risk assessment tools are typically used. There is a clear need to understand the risk posed by individuals who have, perhaps, never committed a violent act, or never appeared to be violent or threatening. There are many examples of such individuals from everyday news—Anders Behring Breivik, who took a ferryboat to a Norwegian Island and killed 77 people, most of them young adults; James Holmes, the Colorado neuroscience graduate student who killed 12 people in a movie theatre and wounded 58; and Seung-Hui Cho, who killed 32 people at Virginia Polytechnic Institute and State University.[2] In addition to those who go on rampages to kill many people, there are those who stalk and kill an ex-wife or girlfriend, and those who kill their lawyer or doctor or employer they believe has mistreated them. Then there are the school shooters. Many of these homicidal individuals kill themselves after their acts. This illustrates the close connection between suicide and homicide in some individuals. Although many of these individuals were never seen by mental health professionals, some were, and their potential violence risk was missed or mishandled. For example, James Holmes was being seen by a campus psychiatrist, who alerted campus police about his potential dangerousness, but it was determined that it was "out of their jurisdiction," after he failed his oral examinations and dropped out of graduate school a few weeks prior to the rampage.

Conventional psychology has been cautious about predictions of violence risk in individuals who have never acted out violently, because of fears about the inaccuracy of such predictions and the cost to the individual of possibly impeding their freedom. However, there has been an increasing expectation on mental health professionals to have the skill to recognize a dangerous person or a person in a dangerous mental state. Days after the Newtown, Connecticut shooting of 20 children, there was an almost instantaneous call for mental health services that could predict or prevent such atrocities (Altimari, January 21, 2013). In the United States, when there is a formal threat to harm another, most mental health professionals must give so-called *Tarasoff* warnings to an intended victim or victims. The *Tarasoff* case from 1976 (*Tarasoff v. The Regents of the University of California*, 1976) is instructive, even today.

The *Tarasoff* Doctrine

Tatiana Tarasoff was a student at the University of California, Berkeley in the late 1960s. Tatiana was killed by a fellow student, Prosanjit Poddar, after she rebuffed his romantic interest. The following facts were taken from Poddar's appeal to the California Supreme Court (*People v. Poddar*, 1974). Poddar was from an "untouchable" caste in India. He came to the UC Berkeley campus as a graduate student in 1967 and lived at the International House. In the following year, he attended folk dancing classes and it was there he met Tatiana. She was a friendly girl. At the New Year's dance at the International House, in the spontaneity of the moment, she kissed him. Poddar interpreted this as a sign of a serious relationship. She told him she was not interested in a relationship with him. Stunned, he appeared to go into a clinical depression, neglecting his studies, his appearance, and his health. Over the next several months, his mental state deteriorated.

He saw Tatiana occasionally, at public functions, and when he could engage her in conversation, he tape-recorded her—tapes which he listened to over and over in order to attempt to ascertain why she didn't love him. During the summer months Tatiana went abroad to study. A friend of Poddar convinced him to seek treatment, and he went to the UC student health service, where he was prescribed an antipsychotic. Poddar told his outpatient psychologist that he was in love with an unnamed girl and he believed he would have to kill her to end his obsessive thoughts about her. The psychologist found out from a third person that Poddar had been considering buying a gun, and he became concerned about Poddar's potential for violence. The psychologist then consulted with his supervising psychiatrist and the psychiatrist who had prescribed an antipsychotic. Together they decided to call and write to the campus police, asking them to apprehend Poddar. They told the police that Poddar was suffering from paranoid schizophrenia, acute and severe, and they were asking the police to civilly commit Poddar. At that time, in California, there was law permitting the involuntarily hospitalization of individuals who were deemed dangerous to themselves or others, or gravely disabled. However, the police found Poddar to be rational and they did not detain him. They simply told him to stay away from Tatiana.

Two months later, Poddar killed Tatiana. He went to her home armed with a pellet gun and a kitchen knife, and he found her home alone. She refused to speak to him. He grabbed her, and she struggled, whereupon he shot her with the pellet gun, she ran from the house, and he caught her and stabbed her 14 times. He then returned to her house and called the police. Poddar was convicted of second degree murder and sentenced to California State Prison for the statutory term, 15 years to life (*People v. Poddar*, 1974). His conviction was reversed, on appeal, and he was allowed to leave the country after having served only 5 years.

Tatiana's parents sued the Regents of the University of California on two grounds: (1) the Student Health Service had failed to detain a patient who was a danger to others, under the Lanterman-Petris-Short Act (1967);[3] and (2) that Poddar was released without warning Tatiana or her parents that she was in grave danger. The UC Regents and the doctors argued that they had no duty of care toward Tatiana because she was not their patient. The California Supreme Court disagreed and ruled that the treatment providers should have determined that Poddar represented a serious danger to Tatiana and they failed to exercise reasonable care to protect her from that danger (*Tarasoff v. The Regents of the University of California*, 1976). The Supreme Court stated:

> Where the patient has communicated to the psychotherapist a serious threat of physical violence against a reasonably identifiable victim or victims, it is the psychotherapist's duty to make a reasonable effort to communicate the threat to the victim(s) and to a law enforcement agency and take reasonable action to protect the victim. The discharge of this duty may require the therapist to take one or more of various steps, depending upon the nature

of the case. It may call for him to warn the intended victim or others likely to appraise the victim of the danger, to notify the police, or to take whatever other steps are reasonably necessary under the circumstances.

The California Legislature subsequently passed legislation refining the language of *Tarasoff* and limiting the psychotherapist's liability, stating:

> No cause of action shall arise against . . . any . . . psychotherapist in failing to warn of and protect from a patient's threatened violent behavior or failing to predict and warn of and protect from a patient's violent behavior, except where the patient has communicated to the psychotherapist a serious threat of physical violence against a reasonably identified victim. . . . If there is a duty to warn and protect under the limited circumstances specified above, the duty shall be discharged by the psychotherapist making reasonable efforts to communicate the threat to the victim . . . and to a law enforcement agency.

More recently, the California Court of Appeals expanded *Tarasoff* in *Ewing v. Goldstein* (2004) and *Ewing v. Northridge Hospital* (2004). These rulings resulted from the killing of Keith Ewing, the new boyfriend of the shooter's ex-girlfriend. Gene Colello had become despondent over the break-up with his girlfriend and told his father that he would kill Ewing. His father relayed that threat to his son's psychotherapist, Dr. Goldstein, who urged him to take Gene to Northridge Hospital. Colello was admitted to the hospital as a voluntary patient. His father also told the intake worker about the threat his son had voiced. Colello was released the following day. One day later, he shot and killed Ewing and then killed himself. Ewing's parents filed suit, alleging that Colello posed a danger to their son that had been foreseeable by both the psychotherapist and the hospital, a threat that they failed to communicate to Ewing. The California Court of Appeals (*Ewing v. Goldstein*, 2004 and *Ewing v. Northridge Hospital*, 2004) held that the defendants (Dr. Goldstein and Northridge Hospital) did have a duty to warn based on the statements by Colello's father. The Appellate Court ruled that the California legislature did not intend to shield a therapist from suit in such a situation because, for the sake of public safety, it would want a therapist to seriously consider a communication "from a family member to the patient's therapist" in deciding whether a *Tarasoff* warning was needed. The case was appealed to the California Supreme Court, but the Court declined to review the case, so this stands as current California case law (Fridhandler, 2005).

States in the US differ in the language of their *Tarasoff* legislation. According to a review by Herbert and Young (2002), 27 US states, following *Tarasoff*, impose a mandatory duty to warn, although the precise requirements of the duty vary considerably. Nine states, plus the District of Columbia, accord psychotherapists permission to warn without explicitly imposing a duty to warn. Virginia flatly rejects *Tarasoff*. The 13 remaining states and the Federal Government have no definitive law on the issue. In California, as well as many other states, if the patient/person is deemed to be a danger to self or others, the next step is voluntary or involuntary hospitalization. Each jurisdiction in the United States has its own statutes for involuntary hospitalization (Lenell, 1977).

In The Netherlands, there is as yet no legislation similar to the *Tarasoff* rule (de Ruiter, 2011). The confidentiality of the therapist-client relationship has thus far taken precedent over the wish to protect possible future victims. In recent years, the debate on this issue again became quite vehement after the first mass shooting in a shopping center occurred in the city of Alphen aan den Rijn in The Netherlands on Saturday April 9, 2011. Twenty-four-year-old Tristan van der Vlis spent less than 15 minutes walking through the shopping center where people were shopping for their weekend groceries on this sunny spring Saturday morning. He killed seven people (including himself) and seriously injured 17. He used the firearms he legally possessed (he was a member of a shooting association), including a semi-automatic rifle. He wore a bomber jacket, camouflage pants, and a bulletproof vest during the rampage, emulating the attire previous spree killers had worn (Langman, 2012). Soon after the mass killing, it became clear that Tristan had a psychiatric history. In 2006, he had been civilly committed for 10 days because of a suicide attempt. In 2008, he also made two attempts at killing himself. He was a member of a shooting club, just like his father and in legal possession of five firearms. The Netherlands Institute of Forensic Psychiatry and Psychology (NIFP), a unit under the Department of Justice, was asked to perform a psychological autopsy on the Tristan case. A summary of the report was published on the NIFP website in July 2011, but the entire report was not made public "for privacy reasons" (www.nifp.net). The summary stated that Tristan was suffering from paranoid Schizophrenia and that this disorder was of paramount importance in causing the attack. Tristan's parents had become increasingly worried about their son's condition, although he had been putting up a façade of good mental health. Tristan was noncompliant with his medication. Ultimately, he saw no other solution than to commit suicide, but not until he had punished God by killing his creatures. Tristan's main delusion was that he denounced the Christian God and was convinced he had found a better God and he had also written a new Bible.

It is remarkable that the mental health center where Tristan had been in treatment did not release his medical records, not even after his parents had given consent to do so. The center defended its decision on grounds of (medical) confidentiality. This unwillingness to share medical information also rendered the NIFP psychological autopsy report incomplete. The contrast with the culture in the US surrounding homicide/suicide cases could not be greater. For instance, in the case of the Korean student Cho, the State of Virginia released a comprehensive report documenting his life history, the course of his psychiatric symptoms, and the treatment he received, including the decisions made to manage his risk (Virginia Tech Review Panel, 2007). The main objective of such a detailed review report is to learn from the analysis, so that hopefully future attacks can be prevented. The Virginia Tech report comprises 147 pages, excluding numerous appendices, and is published on the Internet. This stands in stark contrast to the two-page summary on the Internet of the NIFP report on the Dutch Tristan case.

The Dynamics of Homicide

Both violence risk assessment and threat assessment target events that are relatively rare; they are "low base-rate" events and thus difficult to predict. What follows is a summary of known background dynamics of different types of low base-rate homicide. The empirical knowledge base on these types of extreme violence is less extensive than it is for high base-rate phenomena, such as interpartner violence.

Mass Murder

Mass murder is defined as the killing of multiple people—usually defined as four—in a rampage, in a short period of time (Fox & Levin, 2012). It is distinguished from serial murder, where killings are carried out over a period of time, often with a sexual motive. The number of cases of mass murder seems high, based on the quick reporting of such cases in the worldwide media. Statistics seem to clearly indicate that this phenomenon is much more frequent in the United States, where access to guns is easy. As the Anders Breivik case indicates, such horrible events can occur in Europe as well, although some countries have few mass murders. De Ruiter (2011) recently reviewed all mass murder cases (N = 18) that occurred in Europe during the period 2000–2009 and found that Finland (2) and Germany (5) were overrepresented. Between 1976 and 2010, the United States experienced 645 mass murder events, where at least four victims were killed; this is about 20 US cases per year (Fox, 2007). Because the number of cases is not large in an absolute sense, and a proportion of the perpetrators kill themselves after their attack, it is difficult to conduct formal research on this population. Hempel, Meloy, and Richards (1999) combed 50 years' of psychiatric, psychological, and criminological databases from the United States and Canada, reviewing scientific articles, books, videotapes, audiotapes, newspapers, and interviews with law enforcement officers, victims, and acquaintances of perpetrators. They identified 30 mass murderers who had committed their crimes between 1949 and 1998. This is the only large-scale study of this type of crime and provides important demographic and clinical information about these perpetrators.

- All of the mass murderers were male and the majority were Caucasian. Their mean age was 38.3.

- Sixty-seven percent of the group were divorced or never married. Ninety-four percent could be described as "loners," defined as spending most of their time alone.
- Sixty-three percent were unemployed at the time of the murders. Half had been employed in blue collar jobs, 30 percent had professional occupations.
- Forty-seven percent had served in the military—an important variable because of their acquired familiarity with weapons.
- Fifty percent had a documented psychiatric history, defined as at least one psychiatric hospitalization or one visit with a mental health professional before the mass murder. The most common Axis I diagnoses were paranoid Schizophrenia, Delusional Disorder, and Major Depression. Forty percent evidenced psychotic symptoms at the time of the mass murder, usually paranoid and/or persecutory delusions. An additional 27 percent exhibited behavior suggestive of psychosis.
- Forty-three percent had a history of violence, defined as at least one violent act against a person or animal prior to the mass murder.
- On Axis II, Cluster A and B traits and disorders predominated. Fifty percent exhibited antisocial traits, 37 percent paranoid traits, 40 percent narcissistic traits, 17 percent schizoid traits, 10 percent depressive traits, and 7 percent demonstrated schizotypal traits. Obviously, some individuals were categorized as having more than one type of personality trait.
- Alcohol was consumed by only 10 percent of the perpetrators prior to the killings; there was no information on use of drugs.
- The most common precipitating event was job-related (50 percent) and involved termination, envy of another's promotion, confrontation by an employer, denial of a job reinstatement, bankruptcy, denial of tenure, and anger at employers for employment disability leave. The second-most common precipitant was related to a close relationship (23 percent) and involved actual or perceived abandonment, jealousy, erotomanic beliefs, or child custody or support issues.
- Fifty-three percent committed suicide after the murders; 33 percent were captured; 10 percent were killed.

The authors report additional findings which are particularly important for threat assessment. Thirty-three percent of the murderers had previously made a specific threat against others. These were made either verbally or in writing and clearly described the future mass murder as to location, victims, and/or time. Twenty-three percent made a generalized threat. This was defined as lacking a specific location or victim pool. These included statements such as "I am going hunting" and "Society had their chance."

Mass murderers had often been stockpiling weapons, ammunition, and battle gear. The authors write:

The number of weapons brought to the mass murder ranged from one to 11, with a mean of 3.1. Weapons and other paraphernalia included semi-automatic pistols, semi-automatic rifles, revolvers, bolt-action rifles, hunting knives, a samurai sword, shotguns, nylon cord, shooting glasses, ear plugs, hand grenades, materials to manufacture homemade bombs, black talon bullets, machine guns, silencers, flammable liquids, karate throwing stars, gas masks, bullet-proof vests, binoculars, machetes, charcoal lighter fluid, rope, hatchets, and matches.

(p. 217)

Also, the authors found that 63 percent of the men were preoccupied with weapons or war regalia, defined as spending a significant amount of time around themes of war and violence. They write:

Behaviors included ownership of a large number of weapons such as guns and knives; ownership of large numbers of audio, visual, and reading materials with war, terrorism, or weapons as the main theme; ownership and frequent wearing of military uniforms and combat fatigues; frequent trips to a gun range; practicing martial arts at inappropriate times and places; prophetically violent bumper stickers such as "You'll get my gun when you pry it from my cold, dead fingers"; excessive verbiage focusing on themes of weaponry and violence; evidence of grandiose fantasies centering on war and weaponry; infatuation with Nazi regalia; idealizing famous fictional and nonfictional violent characters; and setting up a gun range inside one's home.

(p. 215)

The preoccupation with themes of violence and the collection of weapons and battle gear are important and observable features that can be used in threat assessment, as can the individual's interpersonal stance and world view. The authors note, "The interpersonal histories of mass murderers suggest a paranoid-schizoid position toward others and the world: a perception of others as persecutory and malevolent objects along with the absence of a desire, and perhaps a capacity, to form affectional bonds" (p. 219). These individuals, they note, have a particular tendency to externalize blame. They state that this "predicts the accumulation and incubation of insults over time, magnified through the lens of hypervigilance, and washed in feelings of anger and resentment" (p. 219).

Fox and Levin (2012) reviewed cases reported in printed media in the United States from a sociological perspective and made similar findings about mass murderers. They report 95 percent of mass killings to be committed by men. The mass murderers tend to be loners and feel alienated from others. They often have histories of being rejected, feeling humiliated and worthless. Over time, they develop resentment, and they externalize their anger onto others—sometimes specific individuals such as co-workers, but sometimes in a more global way in the form of anger at "the world." They have impaired empathy for others and often feel contemptuous of others. They may be set off by an event that seems to them like a catastrophic failure. The case of James Holmes is illustrative in this regard, as he had failed an important oral exam in his graduate program and left the course before his rampage in a Colorado movie theatre. Their homicidal ideation involves fantasies of killing. They may stockpile ammunition and engage in planning and dress rehearsals. Often, at the time of their acts, they are in complete control of their emotions and know exactly what they want to do. They rarely hear voices, although they may have delusions. They are often nihilistic and don't expect to live after their rampage. They will shoot until shot down, or kill themselves as police are closing in. In the eyes of the perpetrator, the shooting may bring immortality and the rampage is their crowning achievement.

A lack of explicit threats of violence is common to workplace violence (Meloy et al., 2011) and to the targeted killing of political and celebrity victims (Fein, Vossekuil, & Holden, 1995). Southerland, Collins and Scarborough (1997) analyzed public records of 282 lethal workplace attacks and found that just 27 percent of the perpetrators had previously threatened violence. Fein et al. (1995) note, "The assumption of many writers is that those who make threats pose threats. While some threateners may pose threats, sometimes those who pose threats do not make threats" (p. 330). In their research on assassins of political figures, they found that fewer than a tenth of the assassins and near-lethal attackers they studied communicated a direct threat to the target or a law enforcement agency. While there may be an absence of direct or implicit threats in targeted violence, Meloy and colleagues (2011) note that there are often behaviors that "warn" of increasing threat. They define "warning behaviors" as factors which constitute change and are evidence of increasing or accelerating risk. Emphasizing that their typology of warning behaviors is rationally derived and needs further empirical research, they include:

(1) pathway warning behavior—behavior that involves research, planning, or preparation for an attack;
(2) fixation warning behavior—behavior that indicates a pathological preoccupation with a person or a cause. This is often accompanied by social or occupational deterioration;
(3) identification warning behavior—behavior that indicates a desire to be a "pseudo-commando," identify with previous attackers or assassins, or identify oneself as an agent to advance a particular cause or belief system;
(4) novel aggression warning behavior—behavior that is new for the person but may be used to test the ability to commit a violent act;
(5) energy burst warning behavior—an acceleration of goal-directed behavior involving the target;
(6) leakage warning behavior—communication to a third party of an intent to commit harm to a target;[4]

(7) last resort warning behavior—increasing desperation or distress, feeling that there is no alternative other than the act, and that the consequences are justified;

(8) directly communicated threat warning behavior. A written or oral threat that implicitly or explicitly states a wish or intent to harm the target.

School Shooters

The mass murders studied above contained a few rampages at college campuses, but there is additional insightful research about adolescents who went on killing rampages on their high school campus (Vossekuil, Fein, Reddy, Borum, & Modzeleski, 2002). Researchers from the US Secret Service and the Department of Education explored all searchable databases maintained in the public domain to identify incidents meeting the definition of a school shooting.[5] They identified 37 incidents of targeted school violence involving 41 attackers that occurred in the United States between 1974 and 2000. In addition to information in the public domain, the authors were able to conduct supplemental interviews with 10 of the perpetrators of school-based attacks. Two or more reviewers reviewed data about (1) motives and plans; (2) mental state; (3) life circumstances; (4) other relevant factors. There was no single "profile" of a student who engaged in targeted school violence. They found:

- The age of the school shooters ranged from 11 to 21 years, with most attackers between the ages of 13 and 18. Three-quarters of the attackers were white.
- Very few of the attackers were known to be failing in school (5 percent). The largest group (41 percent) was doing well in school at the time of the attack, generally receiving As and Bs in their courses.
- Few attackers had no close friends (12 percent). Twenty-seven percent socialized with fellow students who were disliked by most mainstream students or were considered to be part of a "fringe" group. One-third of attackers had been characterized by others as "loners," or felt they were loners. The largest group (41 percent) appeared to socialize with mainstream students or were considered mainstream students themselves.
- Sixty-three percent had never or rarely been in trouble at school. Only a few (10 percent) had ever been expelled from school.
- Almost two-thirds (71 percent) of the attackers felt persecuted, bullied, threatened, attacked, or injured by others prior to the incident. In several cases, individuals had experienced bullying and harassment that was long-standing and severe.[6]
- Only 34 percent of attackers had ever received a mental health evaluation, and fewer than one-fifth had been diagnosed with mental or behavioral disorders prior to the attack.

- Although most attackers had not received a formal mental health evaluation or diagnosis, most (78 percent) exhibited a history of suicide attempts or suicidal thoughts at some point prior to their attack. More than half (61 percent) had a documented history of feeling extremely depressed or desperate.
- Over half (59 percent) demonstrated some interest in violence through movies, video games, books, and other media. The largest group of attackers (37 percent) exhibited an interest in violence in their own writings such as poems, essays, or journal entries.
- Few had a prior history of violence towards other people (31 percent) or animals (12 percent).
- Most were considered to have difficulty coping with significant losses or personal failures. Ninety-eight percent had experienced or perceived some major loss prior to the attack. These included loss of status, loss of a loved one or a significant relationship, a major illness in self or significant other.
- The school-based attacks were rarely impulsive. They were typically thought out and required some degree of advance planning. In many cases, the attacker's observable behavior prior to the attack suggested he might be planning or preparing for a school attack.
- In terms of motive, 61 percent of targeted shootings appeared to be driven by revenge, but most of the attackers had multiple motives, including attention or recognition seeking, desperation, or a misguided belief that it was going to solve their problem.
- In 81 percent of the cases, at least one person had information that the attacker was thinking about or planning the school attack. In 59 percent of the cases, more than one person had information about the attack before it occurred. These other persons were usually peers.
- Most did not express direct threats before their attack, only 17 percent did.
- Almost all (93 percent) engaged in some kind of behavior prior to the attack that caused others to be concerned about them.
- In 44 percent of the cases, the attackers were influenced by other students, that is, dared or encouraged by others to attack.
- Most attackers had access to weapons prior to the attack. Sixty-three percent had a known history of weapon use including knives, guns, and bombs. Over two-thirds of the attackers acquired the guns used in their attacks from their own home or that of a relative.

Domestic Violence Homicides

Few clinicians, even forensic clinicians, will be in a position to triage a mass murderer or a school shooter before their act. It is much more likely that a mental health practitioner working in a hospital or clinical setting, or even in private practice, will be confronted with the need for threat assessment in a domestic violence case. Such was the case in *Hedlund v. The Superior Court of Orange County*

(1983). In this case, a psychological assistant (Ms. Hedlund) at a local university clinic was seeing a man and woman, LaNita and Stephen Wilson, in treatment. Stephen threatened to harm LaNita and the therapist warned her of the threats but reportedly did not advise her of the potential dangerousness. Ultimately, the man ran the woman and their son off the road in her car and then shot her, leading to the loss of a leg. The woman sued the therapist and the clinic, claiming that they did not warn her of the danger to herself or her son. The Supreme Court of California held that the therapist and clinic owed a duty to warn, not only to the woman but also to her son. The Court held that the potential threat to the boy was foreseeable because children are not usually far from their parents. This extended the *Tarasoff* ruling to a "foreseeable" bystander in a close relationship to the victim of an assault. They said a therapist has a duty to exercise a reasonable degree of skill, knowledge, and care ordinarily possessed and exercised by members of that profession under similar circumstances in making a prediction about the likelihood of a client acting dangerously to others.

California has seen many domestic violence cases where a violent and estranged man has killed his wife and sometimes members of her family. Perhaps the most remarkable case was that of a 45-year-old Stockton, California marriage counselor who specialized in anger management who killed his ex-wife, her sister, and her aunt before shooting himself (CBS News, October 24, 2012). The danger in domestic violence (Intimate Partner Battering or IPB cases) is real. According to the US Department of Justice, in the last decade, intimate partners committed 14 percent of all homicides in the US. Women made up around 70 percent of victims killed by an intimate partner, and this was twice the rate of males killed by intimate partners (Catalano, Smith, Snyder, & Rand, 2009). The killing of a woman by her intimate partner or former partner accounts for 40 to 50 percent of all deaths of American women killed (Monckton, 2012). Interpartner homicide (IPH) perpetrators are mostly men (82.7 percent) and a large number (42 percent) committed suicide after following through with the homicide (Garcia, Soria, & Hurwitz, 2007). Divorced or separated individuals had the highest rates of IPH (Rennison & Welchans, 2000). Occasions when a parent kills his partner and children are termed "familicide" (see Chapter 2, this book, for a case of familicide in which the husband did not have a history of spousal battering). Research on intimate partner homicide has demonstrated that the majority of these homicides (65–70 percent of the cases where the female partner is killed, 75 percent of cases where the male partner is killed) are preceded by intimate partner violence against the female partner (Campbell et al., 2003);[7] this was the finding of an 11-city study of risk factors for intimate partner femicide with 220 femicides and a control group of 343 battered women. Seventy-two percent of the IP femicides were preceded by IPB by the male partner before he killed his female partner. This makes a history of intimate partner violence the most important risk factor for intimate partner homicide. Sharps and colleagues (2001) found that in up to 83 percent of homicides in the United States, one or both partners had contact with the criminal justice system, victim assistance programs, and/or health care agencies in the year prior to the homicide. This raises important questions about risk and threat assessment. Sharps et al. (2001) also found that of femicides sampled, 23 percent of the women were beaten while pregnant. In a subsequent study, McFarlane, Campbell, Sharps, and Watson (2002) found a statistically significant association between abuse during pregnancy and attempted/completed femicide (Odds Ratio = 3.7). Black women, compared with white women, had a threefold increase in the risk of abuse during pregnancy and attempted/completed femicide (Odds Ratio = 3.6).

Stalking and harassment occurred in 70 to 90 percent of 200 actual and attempted femicides in 11 US cities (McFarlane et al., 1999). The forms of stalking with the strongest association with IP femicide were: following the woman to work or school, destruction of her property, and leaving threatening messages on her telephone. Since stalking is often reported to police agencies, this is another important source of information for assessing risk of extreme/lethal violence.

From the earliest days of research on IPH, it was clear that when an abused woman attempts to leave an abuser, the violence risk increases. Campbell and colleagues' 11-city study (Campbell et al., 2003) found that 55 percent of the intimate partner femicide victims were estranged from their partners when killed. The authors concluded that estrangement in the prior year increased the risk of femicide by an Odds Ratio of 3.64. When the perpetrator was highly controlling and there was estrangement, the adjusted Odds Ratio increased to 5.52. Wilson and Daly (1993) and Wilson, Johnson, and Daly (1995) found that the first 3 months after separation was the time of most risk, and for the women killed, the killing was usually in the first year after separation (Campbell et al., 2003).

Campbell et al.'s study (2003) further delineated risk factors for IPH. They found unemployment of the perpetrator to increase the risk of IP femicide by an Odds Ratio of 4.42. Sharps et al. (2001) found that 51 percent of the perpetrators of 252 intimate partner homicides were unemployed. Alcohol abuse on the part of the man, but not the woman, was also a risk factor. This was supported by Lipsky, Caetano, Field, and Larkin (2005) who reported that heavy drinking by the male partner increased the risk of IPH by 5 times. Male offenders were more likely than their female victims to drink alcohol or use drugs at the time of the incident. Campbell et al. (2003) found that 70 percent of the male perpetrators were using drugs and/or alcohol at the time of the homicidal incident. Guns in the home were another risk factor: guns were used in IPH by two-thirds of spouses and ex-spouses (Bureau of Justice, 2006). In the 11-city homicide study, perpetrator access to a gun increased the risk of femicide by an Odds Ratio of 5.38. Actual use of a gun during the worst incident of IPH drastically increased the risk of that incident of abuse being fatal, with an odds ratio of 41.38. Forced sex was associated with IP femicide in the 11-city study (Campbell et al., 2003), as was prior strangling. A study of women in Chicago killed by an intimate partner during a 2-year period found that nearly a quarter were killed by strangulation

(Block et al., 2000). Non-fatal strangulation prior to the femicide was reported in 43 percent of the femicides in the 11-city study (Campbell et al., 2003).

Campbell, Glass, Sharps, Laughon, and Bloom (2007) have published an assessment tool to help battered women determine the level of risk in their relationship. This Danger Assessment checklist includes items which were derived from their research. It is a helpful guide for clinicians attempting to evaluate the risk of extreme/lethal violence in an IPB case. It can be accessed online at *www.dangerassessment.com.*

Homicide and Suicide

It is clear from the above that individuals from each class of violence (workplace, school, IPH) may kill themselves when their rampage is over. Fifty-three percent of mass murderers committed suicide, and over two-thirds of school shooters had suicidal ideation prior to their acts (Vossekuil et al., 2002). This underscores the despair, hopelessness, and nihilism of individuals who commit mass murder. It seems likely that most made the decision to die and decided to take people they perceived as responsible for their misery down with them. Mass shooters who were alive to be interviewed often said that they had not made plans about what to do after their killing rampage (Fox & Levin, 2012). Some were clear that they did not care what happened to them.

What about suicide in interpartner homicides? In one study of 178 cases, 42 percent of male IPH perpetrators committed suicide after following through with the homicide (Biroscak, Smith, & Post, 2006). In Campbell et al.'s (2003) 11-city study, a femicide followed by a suicide occurred in approximately 30 percent of femicides. This pattern was almost never seen when women killed a partner. When all homicide-suicide cases in the United States are examined, at least 74 percent involve intimate partners (Campbell et al., 2007; Violence Policy Center, 2006). In the 11-city study of IP homicides, the distinguishing factors in the 30 percent of cases in which the perpetrator killed himself were prior threats of suicide and a history of poor mental health in the perpetrator (Koziol-McLain et al., 2006.)

Clearly only a portion of these individuals present themselves to mental health settings, and only a portion make specific threats to harm another. However, it should be routine that a person triaged with suicidal ideation should be questioned closely about homicidal ideation, especially where there is an indication of resentment and externalization of blame.

The Case of Mr. S.

Mr. S. was a 30-year-old man of mixed Hispanic and Anglo-Saxon heritage who was evaluated 1 month after his arrest for the killing of his estranged wife. She was found strangled, lying fully clothed in her bed, with the couple's wedding picture on her chest. The autopsy revealed the cause of death to be strangulation, and she had slight anal tears. When Mr. S. was arrested, police found a suicide note in his car and several unsent letters to his wife, of various dates.

The couple had been estranged for about 3 months. Mrs. S. had moved to a guest house with their two daughters, and Mr. S. came about once a week to pick up the children for his visits. Mr. S. was 25 years old when he met his wife, who was just 15 at the time. Mr. S. earned a good living working in construction, and he was thrilled by the births of his daughters and was active in child care. There were, however, reports of interpartner violence prior to the couple's separation. On one occasion, Mr. S. ripped his wife's sweater as she pulled away from him and tried to flee. On another occasion, he pushed her and she fell off a step onto a porch, injuring herself. On that occasion, Mr. S. was worried that his wife would disclose what had happened, so he locked her in their bedroom until she promised she wouldn't. However, Mrs. S. had told her girlfriend that she was afraid of her husband.

The couple separated in early December. Mr. S.'s mother recalled that he seemed particularly forlorn that Christmas. He was living in the couple's very bare former home, "with a little bare Christmas tree." He talked to his family about his concerns that his daughters would have a stepfather and his fears that their mother would expose the girls to harm. His family knew he was spending a lot of time driving around in his car, and they suspected he was drinking more. His mother said, "He was very depressed, crying all the time." Mr. S. recalled that he couldn't sleep and he drank until he passed out. Also, Mr. S. quit his job. He said he couldn't bear to be around his work friends because they acted like everything was normal. He couldn't tell them about his separation. He said he would drive to an old work site, where he had helped build a particularly nice house, and he would sit in his car and recall happier times. He didn't like to be alone at his house and only returned every third day or so, to shower and pet the family cat. He shaved his head and eyebrows, he said, because he hated himself.

Mr. S.'s family became aware that he was suicidal in early February. Mrs. S. had called his mother and asked for help getting him to the hospital. When his mother saw him, she said, "It looked like he had been crying and drinking for days." The family took him to a large university-based teaching hospital. His mother said, "They interviewed him but not us. They said they were going to keep him. We thought it would be 72 hours at least, but they released him the next morning. They told him he should get outpatient therapy and gave him a referral."

Mr. S. said that after his release from the hospital, he found his father's gun, and he began to imagine scenarios of his own death. In about March, his sister's husband found him hiding in the closet of his house. He seemed disheveled and frightened. They took him to their house, and when they moved his car, they found the gun hidden under the seat. Three weeks passed, and they thought his mood was improving. He did not start outpatient therapy, instead making excuses.

His hair was growing back. They knew he was still drinking a lot. He couldn't sleep and he would stay on the computer until very late at night. He talked about his children a lot.

On the day of the homicide, Mr. S. went to his wife's house to pick up his children but found that they had gone to spend the night elsewhere. He said he and his wife talked. While he was there, the telephone rang and it was a male voice. Mr. S. argued with his wife and he began to strangle her. He said, "all of a sudden, she was limp in my arms." He recalled feeling overwhelmingly sad, and he placed the framed picture of their wedding, which was nearby, on her chest. He claimed he does not remember sexually assaulting her.

Mr. S. returned to his sister's. He told her what he had done and asked her to take care of his girls. He asked her to drop his wedding ring in his coffin, and he left. When he was found by police, he was in possession of a large quantity of over-the-counter medication which he had not yet taken. Several notes were found. One said, "If found dead, please call my mother, Rena. Please try to keep it from my kids as long as possible." Another said, "Been writing for a while so forgive me for not going into much detail. I can't cope anymore and I have to go now. I must apologize for my lack of involvement in all of your lives, but I do love all of you."

Several were written to his estranged wife, but had dates indicating they were written before the homicide. They had two themes which alternated, one pleading and the other angry. One said:

> Been driving for a while and I miss you. I'm so lonely. I can't go on by myself and I don't think you care enough to keep me alive. I don't know what the after world is gonna be like but if it allows me to think, I will always think of you. Sorry for all the pain. You knew how much it hurt me when you go out and yet you insisted to do it every week, no matter what. I think if you would have shared some of your precious time with me and showed an interest in me and what was going on, things would have been different.

Another said:

> Basically I'm tired. I really don't like the way you are living your life and how easy you let everything go, and all the lies and hiding of shit all the time, even though we're not together any more. I deserve to be treated with some respect, and I get none. Fuck you, bitch. I hope you die a painful and lonely person who never finds happiness, and I hope the girls grow to hate you for what you've done, just to be able to date and go out with other guys and have your freedom. It was at our family's cost. I can't see how you fucking sleep at night, you piece of shit. The way you're going, you will probably get AIDS or be raped by someone, and you'll deserve every bit of it.

None of the notes found made direct threats to harm his wife, but the writings reveal his dramatic mood shifts or "splitting," projecting blame on his wife for the failure of their marriage, and ultimately objectifying her and rationalizing harm to her. The last two notes quoted above were in his car at the time he was taken to the emergency psychiatric setting, and could have provided useful information to the mental health staff had they been shared by the family.

Mr. S. was seen within about 1 month of his arrest for the murder of his wife. He was evaluated as part of a pretrial forensic mental health evaluation, at the request of the defense. He was incarcerated in the county jail at the time. Mr. S. was cooperative with evaluation procedures, which included psychological testing with the Minnesota Multiphasic Personality Inventory (MMPI-2), the Millon Clinical Multiaxial Inventory (MCMI-III), the Structured Inventory of Reported Symptoms (SIRS), and the Rorschach Inkblot Method. The entire criminal file was available and carefully reviewed.

In the forensic clinical interviews, Mr. S. expressed remorse and extreme sadness about the death of his estranged wife, particularly because of its likely effect on their two young daughters. He was frequently tearful despite receiving anti-depressant medication. He reported extremely poor sleep and intrusive recollections of both happy and sad times with his wife and children.

Pertinent to the evaluation was the fact that Mr. S. came from a home where he was a frequent witness to domestic violence. His father, a construction worker, beat his mother and beat him, and his sister as well, to the point that they were all fearful when his father was due to arrive home from work. Mr. S. had left home at 17 and joined the military to get away from his father. Also, Mr. S. had a first marriage when he was very young. Although there was no known domestic violence in that relationship, when the marriage failed, Mr. S. became depressed and talked about feeling like a failure. A second failed marriage clearly intensified these feelings.

Psychological tests are frequently used in forensic pretrial evaluations. Their use in predicting violence, in and of themselves, has been criticized (Reddy et al., 2001). The two personality inventories—MMPI-2 and MCMI-III—indicated that Mr. S. was in a Major Depressive Episode. Given the history provided by his family, of some 6 months of worsening depressive symptoms, plus his emergency psychiatric hospital records, it seemed reasonable to believe that Mr. S. was clinically depressed at the time of the homicide. A review of his test profiles revealed additional important information about the severity and features that are particularly associated with violent acting out (see Figure 9.1).

The MMPI-2 profile is valid. His elevation on Fb is likely due to varying concentration towards the end of the test and an elevated Fb does not invalidate the profile. It is noteworthy that Mr. S. did not elevate on the malingering scales of the SIRS. The MMPI-2 clinical scales are quite elevated. The highest elevation —on scale 8—is a T-score of 100. The Harris-Lingoes analysis indicates that the elevation is largely due to item clusters Emotional Alienation and Lack of Ego

Mastery, Conative and Cognitive. These indicate he has endorsed items surrounding the experience of loss of control of both thoughts and emotions and feeling not himself. His second-highest elevation is on scale 7, at a T-score of 98. This is associated with a brooding, dark, ruminative quality, and a fearful, worrying tendency. The 8–7 and 7–8 person, according to Friedman, Lewak, Nichols, and Webb (2001) is filled with worry and tension. Their excessive introspection may appear confused as well as highly emotional. They are unable to think or concentrate efficiently and their distress is so great that insomnia and suicidal thoughts are highly likely. Suicide attempts can be bizarre. These individuals are shy and feel inadequate and interpersonally sensitive, particularly where heterosexual relations are concerned. Many drink in order to relax. They are chronically on-edge, as if anticipating a disaster, and are extremely quick to feel criticized, judged, or somehow defective. When scale 8 is higher than 7, as it is here, they will show more psychotic-like symptoms and an even greater fixed belief that they are damaged and defective.

Mr. S.'s MMPI-2 profile has other significant elevations. Scale 6 has a T-score of 90, and scale 4 a T-score of 82. The Harris-Lingoes subscales of scale 6 load on Persecutory Ideas (T = 82) and Poignancy (T = 75). The Poignancy elevation indicates that Mr. S. is extraordinarily sensitive and easily hurt. The elevation on Persecutory Ideas indicates that he responds to this hurt with anger and resentment, blaming others for his suffering. This is, of course, evident in his writings to his estranged wife, where he blames her for breaking up their family rather than volunteering wrong on his part. The externalization of blame and resentment is particularly associated with violent acting out in domestic violence situations. Mr. S.'s elevation on scale 4 (T = 82) is also of concern, as it indicates a clear potential for acting-out. What if Mr. S. had been given the MMPI-2 in the emergency room? It is possible and even likely that this same profile would have emerged. The psychologist would have seen that Mr. S. was extraordinarily distressed and sad, that he did not feel in control of his ruminative thoughts, or his extremely distressed emotions, that he had a marked tendency to externalize blame and a considerable potential for acting out. At a minimum, this could have spurred an in-depth conversation with Mr. S. about his anger at his estranged wife and possible homicidal fantasies.

Mr. S.'s MCMI-III profile is very consistent with the MMPI-2 (see Figure 9.2). His highest Axis I scale is Major Depressive Disorder (Base Rate = 99), and he also scores very elevated on Thought Disorder (BR = 81), indicating a severe depressive state with significant distortions in thinking. His personality pattern scales indicate a combination of dependent, depressive, and self-defeating features. While he is not elevated on Paranoid, he is significantly elevated on Borderline, which is consistent with poorly controlled emotion, periods of rage, and the splitting which was evident in his notes to his estranged wife.

A Rorschach was given to further explore Mr. S.'s reality testing and the degree to which his controls and stress tolerance were impaired. The Rorschach was

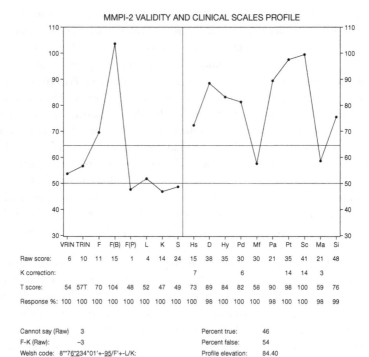

MMPI-2 VALIDITY AND CLINICAL SCALES PROFILE

	VRIN	TRIN	F	F(B)	F(P)	L	K	S	Hs	D	Hy	Pd	Mf	Pa	Pt	Sc	Ma	Si
Raw score:	6	10	11	15	1	4	14	24	15	38	35	30	30	21	35	41	21	48
K correction:									7			6			14	14	3	
T score:	54	57T	70	104	48	52	47	49	73	89	84	82	58	90	98	100	59	76
Response %:	100	100	100	100	100	100	100	100	100	98	100	100	100	98	100	100	98	99

Cannot say (Raw)	3	Percent true:	46
F-K (Raw):	−3	Percent false:	54
Welsh code: 8**76*234"01'+−95/F'+−L/K:		Profile elevation:	84.40

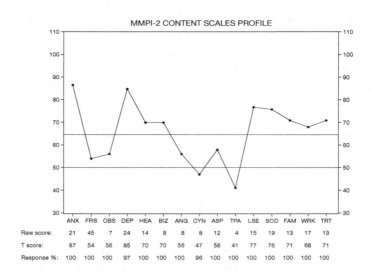

MMPI-2 CONTENT SCALES PROFILE

	ANX	FRS	OBS	DEP	HEA	BIZ	ANG	CYN	ASP	TPA	LSE	SOD	FAM	WRK	TRT
Raw score:	21	45	7	24	14	8	8	8	12	4	15	19	13	17	13
T score:	87	54	56	85	70	70	56	47	58	41	77	76	71	68	71
Response %:	100	100	100	97	100	100	100	96	100	100	100	100	100	100	100

FIGURE 9.1 MMPI-2 Profile for Mr. S.

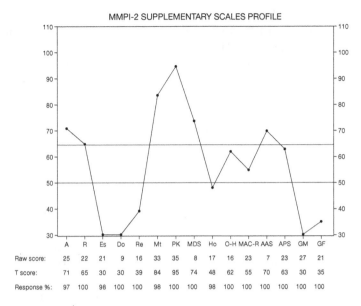

MMPI-2 SUPPLEMENTARY SCALES PROFILE

	A	R	Es	Do	Re	Mt	PK	MDS	Ho	O-H	MAC-R	AAS	APS	GM	GF
Raw score:	25	22	21	9	16	33	35	8	17	16	23	7	23	27	21
T score:	71	65	30	30	39	84	95	74	48	62	55	70	63	30	35
Response %:	97	100	98	100	100	98	100	100	98	100	100	100	100	100	100

FIGURE 9.1 *continued*

administered and scored according to the Comprehensive System (Exner, 2003). Mr. S. gave 31 responses, and his Lambda was .19, indicating an infusion of emotion into his responses. To begin with, he had 15 Blends, a number of which were color-shading blends or shading-shading blends, indicating a confusing mix of emotions. His 8 m (inanimate movement) responses indicate profound feelings of helplessness and feeling controlled by external events. His responses contained significantly more shading than the average person: 4 C' responses, 2 Texture responses, 1 Vista, and 12 diffuse shading (Y) responses. His color responses were only slightly modulated by form, also suggesting poor capacity to control emotion. The Four-square, which examines capacity for control and tolerance for stress, indicated that Mr. S.'s level of experienced stress greatly outstripped his coping resources. His D-score of 7 compared to an adjusted D of 0 indicated that, for Mr. S., the separation from his wife and the loss of his work were too overwhelming for his relatively fragile personality structure.

The Rorschach protocol also demonstrated very poor reality-testing (X+% = .39, F+% = .40, X–% = .23). His WSum6, measuring irrational thinking, was 53, influenced largely by fabulized combinations. His many personalized (PER) responses, which were form failures and infused with bizarre content, clearly indicated psychosis. Mr. S. scored in the clinical range on the Depression Index (DEPI) and had a score of 10 on the Suicide Constellation (S-CON), where the cut-off for significant concern is 8.

The content of Mr. S.'s Rorschach responses offered a glimpse into his ruminations. On the first Rorschach card, he picked up his two hands, made a choking motion, and said: "These look sort of like hands, coming toward something." His gesture suggested strangling. He then saw "tadpoles, with two little hands, developing." Next, still on Card I, he saw "a skeleton or a rib cage which looks transparent, with thin flesh and you can see the interior of the body." This was only one of several responses of a "transparent" body, which suggests his experience of vulnerability. Finally, he gave a response with reference to his childhood: "This looks like dark clouds on a nasty day, moving, like when I was in Alabama on the porch of my house. It would be dark real quick and the clouds would come, and you would definitely be close to your storm shelter." This could have been describing the emotional climate of his home as well, and captures the experience of children living in homes with a violent father. There was a second highly similar "weather" percept, where he saw "dark clouds on a stormy night, a scary night, scary like in a werewolf movie." His responses frequently contained the theme of impending evil. For example, on Card III, he gave an elaborate response about two tribal people frantically drumming to keep evil spirits away.

The protocol contained a fair share of gruesome percepts. On Card II, he saw "smeared blood, like when you cut your finger." On Card IV he saw a creature with its hands and head cut off, "actually burnt off like they were on fire." On Card VI, he saw "a slide of cancer cells." On Card VIII, he saw lizards, but their tails were "melted" because "it looks like a real hot day." On Card IX, he saw a witch with burning fingers, an x-ray of dark lungs "like those that have been damaged by smoking." He also saw flesh with "some sort of disease, like cancer or something." On Card X, he saw "poisonous fish." These responses show an intense preoccupation with threat to safety and hypervigilance to harm both from within and without.

Mr. S. showed virtually no capacity to see Popular percepts (P = 1). Almost every card was seen through a prism of fear, threat, and annihilation. While it would have been extremely unlikely for emergency room staff to give a Rorschach test, had Mr. S. been seen in a counseling center or therapist's office, where Rorschachs are more likely to be administered, his extremely impaired reality testing, poor emotional modulation, and preoccupation with percepts of damage and threat would have signaled the profound degree of his psychiatric deterioration. He certainly showed many signs of being a danger to himself. This, coupled with the letters about his estranged wife, signaled the danger of a potential homicide.

Legal Issues for the Case of Mr. S.

For an individual such as Mr. S., expert testimony would typically center around the degree to which his thinking and capacity for control were impaired. In most jurisdictions in the United States, expert witnesses cannot give an "ultimate

MILLION CLINICAL MULTIAXIAL INVENTORY – III
CONFIDENTIAL INFORMATION FOR PROFESSIONAL USE ONLY

PERSONALITY CODE: 8B 2B 3 2A ** 1 8A * 6A 6B + - ' ' // C ** S * //
SYNDROME CODE: B D A ** R H * // CC ** SS * //
DEMOGRAPHIC: 112765/CI/M/30/W/W/12/MA/IL/-----/--/-----/

CATEGORY		SCORE		PROFILE OF BR SCORES				DIAGNOSTIC SCALES
		RAW	BR	0	60	75	85	115
MODIFYING INDICES	X	126	76					DISCLOSURE
	Y	3	15					DESIRABILITY
	Z	25	85					DEBASEMENT
CLINICAL PERSONALITY PATTERNS	1	15	84					SCHIZOID
	2A	18	86					AVOIDANT
	2B	16	93					DEPRESSIVE
	3	17	91					DEPENDENT
	4	2	8					HISTRIONIC
	5	4	17					NARCISSISTIC
	6A	10	71					ANTISOCIAL
	6B	9	61					AGGRESIVE (SADISTIC)
	7	5	23					COMPULSIVE
	8A	13	80					PASSIVE-AGGRESSIVE
	8B	18	101					SELF-DEFEATING
SEVERE PERSONALITY PATHOLOGY	S	16	76					SCHIZOTYPAL
	C	20	89					BORDERLINE
	P	5	59					PARANOID
CLINICAL SYNDROMES	A	12	94					ANXIETY DISORDER
	H	13	79					SOMATOFORM DISORDER
	N	3	35					BIPOLAR: MANIC DISORDER
	D	17	96					DYSTHYMIC DISORDER
	B	18	104					ALCOHOL DEPENDENCE
	T	2	29					DRUG DEPENDENCE
	R	17	82					POST-TRAUMATIC STRESS
SEVERE SYNDROMES	SS	18	81					THOUGHT DISORDER
	CC	20	99					MAJOR DEPRESSION
	PP	2	59					DELUSIONAL DISORDER

FIGURE 9.2 MCMI-III for Mr. S.

opinion" about whether Mr. S. could or could not premeditate and deliberate. However, the psychological test data illustrate impairments that his lawyer might use to argue that his capacity to premeditate and deliberate, or, even more, his ability to form "intent" was impaired. There was little actual evidence that this crime was premeditated. It appeared, instead, to have resulted from the immediate sense of threat which came from hearing another man's voice on the telephone and the dramatically reduced emotional control presented by Mr. S.'s mental condition. As it happened, Mr. S. pled guilty to second degree murder. No legal action was filed on behalf of the dead woman, although her family might reasonably have argued that the psychiatric staff at the university hospital failed to adequately assess the risk of serious violence. Even the family of Mr. S. was stunned by the lack of psychiatric care offered when they tried to get him help. Of course, the hospital staff did not hear a direct threat to harm, and the indirectly threatening letters were never in their possession. Still, Mr. S. presented with a number of features seen in perpetrators of femicide. He experienced the loss of his wife and children as devastating, a life event from which he would not recover. He was unemployed. He was drinking heavily. He had a Major Depression with suicidal ideation. He had access to a gun. Most important, he externalized blame to his estranged wife, and this morphed into devaluing and objectifying her.

Summary and Implications

With so many recent mass shootings and tragic interpartner homicides, it is likely that the expectations for mental health professionals as assessors of violence risk will be evolving. This chapter presents findings on several subtypes of homicide and homicide-suicide. Looking at the most general risk factors, Litwack, Zapf, Groscup, and Hart (2006) note that certain combinations of variables have received empirical support as predictors of these acts. These are:

(1)   active psychotic symptoms plus substance abuse plus a history of violence or current hostile attitudes;
(2)   the presence of delusional beliefs about significant others and specific personal targets;
(3)   severe and chronic self-destructiveness;
(4)   command hallucinations to commit violence;
(5)   violent fantasies and poor controls;
(6)   erotomania, especially with a history of antisocial behavior;
(7)   recent and currently active narcissistic injury;
(8)   anger, externalization of blame, and lack of empathy.

Those who commit mass murder and targeted school violence have some traits or features in common. In the adult group, the mostly middle-aged men were described as loners or alienated. In the adolescent group, the mostly male teenagers seemed to have friends, although they and their friends were often described as misfits. Both the adult mass killers and the adolescent school shooters had experienced some form of failure, such as a recent significant loss or perception of injury, or chronic unemployment or recent work failure. This underscores the importance of failure in contemporary culture, particularly for males. In both the adult and adolescent groups, there was a high prevalence of resentment and externalization of blame, which is a clear precursor for mass killing. Finally, in both the adult and adolescent groups there was an interest in, if not preoccupation with, violence. In both adult and adolescent groups, a minority of mass killers made overt threats, but there was "leakage" about impending acts, and there was a clear increase in behavior that suggested an impending act (usually an increase in collecting weapons, ammunition, or supplies).

The IPH perpetrators are similar to the mass killers in some respects and different in others. Rather than alienation from others, they have significant abandonment fears. Separation or divorce is the trigger, as it was in Mr. S., for profound feelings of failure and despair. Similar to the other two groups, however, they externalize blame and have strong feelings of resentment. Campbell's 11-city study (Campbell et al., 2003) indicates that they have a high degree of unemployment (likely fueling their feelings of failure). Like the other two groups, they often have acquired weapons.

Caution is urged in the assessment of future violence risk. The research findings on mass killers, targeted school violence perpetrators, and IPV perpetrators should not be used to profile individuals and make predictions from a profile. The state of the art in the prediction of danger involves structured professional judgment, which employs known risk factors as well as the static and dynamic factors present in an individual evaluation. Reddy et al. (2001) propose a model of threat assessment which takes many aspects into account:

(1) possible motivations for violence;
(2) communication about ideas and intentions;
(3) unusual interest in targeted violence;
(4) evidence of attack-related behaviors and planning;
(5) mental condition;
(6) level of cognitive sophistication or organization to formulate and execute an attack plan;
(7) recent losses, such as loss of status;
(8) consistency between communications and behaviors;
(9) concern by others about the individual's potential for harm;
(10) factors in the individual's life or situation that might increase or decrease the likelihood of an attack.

The study of targeted school violence (Vossekuil et al., 2002) indicates that there are often many windows into the thoughts and planning of potential school violence perpetrators. Written materials such as journals, emails, and Internet postings can be a rich source of ideation. Individuals triaged in mental health settings might be asked to share their journals, artwork, or Internet postings. These can be an extremely useful addition to data from psychological testing and interviewing. We can only speculate how mental health professionals might have changed their evaluation of Mr. S. had they had access to his notes to his estranged wife, his MMPI-2 profile, and the findings from the Rorschach.

Currently, mental health professionals are only responsible for direct threats to an intended target. Public outrage, at least in the United States, may come to call mental health practitioners to task for evaluating threat that is not explicit but about which we have warning through behavior and perhaps "leakage," or from positive clinical signs of danger. In understanding the psychological make-up of individuals who commit these extremely violent acts, we assist others to attend to warning signs and perhaps make referral to mental health care and hopefully thereby reduce the number of these acts.

Notes

1   This chapter is dedicated to victims of mass shootings—among them, Irma, my friend and Spanish interpreter, who was a young poet and the first member of her Mexican-American family to attend college when she was among the shooting victims of Charles Whitman at the University of Texas, Austin. Whitman killed 14 and wounded 31, shooting from a tower on the campus, before being shot by police (Lea, 2007). Irma survived but had to learn to talk again and lost her hopes of becoming an English professor.

2   In the month it took to write this chapter, 4 more mass shootings occurred in the United States. A 20-year-old gunman killed 2 people and himself, after shooting over 60 rounds inside the food court of an upscale shopping mall in Portland, Oregon. A 24-year-old gunman stormed an elementary school in Newtown, Connecticut, killed 20 first-grade pupils, the school principal, the school psychologist, and 4 other adults, after previously having killed his mother. Aaron Alexis, a government contractor, entered a US Naval supply yard and opened fire on civilian employees, killing 12 and wounding 3 others before he was killed by police. Finally, a 22-year-old man hunted Transportation Security Administration agents at Los Angeles International Airport, killing 1 and wounding numerous others.

3   The Lanterman-Petris-Short Act is statutory law in California that allows involuntary hospital commitment for individuals deemed to be a danger to themselves or others, or gravely disabled. It was enacted in 1967 and is known as California Welfare and Institutions Code 5150. It outlines a series of legal hearings meant to guard against indefinite involuntary confinement.

4   Fein et al. (1995) note that while their population of assassins and near-lethal attackers did not directly threaten the target, nor warn law enforcement, about two-thirds made some threat about their targets in the days, weeks, or months before their attacks, often by letting someone know or by writing notes, letters, or journals that described their thinking and state of mind.

5   The common definition of a school shooting is an incident in which gun violence occurs at an educational institution, committed either by a student or by an intruder.

6   In one case, most of the attacker's schoolmates described the attacker as "the kid everyone teased." In witness statements from that incident, schoolmates alleged that

nearly every child in the school had at some point thrown the attacker against a locker, tripped him in the hall, held his head under water in the school pool, or thrown things at him.

7   Intimate Partner Femicides or Femicides are cases where a woman is killed by a male partner. These acts have also been termed Uxoricide.

References

Altimari, D. (2013, January 21). Legislature considers big changes in mental health policy after Newtown. *The Courant*. http://articles.courant.com/2013–01–21/news/hc-newtown-mental-health-20130118_1_mental-health-mental-illness-social-workers.

Biroscak, B. J., Smith, P. K., & Post, L.A. (2006). A practical approach to public health surveillance of violence deaths related to intimate partner relationships. *Public Health Report, 121*, 393–399.

Block, C. R., Devitt, C. O., Fonda, D., Fugate, M., Marting, C., McFarlane, J., et al. (2000). *The Chicago women's health study: Risk of serious injury or death in intimate violence. A collaborative research project*. Washington, DC: US Department of Justice, National Institute of Justice.

Bureau of Justice (2006). *Homicide trends in the US: Intimate partner homicide*. Washington, DC: Author.

Campbell, J. C., Webster, D., Koziol-McLain, J., Block, C. R., Campbell, D. W., Curry, M. A., et al. (2003). Risk factors for femicide in abusive relationships: Results from a multisite case control study. *American Journal of Public Health, 93*, 1089–1097. doi: 10.2105/AJPH.93.7.1089.

Campbell, J. C., Glass, N., Sharps, P. W., Laughon, K., & Bloom, T. (2007). *Intimate partner homicide: Review and implications of research and policy*. Thousand Oaks, CA: Sage.

Catalano, S., Smith, E., Snyder, H., & Rand, M. (2009). *Female victims of violence*. US Department of Justice.

CBS News (2012, October 24). News bulletin.

Ewing v. Goldstein, 120 Cal. App. 4th 804 (2004).

Ewing v. Northridge Hospital Medical Center, 120 Cal. App. 4th 1289 (2004).

Exner, J. E. (2003). *The Rorschach: A comprehensive system. Vol. 1: Basic foundations and principles of interpretation* (4th ed.). Hoboken, NJ: Wiley.

Fein, R. A. & Vossekuil, B. (1999). Assassination in the United States: An operational study of recent assassins, attackers, and near-lethal approachers. *Journal of Forensic Sciences, 44*, 321–333.

Fein, R., Vossekuil, B., & Holden, G. (1995). *Threat assessment: An approach to prevent targeted violence* (NCJ 155000) Washington, DC: U.S. Dept. of Justice, Office of Justice Programs, National Institute of Justice.

Fox, J. A. (2007, April 17). Why they kill. *Los Angeles Times*.

Fox, J. A. & Levin, J. (2012). *Extreme killing: Understanding serial and mass murder* (2nd ed.). Los Angeles: Sage.

Fridhandler, B. (2005, January). Ewing v. Goldstein decision summary. *The San Francisco Psychologist*. San Francisco, CA: San Francisco Psychological Association.

Friedman, A. F., Lewak, R., Nichols, D.S., & Webb, J. T. (2001). *Psychological assessment with the MMPI-2*. Mahwah, NJ: Lawrence Erlbaum Associates.

Garcia, L., Soria, C., & Hurwitz, E. L. (2007). Homicides and intimate partner violence: A literature review. *Trauma, Violence and Abuse, 8*, 370–383. doi: 10.1177/15248380 07307294.

Hedlund v. The Superior Court of Orange County, 669 P 2d 41 (1983).

Hempel, A. G., Meloy, J. R., & Richards, T. C. (1999). Offender and offense characteristics of a nonrandom sample of mass murderers. *Journal of the American Academy of Psychiatry and the Law, 27*, 213–225.

Herbert, P. B. & Young, K. A. (2002). Tarasoff at twenty-five. *Journal of the American Academy of Psychiatry and Law, 30*, 275–281.

Klein, E. (2012, December 14). Twelve facts about guns and mass shootings in the United States. *The Washington Post.*

Koziol-McLain, J., Webster, D., McFarlane, J., Block, C. R., Curry, M. A., & Ulrich, Y. (2006). Risk factors for femicide-suicide in abusive relationships: Results from a multi-site case control study. *Violence and Victims, 21*, 3–21. doi: 10.1891/vivi.21.1.3.

Langman, P. (2012). *Waarom jongeren moorden* [Why kids kill]. Utrecht, The Netherlands: Kok.

Lanterman-Petris-Short Act (1967). California Welfare and Institutions Code SS 6000(b), 6002, 6005, & 6006.

Lea, S. R. G. (2007). *The Charles Whitman murders.* Denton, TX: University of North Texas Press.

Lenell, M. (1977). The Lanterman-Petris-Short Act: A review after ten years. *Golden Gate University Law Review, 7*, 733–764.

Lipsky, S., Caetano, R., Field, C. A., & Larkin, G. L. (2005). Psychosocial and substance-use risk factors for intimate partner violence. *Drug and Alcohol Dependence, 78*, 39–47. doi: 10.1016/j.drugalcdep.2004.08.028.

Litwack, T. R., Zapf, P. A., Groscup, J. L., & Hart, S. (2006). Violence risk assessment: Research, legal, and clinical considerations. In I. B. Weiner & A. K. Hess (Eds.), *The handbook of forensic psychology* (3rd ed.), pp. 487–533. New York: Wiley.

McFarlane, J., Campbell, J., Sharps, P., & Watson, S. (2002). Abuse during pregnancy and femicide: Urgent implications for women's health. *Obstetrics and Gynaecology, 100*, 27–36.

McFarlane, J., Campbell, J. D., Wilt, S., Sachs, C., Ulrich, Y., & Xu, X. (1999). Stalking and intimate partner femicide. *Homicide Studies, 3*, 300–316. doi: 10.1177/1088 767999003004003.

McSherry, B. & Keyzer, P. (2011). *Dangerous people: Policy, prediction, and practice.* New York: Routledge.

Meloy, J. R., Hoffmann, J., Guldimann, A., & James, D. (2011). The role of warning behaviors in threat assessment: An exploration and suggested typology. *Behavioral Sciences and the Law, 30*, 256–279. doi: 10.1002/bsl.999.

Monckton, S. J. (2012). *Murder, gender and the media: Narratives of dangerous love.* New York: Palgrave Macmillan.

Otto, R. K. & Douglas, K. S. (2010). *Handbook of violence risk assessment.* New York: Taylor & Francis.

People v. Poddar, 10 C3d 750 (1974).

Reddy, M., Borum, R., Berglund, J., Vossekuil, B., Fein, R., & Modzeleski, W. (2001). Evaluating risk for targeted violence in schools: Comparing risk assessment, threat assessment, and other approaches. *Psychology in the Schools, 38*, 157–172.

Rennison, C. M. & Welchans, S. (2000). *Intimate partner violence* (Special Report). Washington, DC: US Bureau of Justice Statistics.

de Ruiter, C. (2011). Massamoorden in Europa [Mass murder in Europe]. In P. Langman, *Waarom jongeren moorden: Met een bijdrage van Corine de Ruiter over jonge daders van schietincidenten in Europa* [Why kids kill: With a contribution by Corine de Ruiter on young perpetrators of mass shootings in Europe], pp. 283–314. Utrecht, The Netherlands: Kok.

Sharps, P. W., Koziol-McLain, J., Campbell, J. C., McFarlane, J., Sachs, C. J., & Xu, X. (2001). Health care providers' missed opportunities for preventing femicide. *Preventive Medicine, 33*, 373–380. doi: 10.1006/pmed.2001.0902.

Southerland, M., Collins, P., & Scarborough, K. (1997). *Workplace violence: A continuum from threat to death.* Cincinnatti, OH: Anderson.

Tarasoff v. Regents of the University of California, 17 Cal. 3d 425 (1976).

US Department of Justice (1998, March). *Violence by intimates: Analysis of data on crimes by current or former spouses, boyfriends, and girlfriends.* Washington, DC: Author.

Violence Policy Center (2006). *American roulette: Homicide-suicide in the United States.* Washington, DC: Author.

Virginia Tech Review Panel (2007). *Mass shootings at Virginia Tech April 16, 2007. Report to Governor Kaine, Commonwealth of Virginia.* www.governor.virginia.gov/tempcontent/techPanelReport-docs/FullReport.pdf.

Vossekuil, B., Fein, R., Reddy, M., Borum, R., & Modzeleski, W. (2002). *The final report and findings of the safe school initiative: Implications for the prevention of school attacks in the United States.* Washington, DC: US Department of Education, Office of Elementary and Secondary Education, Safe and Drug-Free Schools Program and US Secret Service, National Threat Assessment Center.

Wilson, M. & Daly, M. (1993). Spousal homicide risk and estrangement. *Violence and Victims, 8*, 3–15.

Wilson, M., Johnson, H., & Daly, M. (1995). Lethal and nonlethal violence against wives. *Canadian Journal of Criminology, 37*, 331–362.

10

MISTAKES OR MALPRACTICE

Ethics in the Practice of Forensic Psychological Assessment

Corine de Ruiter and Nancy Kaser-Boyd

Forensic mental health assessment (FMHA) is challenging in many ways. Interviewing individuals charged with a crime means careful informed consent, scrupulous record-keeping, carefully chosen assessment methods, vigilance to civil and legal rights, and attention to boundaries—boundaries of competence and boundaries of information disclosure. The FMHA evaluator must be able to communicate with individuals with mental health problems, procriminal attitudes and/or behaviors, and also with defense lawyers, public prosecutors, judges, and, in the US, with juries. Written communication must be clear, with careful attention to detail, accuracy, and transparency. Reasoning must be clear, alternative hypotheses must be discussed and ruled out. The FMHA practitioner must know the law in her jurisdiction and the definitions of legal terms. Mistakes are probably inevitable, as in any type of professional work, but hopefully they will not rise to a level that would be considered malpractice. In the legal arena, especially in criminal court, the consequences of poor judgment or violation of ethical standards can be enormous.

The American Psychological Association has been very clear about the ethics for psychologists. The five APA general ethical principles include beneficence and nonmaleficence, fidelity and responsibility, integrity, justice, and respect for people's rights and dignity (American Psychological Association, 2002). The Dutch Institute of Psychologists NIP modeled its Code of Professional Ethics on the APA Code.[1] The ethical principle of beneficence and nonmaleficence is intended to protect the well-being of individuals with whom psychologists work. The findings of an FMHA as they are written up in a forensic report can have a significant bearing on the outcome of legal proceedings to determine a defendant's liberty, and this bears on the core value of freedom that underlies basic human rights (Vess, 2011).

Forensic psychologists are guided by clear and specific ethical principles (American Psychological Association, 1991, 2013). The primary responsibility of the forensic assessment expert is to provide accurate and objective information relevant to the legal issues at hand (Doyle & Ogloff, 2009). The APA Specialty Guidelines for Forensic Psychologists

> apply in all matters in which psychologists provide expertise to judicial, administrative, and educational systems including, but not limited to, examining or treating persons in anticipation of or subsequent to legal, contractual, administrative, proceedings; offering expert opinion about psychological issues in the form of *amicus* briefs or testimony to judicial, legislative or administrative bodies; acting in an adjudicative capacity; serving as a trial consultant or otherwise offering expertise to attorneys, the courts, or others; conducting research in connection with, or in the anticipation of, litigation; or involvement in educational activities of a forensic nature.
>
> (American Psychological Association, 2013)

This chapter will review two cases, one from each author, where significant mistakes were made. "Mistake" implies an inadvertent error and is used here because we assume that the psychologists in question might contend that nothing in their training pointed out such errors in methods, or that they strongly believed their methods to have been acceptable. This may seem hard to believe when a psychologist has received forensic training. In some of the content, the reader may see flagrant disregard for ethical and forensic standards, more clearly mal-practice. Both of the cases we present had very serious and adverse legal consequences.

Case 1: Misuse of Psychological Tests

Miguel, an 18-year-old who had migrated to the US with his family from El Salvador when he was 12, was accused of the murder of a 34-year-old man in a local park. The victim was tied up and he had been stabbed 60 times. Other evidence from the scene suggested there had been sexual activity. The victim's family frantically called his cellphone, and each time they called, a young man answered. Investigators ultimately tracked the phone to Miguel. When police investigators interviewed Miguel, he waived his Miranda rights and said that he had known the victim for 3 years. After over an hour of questioning, during which he denied culpability, he admitted that he had killed the victim. In halting English, he said that he did this because the victim did "something bad" to him. He ultimately disclosed that, on his fifteenth birthday, when he was out celebrating with friends, he had met the victim, then 32 years old, and the man had told him he would take him out and show him a good time. Instead, he took him to a motel, where he gave him enough alcohol to cause Miguel to pass out. When he awoke the next morning, he said he felt "groggy" and his body (specifically, his anus) hurt. The man then showed him pictures on a laptop of him sodomizing Miguel. While Miguel had already come out as a gay man, there is an immense gap between consenting sexual acts and those which are forced and are experienced as profoundly demeaning. Miguel told how, in addition, the man had continued to call him, and told him that he had to answer his calls because "he knew where my family lived." There was multiple subsequent contact between the two. The older man insisted that Miguel dress like a woman, and the forced sexual acts continued. Miguel began to decompensate mentally. He became depressed and frequently thought of suicide. He started to abuse drugs, sometimes in a bizarre way, for example, by ingesting cleansing fluids or mixing rubbing alcohol with juice. He often thought of suicide; for example by jumping off a freeway overpass. He also became a regular user of street drugs, including marijuana, methamphetamine, and cocaine. He began to hear voices. Sometimes they told him to use drugs, sometimes to kill himself, and sometimes to kill the older man. His school performance became poor and he was frequently tardy or absent.

Miguel told police investigators that he could not get rid of the voice telling him to kill his tormenter. He told them how he developed a plan to kill him, and how he planned it to occur on his birthday, 2 years from the date on which he was raped. He asked the man to take him out to eat on his birthday, then suggested they go to a park where they could play "games." He convinced the man to be tied up for sex, and then he began his attack. When the attack was over, he left the park, taking the man's cellphone. He was apprehended weeks later, when, as noted, he confessed. Because he was still a juvenile, he was housed at a juvenile detention facility.

One of the authors (NKB) was retained by the defense to evaluate Miguel's personality and mental health. The evaluation occurred approximately 2 years after the homicide, when Miguel was already 20 years old. This may seem surprising but can occur in jurisdictions where the courts are flooded with cases. A second psychologist was retained by the defense to evaluate Miguel's cognitive and neuropsychological functioning. Miguel was still learning to speak English. Although he said he preferred to speak and read English, and he did have some ability to do so, the evaluation was conducted along with a Spanish interpreter. This is an important practice for the evaluator, because subtle differences in meaning can exist between different languages, and a defendant who is interviewed in a foreign language may be put in a disadvantageous position. The interpreter stood by to interpret words or meanings that Miguel did not understand. Miguel had been in the Los Angeles Public School system for 6 years, and he had acquired a good deal of spoken English; however, it is often the case that there are words or concepts that are not understood. For a person whose English is less good, it is clearly preferable for an attorney to find a Spanish-speaking forensic psychologist who speaks the language fluently, but this is not always easy to do. In Los Angeles, alone, there are 39 different languages spoken (Mohan & Simmons, 2004), and there are not enough psychologists with training in these languages. The forensic neuropsychologist brought in a Spanish-speaking psychologist to test Miguel's academic achievement levels. Using a standardized test, he determined that Miguel read Spanish at the sixth grade level, and his comprehension of concepts was also at the sixth grade level. The neuropsychologist tested Miguel's reading in English and found it also at about sixth grade level. Given this, it did not seem that his reading comprehension was good enough to complete the Minnesota Multiphasic Personality Inventory (MMPI-2), which is widely used in FMHA in the United States and requires at least an eighth grade reading level according to the test manual (Butcher, Dahlstrom, Graham, Tellegen, & Kaemmer, 1989). Instead, I administered the Millon Clinical Multiaxial Inventory (MCMI-III; Millon, 1994), which requires a reading level of sixth grade, and is substantially shorter than the MMPI-2 while still offering a broad view of potential diagnoses. The MCMI-III is available in English and Spanish, and Miguel had the two versions to read before answering, plus the assistance of the interpreter who sat with him. The forensic interview with Miguel revealed additional details about the effects of the ongoing abusive relationship which Miguel had with the victim. It appeared from the interview that Miguel might have Posttraumatic Stress Disorder (PTSD). Consequently, the Detailed Assessment of Posttraumatic Stress (DAPS; Briere, 2001), which requires a sixth grade reading level, and the Trauma Symptom Inventory (TSI; Briere, 1995), which the manual indicates requires a fifth to seventh grade reading level, were also administered. Neither of these instruments is available in Spanish, so the interpreter sat nearby to help when Miguel asked for clarification. The results of these tests will be discussed in the context of the prosecution expert's opinions below.

While it is not typical in the US to have an expert on both sides of a case, some cases call for this because of a crime that is especially heinous, or a family that is vocal and pushing for conviction. This was such a case. The prosecution hired its own psychologist. While each defense psychologist had interviewed Miguel on more than one occasion and administered a battery of tests (the neuropsychologist administered 18 tests of cognitive and neuropsychological functioning), the prosecution expert had just one interview and on the same day administered part—the first 364 items—of the MMPI-2. The expert stated that he spoke Spanish and was willing to conduct the interview in Spanish but that the defendant chose to speak English. He did not address whether there were words or concepts that had to be explained in Spanish, which contradicted the experiences with Miguel of both defense psychologists. The prosecution expert was aware that the Spanish-speaking psychologist working with the forensic neuropsychologist opined that Miguel's reading ability *in Spanish* was at the sixth grade level, and not any higher in English, yet he administered the MMPI-2 to Miguel. In his report, he made

Valid Profile

PERSONALITY CODE: 2B ** - * 3 1 6A 2A 8A 6B + 8B 7 '' 5 4 ' ' // S P ** - * //
SYNDROME CODE: R A N B ** T * // PP ** SS * //
DEMOGRAPHIC: T/-----/10/-----/

CATEGORY		SCORE		PROFILE OF BR SCORES				DIAGNOSTIC SCALES
		RAW	BR	0	60	75	85	115
MODIFYING INDICES	X	169	99					DISCLOSURE
	Y	11	51					DESIRABILITY
	Z	22	80					DEBASEMENT
CLINICAL PERSONALITY PATTERNS	1	15	66					SCHIZOID
	2A	16	65					AVOIDANT
	2B	21	91					DEPRESSIVE
	3	17	73					DEPENDENT
	4	13	25					HISTRIONIC
	5	13	34					NARCISSISTIC
	6A	16	66					ANTISOCIAL
	6B	18	61					AGGRESIVE (SADISTIC)
	7	18	36					COMPULSIVE
	8A	16	65					PASSIVE-AGGRESSIVE
	8B	10	56					SELF-DEFEATING
SEVERE PERSONALITY PATHOLOGY	S	24	98					SCHIZOTYPAL
	C	16	70					BORDERLINE
	P	22	93					PARANOID
CLINICAL SYNDROMES	A	19	102					ANXIETY DISORDER
	H	8	59					SOMATOFORM DISORDER
	N	17	88					BIPOLAR: MANIC DISORDER
	D	13	72					DYSTHYMIC DISORDER
	B	15	85					ALCOHOL DEPENDENCE
	T	17	82					DRUG DEPENDENCE
	R	21	105					POST-TRAUMATIC STRESS
SEVERE SYNDROMES	SS	19	75					THOUGHT DISORDER
	CC	15	68					MAJOR DEPRESSION
	PP	16	105					DELUSIONAL DISORDER

FIGURE 10.1 Test Results of Miguel's FMHA.

Profile of DAPS™ *T* Scores

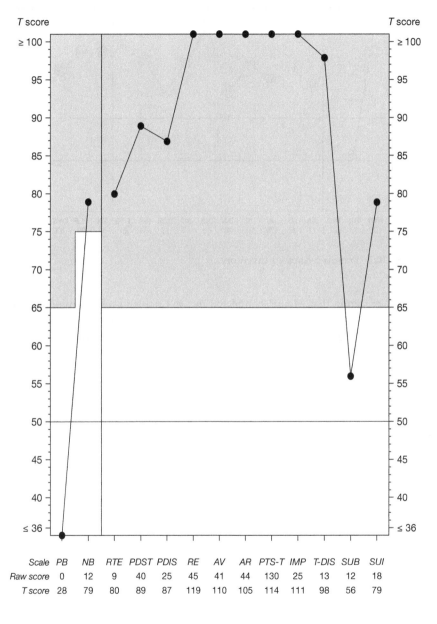

Scale	PB	NB	RTE	PDST	PDIS	RE	AV	AR	PTS-T	IMP	T-DIS	SUB	SUI
Raw score	0	12	9	40	25	45	41	44	130	25	13	12	18
T score	28	79	80	89	87	119	110	105	114	111	98	56	79

●— 06/27/2010

FIGURE 10.1 *continued*

= Raw score

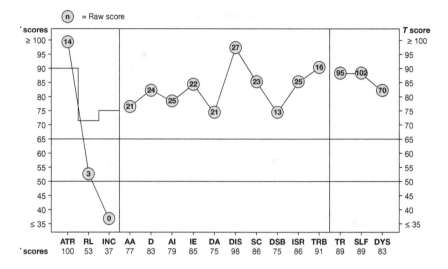

FIGURE 10.2 Trauma Symptom Inventory.

a point of stating that Miguel completed the 364 items in just 75 minutes and thus seemed to have no problem understanding and answering the questions. In reality, this is the average amount of time it takes an individual of average reading ability to complete the entire test. Since the defendant, by the prosecution expert's account, was having no trouble completing the MMPI-2, it was not clear why the test was not finished nor why the prosecution expert stopped with the test administration when he did. We note that the only acceptable short form of the MMPI-2 is 370 items (Friedman, Lewak, Nichols, & Webb, 2001; Pope, Butcher, & Seelen, 2006). He never returned to allow Miguel to complete the test, nor to give Miguel any other test. It was, therefore, surprising when his report was submitted with marked emphasis on malingering. He asserted that Miguel had malingered on the three tests of the defense psychologist as well as on the MMPI-2 which he had administered. He diagnosed Miguel with Borderline Personality Disorder with Antisocial Features. He said he doubted that Miguel had been raped and likely had created that as a story to justify the killing. He also said that there was no specific set of symptoms on psychological tests which is unique to rape or other traumas, though there is a substantial assessment literature on this topic (Armstrong & Kaser-Boyd, 2003; Briere, 1997; Briere & Elliott, 1997; Klotz Flitter, Elhai, & Gold, 2003; Nash, Hulsey, Sexton, Harralson, & Lambert, 1993; Rogers, Sewell, & Salekin, 1994).

The focus of the ethics questions in this case revolved around the inappropriate administration of the MMPI-2 and the prosecution expert's subsequent inaccurate interpretation of the MMPI-2 results. Serious concerns are also evident in the prosecution's expert's conclusions that Miguel was a malingerer, based on inaccurate interpretation of the MMPI-2 and other test protocols and his lack of knowledge about the symptoms of trauma and research on the test results of individuals with histories of trauma.

The raw data that formed the basis of the prosecution expert's opinion was requested and received. In the United States, each side must turn over their clinical notes and test results in a timely fashion, usually 30 days before the trial begins. This is called the "Discovery" process. The prosecution expert sent the partially completed test to a well-known computer scoring company,[2] which dutifully provided an interpretation of the incomplete test protocol. The Caldwell Report began as follows:

> He did not answer 203 items on the inventory. Consequently, many of the scales were incomplete. His scores were pro-rated in order to estimate how many more items he would likely have answered in the scored direction if he had completed all of the items. The following was based on the completed scales plus his pro-rated scores on the incomplete scales.

This caveat appeared nowhere in the prosecution expert's report, which violates the Speciality Guidelines for Forensic Psychologists, principle 10.02 Selection and Use of Assessment Procedures which states:

> Forensic practitioners use assessment instruments whose validity and reliability have been established for use with members of the population assessed. When such validity and reliability have not been established, forensic practitioners consider and describe the strengths and limitations of their findings.
>
> (American Psychological Association, 2013, p. 15)

The prosecution expert used some of the pro-rated scales as a basis for final diagnostic judgments of considerable import. For example, the Caldwell Report stated: "He made a great many atypical and rarely given responses to the items occurring in the last half of the inventory (Scale Fb)." The well-trained user of the MMPI-2 knows that most of the Fb items are in the second half of the test. Let's look more closely at these items. The Fb-scale has the following items: (Endorsed True) 281, 291, 303, 311, 317, 319, 322, 323, 329, 332, 333, 334, 387, 395, 407, 431, 450, 454, 463, 468, 476, 478, 484, 489, 506, 516, 517, 520, 524, 525, 526, 528, 530, 540, 544, 555; (Endorsed False) 183, 404, 501. Counting the Fb items that occur among the 364 items administered to Miguel, we find 12 true and 1 false, i.e., 13 out of the 40 items of the Fb scale. In other words, the statement "He gave a great many atypical and rarely given responses to the items occurring in the last half of the inventory" is meaningless, since he did not complete, and was not asked to complete the last 203 items of the test. The prosecution expert turned the Caldwell Report over in the process of "Discovery," and wrote his report without any explanation that many of the interpretive comments therein were unreliable and inaccurate due to pro-rating. In addition, he referred to the Caldwell interpretive service as a "laboratory" and used the term "laboratory analysis," which elevated its status with a false impression of something more akin to a blood test.

Next, the Caldwell Report states, after analyzing VRIN and TRIN and concluding that there was no reading issue to explain the test results:

> Considering Scales L, F, K, and Ds, he made excessively many atypical and rarely given responses to the inventory. His profile could be grossly over-elevated because of deliberate malingering, severe pathology, acute panic, or an extreme plea for help.

The prosecution expert pounced on the words "deliberately malingering." Although his report mentioned the rest of the sentence—"possible severe pathology, acute panic, or an extreme plea for help"—he said he doubted that any of these were possible as they were not apparent during his one interview with Miguel. He was aware, however, that the defendant had been diagnosed in juvenile hall with Psychotic Disorder NOS and Posttraumatic Stress Disorder, Chronic Type. He was aware, after reading both defense experts' reports and the juvenile hall medical records, that the defendant was seen as a young man with a complicated trauma history who had a tendency to slip into psychotic episodes.

The prosecution expert's report also failed to show that he had familiarity with the effects of sexual trauma, and, more particularly, the effects in male sexual abuse victims. There are several review articles on these effects (Dhaliwal, Gauzad, Antonowicz, & Ross, 1996; Dube et al., 2005; Ray, 2001; Valente, 2005). Dhaliwal and colleagues (1996) note the common finding of depression among male sexual abuse survivors; the patient group invariably presents with more sexual identity confusion, more substance abuse, more anger, and more suicidal ideation. Dhaliwal et al. indicate that male survivors are more likely to externalize their distress, in contrast with female survivors, who are more likely to develop internalizing symptoms. Dorais (2002) elaborates on the acting out of male sexual abuse survivors, noting a greater tendency to identify with the aggressor and transform into an avenger and to turn to prostitution. Holmes & Slap (1998) found that sexually abused boys have two to four times higher risk than their normal counterparts for clinical sequelae such as mood disorders, Posttraumatic Stress Disorder, Borderline Personality Disorder, eating disorder, aggressive behavior, school problems, paranoia, running away, and dissociative symptoms. There is also published research on the common test profiles of sexual abuse victims. For example, in comparison with matched controls, Hunter (1990) and Hunter (1991) found that male sexual abuse survivors scored higher on scales F, K, 1, 2, 5, 6, 7, and 8. Olson (1990), also comparing a male sexual abuse victim group to matched controls, found them to score significantly higher on scales 4, 5, 6, 7, and 8. This research indicates that male sexual abuse survivors have a combination of psychiatric symptoms which include severe disruptions of reality testing and emotional control.

The "mistake," or perhaps even "malpractice," of the prosecution expert went beyond the incompetent use of the MMPI-2 and other tests and the lack of knowledge about the effects of trauma. With the awareness that several other mental health professionals (including the head psychiatrist at the juvenile detention center) believed the defendant to have severe PTSD and trauma-related psychosis, he did not bother to educate himself about how a person with a trauma-related disorder with psychotic features might perform on psychological tests. Let us take the MMPI-2. Bona fide psychiatric patients tend to produce MMPI-2 profiles with high F scales (Greene, 1991). A number of researchers have noted that individuals with traumatic histories also produce MMPI-2 profiles with quite elevated F scores (Kahn, Welch & Zillmer, 1993; Rhodes, 1992; Wilson & Walker, 1990). The most authoritative study on this issue to date is a meta-analysis of the MMPI-2 and malingering, surveying 62 MMPI-2 feigning studies (Rogers, Sewell, Martin, & Vitacco, 2003), which concludes:

> Patients with PTSD have marked elevations on F (Mean = 86.31). [. . .] A major concern for practitioners is whether certain diagnostic groups, such as bona fide patients with schizophrenia and PTSD, are likely to have markedly elevated scores on validity indicators. Such elevations are likely to lead to misclassifications.
>
> (p. 172)

The prosecution expert took each of the defense expert's test results, the MCMI-III, the TSI, and the DAPS and opined that they were malingered. He said that all of the tests "were strongly suspicious of exaggeration or malingering and raised serious doubts about his credibility."

The defendant produced a relatively elevated profile on the MCMI-III, with Disclosure at a base rate of 99. He has elevated scores on Delusional Disorder, Posttraumatic Stress Disorder, Anxiety, Drug and Alcohol Dependence, and Depressive Personality type. The computer-generated narrative states: "The offender's response style may indicate a broad tendency to magnify the level of experienced illness or a characterological inclination to complain or to be self-pitying. On the other hand, the response style may convey feelings of extreme vulnerability that are associated with an episode of acute turmoil." The prosecution expert quoted the first half of the statement from the computer-generated narrative (up to "on the other hand"). The second half he attributed to the defense expert rather than to the computer-generated narrative. He chose to believe that the results indicated malingering rather than vulnerability and turmoil, again showing poor insight into victims of severe and repetitive sexual abuse (Herman, 1992). It is important to note that if patients with trauma histories show elevations on scale F (and other validity scales in the direction of "faking bad") of the MMPI-2, it is logical to expect a similar validity profile on the MCMI or other tests of psychopathology. In fact, I found this to be true in a research study comparing genuine versus malingered Battered Woman Syndrome (Kaser-Boyd, 2004).

Next, on the TSI, the prosecution expert noted that the Atypical Response (ATR) scale had a T-score of 100. The 6-page computer-generated scoring summary had statements on two of these pages addressing the ATR score, but this expert quoted only the one which was on page 3 and stated: "the T Score exceeds validity cutoff score. It is recommended that the TSI be considered invalid." However, on page 2 of the print-out, it stated: "TSI protocols completed by individuals with psychotic symptoms may require special interpretation or may be invalid. Please see the TSI Professional Manual." Since Miguel had been diagnosed with psychotic symptoms in the past and was prescribed antipsychotic medication at the juvenile detention center, a careful forensic psychologist would be expected to go on to read the TSI manual (Briere, 1995). The manual states:

> Extreme overendorsement of ATR items may [. . .] indicate an attempt to present oneself as especially symptomatic or may represent a psychotic condition, either of which can invalidate the TSI. [. . .] It is likely that chronic substance abuse, with its tendency to produce unusual experiences may also be a factor in high ATR scores [. . .] Some extremely traumatized individuals, by virtue of experiencing intrusive sensory symptoms and dissociative states, can have especially elevated valid scores on ATR.
>
> (p. 11)

A forensic evaluator would also need to understand that Miguel's TSI was being compared to a normative sample that consisted of a non-clinical, community sample that mailed back surveys. Childhood experiences of interpersonal violence, including child abuse and other forms of assault, were reported by 31 percent of these men and 43.3 percent of the women; adult interpersonal victimization was reported by 34 percent of men and 43.6 percent of women (p. 29). However, according to the test manual, these were individuals who were not currently in treatment nor in active distress. It is clear that the normative sample was much different, and likely much less severely impaired than Miguel, which could certainly explain his elevation on Atypical Responses. Finally, the elegant meta-analysis of Rogers and colleagues (2003) indicated that patients with serious traumatic histories show elevations on the malingering scales of the MMPI-2, thus it seems wise to extrapolate from this that they might also show elevations on the atypical items of the TSI.

The statements by the prosecution expert about the DAPS and the problems with his analysis are virtually the same as with the TSI. The computer-generated narrative states:

The respondent's T-score on the Negative Bias (NB) scale is elevated, indicating that he endorsed items that were rarely endorsed by traumatized individuals in the standardization sample. He may be attempting to present himself as especially symptomatic, may be randomly responding, or may be experiencing an unusual number of atypical symptoms. The possibility of psychosis or mania also should be ruled out.

(p. 5)

Again, making reference to the test manual is a crucial step in understanding, first, who is in the normative group, and, second, that Miguel is much more disturbed that most individuals with Posttraumatic Stress Disorder, as exhibited by his use of dangerous substances to self-medicate, hearing voices, and contemplating bizarre ways to die. The normative sample for the DAPS was similar to that for the TSI. It was a non-clinical sample who completed a mailed set of questionnaires including the DAPS and the Traumatic Events Survey (TES; Elliott, 1992); the final pool of subjects reported at least one DSM-IV-TR-level traumatic event in the past. The normative sample was referred to as the "trauma–exposed general population participants." (p. 33). The manual states,

> T-scores from 50 to 60 on the DAPS are considered average for trauma-exposed individuals. It should be noted, however, that a T-score of 50 (in a valid protocol) rarely indicates significant symptomatic distress because many trauma-exposed individuals in the general population are relatively asymptomatic, either due to the passage of time since the event or because the trauma was not severe enough to produce lasting stress.
>
> (p. 17)

Again, Miguel is clearly more seriously disturbed than the normative trauma population and therefore we would expect him to endorse more items on the Negative Bias scale. The caveat listed about the NB scale is similar to the one in the TSI manual:

> extreme overendorsement of NB items may indicate an attempt to present oneself as especially symptomatic or, in some instances, may represent a psychotic or manic condition, any of which can invalidate the DAPS results. It is likely that chronic substance abuse, with its tendency to produce unusual experiences, also may be a factor in higher NB scores.
>
> (p. 18)

There was no indication that the prosecution expert considered the information from the two test manuals. Instead, his report concluded that Miguel had malingered on the MMPI-2 he administered and also on all three psychological tests that the defense had administered. The *coup de grace* was this psychologist's statement that he did not believe that Miguel had been raped by the dead man. He said he found the rape story implausible and further made questionable because Miguel continued to have sex with the man, and because Miguel admitted he had subsequently had sex with many men.

As is often the case, there was no external "proof" that Miguel had been raped by the dead man. It was reality, however, that the man was an adult and Miguel was a young teenager. It was also the case that Miguel had been closely observed by mental health practitioners in juvenile hall, and they did not question his credibility about having been a sexual abuse victim. Pointing to Miguel's chaotic sexual life as "proof" that he was not raped demonstrated the prosecution expert's lack of training and experience with sexual abuse survivors.

The impact of the prosecution expert's testimony on the jury was considerable. The young defendant was already struggling with the negative projections of *immigrant, homosexual, cross-dresser, promiscuous,* and *killer.* Added to the list, after this expert's testimony, was *malingerer.* The jury could not sort through the technical, contradictory details offered by the two defense experts and the prosecution expert. Miguel was convicted of first degree murder and, though just 17 when he committed the killing, will likely spend 25 years to life in prison.

Conclusions to Case 1

It is not the intent of the authors to label another expert unethical or to suggest that his work constituted malpractice. In considering the issues presented here, we conclude with a review of the relevant ethical guidelines.

> 2.09 *Appropriate use of Services and Products*: Forensic practitioners are encouraged to make reasonable efforts to guard against misuse of their services and exercise professional discretion in addressing such misuses.

> 9.01 *Use of Appropriate Methods*: Forensic practitioners strive to utilize appropriate methods and procedures in their work. When performing examinations, treatment, consultation, educational activities, or scholarly investigations, forensic practitioners seek to maintain integrity by examining the issue or problem at hand from all reasonable perspectives and seek information that will differentially test plausible rival hypotheses.

> 10.02 *Appropriate Use of Assessment Procedures*: Forensic practitioners use assessment procedures in the manner and for the purposes that are appropriate in light of the research on or evidence of their usefulness and proper application.

> 11.01 *Accuracy, Fairness, and Avoidance of Deception*: Forensic practitioners make reasonable efforts to ensure that the products of their services, as well as their own public statements and professional reports and testimony, are

communicated in ways that promote understanding and avoid deception. . . . When providing reports and other sworn statements or testimony in any form, forensic practitioners strive to present their conclusions, evidence, opinions, or other professional products in a fair manner.

Case 2: Inaccurate Test Interpretation and Failure to Consider Alternate Hypotheses

In November 1998, the 52-year-old landlady of a bed-and-breakfast inn, Marian E.,[3] was sentenced to 6 years' imprisonment and mandated treatment on behalf of the state, on account of a double homicide. Two dead bodies had been found on her premises, one in canvas under some shrubbery, the other buried in the yard. Both corpses showed signs of a violent death. Marian always denied any involvement in these killings. She was arrested on Christmas Eve of 1997, after a local carpenter informed the police. The carpenter claimed Marian had approached her and had asked him for help because she had killed one of her guests.[4] Marian was sent to the Psychiatric Observation Clinic (POC) of the Dutch Ministry of Justice for FMHA (see Chapter 2 for further information on the procedures of this POC). In 2006, when Marian was staying in a forensic psychiatric hospital, CdR was asked to conduct an independent FMHA by Marian's defense counsel. In the context of this new evaluation, CdR also reviewed the original FMHA from the POC.

The POC report dates from June 12, 1998, around 6 months after her arrest. The raw test material obtained from counsel had been administered in April. The conclusion of the POC report reads:

> Accused is a 52-year-old woman, who was suffering from a Psychotic Disorder, already before the criminal acts, if proven. The Psychotic Disorder was expressed in the incapacity to maintain boundaries, to maintain order and planning in daily living, and finally, in the consistent and incorrigible idea that she was being treated wrongfully by the local authorities. The Psychotic Disorder from which she is suffering has seriously diminished her capacity for aggression regulation and her moral judgment [. . .]. At the time of the criminal acts she was suffering from such mental incapacity that, when she is proven guilty, she can be considered diminished responsible for these acts. [. . .] The probability that the defendant would commit serious aggressive acts in the future, according to a similar crime scenario as in the presently alleged offenses, is deemed high.

What is remarkable about the latter conclusion is that the purported "crime scenario," including trigger(s) and motive for the offending behavior, is not described anywhere in the FHMA report. This is not surprising given the fact that Marian says she doesn't know anything about the dead bodies, and the police investigative efforts also gave limited evidence for such a scenario (Acda et al., 2006).

The central conclusion of the POC report is that Marian was suffering from a psychotic disorder, and this disorder, in combination with the judgment of high recidivism risk, resulted in advice of diminished responsibility and a mandated treatment order to the court. Obviously, this conclusion should be based on objective test results and collateral data. Thus, CdR started her review of the test results and test interpretation. The POC psychologist administered nine different tests. The first four assessed cognitive functioning, including intelligence, visual organization, and visual memory. Because the psychologist hypothesized, on the basis of the outcome of these more global cognitive tests that Marian might suffer from neurocognitive dysfunction, a more extensive neuropsychological assessment was performed. The latter did not reveal any neurocognitive deficiencies and her total IQ was 124, which is in line with her Master's level university education and her former successful career as a marine biologist. This chapter will focus mainly on the results from the MMPI-2 and the Rorschach Inkblot Method (RIM), since these two tests in consort provide the most relevant information regarding a possible psychotic disorder. For instance, the RIM has been found to be able to detect psychotic symptoms even when still at a preclinical or less severe stage (Metsänen et al., 2004; Smith, Baity, Knowles, & Hilsenroth, 2001).

MMPI-2

The validity profile of Marian's MMPI-2 does not reveal evidence of distorted responding.

The MMPI-2 clinical scales point to the presence of family conflicts. Marian reports feelings of vulnerability and distrust, a lack of support, and disappointment about this. The elevated score on the Depression scale (scale 2) indicates Marian is experiencing feelings of hopelessness and distress. She feels tired and has difficulty concentrating. There is no evidence for antisocial attitudes or an antisocial lifestyle in her profile. Often, elevated scores on the MMPI-2 clinical scales are interpreted as evidence of structural character pathology. This may be correct, but it may also be incorrect. At all times, the psychologist should consider the role of situational circumstances and the assessment context as a possible reason for an elevated profile. In the case of Marian, there were some notable test findings which supported such a contextual interpretation. Of all three elevated clinical scales, mostly the Harris-Lingoes subscales, which are highly sensitive to situational stress (e.g., scale 8, Friedman et al., 2001), showed elevations. This means the hypothesis that the elevations on the main clinical scales are to a large extent situationally determined should be carefully considered. Note that by the time of her FMHA in the POC, Marian had been incarcerated already for several

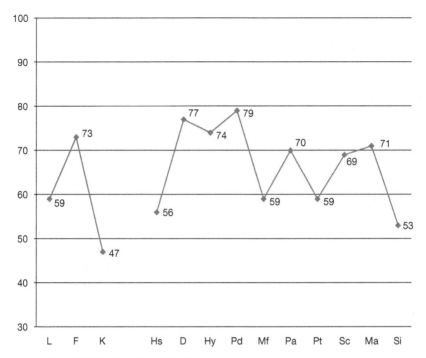

FIGURE 10.2 MMPI-2 Profile of Marian E.

months. She had been subjected to long and harsh interrogations by police officers who were convinced that she was guilty. The prosecution had requested the FMHA at the POC because this defendant did not confess to the killings, but seemed "strange" to them.

What does the POC psychologist write in her report about Marian's personality, based on these raw test data? She states: "She tends to maintain relationships with marginal, antisocial functioning individuals. The defendant's antisocial attitudes appear to be satisfied in this manner." The POC psychologist further contends that: "Repressed anger at her family members plays a role." This interpretation is contrary to her elevated score on the Familial Discord scale, which shows that Marian actually *admits* she has overt conflicts with and feelings of anger towards family members. Admitting angry feelings and repressing them are diametrically opposite.

Three other MMPI-2 clinical scales show elevations: Mania (Ma), Paranoia (Pa), and Schizophrenia (Sc). The Ma scale and its subscales point at Marian's openness to experience and adventurousness. Her life course shows this: she has worked in the US and Scotland, created a new educational program in environmental sciences at a university in The Netherlands, and started the bed-and-breakfast inn close to the ocean in her late 40s. She tends to be stubborn and shows a lack of patience with persons who cannot keep up with her pace. The elevated Pa scale indicates distrust: Marian experiences the world as an unsafe place. Whether the paranoia has a psychotic coloring, in the form of paranoid ideas of reference or paranoid delusions, can be gauged by also examining the score on the Bizarre mentation (BIZ) scale. Her BIZ score is within the normal range; thus, it is unlikely that her distrust has a delusional-paranoid quality. The elevated Pa scale could be related to situational aspects besides her personality and/or psychopathology. On items such as: "I believe I am being plotted against" (138) and "No one seems to understand me" (22), Marian's response is affirmative. But if she is indeed innocent, then these affirmative responses should be interpreted as signs of mental health instead of psychopathology. This last, alternative interpretation is not mentioned by the POC psychologist. On the contrary, she writes that Marian is: "[. . .] to a serious degree paranoid, angry and avoidant. She ruminates a lot and is angry about real or imagined injustice she has suffered. This is paired with ideas of reference and/or paranoid delusions."

The Sc scale also shows a clinical elevation. Although the scale's name is Schizophrenia scale, it should never be used on its own to arrive at a diagnostic conclusion of Schizophrenia or psychosis. Many individuals with the Sc-scale as the highest one are not psychotic (Friedman et al., 2001, p. 132). The individual may be experiencing a personal crisis instead of serious psychopathology. An analysis of the Harris-Lingoes subscales of the Sc scale can help determine the most likely interpretation. The first subscale (T-score = 66) indicates feelings of loneliness, being misunderstood, and cut off from family and friends. On the third subscale (T = 71), Marian shows problems with concentration and memory. The fourth subscale indicates a lack of (mental) energy (T-score = 75). The subscale Bizarre sensory experiences (T-score = 63), which is most closely related to psychotic symptoms such as delusions and hallucinations, is not clinically elevated in Marian's profile.

Again, the possibility that the elevation on the Sc scale is caused by the situational context cannot be ruled out. However, the POC psychologist has no doubt that Marian is suffering from serious psychopathology: "The content of her thoughts is often unusual and unconventional. [. . .] Besides paranoid thoughts, she is also revealing incoherent thinking and loose and chaotic thoughts occur frequently."

RIM

Accurate interpretation of a performance-based personality test, such as the RIM, is highly dependent upon accurate coding of the subject's responses. Available empirical studies indicate that trained raters can reliably score according to the coding instructions of the Comprehensive System (CS; Exner, 2003; Meyer et al., 2002; Viglione & Taylor, 2003).

Client Name: Marian	Gender: Female	Test Date: May 1998
Client ID:	Date of Birth:	Description:

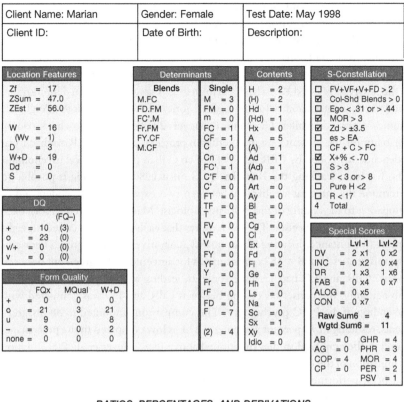

RATIOS, PERCENTAGES, AND DERIVATIONS

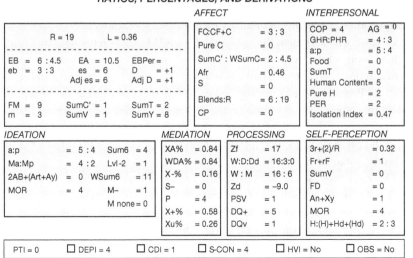

FIGURE 10.3 Rorschach CS Structural Summary of Marian E. based on Consensus Scoring by CdR and LC.

Meyer, Mihura, and Smith (2005) examined the inter-rater reliability of Rorschach CS interpretations across four datasets among three to eight clinicians. They found the level of interclinician interpretive reliability for the CS was similar to findings from meta-analyses of inter-rater reliability in other areas of psychology and medicine (Meyer et al., 2005). A recent study on the inter-rater reliability of the newly developed Rorschach Performance Assessment System demonstrated good to excellent reliability for the large majority of the system's codes (Viglione, Blume-Marcovici, Miller, Giromini, & Meyer, 2012). In order to check coding reliability for the present case, the verbatim protocol of Marian's Rorschach was independently coded by CdR and by Dr. Leo Cohen (LC), a clinical psychologist who has been teaching the Rorschach CS since 1986. This made it possible to determine the inter-rater reliability between two experienced CS coders and to compare it to the coding of the POC psychologist. Marian produced a Rorschach protocol with 19 responses. The CS requires that each response is coded on eight aspects (for instance, location, form quality, cognitive special score). Theoretically, this creates $19 \times 8 = 152$ opportunities for agreement/disagreement between coders. CdR and LC had 13 disagreements, leading to a 91 percent agreement. Subsequently, the consensus coding between CdR and LC was compared with the coding of the POC psychologist. This comparison amounted to 38 disagreements, resulting in 75 percent agreement. This is low compared to the percentages found in the empirical studies mentioned above (e.g., Meyer et al., 2002). Upon examination of the original coding, it was apparent how sloppy the original coding had been performed. Even relatively straightforward CS variables, such as the coding of Populars, which can be easily looked up in the coding workbook, were missed. The large number of coding errors has serious implications for the interpretation of Marian's Rorschach by the POC psychologist.

First, we will document the outcome of the RIM based on the new consensus coding. None of the main clinical indices, such as the Depression index, Coping Deficit index, Perceptual Thinking index (PTI) and Hypervigilance index, is positive. Positive scores on these indices often signal the presence of serious psychopathology. Marian's score on the PTI, an index that indicates poor reality testing and psychotic experiences, is 0. Obviously, this finding is out of line with the POC psychologists's description of Marian as "a person who is hindered by a chronic paranoid psychosis."

There are more grave discrepancies. The cluster Stress tolerance reveals that Marian has an adequate level of resources to handle day-to-day stressors. She is stable, non-impulsive, and modulates her feelings adequately. The statements of the POC psychologist run counter to these findings: "The accused has problems retaining control over her impulses and behavior." The POC psychologist concludes that Marian is suffering from a personality disorder with narcissistic and histrionic features, paired with a chronic paranoid psychosis. After interpreting the original MMPI-2 and RIM, the basis for this conclusion remains elusive.

The diagnostic conclusion can only be understood in light of serious flaws in MMPI-2 interpretation and RIM coding and subsequent interpretation. Of further note is the fact that *nowhere* in the POC report can clear descriptions of Marian's psychotic symptomatology be found. In other words, the content of her supposedly bizarre and paranoid ideation is never described.

When asked to perform an independent FMHA of Marian in 2006, her file contained reports from two psychiatrists and one psychologist who had conducted a second opinion during the interval between her conviction in 1996 and 2006. None of these experts had found any evidence of psychopathology (no personality disorder, no psychotic disorder) in Marian's case, neither in the present nor in the past. In CdR's FMHA of Marian, this evidence was also absent.

The courts in The Netherlands review the necessity for continuation of the TBS-order for an individual every one or two years. None of the experts that testified as to the absence of any disorder in Marian's case were influential in leading the court to terminate her TBS. Ultimately, her TBS was terminated on the request of the forensic hospital in the spring of 2012 because the hospital staff advised the court that she was cured now. Marian is now studying her file and preparing an appeal for a reopening of her case.

General Discussion

Both the above cases illustrate the consequences of a lack of competence in the use of psychological tests and the failure to consider rival hypotheses. As such they fall under the heading of unethical practice, i.e., the opinions and determinations were reached in an inappropriate manner (Bush, Connell, & Denney, 2006). What seems also apparent in both cases is that the psychologists failed to examine the issues from perspectives that differed from those of the referring party. The prosecution expert from Case 1 seemed to have fallen prone to the prosecutor's opinions. The POC psychologist, though appointed by the court, seemed unable or unwilling to consider the option that Marian's refusal to confess to the crimes might be bona fide.

A lack of competent test administration and interpretation is a serious shortcoming but can be repaired by means of continuing education and peer consultation. The need for specialized forensic psychological education cannot be overestimated. We have also found it essential to maintain the quality of our forensic casework to attend annual scientific meetings with ample opportunity for consultation with other forensic psychologists with an assessment practice. We encourage forensic mental health practitioners to research issues pertinent to their case, such as the presentation of a particular disorder on particular tests. FMHA also makes increasing demands on cultural competency of forensic psychologists and we believe reading and consultation with experts in this area is essential to good forensic assessment.

A major issue that is more difficult to tackle just by means of continuing education is the impact of bias. This seems to pose the greatest risk of ethical misconduct in forensic psychology (Bush et al., 2006). Because forensic work is often concerned with cases in which moral values play a large role, forensic psychologists must be continually aware of the possible impact of personal opinions on their professional work. Sometimes, this may mean the forensic psychologists need to decide not to take on a certain case. For example, when CdR's child was still at a young age, she did not take on cases of child molestation, as she was doubtful if she would be able to view these objectively. It is beyond the scope of the present chapter to provide a comprehensive review of all forms of bias, which may compromise the quality and ethics of forensic practice. The reader is kindly referred to the work of Bush et al. (2006; especially chapter 5) for an insightful discussion of these bias issues and of ways to address these proactively. Forensic practice is demanding, and rightfully so, because the opinions offered by psychologists may play a determining role in far-reaching legal decisions.

Notes

1   The latest update of this Ethics Code (2008) is available in English: www.psynip.nl/website-openbaar-documenten-nip-algemeen/code-of-ethics-for-psychologists.pdf.
2   Caldwell Report, which is based on the research of Alex Caldwell, PhD.
3   This case was previously described in a Dutch article (de Ruiter, 2007). Marian E. gave permission to use her test findings and other case material for publication.
4   In a publication in the Dutch Legal Journal, Acda and colleagues (2006) provided evidence for the limited credibility of the carpenter's statements and for other problematic aspects of the evidence in Marian's case. They concluded the case has all the elements for a miscarriage of justice.

References

Acda, P. B. A., Geraerts, E., Henkes, A. B. M., Horselenberg, R., Hoynck van Papendrecht, H. P., & van Koppen, P. J. (2006). Anatomie van een dubieuze veroordeling: De Anjummer pensionmoorden [Anatomy of a dubious conviction: The Anjum bed-and-breakfast murders]. *Nederlands Juristenblad* [Netherlands Legal Journal], *81*, 1558–1564.

American Psychological Association (1991). Specialty Guidelines for Forensic Psychologists. *APA Monitor, 22*, 22.

American Psychological Association (2002). Ethical principles of psychologists and code of conduct. *American Psychologist, 57*, 1597–1611. www.apa.org/ethics/code/code.pdf.

American Psychological Association (2013). Specialty Guidelines for Forensic Psychologists. *American Psychologist, 68*, 7–19. doi: 10.1037/a0029889.

Armstrong, J. & Kaser-Boyd, N. (2003). Projective assessment of trauma. In M. Hilsenroth & D. Segal (Eds.), *Objective and projective assessment of personality and psychopathology* (pp. 500–512). New York: Wiley.

Briere, J. (1995). *Trauma symptom inventory: Professional manual.* Lutz, Florida: Psychological Assessment Resources.

Briere, J. (1997). *Psychological assessment of adult posttraumatic states.* Washington, DC: American Psychological Association.

Briere, J. (2001). *Detailed assessment of posttraumatic stress: Professional manual.* Lutz, FL: Psychological Assessment Resources, Inc.

Briere, J. & Elliott, D. M. (1997). Psychological assessment of interpersonal victimization effects in adults and children. *Psychotherapy, 34,* 353–364.

Bush, S. S., Connell, M. A., & Denney, R. L. (2006). *Ethical practice in forensic psychology: A systematic model for decision making.* Washington, DC: American Psychological Association.

Butcher, J. N., Dahlstrom, W. G., Graham, J.R., Tellegen, A., & Kaemmer, B. (1989). *MMPI-2: Manual for Administration and Scoring.* Minneapolis, MN: University of Minnesota Press.

Dhaliwal, G. K., Gauzad, L., Antonowicz, D. H., & Ross, R. R. (1996). Adult male survivors of childhood sexual abuse: Prevalence, sexual abuse characteristics and long-term effects. *Clinical Psychology Review, 16,* 619–639. doi: 10.1016/S0272-7358(96)00018-9.

Dorais, M. (2002). *Don't tell: The sexual abuse of boys.* Quebec: McGill-Queens.

Doyle, D. J. & Ogloff, J. R. P. (2009). Calling the tune without the music: A psycho-legal analysis of Australia's post-sentence legislation. *Australian and New Zealand Journal of Criminology, 42,* 179–20.

Dube, S. R., Anda, R. F., Whitfield, C. L., Brown, D. W., Felitti, V. J., Dong, M., & Giles, W. H. (2005). Long-term consequences of childhood sexual abuse by gender of victim. *American Journal of Preventive Medicine, 28,* 430–438. doi: 10.1016/j.amepre.2005.01.015

Elliott, D. M. (1992). *Traumatic events survey.* Unpublished psychological test, Harbor-University of California-Los Angeles Medical Center.

Exner, J. E., Jr. (2003). *The Rorschach: A comprehensive system: Volume 1. Basic foundations and principles of interpretation* (4th ed.). Hoboken, NJ: Wiley.

Friedman, A. F., Lewak, R., Nichols, D. S., & Webb, J. T. (2001). *Psychological assessment with the MMPI-2.* Mahwah, NJ: Erlbaum.

Greene, R. L. (1991). *The MMPI-2/MMPI: An interpretive manual.* Boston: Allyn & Bacon.

Herman, J. L. (1992). Complex PTSD: A syndrome in survivors of prolonged and repeated trauma. *Journal of Traumatic Stress, 5,* 377–391. doi: 10.1002/jts.2490050305.

Holmes, W. C. & Slap, G. B. (1998). Sexual abuse of boys: Definition, prevalence, correlates, sequelae, and management. *Journal of the American Medical Association, 280,* 1855–1862. doi: 10.1001/jama.280.21.1855.

Hunter, J. A. (1991). A comparison of the psychosocial maladjustment of adult males and females sexually molested as children. *Journal of Interpersonal Violence, 6,* 205–217.

Hunter, M. (1990). *Abused boys: The neglected victims of sexual abuse.* Lexington, MA: Lexington Books & D. C. Heath and Company.

Kahn, F. I., Welch, T. L., & Zillmer, E. A. (1993). MMPI-2 profiles of battered women in transition. *Journal of Personality Assessment, 60,* 100–111.

Kaser-Boyd, N. (2004). Battered woman's syndrome: Clinical features, evaluation, and expert testimony. In B. J. Cling (Ed.), *Sexualized violence against women and children* (pp. 41–70). New York: Guilford.

Klotz Flitter, J. M., Elhai, J. D., & Gold, S. N. (2003). MMPI-2 F scale elevations in adult victims of child sexual abuse. *Journal of Traumatic Stress, 16,* 269–274.

Metsänen, M., Wahlberg, K.-E., Saarento, O., Tarvainen, T., Miettunen, J., Koistinen, P., Läksy, K., & Tienari, P. (2004). Early presence of thought disorder as a prospective sign of mental disorder. *Psychiatry Research, 125,* 193–203. doi: 0.1016/j.psychres.2004.01.002.

Meyer, G. J., Hilsenroth, M. J., Baxter, D., Exner, J. E., Jr., Fowler, J. C., Piers, C. C., & Resnick, J. (2002). An examination of interrater reliability for scoring the Rorschach Comprehensive System in eight data sets. *Journal of Personality Assessment*, 78, 219–274. doi: 10.1207/S15327752JPA7802_03.

Meyer, G. J., Mihura, J. L., & Smith, B. L. (2005). The interclinician reliability of Rorschach interpretation in four data sets. *Journal of Personality Assessment*, 84, 296–314. doi: 10.1207/s15327752jpa8403_09.

Millon, T. (1994). *MCMI-III: Manual*. Minneapolis, MN: National Computer Systems.

Mohan, G. & Simmons, A. M. (2004, June 16). Diversity spoken in 39 languages. *Los Angeles Times*. Los Angeles: Times Publishing.

Nash, M. R., Hulsey, T. L., Sexton, M. C., Harralson, T. L., & Lambert, W. (1993). Long-term sequelae of childhood sexual abuse: Perceived family environment, psychopathology, and dissociation. *Journal of Consulting and Clinical Psychology*, 61, 276–283.

Olson, P. E. (1990). The sexual abuse of boys: A study of the long-term psychological effects. In M. Hunter (Ed.), *The sexually abused male* (pp. 137–152). Lexington, MA: Lexington Books & D. C. Heath and Company.

Pope, K. S., Butcher, J. N., & Seelen, J. (2006). *The MMPI, MMPI-2, and MMPI-A in court: A practical guide for expert witnesses and attorneys* (3rd ed.). Washington, DC: American Psychological Association.

Ray, S. L. (2001). Male survivors' perspectives of incest/sexual abuse. *Perspectives in Psychiatric Care*, 37, 49–59.

Rhodes, N. R. (1992). Comparison of MMPI psychopathic deviate scores of battered and non-battered women. *Journal of Family Violence*, 7, 297–307. doi: 10.1007/BF00994620.

Rogers, R., Sewell, K. W., & Salekin, R. T. (1994). A meta-analysis of malingering on the MMPI-2. *Assessment*, 1, 227–237.

Rogers, R., Sewell, K. W., Martin, M. A., & Vitacco, M. J. (2003). Detection of feigned mental disorders: A meta-analysis of the MMPI-2 and malingering. *Assessment*, 10, 160–177. doi: 10.1177/1073191103010002007.

de Ruiter, C. (2007). Een dubieuze gedragskundige rapportage bij een ontkennende verdachte. De casus van de Anjummer pensionmoorden [A dubious forensic mental health report on a nonconfessing defendant: The case of the Anjum bed-and-breakfast murders]. *Proces*, 86, 136–145.

Smith, S. R., Baity, M. R., Knowles, E. S., & Hilsenroth, M. J. (2001). Assessment of disordered thinking in children and adolescents: The Rorschach perceptual-thinking index. *Journal of Personality Assessment*, 77, 447–463. doi: 10.1207/S15327752JPA 7703_06.

Valente, S. M. (2005). Sexual abuse of boys. *Journal of Child and Adolescent Psychiatric Nursing*, 18, 10–16. doi: 10.1111/j.1744–6171.2005.00005.x.

Vess, J. (2011). Ethical practice in sex offender assessment: Consideration of actuarial and polygraph methods. *Sexual Abuse: A Journal of Research and Treatment*, 23, 381–396. doi: 10.1177/1079063210382045.

Viglione, D. J. & Taylor, N. (2003). Empirical support for interrater reliability of Rorschach comprehensive system coding. *Journal of Clinical Psychology*, 59, 111–121. doi: 10.1002/jclp.10121.

Viglione, D. J., Blume-Marcovici, A. C., Miller, H. L., Giromini, L., & Meyer, G. (2012). An inter-rater reliability study for the Rorschach performance assessment system. *Journal of Personality Assessment*, 94, 607–612. doi: 10.1080/00223891.2012.684118.

Wilson, J. P. & Walker, A. J. (1990). Toward an MMPI trauma profile. *Journal of Traumatic Stress*, 3, 151–168. doi: 10.1002/jts.2490030111.

11

FORENSIC REPORT WRITING

The Science and the Story

Corine de Ruiter and Nancy Kaser-Boyd

Most clinical psychologists who enter the legal arena to conduct forensic mental health assessments (FMHAs) have been trained in clinical assessment report writing. There are excellent text books on psychological assessment, which provide guidelines for writing these types of assessment reports (e.g., Groth-Marnat, 2009). Forensic report writing requires the "unlearning" of some of these guidelines because the forensic report is meant to present the trier of fact with an expert's opinion with regard to a psycholegal question with the aim of serving the truth. Most clinical assessment reports are written on behalf of the assessee; forensic reports in criminal cases are written for the court, the attorney or the public prosecutor's office. In clinical evaluations, the assessee–evaluator relationship is bound by confidentiality privilege, as laid down in professional ethics codes (see Chapter 10), which means the assessee has the right to block disclosure of the report to third parties. In FMHA, reports are written on request of a third party, which means the report most likely will be disclosed, particularly when the assessment is court-ordered. The fact that FMHA reports will be read by individuals who are not mental health professionals, but by legal professionals and laypeople who are unfamiliar with clinical jargon, means this should be kept to a minimum or explained. The FMHA report in criminal cases may become part of the public domain, which requires careful concern of inclusion of particularly private information which may not be strictly necessary in the report. Finally, the FMHA report, more so than the clinical report, should make a clear distinction between facts and interpretations or inferences, since the trier of fact needs to be able to consider the evaluator's data and his reasoning. In this chapter, we will present empirical research on the quality of forensic reports, discuss the essential qualities of a good forensic report and common errors, with examples from practice. A special section will be devoted to writing about the outcome of violence risk assessment in forensic reports.

Research on Forensic Reports

Reports of FMHA are meant to serve as evidence in court, which requires careful attention to both their *content* and *form* (Ireland, 2008). Compared with empirical studies on forensic assessment and its instruments, there is a rather limited research base on forensic report writing (Griffith, Stankovic, & Baranoski, 2010). A review of 10 studies that examined the quality of forensic reports (Wettstein, 2005) revealed six of these studies actually examined forensic reports to identify the frequency of various strengths and weaknesses in terms of their content and form. Four of these six studies (Christy, Douglas, Otto, & Petrila, 2004; Hecker & Steinberg, 2002; Robbins, Waters, & Herbert, 1997; Skeem, Golding, Cohn, & Berge, 1998) revealed that evaluators mostly reported relevant data, and the psycholegal question was often addressed adequately, but the reports often failed to include the evaluator's reasoning about the link between the data and the evaluator's opinion about the psycholegal question (the first forensic report in the case of Marian E., presented in Chapter 10, provides a pertinent example). Forensic reports must describe transparently how the psycholegal opinion is supported (or not) by the data presented and state the logical reasoning by which the evidence leads to the opinion (e.g., Conroy, 2006; Heilbrun, 2001; Melton, Petrila, Poythress, & Slobogin, 2007). Interestingly, this same problem was the most frequent mistake made in a recent study by Grisso (2010) on a sample of forensic reports (N = 62) that had been submitted to the American Board of Forensic Psychology by 36 candidates for forensic board certification. A panel of forensic mental health practitioners had reviewed the reports, which resulted in non-acceptance of these reports. The reviewers' evaluations of the reports were used to create an inventory of discrete types of "problems" encountered in the reports. Table 11.1 (Grisso, 2010) provides the top 10 most frequent problems noted in the rejected reports.

In The Netherlands, van Esch (2012) examined 194 pretrial forensic reports of defendants adjucated in the Dutch criminal justice system in 2001. She noted that only a small percentage (30 percent) of forensic mental health evaluators compared the version of the offense that the defendant gave with data from other sources. Even more concerning was the fact that she found that a number of topics that should have been part of the interview with the defendant were not covered in every forensic report: an interview about the alleged offense(s), criminal history, somatic aspects, substance use, substance use before/during the alleged offense, and the mental health history. In The Netherlands, professional ethics guidelines (Netherlands Institute of Psychologists, 2008) prescribe that a draft psychological report should be discussed with the assessee, the assessee should be given the opportunity to read the draft report and to make suggestions for correction of facts, if applicable. Van Esch (2012) noted that only one in five forensic mental health evaluators had discussed the report with the defendant.[1]

TABLE 11.1 Most Frequent Faults in Forensic Report Writing (Percent of Reports in Which They Were Identified)

1. *Opinions without sufficient explanations*
   (56 percent)
   Major interpretations or opinions were stated without sufficiently explaining their basis in data or logic (regardless of whether the report's data could have sustained the opinion)

2. *Forensic purpose unclear*
   (53 percent)
   The legal standard, legal question, or forensic purpose was not stated, not clear, inaccurate, or inappropriate

3. *Organization problems*
   (36 percent)
   Information was presented in a disorganized manner (usually without a reasonable logic for its sequence)

4. *Irrelevant data or opinions*
   (31 percent)
   Data and/or some opinions included in the report were not relevant for the forensic or clinical referral questions

5. *Failure to consider alternative hypotheses*
   (30 percent)
   Data allowed for alternative interpretations, while report did not offer explanations concerning why they were ruled out (often response style/malingering alternative, sometimes diagnostic)

6. *Inadequate data*
   (28 percent)
   The referral question, case circumstances, or final opinion required additional types of data that were not obtained or were not reported, and for which absence was not explained in report

7. *Data and interpretation mixed*
   (26 percent)
   Data and interpretations frequently appeared together in section that reports data

8. *Overreliance on single source of data*
   (22 percent)
   An important interpretation/opinion relied wholly on one source of data when corroborating information from multiple sources was needed (often overreliance on examinee's self-report)

9. *Language problems*
   (19 percent)
   Multiple instances of jargon, biased phrases, pejorative terms, or gratuitous comments

10. *Improper test uses*
    (15 percent)
    Test data were used in inappropriate ways when interpreted and applied to the case, or tests were not appropriate for the case itself

Note: Adapted from "Guidance for improving forensic reports: A review of common errors" by T. Grisso, 2010, *Open Access Journal of Forensic Psychology*, 2, pp. 110–111.

Similar to the findings reported in research on the quality of forensic reports from the US (e.g., Grisso, 2010; Wettstein, 2005), van Esch found that the majority of the forensic reports lacked clear and transparent reasoning to support the evaluator's conclusion. Obviously, this type of research (Grisso, 2010; van Esch, 2012) offers us guidance to improve our forensic report writing skills, and this will be the focus of the next part of this chapter.

Essential Qualities of a Good Forensic Report

Griffith, Stankovic, and Baranoski (2010) conceptualized the forensic mental health report as a performative narrative. The written report is the "practice-product" of the forensic mental health professional (p. 32), the mastery of which is essential because the report may have significant influence on the legal outcome for the assessee involved. Forensic evaluators must organize information from interviews, psychological tests, documents, and collateral sources into a coherent narrative. Forensic reports tell a story that accounts for the most compelling and valid data that answer a psycholegal question. Griffith et al. (2010) argue that it is important that forensic report writers position themselves as characters in their own stories (Peterson & Langellier, 2006). The forensic evaluator is an expert witness who writes a narrative, guided by the ethical requirement to be objective and transparent, but also prone to heuristic biases and ethical failure. Being conscious of this aspect of forensic report writing is crucial to avoid common pitfalls, such as pejorative and premature labeling (see Chapters 6 and 8, for instance) and relying too much on eyewitness accounts (e.g., those in the police file) that may be false. In other words, continuous reflection on the science and art of forensic report writing requires formalized consideration of how one uses words in the creation of the report (Resnick, 2006).

As is clear from the above research review, the main problems with forensic reports concern content, not form, although the two are obviously intertwined. If a report is badly structured, it will be more difficult for the trier of fact to distill the essential information. One could argue that an adequate form and structure of the report is a necessary but not sufficient condition for a good quality report. Over the years, many scholars in forensic mental health have provided guidelines for the organization of forensic reports (e.g., Gagliardi & Miller, 2008; Heilbrun, 2001; Heilbrun, Marczyk, & DeMatteo, 2002; Melton et al., 2007). Two sources provide samples from forensic reports with reflection and discussion which we have found very insightful (Heilbrun et al., 2002; Melton et al., 2007). Here we summarize the basic structure of a forensic report in criminal cases, which may need to be amended, depending on the particular jurisdiction in which the assessor is working. Obviously, a forensic report has a format that is tailored to answering the psycholegal question at hand. A comprehensive checklist that is particularly helpful is provided by the University of Massachusetts Medical School, with separate guidelines for Criminal Responsibility and Competency to Stand Trial (www.umassmed.edu/forensictraining/Reports/).

A forensic report starts with a title page which contains key identifying information concerning the assessee, the evaluator's name, date of the report, and the referral source (court, defense counsel, district-attorney). In order to keep in line with the temporal order of the evaluation, it is good practice to start the report with the referral question. For instance, if the assessee has been convicted for manslaughter by the court in first instance, and the evaluator has been asked to conduct a second opinion FMHA by the Court of Appeal, as is possible in The Netherlands, this should be described to provide the reader with the context of the report. In the US, it is good practice to begin the report with the referral question, and the actual criminal charge. Early in the report, there should be a description of the manner in which the assessee was informed of the purpose of the evaluation and the limits of confidentiality. The latter is especially relevant when the report is prepared for the court or other public institution; when an attorney is the referral source, the attorney and the assessee decide on the release of the report (Gagliardi & Miller, 2008). How the assessee was informed about the collection of information from collateral sources, for instance the interviewing of third parties or the retrieval of medical records, should also be described in the report.

The next part of the forensic report provides factual information on the actual FMHA. The report needs to present information on where (e.g., in a prison, at the evaluator's office), on which dates, and for how long the evaluator performed the assessment. A listing of test instruments used should be provided, possibly with some basic information on the purpose and properties of these instruments in an appendix. Providing this information is important as it supports the transparency of the FMHA. Subsequently, a listing of collateral information sources is required, both documents and oral interviews with collaterals. It is also relevant to report information sources that were sought, but could not be retrieved, and the possible limitations this may entail.

In the structured pretrial forensic reporting format provided by The Netherlands Institute of Forensic Psychiatry and Psychology (NIFP, 2014), which has the status of a recommendation not a prescription, the subsequent section of the report concerns "Relevant information from the legal documentation." What is "relevant" is strictly up to the evaluator, which obviously leaves a lot of room for subjective judgment. In a pretrial FMHA in both The Netherlands and the US, the psycholegal questions are generally fixed and concern mental state at the time of the offense, relationship between mental disorder and offense, future violence risk, and treatment recommendations, when applicable. The evaluator will read the legal documentation with these referral questions in mind, noting for instance eyewitness statements of the alleged offense, observations of the defendant's loved ones in the weeks prior to the alleged offense, and observations of police officers upon arrest and during interrogations. It is advisable, if at all possible, to gain access to the actual recordings of the interrogations in order to obtain an objective judgment (see Chapter 6). Both in the US and in The Netherlands interrogations are frequently videotaped, permitting an evaluation of the assessee's mental status at the time of interrogation. It is highly relevant to compare the offense and the defendant's behavior at that time, as it arises from the legal documentation, with the information gathered during the interview with the defendant at the time of the FMHA, and we recommend separating the two in the forensic report. In this way, it is clear to the trier of fact how the evaluator has arrived at her final conclusion, because she will have to compare and contrast conflicting data in a later summary section in the report. In some cases, the two versions are quite different, and the evaluator will not be able to decide on their reliability and validity. In such a case, the evaluator will need to describe clearly the discrepancies, and may need to conduct further interviews with the assessee. In The Netherlands, where most experts are court appointed and where the legal decision on guilt and the issue of criminal responsibility are dealt with in a single trial (Chapter 1), it is customary in such cases for experts to answer the referral questions for the two versions or scenarios separately, and it will be up to the trier of fact to come to an ultimate legal decision.

After having summarized the relevant information from the legal file, the actual clinical part of the FMHA is covered in the report. This section usually starts with a history taken during the interview with the assessee, and can best be reported under separate headings for ease of locating this information: family, early childhood, school and work, relationships, medical, psychosexual, substance use, psychiatric, criminal, social (finances, housing). When Mental State at the time of the Offense (MSO) is part of the referral question, details from the interview with the assessee on this issue need to be reported. We have found the semi-structured interview accompanying the Psychopathy Checklist-Revised (PCL-R; Hare, 2003) helpful in this regard because it contains all the relevant questions under the section Current Offense, for instance, what happened?; what did you do?; what did you think/feel?; was the offense planned or impulsive?; were you under the influence of substances when you committed the offense?; how come you got arrested? However, it is important in the forensic interview to provide time for the assessee to give her narrative of what occurred, and why, because at other times when asked to give her story, her account may have been limited by directive questions. In closing, questions can then be asked about aspects of the account that are not clear, or about inconsistencies.

A brief section on appearance and behavior, often called the Mental Status Examination (MSE), can be entered before the psychosocial history or here. On the issue of whether a traditional MSE (global description of orientation in time, person and place; mood; memory; intelligence level; ideation) should be a part of a forensic report there is no consensus among scholars. Gagliardi and Miller (2008), for instance, opt to not include a MSE because it usually contains clinical jargon and its validity is limited to the moment it was taken. On the other hand, Heilbrun, Grisso, and Goldstein (2009) suggest reporting "appearance, mood, behavior, sensorium, intellectual functioning, thought" (p. 116). Importantly, the focus in this section of the report should be on aspects which are relevant to the psycholegal questions. We have seen forensic reports which describe an assessee's appearance in detail, including types of tattoos, running the risk of prejudicing the assessee. The general attitude of the assessee during the evaluation needs to be described, as this may be relevant in relation to the interpretation of other findings from the FMHA (e.g., level of cooperation/openness; ability to remain on-topic). Beware of putting too much emphasis on particular incidents that happened during the assessment in the report because the focus should be on patterns of behavior. However, sometimes, an assessee may present quite differently on different occasions during the FMHA, and these differences may point out relevant symptoms of mental disorder.

In the next section, the findings from the psychological tests are reported. The tests used are listed and geared towards the psycholegal questions at hand. The importance of using multiple test instruments to assess the functional capacities (Grisso, 2003) relevant to the psycholegal issue cannot be overestimated. For example, the personality trait of impulsivity, which is highly relevant for the assessment of the risk of future violence, can be assessed by means of self-report, an interview with significant others, and a psychological or neuropsychological test. When the different data sources concur, the evaluator can draw firm and clear conclusions; when they do not, their disagreement should be disclosed. We advise against the reporting of numerical test findings because they may be misleading (all psychological tests have a standard error of measurement) and legal professionals have a tendency to misinterpret cut-off scores. On personality tests, a term such as "clinically significant" is appropriate; a cut-off score for the test could be explained in a footnote. With a test that may unfairly depict an assessee, even more caution is warranted. For example, since the introduction of the PCL-R in The Netherlands, it has become very difficult to get forensic patients with PCL-R scores > 26 past review boards for unsupervised leave, because in research on the predictive validity of the PCL-R in The Netherlands a total score of 26 was used as the cut-off for psychopathy (Hildebrand, de Ruiter, & Nijman, 2004; Hildebrand, de Ruiter, & de Vogel, 2004). When the PCL-R is used in the FMHA, we recommend reporting the personality traits the instrument has uncovered, including examples of behaviors which reveal the trait. We never use the term "psychopath" in a forensic report because of its negative connotation and because the term is too general and therefore not informative. We describe the PCL-R personality criteria (Affective, Interpersonal, and Behavioral facets) on which a 2 was scored; these traits are definitely present. We not only mention the trait, but also a number of the specific behavioral examples on which the score is based. For example:

Frank tends to manipulate others for personal gain. He cheated for years, to get social welfare benefits while he also held a job. During his work as a taxi driver, he also manipulated clients in order to get more rides.

Frank boasts about the criminal and non-criminal successes in his life. He is extremely self-righteous, and doesn't feel any shame or regret about his violent crimes (note that he previously served a 6-year prison term for manslaughter) and his chaotic lifestyle. On the contrary, he talks with pride about his last offense (attempted homicide).

The subsequent section, which we term "Diagnostic considerations," integrates the findings from the different data sources (file documents, clinical observation, interviews with collaterals, test findings) into a coherent picture, with the psycho-legal question in mind. For instance, in relation to limitations in functional capacities relevant for assessing criminal responsibility, the report needs to include inform-ation on aspects such as reality testing (including the presence of hallucina-tions or delusions or paranoid ideation), important affective states (fear, anger), impulse control and aggression regulation, ability to think about right and wrong, capacity for empathy, procriminal attitudes, etc. A classification in terms of DSM or ICD (International Classification of Diseases) may or may not be a part of this section. If the assessee does meet criteria for a psychiatric classification, it is import-ant to list the criteria the assessee meets and the basis for this. When there are discrepancies between different data sources, these should be mentioned and, if possible, explained. Differences in diagnosis are common when the assessee has been in treatment in multiple locations (e.g., community mental health center, county jail, prison, or private practitioner; see Chapter 4 for a pertinent example case). This is often the case where the person making the diagnosis in that set-ting has spent a relatively brief time evaluating the assessee. Diagnosis can also vary depending on the evaluator's training and experience. For example, many diagnostic work-ups look only at presenting symptoms in making the diagnosis rather than taking a detailed history of the disorder, including its genesis (the "snapshot" of the assessee rather than a videotape of her life). In cases where there have been multiple diagnoses, the report should explain the FMH evaluator's reasoning for settling on her diagnosis.

The final section, before the actual answers to the psycholegal questions are presented, contains the "Forensic analysis." The content of this analysis obviously depends on the psycholegal questions posed, but should always contain scientific reasoning in assessing the causal connection between clinical condition, functional capacities, and the legal test. In an MSO report, topics to be covered are the temporal and causal link between deficient functional capacities and the alleged offense in terms of feeling, thought, and behavior. In a risk assessment report, the risk and protective factors present should be identified, including their possible interaction, all placed in the context of the individual case. In this section, citation of relevant research can help support the argumentation, and these sources should be mentioned in footnotes or in an appendix. Grounding of the forensic analysis in findings from the scientific literature (e.g., findings of group data on individuals with similar psychopathology or offending behavior; pertinent case studies) is an essential aspect of FMHA and forensic report writing, although often overlooked. Knowledge of the research literature has helped us gain a deeper understanding of our forensic cases, as demonstrated in the chapters in this book. Forensic analysis requires critical thinking. What constitutes acceptable evidence for or against your conclusion/opinion? What other explanations might there be for the evidence? For every opinion in your report ask yourself: how do I know that? We have found this to be both the most challenging and the most interesting part of FMHA.

The final part of the forensic report should contain a brief answer to the psycholegal questions. In the US, in contrast to The Netherlands, there is a long tradition of scholarly discussion of whether the forensic report may (Rogers & Shuman, 2000) or may not (Grisso, 2003; Heilbrun, 2001) include an opinion on the ultimate legal issue, since in most jurisdictions in the US, the FMH evaluator is not permitted to testify to the ultimate legal issue. In practice this is more of a theoretical exercise because a clear description in the written report of the reasoning how the evaluator came to her opinion on the psycholegal questions is to an extent an ultimate issue opinion, albeit not stated as such. Evaluators should end their report with their signature, possibly preceded by a declaration affirming the authenticity or truthfulness of their professional opinion (Gagliardi & Miller, 2008). In The Netherlands, the standard declaration is: "Undersigned declares to have abided by the Code for Forensic Experts and to have written this report truthfully, completely and to the best of her knowledge."[2]

Forensic reports should be as brief as possible, but as long as needed. Triers of fact, whether judges or juries, are pressed for time, and overly wordy and redundant reports will irritate them and/or make them miss the essence. The only way to write a concise and compelling report is through rigorous editing, as one does with a scientific paper. As we have noted above in several examples, choice of words matters. Jargon should be avoided as much as possible. The same goes for words with a prejudicial connotation, such as: denied, refused, claimed. In a workshop on forensic report writing,[3] Drs. Anita Boss and Julie Gallagher provided some instructive writing exercises to assist forensic psychologists in explaining technical terms to a lay reader. For example:

> *Formal thought disorder*: thinking that is illogical and that jumps from one topic to the next without a logical connection between the two. [provide examples from the interview with the assessee]

> *Suicidal ideation*: the person has thoughts of suicide. [then provide examples: Thoughts? Plans? Actual acts?]

A forensic report tells a story that accounts for the salient findings and answers the psycholegal referral question (Karson & Nadkarni, 2013). Only valid data should be considered and reported. If certain file documentation is erroneous, for instance, because it is based on only one information source (see Chapter 1, pp. 13–14 for an example) it should be omitted from the report. Do not simply copy the interpretations and diagnostic conclusions from previous mental health reports, but remain close to the data (i.e., observations, test findings). In a recent paper, Allan and Grisso (2014) demonstrated how ethical principles can guide us in the way we write forensic reports. Taking the Specialty Guidelines for Forensic Psychology of the American Psychological Association (2013) as a starting point, they explain how the principles of Beneficence and Non-Maleficence, Fidelity and Responsibility, Integrity, Respect for the Rights and Dignity of Persons, and Justice and Fairness can help improve the quality of forensic reports. They provide many excellent examples of forensic report writing that does and does not abide by these principles, and is a helpful resource both to the novice and the experienced writer. Notwithstanding the fact that the forensic report is not commissioned by the assessee, he or she is at the center of the decision making, and the evaluator has an ethical obligation to him or her (Mills, Kroner, & Morgan, 2011). At the closing of this chapter, the forensic report NKB provided on the request of the Deputy Public Defender on Mr. H., described in Chapter 5 of this book, is given as an example.

Violence Risk Assessment in Forensic Reports

Communicating the outcome of violence risk assessment in such a way that the legal decision maker understands and uses this communication in the way it was intended, is one of the most challenging aspects of forensic report writing. Violence risk communication has been subjected to empirical investigation to a much lesser extent than the psychometric qualities of violence risk assessment tools, although it is arguably just as important. Effective violence risk communication assists the trier of fact in reaching a fair decision regarding risk management, release, and/or rehabilitation of the assessee. In this section, we will first provide a brief review of the present state of the research literature on violence risk communication, revealing the ongoing debate among scholars on this issue. Subsequently, we will offer a number of guidelines for violence risk communication in forensic reports based on our current level of knowledge.

Research on Violence Risk Communication

Broadly speaking, the scholarly literature can be divided into two disparate models of violence risk communication: the prediction and the prevention model. According to the prediction model, violence risk should be communicated in terms of frequency or probability estimates (e.g., Harris & Rice, 2007) on the basis of actuarial risk assessment tools. The prevention model (e.g., Douglas & Kropp, 2002) proposes that violence risk communication should focus on presenting categorical estimates of risk (e.g., low, moderate, high), including a listing of relevant risk factors emphasizing dynamic, changeable risk factors and the identification of risk management strategies that could decrease the risk. Structured professional judgment tools, such as the Historical Clinical Risk Management-20 (Webster, Douglas, Eaves, & Hart, 1997; Douglas, Hart, Webster, & Belfrage, 2013), belong to this model. Still others advocate the use of a mixed model for effective risk communication: "(1) establishing an actuarial risk estimate within the context of group norms; (2) identifying central risk factors with particular emphasis on dynamic risk factors; and (3) identifying intervention and risk management strategies that can potentially moderate that risk" (Mills et al., 2011, p. 130). Monahan and Steadman (1996), in comparing violence risk communication with day-to-day weather forecasting and storm warnings, also contend that violence risk communication might be best served by a combination of categorical and probabilistic language in the same message. However, what is effective violence risk communication is ultimately an empirical question, and our database is still rather scant.

One line of research on violence risk communication has examined which type of communication is preferred by forensic psychologists and judges. Both groups of professionals prefer categorical estimates over probability or frequency estimates (Heilbrun, Philipson, Berman, & Warren, 1999; Grann & Pallvik, 2002; Kwartner, Lyon, & Boccaccinni, 2006; Redding, Floyd, & Hawk, 2001). Obviously, preference does not assume accuracy or appropriateness (Scurich & John, 2012). In fact, categorical estimates have become an issue of concern among both legal and psychological scholars. Schopp (1996), partly in response to Monahan and Steadman's (1996) article, objected to the use of a categorical format, because

> the categorical systems of communication currently [. . .] proposed for use in mental health law by Monahan and Steadman (1996) differ from probabilistic systems of communication in that these categorical approaches use discreet categories rather than probability statements and compress the descriptive and prescriptive functions by communicating risk in categories that combine a statement of risk level with a prescription for preventive action.
>
> (p. 941)

In this way, categorical estimates that inherently contain subjective judgment lead to a shifting of decision making from the judiciary to the mental health professional. In addition, categorical estimates provide legal decision makers little incentive to disagree with the evaluator's risk judgment (Scurich & John, 2012).

The opposite is true for probability estimates because here the evaluator only presents the descriptive findings, and the judgment on the ultimate issue (e.g., level of risk; yes/no release on probation conditions; yes/no civil commitment) is left to the discretion of the legal body. Still, probability estimates are not without their own problems. First of all, there are many different ways of communicating probability to reoffend. For instance, there are *probability* estimates, such as: "Mr Z. scored an XX on this risk assessment instrument. Individuals with this score reoffended at 40 percent over a follow-up of 5 years and at 50 percent over 10 years." Another option is *frequency* estimates: "Individuals with a score similar to Mr Z. on the risk assessment instrument reoffended at a rate of 4 out of 10 over a follow-up of 5 years, and at a rate of 5 out of 10 over 10 years." Slovic, Monahan, and MacGregor (2000) compared these two risk communication formats and found the frequency format, compared with the probability format, led to higher perceptions of risk, even though the risk level was held constant. The authors attribute this to judges "imagining the numerator" in the frequency format, which purportedly evokes images of violence. A follow-up study by Monahan et al. (2002) replicated this result, but only for clinicians who worked in forensic settings; they also found that more vivid portrayals of the offense resulted in more conservative decision making. However, one study (Hilton, Harris, Rawson, & Beach, 2005) did not find the difference in decision making between the frequency and probability estimates.

Recently, Scurich and John (2011) have shown that even the subtle way probability estimates are framed impacts decision making. In a study with 303 university students who acted as mock judges, they found that risk framed as a 26 percent probability of violence generally led subjects to authorize civil commitment, whereas the same risk framed in the numerical complement, a 74 percent probability of no violence, generally led decision makers to decide to release. This research revealed that subtle manipulation in the framing of risk estimates is powerful to affect commitment decisions. The general tendency in violence risk communication practice to frame estimates in terms of the probability of violence, will skew decision makers towards false positives. Scurich and John (2011) argue that further research should investigate whether presenting both the risk estimate and its complement, the risk of nonviolence, cancels out the framing effect. If it does, forensic evaluators should become obliged to present both to decision makers. Although Scurich and John (2011) used university students as decision makers, there is no reason to believe that judges are any less susceptible to the effect of framing (Guthrie, Rachlinski, & Wistrich, 2001).

The inherent inaccuracy of risk-only evaluations was cogently argued by Rogers (2000). He stated that "overfocus on risk factors is likely to contribute to pro-fessional negativism and result in client stigmatization" (p. 598). In recent years, there has been an increase in research on protective factors in forensic mental health (e.g., Viljoen, Nicholls, Greaves, de Ruiter, & Brink, 2011; de Vries Robbé, de Vogel, & Douglas, 2013), although in comparison to research on risk factors, it is a mere drop in the ocean. The development of tools for the assessment of protective factors for violence risk, such as the Structured Assessment of Protective Factors for violence risk (SAPROF; de Vogel, de Ruiter, Bouman, & de Vries Robbé, 2012; de Vogel, de Vries Robbé, de Ruiter, & Bouman, 2011) and the

Short-Term Assessment of Risk and Treatability (START; Nicholls, Brink, Desmarais, Webster, & Martin, 2006; Webster, Martin, Brink, Nicholls, & Desmarais, 2009) has eased the path to conduct research on protective factors. Several recent studies have demonstrated that protective factors provide incremental predictive validity over the use of risk factors alone (Ullrich & Coid, 2011; de Vries Robbé et al., 2013). In addition, evidence was found for an interaction effect between risk and protective factors (Lodewijks, de Ruiter, & Doreleijers, 2010; de Vries Robbé et al., 2013): especially in cases of moderate and high risk, protective factors such as commitment to structured leisure activities (Bouman, de Ruiter, & Schene, 2010) and commitment to school (Lodewijks et al., 2010) can act as buffers to mitigate risk. Although the research on protective factors in forensic mental health is "a new frontier" (de Ruiter & Nicholls, 2011), it should alert the forensic evaluator to the importance of taking protective factors into consideration when performing a risk assessment and when designing and implementing a risk management plan, all of which should be included in the risk communication.

Real-world risk assessment evaluations can have dramatic and potentially harmful consequences for the patient/client. For example, when violence risk tools and reports are used to evaluate prison inmates for parole, an unclear or negatively-toned report can put off parole for years. In California, litigation is pending over the Board of Parole Hearings Forensic Assessment Division's alleged failure to use well-validated violence risk assessment tools, for failure in reports to define the meaning of "low," "medium," or "high" risk, for failure to indicate which factors are the basis for such a decision, and for failure to release the raw data so that other psychologists can comment. The manner for distinguishing high, medium, or low risk is unclear and likely inconsistent across evaluators, and the resulting label plays perhaps the most significant role of any aspect of these evaluations in parole consideration. In fact, no prisoner labeled as an overall "high" risk in one of these reports in California has ever been granted parole (*Johnson v. Shaffer*).

Guidelines on Violence Risk Communication

Although the empirical database on violence risk communication is still limited, the emerging evidence points to a need for careful and balanced reporting on risk. In view of this, we would like to suggest the following guidelines:

- When reporting probability estimates derived from static risk assessment tools, note that these estimates are based on static factors only and exclude dynamic risk and protective factors.
- Report both the probability estimate for the negative outcome and for the positive outcome (see Scurich & John, 2012).

- Provide a listing of the important dynamic risk factors and protective factors, and describe if and how these interact.
- Provide information on the context for which the risk assessment is valid (e.g., inpatient setting, supervised leave from a secure facility, community supervision/probation).
- Provide a risk management plan which describes the way in which different risk management strategies reduce risk.

In conclusion, we contend that forensic report writing is both a science and an art, in need of continuing critical reflection by forensic evaluators, because of the impact of these reports on the lives of the assessees. Many types of heuristic biases are continuously challenging evaluators' objectivity. Writing forensic reports in an ethically responsible manner is a professional skill that requires continuous maintenance by means of intercollegial consulting, continuing education and study of the professional and scientific literature.

Sample Forensic Psychological Report on Mr. H.

September 11, 2011

A. D.

Deputy Public Defender
Office of the Los Angeles County Public Defender
Los Angeles, CA 90012

RE: *People v. Mr. H.*, Case # 11111

Dear Mr. D.:

At your request, I have conducted a forensic psychological evaluation of Mr. H., pursuant to Sections 730 and 952 of the Evidence Code. You asked for an evaluation of his general mental condition, and whether his mental condition was related to the crime charged. You also noted that Mr. H. had been sexually assaulted by a male prisoner while incarcerated in State Prison, and you asked whether that might cause him to compulsively exhibit himself to women [i.e., as a compulsion to show he is heterosexual]. You forwarded background information, including:

- Arrest Report on the current charges [dated March 25, 2011].
- Audio Recording of Mr. H.'s Interview by Police Investigators.
- Incident Report dated March 22, 2004, concerning Mr. H.'s mother.
- Long Beach Police Department Report dated October 17, 2010.
- Incident Report dated 4/11/2006.
- Attest Report dated 1/26/2008.
- Medical [Psychiatric] Records from State Prison.

The Allegations

According to the Arrest Report of March 25, 2011, Mr. H. was in the office of a counselor at a technical school he was attending when he unzipped his pants, exposed his penis, and began to rub the tip of his penis while still speaking to the counselor. She yelled for a co-worker, hoping that this would cause Mr. H. to stop and leave her office. The co-worker entered and Mr. H. subsequently left. Mr. H. is charged with Indecent Exposure. The Arrest Report notes that he has prior Indecent Exposure arrests. The Police Report summarizes Mr. H.'s comments, stating: "While at Rampart Station, H. began to make voluntarily spontaneous statements that he 'gets off' by exposing himself to women. He admitted to exposing himself to several hundred women in Long Beach and around Los Angeles. He knew it was wrong, but he knew that women liked it." His written statement is somewhat different, however. It states, "The reason why I did it is because I suffer from an illness and the voices that I here (sic) told me it was okay to do it. I am seeking help about this illness I suffer. I need help."

In the audiotaped interview with police, Mr. H. said that he "suffered from an illness." He said that he exposed himself in 2003 or 2004 and went to jail but he "continued to do it because I got away with it." He did it "on the street, in laundromats, and in parks" around Long Beach and Los Angeles. He said he had been diagnosed Bipolar Disorder and had been prescribed Abilify "because I hear voices telling me to do it." He said "God tells me not to."

He said that on the day in question, he was sitting in the counselor's office, talking to her, and "I just got the urge and did it." He did not think it upset her. He said he had "never done it to a woman who didn't like it." He volunteered that he believed "it helped them with their urges." He said "These women get off on that." He said "Only a couple didn't like it" as "they called the police." He said that he had done this "whenever I get an urge." Overall, he estimated that he had exposed himself 40–50 times, or three or four times a week. He said it had "picked up lately" because "my hormones are getting higher." He said his father told him he needs treatment. He added, here, "it's like a fetish, you know how some men like women to dress up in different attire?" He said "It pleases me so I do it more."

Mr. H. said that he had been on trial previously for this type of conduct. His father's apartment manager "said I tried to call her in the room to have sex." He admitted that his intent was "to have sex with her." He was, however, found not guilty "on all 12 counts."

Mr. H. told the police that he had been written up two or three times for exposing himself while he was incarcerated. He said that he felt "God is obligated to come into my life and take it away from me." He said he "prays about it."

Evaluation

Mr. H. was forensically interviewed on June 17, 2011, in the county jail. He was informed about the nature and purpose of the evaluation. With regard to confidentiality, it was explained that if his attorney decided to submit the report, the matters discussed, and the test results, would no longer be confidential and would be shared with the District Attorney and the Court. He understood the explanations. He replied to questions with considerable detail. He appears to be of at least average intelligence, and he was polite and cooperative. His affect did seem, at times, inappropriate. In particular I noted odd smiling, euphoria [odd given his incarceration], and a kind of energy that suggested the precursors to a manic episode. He also exhibited some preoccupation with religious thought. He said that at times his mind "races." He said he was not taking any medication for his diagnosed Bipolar Disorder and that "God is helping me with it." He paused to ask "If I claim to have a relationship with God, it's not psychotic is it?"

Additional supportive detail of his history of mental disorder was found in his prison medical records. Mr. H. was psychologically tested with the Personality Assessment Inventory (PAI) and the Psychopathic Personality Inventory-Revised (PPI-R). I applied the data collected to the Static-99, a sex offender risk assessment tool. These tests will be described in further detail in the test results section, below.

History

Mr. H. is currently 25 years old [DOB 10/26/85] and is of mixed non-Caucasian ethnicity. Mr. H. is an only child. His family was middle class, and this may account for his relatively good ability to present his history. His father had worked for many years for the US Postal Service. His mother worked "in telecommunications and gets a commission." He states, "I acted out towards my parents as a teenager." He described depression and despair, as well as attempts to fit in with various groups such as athletes and, later, teenagers from the inner city, to which he had to travel. He had sojourns in several psychiatric hospitals as well as Juvenile Hall. He said:

> I've had symptoms since 13, off and on. . . . I was in a hospital as an adolescent—Augustus Hawkins, MLK, and USC—at USC it was an intake and then by the morning I was gone. And in Twin Towers . . . in blue and yellows, they said because of my history, did I want meds.

Asked why he needed to be in the hospital at 13, he said:

> Basically, drugs. I started messing with a lot of different drugs. Also at 12 or 13, I got involved with Black Magic. It was me wanting to know about

it [Black Magic] and at the same time I was trying to do séances to reach into another realm, and with another home boy after I started gang-banging. My parents, they were going through a divorce. I was very emotional. I thought I had something to do with it. I loved my dad, and my mom, too. We were moving a lot, from Bellflower to Norwalk and back to Bellflower. My mom went with her boyfriend, who broke up the marriage. In 2009 she moved to Kansas City, Missouri. My dad stayed in Norwalk for a while and I stayed with him. Then me and my dad moved back to Bellflower and they tried to work out the marriage.

At that time, I started going to Juvenile Hall. [What for?] For assault, vandalism, GTA. I was going to M. High School, but I felt I always had to prove myself. I played football, basketball, and ran track. I was also traveling on my own to Watts, and Nickerson Gardens. I was looking for protection, a figure who could direct me. Also popularity, money, and clothes—the things I saw other kids having. My father was trying to keep me away from that. He wanted me to play football.

This "acting out" included use of drugs, which he states was "mostly marijuana." He said he used cocaine [snorting] "one or two times" and "rock cocaine two or three times." He said that after age 18 he began to use PCP on occasion. His early suicide attempt, he said, was also "acting out." He said "because I attempted suicide, my parents tried to work things out." However, it appears that Mr. H. also began to display bona fide symptoms of serious mental disorder by the age of 16 or 17. He was in a Juvenile Court placement [Penny Lane] when he was psychiatrically hospitalized. He said:

I had graduated from high school and then I had a breakdown. The symptoms came back. I had a psychotic episode with my mom there. I knocked curling irons out of her hands and they burned her. I was hearing voices and seeing things, feeling someone was out to get me. I thought I was doing a séance with another person. I put a pentagram on the floor with a rock and was in like a prayer position, and was trying to pull myself closer to Satan. Before the thing with my mom, I thought Satan was on the TV and that she was in danger and I should try to get her out of the house and I was seeing shadows, and I thought they were going to come in. . . . She didn't know what to do. My dad was out of town.

Mr. H. said he thought that the symptoms at that time might have been influenced by using PCP. It is not clear whether this would have been the cause, or the only cause, as he spent his earlier years, as I can tell from the records, in denial about having a mental disorder. He mentioned that his mother's mother was "Bipolar," suggesting biological roots to his disordered behavior. Mr. H. was criminally charged for assaulting his mother. According to the Incident Report of March 22, 2004, which you provided, Mr. H. was charged with "Assault with force likely to produce great bodily injury." In the Incident Report, she is quoted as stating she was sitting on the couch in the living room of the location, curling her hair with a hot curling iron. Her son approached her as she was curling her hair and told her to stop. She said he was perspiring heavily on his forehead and upper lip and had a blank stare. She refused to stop curling her hair and turned away from him. He called her "Satan" and pushed her back on the couch and began to strangle her by placing both of his hands around her neck. She could not breathe, as he strangled her for several seconds. She began to punch and slap him until she was able to maneuver her left foot parallel to the living room window and broke it with her foot and was able to scream for help. A neighbor called 911, and she struggled to free herself from her son.

Mr. H. remembers this incident in a different way than his mother. He said it didn't happen "in that order." He said: "She was in the bathroom curling her hair. I didn't want her to drop the curler in the water so I grabbed her." Arresting officers felt Mr. H. was displaying symptoms of "being under the influence." They suspected PCP. He states that he took a plea deal and was sentenced to 2 years and one strike.

Mr. H. apparently violated his parole in 2006. According to an Incident Report of 4/11/2006, which you provided, Mr. H. was arrested along with three other young adults in a suspected shooting of a Hispanic man. Mr. H. was on parole for the previous charge, and his parole was violated.

According to the Arrest Report of January 26, 2008, which you provided, Mr. H. was charged with carjacking. According to the report, witnesses observed Mr. H. running up to vehicles and attempting to get into them by overpowering the driver. The first victim said that Mr. H. attempted to jump on top of her hood. He then ran around to the driver's side and attempted to open the driver's door, but it was locked. She got away but observed him attempt to carjack two or three more victims. She observed him to be acting very violent. A witness told police that he observed Mr. H. run up to a vehicle and bang on the hood, then scream "This is a jack! This is a jack! Mafia! Get out of the car." The victim drove off with the suspect hanging onto the car, until he fell off and ran up to another car, repeating the same words. Another witness identified the suspect as Mr. H., a resident of his halfway house. When Mr. H. was interviewed by the police, he said "I wanted to take a car and have a high speed chase." He said he wanted this in order to be famous and be on television. Once again, Mr. H.'s parole was violated.

Mr. H. said he had "numerous psychotic episodes in prison." He said he was treated at Vacaville State Prison, at Salinas Valley State Prison, at Tehachapi, and at Lancaster State Prison, and he received Depakote and Haldol. He states he is now "allergic" to Haldol. He apparently had some sort of attraction to one of his treatment providers but came to feel "that she and her assistant were trying to pull me over to Satan."

Mr. H. said he was released on parole from Salinas Valley State Prison and went to live with his father. He said he was "out for about 1 year." He was then arrested on the carjacking offense, which, as noted, was a parole violation. He said "I was having numerous psychotic episodes but no meds. I was living in a half-way house. I felt if I did the crime, I would be placed in the Russian Mafia, like in 'Training Day'."

He said he received another parole violation and was sent to Lancaster and "went back and forth three times." He said he got treatment at Lancaster "because I was having psychotic episodes there. I got Haldol and Cogentin there."

Mr. H. said he was also sexually assaulted by a male prisoner while he was in Lancaster State Prison. This was in about 2008. He said: "I had a homosexual person in my cell and that person wanted sex and forced me." Asked if he thinks that had an effect on him, he said: "Yes, but I gave it all to God."

You forwarded an Arrest Report describing a report of an indecent exposure on October 16, 2010 in the city of Long Beach at a half-way house. A woman in the half-way house indicated she was outside her residence smoking a cigarette when she observed Mr. H. sitting in a chair facing towards her duplex. She spoke with him casually about work and then observed that he was holding his penis in his hand, making stroking motions that appeared to be masturbation. She asked him what he was doing and he put his penis back in his pants and asked her what she was talking about. When interviewed by the police on that occasion, Mr. H. denied exposing himself, but said he may have adjusted his penis under his clothing while in a seated position talking and smoking with the woman. He said that she had tried to seduce him several times in the past. The manager of the half-way house said that Mr. H. had been reported as grabbing his crotch in front of the female clients at the half-way house and ignored the manager's requests to stop. Police interviewed several clients of the half-way house who had individual experiences with Mr. H. exposing himself. This indecent exposure apparently resulted in a parole violation.

Mr. H. said he was last released from prison in about January of 2011. He said that he had been "out only a little while when this happened [referring to the index offense]." He was being followed by the Outpatient Parole Clinic in Long Beach, but he volunteered that he wasn't taking his medication "like I was supposed to take it."

Apparently when Mr. H. goes into psychotic episodes, he has many troubling thoughts of both a religious and sexual nature. His mind "races." [These are also documented in the prison medical records, which I will summarize, below.] He said:

> I believe that spirits are real and you can be cursed. It's very intense and confusing. I had been suicidal. I cut my wrists on different occasions and tried to hang myself, but I didn't understand what death was. I wanted to talk to God.

His sexual thoughts involve the belief that he is doing a favor to women by showing his penis. Mr. H. told the police that this is a "fetish," and he correctly defined fetish; during the FMHA, he said he could not remember using that word. He also told the police that he found the behavior "gratifying" and that he had done it 40 to 50 times in locations around Long Beach and Los Angeles. He said he did not think it harmed women because "some allowed it and some ignored it. That led me to think that it was OK, and I kind of developed a desire for it." He said that when he was at a half-way house in 2010 "[I]exposed myself to numerous other women."

Mr. H. said that being sexually assaulted in prison by a man "enhanced my sexual drive. I wasn't comfortable with my sexual orientation [in prison] because I am attracted to women and not men, and I do want a wife and children."

The Index Offense

Just shortly out of State Prison, where he had a long, documented sojourn in the mental health sections of the named prisons and was determined to be in need of "triple C" services [CCCMS], he was enrolled at a technical school where the current offense occurred. About this period, he said:

> I was confused on what actually was happening at the time and not fully conscious of what was happening around me. I wasn't fully aware of my surroundings, due to drugs and my past psychiatric history. I've been given numerous psychotic medications and diagnosed Bipolar/Schizophrenia. I had not taken it [Abilify] that day. I was supposed to take it, and I had not taken it in the way I was supposed to take it—two times a day, but I was just taking it when I was remembering. I was hearing voices of God [saying] that I would be accepted into a Mafia if I exposed myself to God.

I noted to Mr. H. that he had actually exposed himself to a female counselor, not to God. Mr. H. listened politely when I explained that women are usually fearful when someone exposes himself, and many women simply freeze with fear. He said he hadn't thought about that. He said he realizes that his behavior was wrong, and he would like to get more mental health treatment.

Prison Medical Records

Mr. H. was deemed, early on in his time in prison, to have a mental disorder. At age 18, he was sent to North Kern State Prison and he was diagnosed Bipolar Disorder and prescribed Depakote and Risperdal. A chart note of November 24, 2005, indicates that, by that date, he was on his fourth hospital admission since August 2005, including August 18 to August 22, October 6 to October 13, November 4 to November 17, and the current one. The prison hospital chart notes, from each admission document bizarre, primitive behavior. He was psychiatrically hospitalized again in January 2005, stating he heard the voice of God. His psychotic episodes appeared to coincide with going off medication. For a time, he told mental health staff he didn't feel he needed medication, or that his parents didn't think he should be on medication. The hospital records I reviewed were approximately 3 inches thick and covered CCCMS treatment all the way up to late 2008. A sample of the bizarre and psychotic behaviors observed includes:

On November 2, 2005, the chart note quotes Mr. H. saying:

> I'm cold. There is evil coming out of me. I've had a lot of spiritual problems. The Devil wants me to kill myself with a razor but I won't. Taking my life would cause spiritual problems for the world.

The note further states, "Patient reports auditory, visual and tactile hallucinations of insects and spiders. Patient is delusional and feels he is possessed. Patient reports paranoid ideas and states people are out to get him."

A chart note of January 12, 2006 states:

> Patient states his suicidal history consisted of three attempts: (1) in 2000 when 16–17 years old, in a group home; (2) in 2001 when 16–17, in jail, when he cut both wrists with a razor blade; and (3) in August 2005 on the Yard, when he cut both wrists with a razor blade.

A chart note of July 13, 2006 quotes Mr. H. as saying:

> I hear voices. Sometimes I talk to Satan and he tells me he's going to kill me, and I pray to Jesus to rebuke him. Sometimes I see ghosts and goblins, demons and devils, and Satan and the anti-Christ. I can talk to the whole world, pretty much tell everybody about everything in their life.

The chart notes more delusional content and grandiosity.

A chart note of July 25, 2006, reports Mr. H. again discussing devils and stating that he cut off the Devil's head. It states, "He has paranoid and grandiose delusions, reports auditory hallucinations. He is acutely Psychotic, and a risk to self and others."

Three days later, he reported that there were spiders in his cell biting him. He was being medicated with Depakote and Risperdal. He began spreading feces on the walls and he urinated on the mattress, he said, to get rid of the spiders and "fight evil."

A chart note of September 17, 2006, indicates that Mr. H. drank disinfectant "because he is feeling suicidal." He told mental health staff that he had not taken his medication for two weeks.

When he was re-incarcerated in 2007, he was again given mental health treatment, again diagnosed with an Axis I Disorder and given Haldol and Cogentin, and also Lithium.

A chart note of October 9, 2007 indicates that he told mental health counselors that he "showed a counselor" his penis "because voices tell me to." He added that listening to his voices "allows Satan to win."

The chart also notes periods of profound depression. In short, there is ample evidence in over 4 years of prison records of an Axis I Disorder, with a major disturbance of emotion, with Manic Episodes, and a major disturbance in thinking, with auditory and tactile hallucinations. These continued while incarcerated, when his access to street drugs was limited.

Psychological Test Results

Mr. H. was assessed with the Personality Assessment Inventory (PAI) and the Psychopathic Personality Inventory-Revised (PPI-R). At the time of testing, he was not receiving psychotropic medication.

The PAI is a 344-item self-report inventory comprising 22 non-overlapping scales that cover a wide range of diagnostic possibilities (e.g., Axis I disorders such as Schizophrenia, and Axis II disorders such as Antisocial Personality Disorder and Borderline Personality Disorder). It offers actuarially-derived indices to evaluate malingering and defensiveness, as well as violence potential and treatment amenability. The PAI was developed with a construct validation approach rather than the empirical correlate method of some other well-known tests (such as the MMPI-2). The PAI has scales that are highly relevant to the assessment questions raised in this evaluation: (1) Does Mr. H. have test results similar to persons with bipolar or manic features?; (2) Does he have other personality features that could be relevant to sexual acting out?; (3) Is he elevated on the Aggression scale?; (4) How does he score on the Violence Potential Index?; (5) Is he likely to cooperate with treatment?

At the time Mr. H. was tested, he was not on medication, and he was housed in the general population. He said he did not want to have a mental disorder. The validity indices of the PAI were somewhat elevated. He was elevated on "Infrequency" suggesting he may have had trouble attending to or interpreting item content, perhaps interpreting items idiosyncratically. He was not elevated on Negative Impression Management, a scale associated with malingering, nor on Positive Impression Management, which is seen in individuals who are "faking good," i.e., answering as if they are more healthy than they are. In short, Mr. H. appears to have been relatively honest in responding to the items of this test.

On the clinical scales of the PAI, Mr. H. obtained two highly significant elevations. These were on scales named Mania and Antisocial Personality Disorder. He obtained lesser but still high elevations on the scales Borderline Personality Disorder and Schizophrenia. Finally, he was elevated on the scales Paranoia and

Aggression. Due largely to the elevation on these two scales, and his elevation on Mania, Mr. H. was considered, at the time of testing (i.e., when not medicated), to reflect a risk of continuing aggression.

The PAI scales can be further analyzed using subscales, which were derived by a statistical procedure that sorts related items within each scale to parse out the symptoms that most caused the elevation. On the Mania scale, Mr. H. scored high on Activity Level and Irritability. He was not elevated on Grandiosity. This finding is significant and points towards racing thoughts, pressured behavior, and a likely intensity of sex drive, such is often seen in Mania. On the subscales of the ASPD scale, Mr. H. was most elevated on Stimulus-Seeking, and he was also elevated on Egocentricity.

The lower but still significant score on the BPD and Schizophrenia scales likely reflect a deviation from normal in emotional control and clear thinking rather than the existence of the full symptoms picture of these disorders.

Taken as a whole, Mr. H.'s highest overall PAI subscales were Activity Level and Stimulus-Seeking, two scales which are highly relevant to level of sex drive.

The PAI results also address the potential for successful treatment. The PAI offers two ways to look at amenability to treatment: (1) openness to treatment and interest in change; and (2) the difficulty of treatment given the diagnosis. Mr. H. clearly has an interest in and motivation for therapy. He acknowledges important problems and believes he has a need for help. Furthermore, he endorses the importance of personal responsibility. He is likely, however, to be a difficult patient due primarily to his mood instability and pressured, impulsive behavior.

The PPI-R was chosen to evaluate the presence of antisocial or psychopathic personality traits because it permits a survey of traits that are a part of this pathological personality disorder, as well as a global score. The presence of a personality disorder could interfere with treatment and especially with treatment compliance. Mr. H. was elevated on content scales Blame Externalization, Carefree Non-Planfulness, and Coldheartedness. On the Factor scales, his highest score was on Self-Centered Impulsivity. What stands out most is Mr. H.'s tendency to be impulsive. He has additional problematic features including a lack of empathy and a tendency to externalize blame.

When the data from the current evaluation were applied to the Static-99, Mr. H. obtained a total of 6 points, which places him in the High Risk category. However, it is important to note that his prior convictions for both sexual and non-sexual violence were for crimes committed while he was also in a manic episode.

To review the questions posed for the psychological testing:

(1) *Does Mr. H. have test results similar to persons with bipolar or manic features?*
Yes, he appears as a person with manic tendencies. He likely has periods of time when he is driven and impulsive. His mind "races" and his reality testing is poor. By history, his manic thought surrounds sexual ideation and behavior.

(2) *Does he have other personality features that could be relevant to sexual acting out?*
Mr. H. points to external factors and believes they control his thoughts and actions; in particular, he has elements of a delusional disorder regarding God and commands from God. When manic he is hypersexual. He does not easily understand how others feel or think (particularly women) and therefore has little awareness of the impact on others of his exposure of his genitals. He can be markedly impulsive when in a manic state.

(3) *Is he elevated on the Aggression scale? How does he score on the Violence Potential Index?*
In his unmedicated state, Mr. H. has a modest elevation on Aggression, though he is not elevated on Physical Aggression. Due largely to his elevations on scales which measure mood instability and impulsivity, he is elevated on violence risk.

(4) *Is he likely to cooperate with treatment?*
He is likely to cooperate with treatment, but treatment may, nevertheless, be challenging, due to his mood instability and impulsivity. Psychological treatment should be an adjunct to pharmacological treatment.

Psychological test results should not be read as dispositive. The forensic psychological evaluation integrates data from psychological tests, case records, and diagnostic interviewing. These results are presented below.

Diagnostic Opinion

It is my opinion that Mr. H. has a serious Axis I Mental Disorder. I agree with prison mental health providers that the disorder is most likely diagnosed Schizoaffective Disorder, Bipolar Type. He is not suffering from Schizophrenia, as his symptoms ebb and flow because of mood symptoms. He is not a case of pure Bipolar Disorder, as at times he has reported hearing voices and has also reported tactile hallucinations. He certainly has episodes where he is completely disorganized, impulsive, and psychotic. At these times, he has bizarre religious delusions, has grandiose ideas, and engages in primitive behaviors such as throwing feces and urine, and masturbating in front of staff. While his behavior suggests a Paraphilia, his sexual preoccupation and acting out is typically present when he has become manic.

The diagnostic criteria for Schizoaffective Disorder are:

A. An uninterrupted period of illness during which, at some time, there is either a Major Depressive Episode, a Manic episode, or a Mixed Episode concurrent with symptoms that meet Criterion A for Schizophrenia [delusions, hallucinations, grossly disorganized behavior].

B. During the same period of illness, there have been delusions or hallucinations for at least 2 weeks in the absence of prominent mood symptoms.

C. Symptoms that meet criteria for a mood episode are present for a substantial portion of the total duration of the active and residual periods of the illness.

The Bipolar Type is diagnosed if the disturbance includes a manic or mixed episode or a mixed episode and major depressive episodes.

In a manic episode, according to DSM-IV-TR, the individual must have at least three of the following:

(1) inflated self-esteem or grandiosity [such as a belief that he killed the Devil, or a belief that one is helping women by exposing one's penis];

(2) decreased need for sleep;

(3) more talkative than usual or pressure to keep talking;

(4) flight of ideas or racing thoughts;

(5) distractibility;

(6) an increase in goal-directed activity, socially or sexually, or psychomotor agitation;

(7) excessive involvement in pleasurable activities that have a high potential for painful consequences (such as sexual improprieties).

The Schizoaffective Disorder diagnosis also indicates that the person has a number of the signs and symptoms of Schizophrenia, such as impaired insight, impaired and illogical reasoning, and impaired judgment.

Legal Opinion

While Mr. H.'s extreme behaviors (e.g., carjacking, indecent exposure) sound volitional, this is largely because he believes he has control over his symptoms (and thus can stop medications and simply pray). In reality, he has a biologically-based and highly heritable disorder that, already at the age of 25, has seen quite a number of psychotic episodes. If he hadn't been a patient of the California prison systems CCCMS program, we probably would know less about his mental disorder. He is more a psychiatric patient than a criminal.

It is clear from the DSM-IV-TR diagnostic criteria that in the manic phase of the disorder there is an increase in sexual and impulsive behavior and an "excessive involvement in pleasurable activities that have a high potential for painful consequences." His episodes of indecent exposure are very much tied to the manic phase of his Schizoaffective Disorder, Bipolar Type. When he does not take his medication, he decompensates and the full manifestation of his manic and psychotic symptoms emerges. His belief that women enjoy seeing his penis and that it "helps them with their urges" is the grandiosity that is seen with the disorder.

Mr. H.'s sexual assault by a male inmate in prison may have enhanced the compulsivity of his urge to expose himself to woman and masturbate, in order to assert his heterosexuality; however, it is intrinsically bound up with the manic phase of his illness.

Mr. H. is amenable to treatment. Treating Mr. H. successfully will depend on medication with the right combination of psychotropic drugs and intensive therapy and case management until he is stable and accepts his need for continuing treatment.

If I can answer additional questions, I will try to do so.

Respectfully submitted,
Nancy Kaser-Boyd, PhD
Diplomate, American Board of Assessment Psychology
Clinical and Forensic Psychologist
Member, Los Angeles County Superior Court Psychiatric Panel

Notes

1   The Specialty Guidelines for Forensic Psychology (American Psychological Association, 2013) do not require discussion of the draft report with the assessee. Guideline 10.05 states:

> **Provision of Assessment Feedback**. Forensic practitioners take reasonable steps to explain assessment results to the examinee or a designated representative in language they can understand. In those circumstances in which communication about assessment results is precluded, the forensic practitioner explains this to the examinee in advance.
>
> (p. 16)

2   In Dutch: Ondergetekende verklaart bij het onderzoek de door haar onderschreven gedragscode voor gerechtelijk deskundigen in acht te hebben genomen en dit verslag naar waarheid, volledig en naar beste inzicht te hebben opgemaakt.
3   "How to write a better forensic report," a half-day workshop by Anita L. Boss, Psy.D. and Julie Gallagher, Psy.D. at the Annual Meeting of the Society for Personality Assessment, March 2014, Arlington, Virginia.

References

Allan, A. & Grisso, T. (2014). Ethical principles and the communication of forensic mental health assessments. *Ethics & Behavior*. Advance online publication. doi: 10.1080/10508422.2014.880346.

American Psychological Association (2013). Specialty guidelines for forensic psychologists. *American Psychologist, 68*, 7–19. doi: 10.1037/a0029889.

Bouman, Y. H. A., de Ruiter, C., & Schene, A. H. (2010). Social ties and short-term self-reported delinquent behaviour of personality disordered forensic outpatients. *Legal and Criminological Psychology, 15*, 357–372. doi: 10.1348/135532509X444528..

Christy, A., Douglas, K., Otto, R., & Petrila, J. (2004). Juveniles evaluated incompetent to proceed: Characteristics and quality of mental health professionals' evaluations. *Professional Psychology: Research and Practice, 35*, 380–388. doi: 10.1037/0735–7028.35.4.380.

Conroy, M. A. (2006). Report writing and testimony. *Applied Psychology in Criminal Justice, 2,* 237–260.

Douglas, K. S. & Kropp, P. R. (2002). A prevention-based paradigm for violence risk assessment: Clinical and research applications. *Criminal Justice and Behavior, 29,* 617–658. doi: 10.1177/009385402236735.

Douglas, K. S., Hart, S. D., Webster, C. D., & Belfrage, H. (2013). *Historical Clinical Risk Management-20 Version 3.* Vancouver, Canada: Mental Health, Law, and Policy Institute, Simon Fraser University.

van Esch, C. (2012). *Forensische gedragskundige expertise in strafzaken* [Forensic behavioral expertise in criminal cases]. Doctoral thesis, Leiden University, Leiden, The Netherlands.

Gagliardi, G. J. & Miller, A. K. (2008). Writing forensic psychological reports. In R. Jackson (Ed.), *Learning forensic assessment* (pp. 539–563). New York: Routledge.

Grann, M. & Pallvik, A. (2002). An empirical investigation of written risk communication in forensic psychiatric evaluations. *Psychology, Crime & Law, 8,* 113–130. doi: 10.1080/10683160208401812.

Griffith, E. E. H., Stankovic, A., & Baranoski, M. (2010). Conceptualizing the forensic psychiatry report as performative narrative. *Journal of the American Acadamy of Psychiatry and the Law, 38,* 32–42.

Grisso, T. (2003). *Evaluating competencies: Forensic assessment and instruments* (2nd ed.). New York: Kluwer Academic.

Grisso, T. (2010). Guidance for improving forensic reports: A review of common errors. *Open Access Journal of Forensic Psychology, 2,* 101–115. www.forensicpsychologyunbound. ws/OAJFP/Volume_2__2010_files/Grisso%202010–2.pdf.

Groth-Marnat, G. (2009). *Handbook of psychological assessment* (5th ed.). Hoboken, NJ: Wiley.

Guthrie, C. P., Rachlinski, J. J., & Wistrich, A. J. (2001). Inside the judicial mind. *Cornell Law Review, 88,* 777–830.

Hare, R. D. (2003*). The Hare psychopathy checklist-revised* (2nd ed.). Toronto, ON: Multi-Health Systems.

Harris, G. T. & Rice, M. E. (2007). Characterizing the value of actuarial violence risk assessments. *Criminal Justice and Behavior, 34,* 1638–1658. doi: 10.1177/009385480730 7029.

Hecker, T. & Steinberg, L. (2002). Psychological evaluation at juvenile court disposition. *Professional Psychology: Research and Practice, 33,* 300–306. doi: 10.1037/0735-7028. 33.3.300.

Heilbrun, K. (2001). *Principles of forensic mental health assessment.* New York: Kluwer Academic/Plenum.

Heilbrun, K., Grisso, T., & Goldstein, A. M. (2009). *Foundations of forensic mental health assessment.* New York: Oxford University Press.

Heilbrun, K., Marczyk, G., & DeMatteo, D. (Eds.) (2002). *Forensic mental health assessment: A casebook.* New York: Oxford University Press.

Heilbrun, K., Philipson, J., Berman, L., & Warren, J. (1999). Risk communication: Clinicians' reported approaches and perceived values. *Journal of the American Academy of Psychiatry and the Law, 27,* 397–406.

Hildebrand, M., de Ruiter, C., & Nijman, H. (2004). PCL-R psychopathy predicts disruptive behavior among male offenders in a Dutch forensic psychiatric hospital. *Journal of Interpersonal Violence, 19,* 13–29. doi: 10.1177/0886260503259047.

Hildebrand, M., de Ruiter, C., & de Vogel, V. (2004). Psychopathy and sexual deviance in treated rapists: Association with sexual and nonsexual recidivism. *Sexual Abuse: A Journal of Research and Treatment, 16,* 1–24. doi: 10.1177/107906320401600101.

Hilton, N. Z., Harris, G. T., Rawson, K., & Beach, C. A. (2005). Communicating violence risk information to forensic decision makers. *Criminal Justice and Behavior, 32,* 97–116. doi: 10.1177/0093854804270630. www.umassmed.edu/forensictraining/Reports.

Ireland, J. L. (2008). Psychologists as witnesses: Background and good practices in the delivery of evidence. *Educational Psychology in Practice, 24,* 115–127.

Johnson v. Shaffer, First Amended Civil Complaint for Declaratory and Injunctive Relief, United States District Court, Eastern District of California, Case No. 2:12-cv-1059 GGH P.

Karson, M. & Nadkarni, L. (2013). *Principles of forensic report writing.* Washington, DC: American Psychological Association.

Kwartner, P. P., Lyon, P. M., & Boccaccinni, M. T. (2006). Judges' risk communication preferences in risk for future violence cases. *International Journal of Forensic Mental Health, 5,* 185–194. doi: 10.1080/14999013.2006.10471242.

Lodewijks, H. P. B., de Ruiter, C., & Doreleijers, T. A. H. (2010). The impact of protective factors in desistance from violent reoffending: A study in three samples of adolescent offenders. *Journal of Interpersonal Violence, 25,* 568–587. doi: 10.1177/088626050933 4403.

Melton, G. B., Petrila, J., Poythress, N.G., & Slobogin, C. (2007). *Psychological evaluations for the courts: A handbook for mental health professionals and lawyers* (3rd ed.). New York: Guilford.

Mills, J. F., Kroner, D. G., & Morgan, R. D. (2011). *Clinician's guide to violence risk assessment.* New York: Guilford.

Monahan, J. & Steadman, H. J. (1996). Violent storms and violent people: How meteorology can inform risk communication in mental health law. *American Psychologist, 51,* 931–938. doi: 10.1037/0003–066X.51.9.931.

Monahan, J., Heilbrun, K., Silver, E., Nabors, E., Bone, J., & Slovic, P. (2002). Communicating violence risk: Frequency formats, vivid outcomes, and forensic settings. *International Journal of Forensic Mental Health, 1,* 121–126. doi: 10.1080/14999013.2002. 10471167.

Netherlands Institute of Forensic Psychiatry and Psychology (2014). Guide for formatting forensic reports. www.nifpnet.nl/Portals/0/Formats%20straf%20jeugd/Format %20straf%20Jeugd%20psycholoog%202010a%20SCHRIJFWIJZER%20met%20GBM. pdf.

Netherlands Institute of Psychologists (2008). *Beroepscode voor psychologen* [Professional code for psychologists]. www.psynip.nl/website-openbaar-documenten-nip-algemeen/ beroepscode-voor-psychologen.pdf.

Nicholls, T. L., Brink, J., Desmarais, S. L., Webster, C. D., & Martin, M. (2006). The Short-Term Assessment of Risk and Treatability (START): A prospective validation study in a forensic psychiatric sample. *Assessment, 13,* 313–327. doi: 10.1177/1073 191106290559.

Peterson, E. E. & Langellier, K. M. (2006). The performance turn in narrative studies. *Narrative Inquiry, 16,* 173–80. doi: 10.1075/ni.16.1.22pet.

Redding, R. E., Floyd, M. Y., & Hawk, G. L. (2001). What judges and lawyers think about the testimony of mental health experts: A survey of the court and bar. *Behavioral Sciences and the Law, 19,* 583–594. doi: 10.1002/bsl.455.

Resnick, P. J. (2006). Principles of psychiatric-legal report writing. In *The Syllabus of the Forensic Psychiatry Review Course.* Brookfield, CT: American Academy of Psychiatry and the Law.

Robbins, E., Waters, J., & Herbert, P. (1997). Competency to stand trial evaluations: A study of actual practice in two states. *Journal of the American Academy of Psychiatry and Law, 25,* 469–483.

Rogers, R. & Shuman, D. (2000). *Conducting insanity evaluations* (2nd ed.). New York: Guilford.

de Ruiter, C. & Nicholls, T. L. (2011). Protective factors in forensic mental health: A new frontier. *International Journal of Forensic Mental Health, 10,* 160–170. doi: 10.1080/14999013.2011.600602.

Schopp, R. F. (1996). Communicating risk assessments: Accuracy, efficacy and responsibility. *American Psychologist, 51,* 939–944. doi: 10.1037/0003–066X.51.9.939.

Scurich, N. & John, R. S. (2011). The effect of framing actuarial risk probabilities on involuntary commitment decisions. *Law and Human Behavior, 35,* 83–91. doi: 10.1007/s10979–010–9218–4.

Scurich, N. & John, R. S. (2012). Prescriptive approaches to communicating the risk of violence in actuarial risk assessment. *Psychology, Public Policy, and Law, 18,* 50–78. doi: 10.1037/a0024592.

Skeem, J., Golding, S., Cohn, N., & Berge, G. (1998). Logic and reliability of evaluations of competence to stand trial. *Law and Human Behavior, 22,* 519–547. doi: 10.1023/A:1025787429972.

Slovic, P., Monahan, J., & MacGregor, D. (2000). Violence risk assessment and risk communication: The effects of using actual cases, providing instruction, and employing probability versus frequency formats. *Law and Human Behavior, 24,* 271–296. doi: 10.1023/A:1005595519944.

Ullrich, S. & Coid, J. (2011). Protective factors for violence among released prisoners: Effects over time and interactions with static risk. *Journal of Consulting and Clinical Psychology, 79,* 381–390. doi: 10.1037/a0023613.

Viljoen, S., Nicholls, T., Greaves, C., de Ruiter, C., & Brink, J. (2011). Resilience and successful community reintegration among female forensic psychiatric patients: A preliminary investigation. *Behavioral Sciences and the Law, 29,* 252–270. doi: 10.1002/bsl.1001.

de Vogel, V., de Ruiter, C., Bouman, Y., & de Vries Robbé, M. (2012). *SAPROF. Guidelines for the assessment of protective factors for violence risk* (2nd ed.). Utrecht: Van der Hoeven Stichting.

de Vogel, V., de Vries Robbé, M., de Ruiter, C., & Bouman, Y. H. A. (2011). Assessing protective factors in forensic psychiatric practice: Introducing the SAPROF. *International Journal of Forensic Mental Health, 10,* 171–177. doi: 10.1080/14999013.2011.600230.

de Vries Robbé, M., de Vogel, V., & Douglas, K. S. (2013). Risk factors and protective factors: A two-sided dynamic approach to violence risk assessment. *Journal of Forensic Psychiatry & Psychology, 24,* 440–457. doi: 10.1080/14789949.2013.818162.

Webster, C. D., Douglas, K. S., Eaves, D., & Hart, S. D. (1997). *HCR-20: Assessing the risk of violence (version 2).* Burnaby, BC: Mental Health, Law, and Policy Institute, Simon Fraser University.

Webster, C. D., Martin, M. L., Brink, J., Nicholls, T. L., & Desmarais, S. L. (2009). *Manual for the Short-Term Assessment of Risk and Treatability* (START) (Version 1.1). Port Coquitlam, Canada: British Columbia Mental Health & Addiction Services.

Wettstein, R. (2005). Quality and quality improvement in forensic mental health evaluations. *Journal of the American Academy of Psychiatry and the Law, 33,* 58–175.

12

PROVIDING EFFECTIVE
EXPERT TESTIMONY

Nancy Kaser-Boyd and Corine de Ruiter

The forensic mental health evaluator in criminal cases will be asked to testify in only a proportion of cases.[1] While this may not be a large proportion, each case must be prepared as if there will be a full hearing on the relevant matters. Following the guidelines for FMHA and report writing outlined in previous chapters should lay the groundwork for competent and ethical expert testimony,[2] but giving testimony is a unique skill for the forensic evaluator.

There is wide variation across the world in whether a case will be tried in front of a jury, a judge, a panel of judges, or a combination of judges and laypeople.[3] Giving testimony and, more particularly, being cross-examined, can be very much like taking a doctoral oral exam, since any type of question can be asked about virtually any aspect of a report or opinion. Providing testimony requires the translation of sometimes complicated psychological concepts into simple language, often peppered with the use of analogies which make concepts more clear. Although it may seem as if testifying before a jury of laypeople is more challenging because of a lack of education and training in psychological science in such laypeople, research has shown that the difference between laypeople and judges in this respect is minimal. For instance, a set of empirical studies by Kovera and McAuliff found that judges and attorneys were unable to detect major flaws (such as lack of a control group or experimenter bias) in expert evidence, while jurors were only slightly better because they did detect the lack of a control group (Kovera & McAuliff, 2000; McAuliff, Kovera & Nunez, 2009; for a review, see McAuliff & Groscup, 2009). Judges and attorneys were also found to be quite unrealistically optimistic about their ability to identify flawed expert evidence. Other research has shown that judges' ruling on the admissibility of evidence appeared to be based more on characteristics of the expert, such as subject-matter knowledge and education, than on those of the evidence (McAuliff & Groscup, 2009; Merlino,

Murray, & Richardson, 2008). The bottom line is that the expert needs to do her best to prepare for court testimony, but the outcome is uncertain.

This chapter provides a review of admissibility rules for scientific evidence in court. These rules are quite distinct and have developed over the years as a result of case law, and they differ per jurisdiction. We offer a summary of the literature on effective expert testimony, by focusing on substantive and stylistic aspects. The 'do's and 'don't's of cross-examination and professional ethics guidelines on expert testimony are reviewed, with examples on how to respond to personal attacks.

Admissibility of Expert Testimony

In most of the states in America, expert testimony is now governed by Federal Rules 702–705:

> **Rule 702**: If scientific, technical, or other specialized knowledge will assist the trier of fact to understand the evidence or to determine a fact in issue, a witness qualified as an expert by knowledge, skill, experience, training, or education, may testify thereto in the form of an opinion or otherwise, if (1) the testimony is based upon sufficient facts or data, (2) the testimony is the product of reliable principles and methods, and (3) the witness has applied the principles and methods reliably to the facts of the case.

> **Rule 703**: The facts or data in the particular case upon which an expert bases an opinion or inference may be those perceived by or made known to the expert at or before the hearing. If of a type reasonably relied upon by experts in the particular field in forming opinions or inferences upon the subject, the facts or data need not be admissible in evidence in order for the opinion or inference to be admitted. Facts or data that are otherwise inadmissible shall not be disclosed to the jury by the proponent of the opinion or inference unless the court determines that their probative value in assisting the jury to evaluate the expert's opinion substantially outweighs their prejudicial effect.

> **Rule 704**: Except as provided in subdivision (b), testimony in the form of an opinion or inference otherwise admissible is not objectionable because it embraces an ultimate issue to be decided by the trier of fact.
>
> No expert witness testifying with respect to the mental state or condition of a defendant in a criminal case may state an opinion or inference as to whether the defendant did or did not have the mental state or condition constituting an element of the crime charged or of a defense thereto. Such ultimate issues are matters for the trier of fact alone.

> **Rule 705**: The expert may testify in terms of opinion or inference and give reasons therefor without first testifying to the underlying facts or data,

unless the court requires otherwise. The expert may in any event be required to disclose the underlying facts or data on cross-examination.

Case law in the US has added to the Federal Rules of Evidence governing admissibility of expert testimony. In the US, the standard for admitting expert testimony is now either the *Frye* standard or the *Daubert* standard. *Daubert* has been adopted in about one-third of the US states, but because these are typically the more populous states, more than half of the US population lives in states and local jurisdictions that are governed by *Daubert* (Hess, 2006).

The *Frye* standard derives from a 1923 case in which the defendant offered the results of a lie detector test, which he claimed demonstrated that he was telling the truth when he denied killing the victim. The court ruled that the evidence was inadmissible because the scientific principles upon which the procedure was based were not "sufficiently established to have gained acceptance in the particular field in which it belongs." This became known as the *Frye* general acceptance test and remained the standard used in both federal courts and state courts around the country for many years. *People v. Kelly* (1976) added to the standard in California: the California Supreme Court laid out what it felt were the main advantages of the *Frye* standard. In a very recent case, the California Supreme Court, *Sargon Enterprises v. University of Southern California* (2012), modified the law to conform to *Daubert* (see below).

The *Daubert* rule came from *Daubert v. Merrill Dow Pharmaceuticals*, a 1993 case involving a birth defect allegedly caused by the use of Bendictin, a medication manufactured by Merrill Dow Pharmaceuticals and used to alleviate morning sickness. The plaintiff alleged that Bendictin had caused a birth defect in her son. The plaintiff's expert was not allowed to testify. The US Supreme Court heard the case and articulated what has become known as the *Daubert* test. The test has four prongs (Hess, 2006):

(1) testability of a theory or technique: the theory's hypothesis or the technique used can be tested, falsified, and refuted;
(2) scrutiny of the scientific community: the theory or technique has been subjected to peer review and publication;
(3) known or potential error rate: the theory or technique has or may have standards controlling the technique's operation (allowing us to know how confident we may be in its conclusions, such as the standard error of measurement);
(4) general acceptance: the theory or technique is generally accepted within a relevant scientific community.

While *Daubert* sounds more stringent than *Frye*, the earlier *Frye* test is considered more conservative. Two subsequent cases added to the case law, resulting in the label *Daubert-Joiner-Kumho* test. *Joiner* and *Kumho* emphasized the "gatekeeper" role of the judge in admitting expert testimony. California's *Sargon Enterprises v. University of Southern California* accepted the language of *Daubert, Joiner* and *Kumho*. Sargon Enterprises contracted with the University of Southern California (USC) to conduct clinical studies on an implant for which they held the patent. Sargon claimed that USC had botched the clinical trials and, as a result, they were unable to market their product. An expert witness calculated their lost profits. USC argued that the calculations were not of the sort reasonably relied upon by experts in the field. The trial judge also opined that the methodology used was unreliable. The Court of Appeal reversed the trial court's ruling, indicating that the judge had abused his discretion in excluding the testimony. USC appealed to the California Supreme Court and the Supreme Court opined that the judge acts as a gatekeeper to exclude expert opinion: "that is (1) based on matter of a type on which an expert may not reasonably rely; (2) based on reasons unsupported by the material on which the expert relies, or (3) is speculative."

The California Supreme Court further cautioned judges not to overstep their authority. The decision on admissibility must not involve choosing between competing expert opinions. Citing *Daubert*, the California Supreme Court stated the gatekeeper's focus must be solely on principles and methodology, not on the conclusions generated. Citing *Kumho*, the California Supreme Court ruled that the gatekeeper's role is to make certain that an expert, whether basing testimony upon professional studies or personal experience, employs the same level of intellectual rigor in the courtroom that characterizes the practice of an expert in the relevant field. In Canada, the case of *R. v. Mohan* (1994) sets forth four factors to consider in the admissibility of expert opinion: relevance, necessity in assisting the trier of fact, absence of any exclusionary rule, and a properly qualified expert. Novel scientific theories or techniques are subjected to special scrutiny to determine if they meet the basic threshold of reliability. In *R v. J.L-J* (2000), the Supreme Court of Canada explicitly adopted the reasoning of *Daubert*.

In Chapter 1, it was explained that The Netherlands does not have the equivalent of the Federal Rules of Evidence or *Daubert, Frye*, etc. standards. It is the trial court that decides on the selection and evaluation of the available evidence, including expert evidence. However, several Dutch Supreme Court rulings caution the courts to critically review the status and quality of expert evidence. For instance, the Anatomically Correct Dolls-decision (HR February 28, 1989, NJ 1989, 748) concerned a case of a defendant accused of child sexual abuse. In this case, the Supreme Court ruled that when a court is confronted with an argued attack upon the reliability of a method used by an expert (in this particular case, the use of Anatomically Correct Dolls), it may not rely upon such evidence as a basis for their decision without providing additional evidence and reasoning why the court deems the method reliable after all (van Kampen, 2003).

In another ruling, the Dutch Supreme Court held that the quality of the expert himself should also be tested (HR January 27, 1998, NJ 1998, 404) when courts are confronted with an attack on the expert (aside from his method). Courts need to establish whether the expert's knowledge concerns research on, and analysis of, the substance of his testimony. The Supreme Court stated that the trial court needs to independently determine the reliability of the expert and his method. In actual practice, the Dutch courts pay very little attention to the quality of the expert's expertise and/or the reliability and validity of their methods. Courts hardly ever peruse the expert's CV before the trial hearing nor ask questions regarding their level of knowledge and experience before the actual expert testimony. This is quite contrary to US trial practice, as can be seen from the criminal trial transcript at the end of this chapter.

Professional Expert Witnesses

Brodsky (1991; 1999; 2004) has published a list of expert testimony maxims, derived from his own experience as an expert witness. Heilbrun, Grisso, and Goldstein (2009) have reorganized these into those that are substantive and procedural, or as Heilbrun, Marczyk, and DiMatteo (2002) note "substantive" and "stylistic." Successful expert witnesses possess both substantive strength and stylistic effectiveness (Brodsky, 1991; Heilbrun, 2001; Heilbrun et al., 2009). Heilbrun and colleagues (2002) define substance as: (1) substantial training and experience; and (2) adequate data, clear reasoning, and knowledge of legal standard(s). Brodsky (1991) defines style as: (1) trustworthiness; (2) dynamism/charisma; (3) comfort in the courtroom; (4) professional demeanor; and (5) clear speaking.

Substantive Strength

The main criterion for substance is the enhancement of the relationship between the FMHA findings and the testimony (Heilbrun, 2001). Grounding in scientific evidence and relevance to the case under consideration are the guiding principles. We will highlight a number of the maxims that we have found particularly helpful and which we have emphasized throughout this book.

First and foremost is the need for a strong link between the FMHA findings and the subsequent court testimony. Interpretations and conclusions drawn from the FMHA may be challenged in court, and it is of great importance to consider all relevant alternative interpretations in the FMHA report, to be prepared for these challenges. The same applies to challenges about a defendant's or plaintiff's faking good and faking bad. The issue of response style should be covered in the FMHA report, with findings supporting or countering a particular response style presented in an objective and fair way. Brodsky also emphasizes the importance of a good working knowledge of the scientific literature, to integrate this into the FMHA and subsequent testimony. Under *Daubert*, experts should be prepared with peer-reviewed research to defend the nature of their theories, principles, and methodologies (Brodsky, 1999). They should read and know the essential scholarly resources in your field, attend lectures/workshops by those scholars, email them with questions, and be prepared to rebut cross-examinations on those topics in a professional way (Brodsky, 2004). Expert witnesses should be prepared to discuss criticisms in the literature of their test methods in a manner that is knowledgeable, candid, and contextual (Brodsky, 2004). Cross-examination about examiner effects and heuristic biases call for the expert to explain how training and standardized procedures diminish such effects (Brodsky, 1991).

Credibility of testimony occasionally can revolve around brief questions and answers. Treat all testimony, even short and apparently insignificant answers, as important enough to think through and answer with care (Brodsky, 2004). Pausing before answering questions creates room for thought and careful responding. Tailoring your preparation for testimony to build on your strengths and to compensate for your weaknesses is a good idea. Memorize what you can. For the gaps that exist in memory and organization, invest heavily in preparing written outlines and memory aids before going to court (Brodsky, 2004). Brodsky (2004) and Heilbrun and colleagues (2009) recommend that the FMHA expert write, or be involved in writing, the examination questions. Be prepared for the opposing attorney to insinuate that this is somehow improper.

Avoiding the use of jargon is important to tell the story of what you have found in a way that makes the technical material accessible and that enhances the judge/jury's understanding of your expert opinion. Building a narrative bridge between your findings and the actual experience of the defendant so that the testimony comes alive to create a meaningful story is essential (Brodsky, 2004).

Some of these maxims, however, seem so straightforward that it is hard to imagine that a forensic mental health professional would not abide by them. Yet we have seen plenty of examples to the contrary during our work as expert witnesses. An important maxim is to agree to be an expert only when genuine expertise is present. This means having the relevant competence, knowledge, and experience. Obviously, this expertise is built over many years of education and forensic-clinical experience. This doesn't mean novice forensic psychologists should not perform FMHAs or provide expert testimony; it just means they should know their professional limitations and seek supervision and consultation with more experienced colleagues when appropriate. Finally, not all questions asked in a court of law can be answered. Sometimes the FMHA findings are equivocal; sometimes there is no scientific evidence to support an expert opinion. In such cases, it is ethical and appropriate for the expert to say he does not know. This is preferable to making up an answer on the spot. CdR once testified in a case of a young woman who grew up in a highly violent home, with an alcoholic father who made numerous attempts on her mother's life, resulting in more than one escape of family members to women's shelters. She testified that the woman's symptoms of Posttraumatic Stress Disorder (PTSD) could be related to these childhood circumstances, as the empirical research on the consequences of witnessing intimate partner violence on the psychological well-being of children shows (e.g., Kitzmann, 2005; Rossman, 1999). The prosecution expert (a psychiatrist) claimed that no such evidence existed, and that only actual physical abuse of the child could be a cause of PTSD symptoms. Citing the relevant research was helpful to the judge.

Stylistic Effectiveness

Good expert testimony is also persuasive and credible. Some of what we know about how juries evaluate the credibility of expert witnesses comes from mock trial research. Brodsky and Griffin (2010) identified four empirically supported domains of courtroom credibility: knowledge, likeability, trustworthiness, and confidence. Brodsky et al. (2009) and Neal et al. (2012) conducted two research studies, collapsing these four traits into two domains: knowledge (competence) and likeability (warmth). In the first study (Brodsky, Neal, Cramer, & Ziemke, 2009), the authors examined the relationship between expert witness likeability and jurors' judgments regarding sentencing the defendant. Two male actors were trained in presenting high and low levels of expert likeability. Likeability was operationalized as the degree to which an expert was friendly, respectful, kind, well-mannered, and pleasant. It was behaviorally defined as (1) a pleasant, smiling facial expression; (2) use of "we" or "us" when referring to groups; (3) demonstration of a less controlling attitude; (4) physical attractiveness; (5) use of informal speech, such as referring to an individual by name; (6) direct eye contact; and (7) truthfulness. The actors offered opinions about the risk potential of the defendant in a mock juror situation where the defendant was facing the death penalty. The participants were 225 students in an introductory psychology class at an American university. For content, the actors used testimony from a state-hired expert witness in a published legal case. Both actors presented themselves as tall, bearded, male professors at a major university with 14 years of experience in psycholegal evaluations and testimony in over 50 cases. They were rated on a witness credibility scale. The authors found that expert likeability influences juror perceptions of credibility in a linear manner. The highly likeable expert was rated as more trustworthy than his less likeable counterpart. However, expert likeability did not influence juror sentencing decisions.

The second study (Neal, Guadagno, Eno, & Brodsky, 2012) explored how male and female experts were perceived when aspects of credibility, knowledge, and likeability were manipulated. In particular, the authors studied warmth as a manifestation of likeability. They hypothesized that competence is driven by perceptions of confidence, skillfulness, and capability, whereas warmth is driven by perceptions of friendliness, good-naturedness, and sincerity. Again, with a mock jury subject pool, using a two by two design (high and low knowledge, high and low likeability), the authors found that experts high on knowledge and likeability were rated as the most credible, whereas experts low on these dimensions were least credible. There were, however, gender differences. Female expert witnesses, overall, received lower ratings on credibility than males. Likeability in a female expert witness did not enhance her credibility over her male counterpart. Women had to be viewed as both warm and competent to compare favorably to men. As in Study 1, credibility of the expert did not influence the mock jurors' ultimate decision.

Kwartner and Boccaccini (2008) analyzed 62 expert witness research studies, some with a mock trial design, and concluded that the four basic principles of effective expert testimony were: clarity, clinical knowledge, case specificity, and certainty. Clarity involves avoiding highly technical language. Some expert witnesses describe this as framing concepts in language that your grandmother would understand. Kwartner and Boccacinni (2008) found that mental health experts were more persuasive when they included information about clinical experience and knowledge. They note that in academia, actuarially-based decisions are considered superior, but in the courtroom, jurors expressed a preference for clinically-based testimony. The best practice is probably to combine clinical and actuarial information. When testimony is research-based, the attorney may have to prepare the jury to be ready to process research-based testimony. Case specificity, that is, whether the expert presents detailed clinical/forensic information about the actual case, may be determined by the lawyer who calls the witness; that is, some testimony is specifically limited to describing a mental health diagnosis and its impact on mental state, for example, the impact of a psychotic state on the ability to plan and deliberate. However, experts presenting the results of an actual evaluation of the defendant were rated more favorably than those providing educative testimony. The authors also found that jurors preferred experts who were willing to draw firm conclusions and, in particular, preferred experts who expressed a high level of confidence in their opinion, but not absolute confidence. The most persuasive expert was found to be one who expressed confidence in their opinion without appearing over-confident or omnipotent.

Rogers, Bagby, Crouch, and Cutler (1990) conducted a number of studies on whether jurors react favorably to experts who address ultimate issues. They found that jurors are most influenced by testimony that clearly and strongly speaks to the decisions they have to make but leaves room for them to exercise their own judgment. This coincides with the findings of Brodsky and colleagues (2009) that jurors reacted favorably to the "likeable" expert witness but made up their own minds regarding the legal issue.

Stylistic aspects of expert testimony can also involve the way the expert dresses, her mannerisms, tone of voice, and use of language. Grisso (1986) notes that while face validity is the weakest form of validity in behavioral science research, it is one of the most important in legal contexts. Heilbrun et al. (2009) note that if the legal decision maker does not consider the evidence seriously because of how it is presented, it does not matter how substantively strong it might be.

Ethical Expert Testimony

The ethics of providing expert testimony are a critical part of the competence that makes for a good expert. Psychological bodies that govern our professional behavior have given us clear guidelines. Foremost are the Ethical Principles for Psychologists and Code of Conduct (American Psychological Association, 2010), which state:

> Psychologists do not knowingly make public statements that are false, deceptive, or fraudulent concerning their research practice, or other work activities or those of persons or organizations with which they are affiliated.
>
> Psychologists do not make false, deceptive, or fraudulent statements concerning (1) their training, experience, or competence; (2) their academic degrees; (3) their credentials; (4) their institutional or association affiliations; (5) their services; (6) the scientific or clinical basis for, or results or degree of success of, their services; (7) their fees; or (8) their publications or research findings. (Principle 5.01)

Principles are more specifically outlined in the Specialty Guidelines for Forensic Psychologists (American Psychological Association, 2013):

> When in their role as expert to the court or other tribunals, the role of forensic practitioners is to facilitate understanding of the evidence or dispute. Consistent with legal and ethical requirements, forensic practitioners do not distort or withhold relevant evidence or opinion in reports or testimony. When responding to discovery requests and providing sworn testimony, forensic practitioners strive to have readily available for inspection all data which they considered, regardless of whether the data supports their opinion, subject to and consistent with court order, relevant rules of evidence, test security issues, and professional standards.
>
> When providing reports and other sworn statements or testimony in any form, forensic practitioners strive to present their conclusions, evidence, opinions, or other professional products in a fair manner. Forensic practitioners do not, by either commission or omission, participate in misrepresentation of their evidence, nor do they participate in partisan attempts to avoid, deny, or subvert the presentation of evidence contrary to their own position or opinion. This does not preclude forensic practitioners from forcefully presenting the data and reasoning upon which a conclusion or professional product is based (Guideline 11.01).
>
> Consistent with relevant law and rules of evidence, when providing professional reports and other sworn statements or testimony, forensic practitioners strive to offer a complete statement of all relevant opinions

that they formed within the scope of their work on that case, the basis and reasoning underlying the opinions, the salient data or other information that was considered in forming the opinion, and an indication of any additional evidence that may be used in support of the opinions to be offered. The specific substance of forensic reports is determined by the type of psycholegal issue at hand as well as relevant laws or rules in the jurisdiction in which the work is completed (Guideline 11.04).

The Specialty Guidelines for Forensic Psychologists[4] outline other important ethical considerations in providing expert testimony, for example, differentiating between observations, inferences, and conclusions (Guideline 11.02); disclosing sources of information and bases of opinions (Guideline 11.03); commenting upon other professionals and participants in legal proceedings (Guideline 11.05); out of court statements (Guideline 11.06); and commenting upon legal proceedings (Guideline 11.07).

Cross-examination

It is easy to feel personally attacked during cross-examination, but the FMHA expert is well advised to remember the words of Hess (2006):

> The law relies heavily on cross-examination as a prophylactic against misleading testimony. The adversarial side can always produce other experts and contradictory evidence to dispel the evidence of the other side's experts. The judge can issue careful jury instructions on the burden of proof. Finally, the judge can exclude testimony found not relevant or whose relevance is outweighed by its emotional inflammation.
>
> (p. 661)

There are many styles of cross-examination of the FMHA expert witness. These can vary based on factors that may have nothing to do with the FMHA expert, factors such as whether the case is high profile, whether there is an opposing expert, or whether the opposing attorney wants to delve into psychological materials to a degree that s/he can ask critical questions. Bank and Packer (2007) summarized typical strategies for cross-examination:

- The opposing attorney[5] may attempt to demonstrate that the expert does not have the requisite expertise.
- S/he may attempt to question the validity of data used, such as the validity of tests, inadequate data collection, etc.
- S/he may emphasize errors in the report, even if they are minor.
- S/he may use the FMHA witness' prior trial or hearing transcripts to look for inconsistent statements.

Some attorneys follow Ziskin and Faust (1988) who wrote a guide for cross-examining psychological and psychiatric expert testimony. Ziskin's material can be organized into domains of attack. First, an attack on the training and background of an expert witness. A common strategy for attacking psychologists is to emphasize that they are not medical doctors, conveying an attitude that there are significant limitations to what psychologists know. This strategy was more effective in previous decades, when psychologists were just beginning to enter the courtroom. Other attacks on training and background might include a lack of board certification or diplomate status, no academic appointment, few or no publications. Since most experts are carefully chosen and "vetted" prior to being retained, it is not very likely that the expert will have a hard time with this line of questioning. Hess (2006) and Brodsky (2004) recommend that the expert witness describe their credentials with modesty but assertiveness. The second line of attack is often on the reliability of diagnosis. In earlier years, before the Diagnostic and Statistical Manual of Mental Disorders (DSM) provided clear criteria, assessors were more likely to disagree. Another frequent attack on diagnosis notes that the diagnostic manual has been revised multiple times and final diagnoses are "voted on" by committees. The expert who is familiar with the epidemiological research that forms the basis for the DSM revisions will be quite able to answer such questions. In any case, diagnostic categories are not at the heart of FMHA. Functional capacities have to be examined in relation to the psycholegal issue(s) at hand, which often means that symptoms and circumstances are more important than diagnoses (Grisso, 2003). One of the authors (NKB) has been cross-examined numerous times with regard to Rosenhan's (1973) research, which is raised to question the reliability of diagnosis as well as the ability of people to "fool" mental health professionals. Rosenhan sent eight simulators to 12 different psychiatric hospitals in an attempt to gain admission. The 12 pseudopatients (a few went to more than one hospital) described the repetitive experience of hearing voices which seemed to pronounce the words "empty," "hollow," and "thud." After admission, all reported that they felt fine and had no more hallucinations. All but one pseudopatient was diagnosed with Schizophrenia; the twelfth was diagnosed manic-depressive. Once admitted, some took extensive notes on the behavior of staff and fellow patients. This was interpreted as a sign of mental illness. Their stays in hospital ranged from 7 to 52 days. One interesting fact was that contact with doctors averaged 6.8 minutes per day, raising questions about just how much information formed the database for the diagnosis.

For a juror or judge who is not educated in the scientific method, the experience of eight "fakers" may seem impressive. However, the expert witness can point out that this was a highly controversial study, with much criticism (Millon, 1975; Spitzer, 1975). To begin with, in modern science an N of 12 is more of an exploratory clinical study than scientific research, and there were no controls. Next, a database of less than 7 minutes would likely not be sufficient for accurate diagnosis, and it would clearly be substantially less time than the expert spent conducting the FMHA assessment.

Next, the attack might be on clinical judgment. Here, the attorney might ask questions surrounding examiner bias, confirmatory bias, examiner effects, or the subjectivity of opinions based on clinical material. Much of the suggested cross-examination questioning by Ziskin surrounded psychological tests, and this material is now very outdated. However, because attorneys are very good at adapting material for their case, and because Ziskin's work includes samples of actual questions and the witnesses' answers, this is good material to review.

Rogers, Bagby, and Perera (1993) note that Ziskin has not followed his own criticisms of expert testimony by experimentally validating his cross-examining techniques, to see if they actually result in diminishing the credibility of the expert witness. Rogers and colleagues (1993) studied the impact of Ziskin's cross-examination strategies in a mock trial design. The study combined two versions of an accused's statement to police, two versions of expert testimony by a psychiatrist, and five cross-examination conditions (inadequacies in training and education, situational influences on interviewing, problems with diagnosis, limitations of clinical judgment, and a control condition). None of the cross-examination strategies exerted a significant effect on ratings of the expert's credibility or on the mock jury's finding of insanity. Cross-examination strategies did exert an effect on the mock jurors' rating of the difficulty in rendering a verdict.

There are other common attacks. Perhaps the most common is that anyone accused of a serious crime, such as murder, might lie about their mental impairment to get out of trouble. For the expert witness, however, the issue is whether the defendant is faking a mental disorder, which can be examined using response style indicators on psychological tests and by adequate use of collateral information. It is the first author's experience that it is most common for attorneys to focus on the specifics of the case; for example, the behavior of the defendant that exhibits consciousness of guilt or inconsistent statements by the defendant. Sadly, this is where the expert might be the most weak. The attorneys most likely have had months to go over Discovery materials, listen to audio or videotapes of the defendant's statements, interview witnesses, and memorize the facts of the case. The typical expert, on the other hand, spends somewhere between 40 and 80 hours on a case, does not visit the crime scene nor handle the physical evidence and is even excluded from observing the testimony of live witnesses. This is a disadvantage which should be handled with the most rigorous reading of the Discovery, examining the photographs, listening to the defendant's statements, and committing to memory the details of the crime. Another area for cross-examination are the possible inconsistencies between what the defendant told the forensic psychologist/expert and what they have said elsewhere, such as in their statement to police, or in trial testimony. The expert is advised to carefully read and compare statements and understand the reason(s) for the inconsistencies. Table 12.1 provides a list of tips we have found useful in preparing for court testimony.

TABLE 12.1 Practical tips to prepare for testimony

---

1. Review the police report and crime scene photographs to refresh memory about the evidence.

2. Review your own report and make a memory sheet about the dates and points you might forget.

3. Review the psychological test results. Check the scoring of each test for accuracy and completeness. Does each test have the date it was administered? Does each test have the defendant's name and birth date?

4. Organize your file into a binder so you will know the location of materials and avoid shuffling through a pile of papers.

5. Prepare to turn over clinical-forensic notes and raw test data in the process of discovery.

6. Organize professional literature that supports your opinions.

7. Read opposing expert's report well before your testimony.

8. Obtain opposing expert's raw test data. Double-check the scoring.

9. Familiarize yourself with opposing expert's background and experience.

10. Review the Specialty Guidelines for Forensic Psychologists, to ensure that you have followed basic principles for an FMHA Evaluation.

11. Provide time to meet with the lawyer who retained you.

12. Consider preparing Direct Examination questions to facilitate the clear presentation of testimony.

Opinions Regarding Persons Not Examined

This is an especially important area in expert testimony which may arise when examining a defendant for the opposing side when there is restricted access or no access to the defendant, or when simply performing a records review. The Ethical Principles for Psychologists and Code of Conduct (2002) state:

> Forensic practitioners recognize their obligations to only provide written or oral evidence about the psychological characteristics of particular individuals when they have sufficient information or data to form an adequate foundation for those opinions or to substantiate their findings (Standard 9.01).

The Specialty Guidelines for Forensic Psychologists supplement this by stating:

> Forensic practitioners seek to make reasonable efforts to obtain such information or data and they document their efforts to obtain it. When it is not possible or feasible to examine individuals about whom they are offering an opinion, forensic practitioners strive to make clear the impact

of such limitations on the reliability and validity of their professional products, opinions, or testimony.

When conducting a record review or providing consultation or supervision that does not warrant an individual examination, forensic practitioners seek to identify the sources of information on which they are basing their opinions and recommendations, including any substantial limitation to their opinions and recommendations (Guideline 9.03).

These latter standards mean that in forensic cases where the access to independent sources of information is limited, definitive diagnostic conclusions are often not possible, and should only be formulated with the caveats mentioned (see the case of Mr. A. at the end of Chapter 1).

We include an actual court transcript from a US criminal case at the closing of this chapter so that the reader can be acquainted with the structure and content of a typical piece of direct testimony and cross-examination. How should you evaluate your own expert testimony? Novice FMHA practitioners may be inclined to evaluate their testimony based on how the jury or trier of fact votes. If the decision is for the opposing side, the FMHA expert may feel that they weren't a very convincing expert witness. It is important to remember that a trial comprises many complex elements, such as the strength of the other witnesses, the skill of opposing attorneys, the rulings regarding admissible evidence by the judge, and, perhaps most important, the technical-forensic evidence (e.g., gunshot wounds, blood evidence, threatening emails, etc.). The FMHA expert should not be invested in the outcome of the trial. Rather, her best work involves presenting clear and objective evidence from psychological science in relation to the psycholegal question concerned.

A Criminal Trial Transcript[6]

Legend: Ms. G. is the Defense Attorney
           Mr. D. is the District Attorney
           Dr. KB is the expert witness

Ms. G: The Defense calls Dr. Nancy Kaser-Boyd.
Deputy: Do you promise to tell the truth, the whole truth, and nothing but the truth?
Dr. KB: I do.
Judge: You may be seated.
Deputy: Please state and spell your name. [Witness complies]

DIRECT EXAMINATION
Ms. G: Doctor, what is your current occupation?
Dr. KB: I am a clinical and forensic psychologist and I am currently an associate clinical professor at the Geffen School of Medicine at UCLA.

Ms. G: What is a clinical and forensic psychologist?

Dr. KB: It is someone who has credentials in both clinical psychology and forensic psychology. Clinical psychology includes the study of abnormal behavior, diagnostic interviewing, psychological assessment, modes of intervention treatment, and treatment planning and evaluation. I'm licensed by the State of California to do psychological assessment, conduct treatment, evaluate treatment, and so forth. A forensic psychologist has additional training and experience in forensic psychology, which is the application of what we know from clinical psychology to questions that courts raise. Courts raise all different kinds of questions. Family court raises questions about parental fitness. Civil Court raises questions about personal injury. Criminal Court raises questions about competency to stand trial, mental state at the time of a trial, considerations for pronouncing sentencing, and so on.

Ms. G: Thank you. What is your professional background?

Dr. KB: [Describes education and training in clinical and forensic, positions held, and current positions.]

Ms. G: Your experiences in inpatient psychiatric wards in different hospitals, does that experience include people with drug-induced psychoses?

Dr. KB: Yes.

Ms. G: As well as people with functional mental illnesses?

Dr. KB: Yes. These days there is a lot of drug use, and some of it results in what we call settled mental illness. In some cases, of course, people improve when they stop taking the drug.

Ms. G: I assume you have testified before in court.

Dr. KB: Yes, I have.

Ms. G: Now, in this case, the case of Mr. S., you were hired by me, correct?

Dr. KB: Correct.

Ms. G: Is it fair to say that you expect to be paid for working?

Dr. KB: Yes.

Ms. G: What are you charging me?

Dr. KB: $180 an hour.

Ms. G: What did you do in terms of preparing to come in and testify and render an opinion in this case?

Dr. KB: I read the investigation reports, and they have Bates-stamped pages, so I had pages 1 through 164, and these included witness and victim statements, as well as an interview with the defendant's mother. After that, I was sent a number of pages from Mr. S.'s social media account. I had his school records, which were pretty extensive, and they also included a note about a psychiatric referral he had in school. I had the report of the psychopharmacologist, and I also watched the movie which was playing in the theatre at the time of the stabbings.

Ms. G: Have you also seen Mr. S.?

Dr. KB: Yes, I saw him on three occasions. I conducted a three-and-one-half-hour interview on August 14, a three-hour interview on September 2, and a two-hour interview and psychological testing on September 13.

Ms. G: Okay. Now, you've already touched on this a little bit, but can you please describe your training and experience and background dealing specifically with drug-induced psychotic symptoms or disorders?

Dr. KB: As an intern at LA County/USC Hospital, many patients on the in-patient units developed psychotic symptoms because of drug use/abuse. Back in those days—the 1980s—it was usually PCP [Phencyclidine], sometimes mushrooms, sometimes crack cocaine. . . . My next experience with psychotic disorders was at Ingleside Hospital, a psychiatric inpatient facility in east Los Angeles. I have also supervised assessment cases at UCLA Medical Center, Neuropsychiatric Institute. In any inpatient unit, you are going to see a mixture of people with drug-induced psychosis and people who have pure mental illness. Also, most of the serious crimes I work on involve drug or alcohol abuse. That's not because I have published on drug abuse. I haven't. But that's just the way crime is in California.

Ms. G: Can you tell us, Dr. KB, what exactly a hallucination is?

Dr. KB: A hallucination is a perceptual experience that doesn't match the reality constraints of the real world. It's a false perception.

Ms. G: And is a hallucination considered a psychotic symptom?

Dr. KB: Yes.

Ms. G: Why is that?

Dr. KB: "Psychotic" means a departure from reality. Experiencing things that are not real, things that are not really there, or not interpreted in the way the person has interpreted it. An example: a person might interpret a shadow as a ghost and might believe the ghost is signaling them to engage in certain behavior. The shadow is there, but it is not a ghost, and of course, there is no signal.

Ms. G: Would a hallucination impair somebody's thinking?

Dr. KB: Yes, hallucinations do impair thinking.

Ms. G: What is a delusion?

Dr. KB: A delusion is a false belief. In our textbooks, it is defined as holding firm to a belief that is not consensually validated by one's peers or social group.

Ms. G: Is a delusion considered a psychotic symptom?

Dr. KB: Yes, it is.

Ms. G: Why is that?

Dr. KB: A delusion is a false belief which can lead a person to do things that are unrealistic for the situation—illogical, bizarre, or not based in reality, and "psychotic" means that reality-testing is impaired. Thinking is illogical and behavior usually follows which is illogical or bizarre.

Ms. G: Is there a difference between a drug-induced hallucination and a hallucination an individual would experience due to pure mental illness?

Dr. KB: Not really.

Ms. G: Is it fair to say that a hallucination is a hallucination?

Dr. KB: Yes. There is a tendency for people who are toxic from a drug to have visual hallucinations, but people with mental illness, such as paranoid schizophrenia, about 20 percent of those individuals do have visual hallucinations. To determine the cause of the hallucinations, you have to take a history.

Ms. G: Can you describe for us the different types of hallucinations?

Dr. KB: Yes. There are auditory hallucinations. Those are usually voices the person feels are outside their head; they are often persecutory; for example, voices telling a person they are worthless, or they are going to fail. They can be frightening—telling the person they are going to die, or they should kill someone. They can be religious; for example, the person can believe he is hearing the voice of God. They can be grandiose; the person could believe, for example, that they are Hitler and voices are directing them to some particular action. There are all kinds of variations on these themes in Methamphetamine abusers. These are all auditory hallucinations.

Then, there are visual hallucinations. As I said, these tend to be more common in toxic states and in straight medical illnesses. For example, problems with the ocular nerve can cause visual hallucinations. Migraine headaches can cause them. We also see them with ingestion of toxic substances, such as LSD or mushrooms. [Expert interrupted before explaining olfactory hallucinations or tactile hallucinations.]

Ms. G: Is it true that hallucinations can make your thinking to be highly unrealistic?

Dr. KB: Yes, there is a bridge between hallucinations and psychosis and unrealistic thinking. When you're responding to a stimulus that's not really there or doesn't mean what you think it means, you are likely going to react in a way that is very unrealistic. It markedly deviates from good reality testing, which is "psychosis."

Ms. G: You indicated earlier that a hallucination can create a false perception. Can you describe for us or explain what you mean by the phrase "false perception"?

Dr. KB: Well, in the realm of criminal behavior, we have people who believe that they hear the voice of God commanding them to kill someone. Okay? It is called a command hallucination. Of course, God isn't telling them to kill someone, but the belief that the voice is real can cause them to engage in violent behavior.

Ms. G: If a person is hallucinating and their thinking is impaired, and they are experiencing false perceptions, is it fair to say their reactions are based on the hallucination and not on reality?

Dr. KB: Yes, a person may respond with behavior and emotion that is consistent with the hallucination. So, let's say, that in the example I just gave that there is a command hallucination, and the person believes it is from God, they might actually kill someone with great vengeance, because they believe it is the voice of God. People can be distraught when they hear voices. They can be frightened. There is always an emotional component to people's behavior, in addition to the cognitive.

Ms. G: Is it fair to say that hallucinations may cause an intense emotional response?

Dr. KB: Yes, because when a person is psychotic, they don't have emotional control. You or I might see a movie. Maybe it provokes us a little bit, maybe it makes us fearful, but we have emotional control. We can calm down. We can tell ourselves this is fiction. The person who is psychotic is impaired in logical thinking and in behavioral control.

Ms. G: Is it possible to predict the content of an individual hallucination?

Dr. KB: I don't think so. They are usually highly personal to that person's experience.

Ms. G: Could a hallucination cause a person to react violently?

Dr. KB: Yes it could.

Ms. G: Why is that?

Dr. KB: Well, if a person is hallucinating something that is frightening to them, or if they have heard voices that tell them to do something, those are examples that could lead to violence.

Ms. G: Is it possible for an individual experiencing a hallucination to stop or prevent the hallucination from happening?

Dr. KB: No. The way to stop a hallucination is to go to a hospital and get antipsychotic medication.

Ms. G: Is it possible for the person experiencing a hallucination to control their reaction to the hallucination?

Mr. D: Objection, your Honor. Relevancy. Lacks foundation.

Judge: Sustained.

Ms. G: Could you describe for us, Dr. Kaser-Boyd, the types of feelings or emotions that people experience when hallucinating?

Dr. KB: It depends on the type of hallucination and what the content of the hallucination is. They can experience themselves as extremely power-ful, or invulnerable. They can experience themselves as extremely vulnerable and threatened. They can experience rage. They can have uncontrolled sexual thoughts or impulses. It pretty much runs the gamut.

Ms. G: Could they be paranoid?

Dr. KB: Yes.

Ms. G: Confused?

Dr. KB: Well, confusion comes with the whole psychotic phenomena. Someone who is hallucinating and psychotic is definitely confused.

Ms. G: Could the hallucinations cause fear?

Dr. KB: Yes.

Ms. G: Could the emotions experienced from the hallucination cause a person to react?

Dr. KB: Yes.

Ms. G: Could these emotions cause violence?

Dr. KB: Yes.

Ms. G: You indicated that a person hallucinating could experience rage. Could the emotion or rage and experience of that hallucination cause them to act out on that rage?

Dr. KB: Yes.

Ms. G: If someone were acting on this rage from a hallucination, would they necessarily remember every single thing they did in their actions?

Dr. KB: No. Memory during psychotic states tends to be very spotty.

Ms. G: Why is that?

Dr. KB: Well, the brain isn't functioning normally, so the brain isn't recording memories the way your brain and my brain might be. Memory requires attention to what's going on, and clear thinking, and usually those are absent. Also, we think of psychotic states as like nightmares. People will wake up and remember the nightmare but usually not every single part of it. There are often parts that they can't recall.

Ms. G: Would you agree that a hallucination places an individual in an altered state?

Dr. KB: Yes.

Ms. G: Is automatic behavior or practiced behavior still possible when you are in that altered state?

Dr. KB: Yes. It depends on what it is, but things that have been learned or even over-learned can often still be carried out when one is hallucinating.

Ms. G: Could driving be an example?

Dr. KB: Yes.

Ms. G: Suppose someone is hallucinating and sees violent imagery. How might that affect them?

Dr. KB: When someone is psychotic and hallucinating, their reality testing is impaired. The barrier between real and not real is already violated, so it could become incorporated into their psychotic thoughts or hallucinations.

Ms. G:	If you were told that a person believed that they could communicate with people on a movie or television screen and control what these other people were doing, would that be consistent with a hallucination?
Dr. KB:	Yes. It would be delusional, and it would be psychotic.
Ms. G:	If you believed you were seeing evil imagery coming out of a movie screen, would that be consistent with a hallucination?
Dr. KB:	Yes.
Ms. G:	Nothing further. Thank you.

CROSS-EXAMINATION

Mr. D:	Good morning, Doctor. Now, I heard a lot of discussion about hallucinations, but let's just clarify something. Your experience, primarily in the criminal courts, is dealing with mental health cases, right?
Dr. KB:	It's not easy to distinguish between mental health problems and drug abuse, because there's a big overlap. Most of the serious, violent cases I've worked on involved drug abuse.
Mr. D:	I understand you testified in cases in which a defendant has pled not guilty by reason of insanity, correct?
Dr. KB:	Some of my cases have involved that plea.
Mr. D:	You understand in this case, there is no mental defense, that's not a defense in this case, right?
Ms. G:	Objection. Relevance.
Judge:	Overruled. You may answer.
Dr. KB:	I definitely understand that.
Mr. D:	You understand that whether or not Mr. S. was a raving psychotic lunatic is completely irrelevant to these proceedings, don't you?
Ms. G:	Objection, vague.
Mr. D:	I will rephrase. Apart from the drugs, independent of any drug-induced hallucination, if Mr. S. stabbed two people in the theatre simply because he was a mentally ill, raving lunatic, that would be completely irrelevant to these proceedings, do you understand that?
Ms. G:	Objection. Relevance. Lacks foundation. How is she supposed to determine that?
Judge:	Overruled. You may answer.
Dr. KB:	It's not relevant here and now because the defense of insanity is not being raised. It might be relevant to general mental state.
Mr. D:	How many people have you seen who have described seeing something that you would classify as a hallucination, and they told you they saw evil images?
Dr. KB:	I have trouble with the way the question is phrased, so I'm going to answer it in the way I think you mean it. How many people have I seen that saw evil images that I thought they were hallucinating.

Mr. D: Yes.

Dr. KB: Many. One hundred. Maybe more.

Mr. D: Let me ask you this. Are you familiar with the DRE program.

Dr. KB: Somewhat.

Mr. D: You have never actually received drug recognition training, is that right?

Dr. KB: That's right.

Mr. D: And you're not familiar with each of the drug classes?

Dr. KB: Well, we study that in my field as well.

Mr. D: How many people on the street have you ever actually spoken to while they were under the influence of hallucinogenic mushrooms?

Dr. KB: I'm not on the street working. I am in a hospital.

Dr. D: So the answer would be zero?

Dr. KB: That's correct.

Mr. D: Let me ask you about your knowledge of Psilocybin. Can you tell the jury what are the general indicators of somebody who is under the influence of Psilocybin?

Dr. KB: They can be fearful, panicky even. They can have a dissociative effect, where things don't feel real. They can have delusions and hallucinations.

Mr. D: Now, you met with the defendant three times in this case, right?

Dr. KB: Right.

Mr. D: Do you recall the defendant telling you that he became interested in junior high school in witchcraft and the supernatural?

Dr. KB: Yes.

Mr. D: Do you recall writing a report that stated he has a history of unrealistic beliefs and non-drug-induced hallucinations and delusions?

Dr. KB: Yes.

Mr. D: So you are not here in this case to tell the jury that whatever hallucination Mr. S. may or may not have experienced was caused by drug use, right?

Dr. KB: I don't think that's right. I think that I formed the opinion that he has a heavy history of using drugs. He gave a report to me of ingestion of Psilocybin mushrooms on that day. He also has a previous history of some mildly psychotic thoughts. Nothing as extreme as what he experienced on this day.

Mr. D: You don't really think you can get inside somebody's mind after seeing them for three times and make a prediction what they were really thinking at a point in time, do you?

Dr. KB: If I believed that would not be possible, I wouldn't be here. Three in-depth interviews are much more than what people receive even when admitted to the hospital. I'm basing it on the history in the records I reviewed that describe his behavior pretty clearly. I'm also basing it, obviously, on what he remembers about his history.

Mr. D: You are not suggesting that you can read minds, are you?

Ms. G: Objection. Argumentative.

Judge: Sustained.

Mr. D: If somebody was hallucinating and psychotic, how would they appear to the people around them?

Dr. KB: It depends on the nature of their hallucination and how much they've lost behavioral control. They might be talking to themselves, or they might just seem to be confused. They might seem unusually angry. They might give off some vibes that they were some kind of scary person, or they might not look terribly different, because it's what's going on in their head that is the psychotic stuff.

Mr. D: Doctor, have you ever been fooled?

Dr. KB: I'm sure I have been. In this context the question would be, have I ever been fooled by someone who was malingering psychosis.

Mr. D: I have nothing further.

RE-DIRECT EXAMINATION

Ms. G: The D.A. asked you if you had ever been fooled by someone you were examining. As a clinical and forensic psychologist, are there steps you take in order to make sure that somebody is not faking or malingering?

Mr. D: Objection. Relevance.

Judge: Overruled.

Dr. KB: Yes, there are.

Ms. G: Did you take those steps in this case? Steps to rule out malingering by Mr. S?

Dr. KB: Yes I did.

Ms. G: What did you do?

Dr. KB: I administered the Structured Interview of Reported Symptoms, called the SIRS, now revised and called the SIRS-2.

Ms. G: Is this a test that is commonly accepted in the field of forensic psychology?

Dr. KB: Yes.

Ms. G: How do you go about administering it?

Dr. KB: [Explains administration and scoring.]

Ms. G: And what did you find?

Dr. KB: According to the cutting scores that are given us in the test manual, he is not malingering or faking a mental disorder.

Ms. G: Thank you, Doctor. Nothing further.

Notes

1   Heilbrun (2001) reports on the basis of anecdotal observations from three US states, that across a range of criminal forensic issues, testimony is presented in about 10 percent of FMHA cases. This frequency will go up in high-profile cases in which the FMHA findings are relevant to the retaining attorney (p. 255).
2   "Expert testimony" here is distinguished from the testimony of a percipient witness, such as an eyewitness or therapist.
3   In the United States, testimony in criminal matters is typically given in front of a jury; the exception is when the defense attorney and the prosecutor agree to a "Court Trial" where a judge makes the decision about guilt or innocence. In The Netherlands, expert testimony in criminal cases is always given in bench trial with three judges.
4   Note the absence of Specialty Guidelines for forensic psychologists in The Netherlands.
5   Note that in the inquisitorial system, there is no opposing attorney, but the expert witness may still be questioned by all parties in a case, including the prosecutor, the defense attorney, and the judge(s).
6   Edited for brevity and to correct grammar.

References

American Psychological Association (2010). *Ethical principles of psychologists and code of conduct* (2002, Amended June 1, 2010). www.apa.ort/ethics/code/index.aspx.

American Psychological Association (2013). Specialty guidelines for forensic psychologists. *American Psychologist, 68*, 7–19. doi: 10.1037/a0029889.

Bank, S. C. & Packer, I. K. (2007). Expert witness testimony: Law, ethics & practice. In A. M. Goldstein (Ed.), *Forensic psychology: Emerging topics and expanding roles* (pp. 421–445). Hoboken, NJ: Wiley.

Brodsky, S. (1991). *Testifying in court: Guidelines and maxims for the expert witness.* Washington, DC: American Psychological Association.

Brodsky, S. (1999). *The expert witness: More maxims and guidelines for testifying in court.* Washington, DC: American Psychological Association.

Brodsky, S. (2004). *Coping with cross-examination and other pathways to effective testimony.* Washington, DC: American Psychological Association.

Brodsky, S. L. & Griffin, M. P. (2010). The witness credibility scale: An outcome measure for expert witness research. *Behavioral Sciences and the Law, 28*, 892–907. doi: 10.1002/bsl.917.

Brodsky, S. L., Neal, T. M. S., Cramer, R. J., & Ziemke, M. H. (2009). Credibility in the courtroom: How likeable should an expert witness be? *Journal of the American Academy of Psychiatry and the Law, 37*, 525–532.

Chang, W. & Ufkes, F. J. (2013). Supreme Court clarifies role of trial judges in determining admissibility of expert testimony. *California Bar Journal.* www.apps.calbar.ca.gov/mcleselfstudy/mcle_home.aspx.

Daubert v. Merrill Dow Pharmaceuticals, 509 U.S. 579 (1993).

Frye v. United States, 54 App. D.C. 46, 47, 293 F. 1013 (1923).

General Electric Company v. Joiner, 522 U.S. 136, 118 S.Ct. 512 (1997).

Glancy, G.D. & Saini, M. (2009). The confluence of evidence-based practice and *Daubert* within the fields of forensic psychiatry and the law. *Journal of the American Academy of Psychiatry and the Law, 37*, 438–441.

Grisso, T. (1986). *Evaluating competencies: Forensic assessment and instruments.* New York: Plenum.

Grisso, T. (2003). *Evaluating competencies: Forensic assessment and instruments* (2nd ed.). New York: Kluwer Academic/Plenum.

Heilbrun, K. (2001). *Principles of forensic mental health assessment.* New York: Kluwer Academic.

Heilbrun, K., Grisso, T., & Goldstein, A. M. (2009). *Foundations of forensic mental health assessment.* New York: Oxford University Press.

Heilbrun, K., Marczyk, G., & DeMatteo, D. (Eds.) (2002). *Forensic mental health assessment: A casebook.* New York: Oxford University Press.

Hess, A. K. (2006). Serving as an expert witness. In I. B. Weiner & A. K. Hess (Eds.), *The handbook of forensic psychology* (pp. 652–697). New York: Wiley.

van Kampen, P. T. C. (2003). Expert evidence: The state of the law in The Netherlands and the United States. In P. J. van Koppen & S. D. Penrod (Eds.), *Adversarial versus inquisitorial justice: Psychological perspectives on criminal justice systems* (pp. 209–234). New York: Kluwer Academic/Plenum.

Kitzmann, K. M. (2005). Domestic violence and its impact on the social and emotional development of young children. *Encyclopedia on Early Childhood Development.* Center of Excellence for Early Childhood Development. www.child-encyclopedia.com/pages/PDF/KitzmannANGxp_rev.pdf.

Kovera, M. B. & McAuliff, B. D. (2000). The effects of peer review and evidence quality on judge evaluations of psychological science: Are judges effective gatekeepers? *Journal of Applied Psychology, 85,* 574–586. doi: 10.1037/0021–9010.85.4.574.

Kumho Tire Co. v. Carmichael, 526 U.S., 119 S. Ct. 1167 (1999).

Kwartner, P. P. & Boccaccini, M. T. (2008). Testifying in court: Evidence-based recommendations for expert-witness testimony. In R. Jackson (Ed.), *Learning forensic assessment* (pp. 565–588). New York: Routledge.

McAuliff, B. D., Kovera, M. B., & Nunez, G. (2009). Can jurors recognize missing control groups, confounds, and experimenter bias in psychological science? *Law and Human Behavior, 33,* 247–257. doi: 10.1007/s10979–008–9133–0.

McAuliff, B. D., & Groscup, J. L. (2009). *Daubert* and psychological science in court: Judging validity from the bench, bar, and jury box. In J. L. Skeem, K. S. Douglas, & S. O. Lilienfeld (Eds.), *Psychological science in the courtroom: Consensus and controversy* (pp. 26–52). New York: Guilford.

Merlino, M. L., Murray, C. I., & Richardson, J. T. (2008). Judicial gatekeeping and the social construction of the admissibility of expert testimony. *Behavioral Sciences and the Law, 26,* 187–206. doi: 10.1002/bsl.806.

Millon, T. (1975). Reflections on Rosenhan's "On being sane in insane places." *Journal of Abnormal Psychology, 84,* 456–461. doi: 10.1037/h0077120.

Neal, T. M., Guadagno, R. E., Eno, C. A., & Brodsky, S. L. (2012). Warmth and competence on the witness stand: Implications for the credibility of male and female expert witnesses. *Journal of the American Academy of Psychiatry and the Law, 40,* 488–497.

People v. Kelly, 549 P. 2d 1240 (Cal. 1976).

R. v. Mohan, 2 S.C.R. 9 (1994).

R. v. J.L.-J., 2 S.C.R. 200 (2000).

Rogers, R., Bagby, R. M., & Perera, C. (1993). Can Ziskin withstand his own criticism? Problems with his model of cross-examination. *Behavioral Sciences and the Law, 11,* 223–233.

Rogers, R., Bagby, R. M., Crouch, M., & Cutler, B. (1990). Effects of ultimate opinions on juror perceptions of insanity. *International Journal of Law and Psychiatry, 13,* 225–232. doi: 10.1016/0160–2527(90)90018-X.

Rosenhan, D. L. (1973). On being sane in insane places. *Science, 179*, 250–258. doi: 10.1126/science.179.4070.250.

Rossman, B. B. R. (1999). Multiple risks for children exposed to parental violence: Family factors, psychological maltreatment, and trauma. *Journal of Aggression, Maltreatment & Trauma, 2*, 207–237. doi: 10.1300/J146v02n02_10.

Sargon Enterprises v. University of Southern California, Cal 4th (212) DJDAR 15846 (November 26, 2012).

Spitzer, R. (1975). On pseudoscience in science, logic in remission, and psychiatric diagnosis: A critique of Rosenhan's "On being sane in insane places." *Journal of Abnormal Psychology, 84*, 442–452. doi: 10.1037/h0077124.

Ziskin, J. & Faust, D. (1988). *Coping with psychiatric and psychological testimony* (4th ed.). Marina del Rey, CA: Law and Psychology Press.

INDEX